TERRY NEWMAN

MARILYN MONROE STYLE

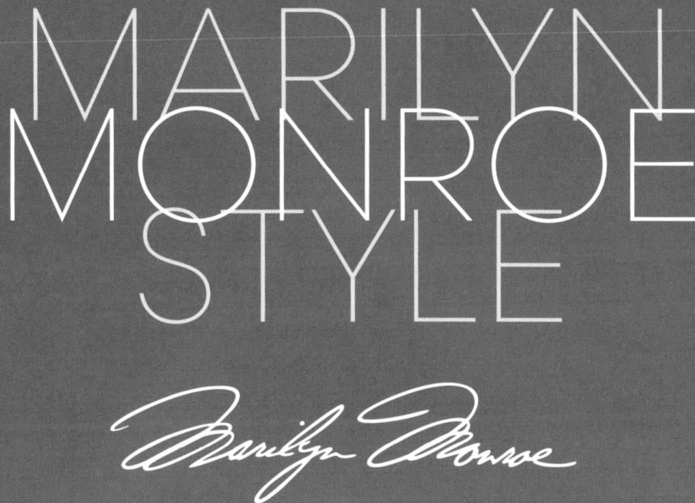

ACC ART BOOKS

THE ESTATE OF MARILYN MONROE, LLC

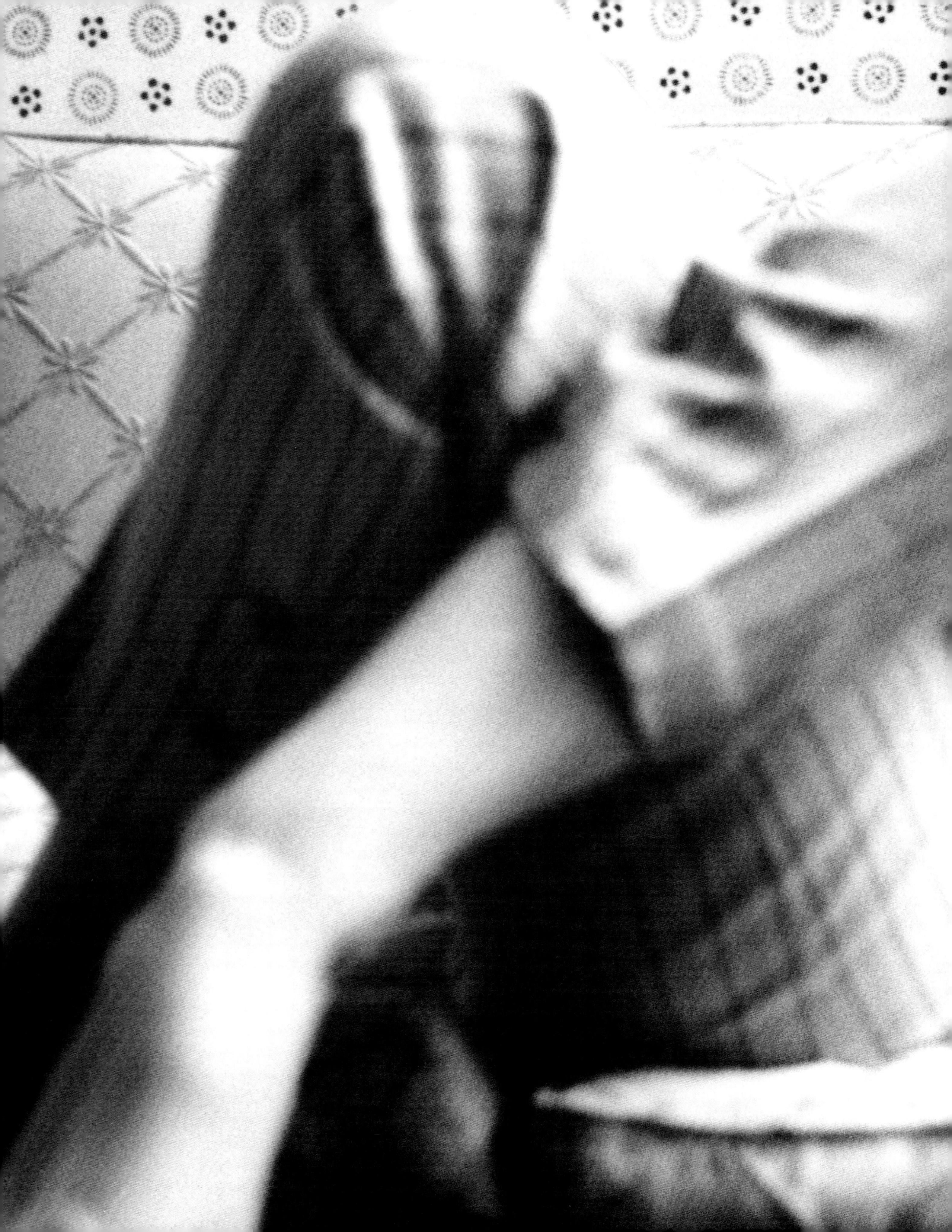

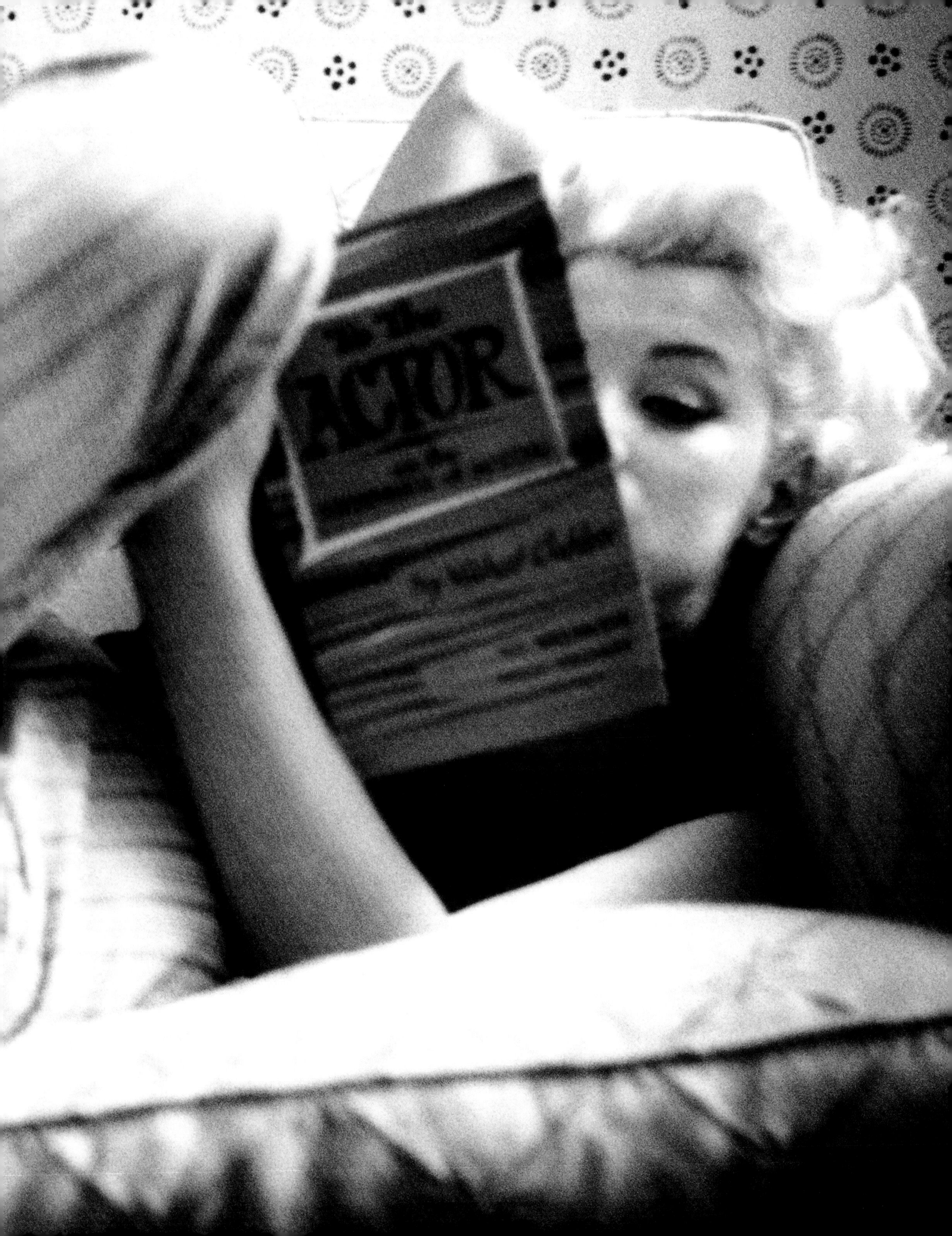
ACTOR

CONTENTS

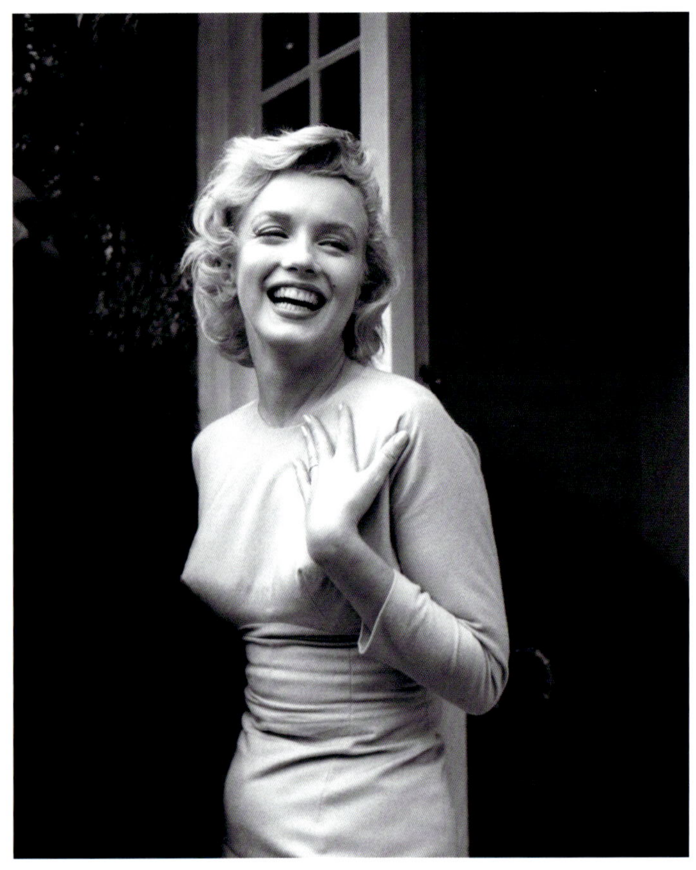

'FIFTY YEARS FROM NOW… THEY MAY LAUGH
AT US FOR OUR PASSION FOR YOUTH, FOR
SOMETHING CALLED GLAMOUR; FOR SLIM
FEMALES WITH SHOULDER-LENGTH MANES,
EXPLOITED BY THE MOVIES, RADIO, PIN-UPS,
AND PRESS, WHO BECAME THE FEMININE
PROTOTYPE OF AN ERA. FOR BEING A TIME IN
HISTORY WHEN THE MANNER OF WEARING
A SARONG, OR A SWEATER, OR A LOCK OF
HAIR, COULD MAKE A WOMAN WORLD-
FAMOUS OVERNIGHT.'

– *Vogue*, 1943

Above: Marilyn outside her home at Englefield Green, Surrey, England, c.1956

FORMATIVE
YEARS

When the Great Depression hit in 1929, Americans would suffer for a decade before then entering the Second World War in 1941, which would last another four years. During this time, economic hardship meant that most women had frugal wardrobes, sewed their own clothes and made do and mended, patching, repairing and upcycling hand-me-downs. Fashion existed but, for many, it shone most brightly in the outfits worn by silver-screen actresses such as Jean Harlow. In *Harlow in Hollywood: The Blonde Bombshell* (2011), Darrell Rooney explains how it was only in 1929 that the first films with sound arrived: 'Jean Harlow was the very first blonde bombshell who spoke and made sound onscreen. Jean Harlow was Marilyn Monroe's idol. If there hadn't been a Jean Harlow, there never would've been a Marilyn Monroe in that way.' Harlow's stage wardrobe for her 1929 film *Saturday Night Kid* was created by legendary costume designer Edith Head, who recalls being 'impressed with her [Harlow's] sensuous body'. She goes on, 'I made the most of it with white satin, cut on the bias […] what she wore in those scenes inspired others to take a second look and realize her knockout potential' (Head, 1983).

The dress was inspired by the work of French couturier Madeleine Vionnet, whose innovative creations draped and celebrated the curves of a woman's body. The 1930s wardrobe moved away from the string-bean boyish silhouette of the '20s, discarded restrictive corsetry and, instead, embraced a more voluptuous shape such as that of Monroe. According to Sarah Berry, professor of film and media, high fashion became accessible through film, its looks translated and made covetable for the millions of filmgoers who would pay a few cents to gaze at figure-hugging frocks that transcended their standard day-to-day wear. She explains how 'the white evening gown, often worn with a white fur

wrap, was an omnipresent signifier of feminine luxury throughout the 1930s, particularly following Jean Harlow's appearance in an Adrian-designed satin version in *Dinner at Eight* (1933)' (Berry, 2000). It is no coincidence that a fur shrug over a slip of a dress would become a signature look of Monroe's when she became one of Hollywood's biggest stars. It was these clothes that Marilyn would grow up pouring over when she went to the cinema, dreaming of becoming an actress, and which would later become the template for her professional stage wardrobe.

In the documentary *Marilyn on Marilyn* (2001), Monroe reveals how one of her foster families used to take her to the cinema in Hollywood every weekend:

> *'I was taken there because they worked during the week, and they worked very hard, and they didn't want to be bothered with a child around the house, I think. You can't blame them. So, I was taken there in the morning and would wait till the movie opened […] for 10 cents I would go in and sit in the first row, and I'd watch all kinds of movies […] and I'd sit there and watch them over and over again till late at night. I was supposed to come out at dark, but of course I didn't know when it was dark.'*

In comparison to the clothes she saw on the big screen, her childhood and teenage closet was meagre. Early photographs show her wearing straightforward, plain pieces reflective of the utility-mode styling of recession and war. For an icon who is known for her onscreen glamour, there is a poignancy in knowing that she grew up poor, unable to afford more than a

A young Norma Jeane, Los Angeles, 1944

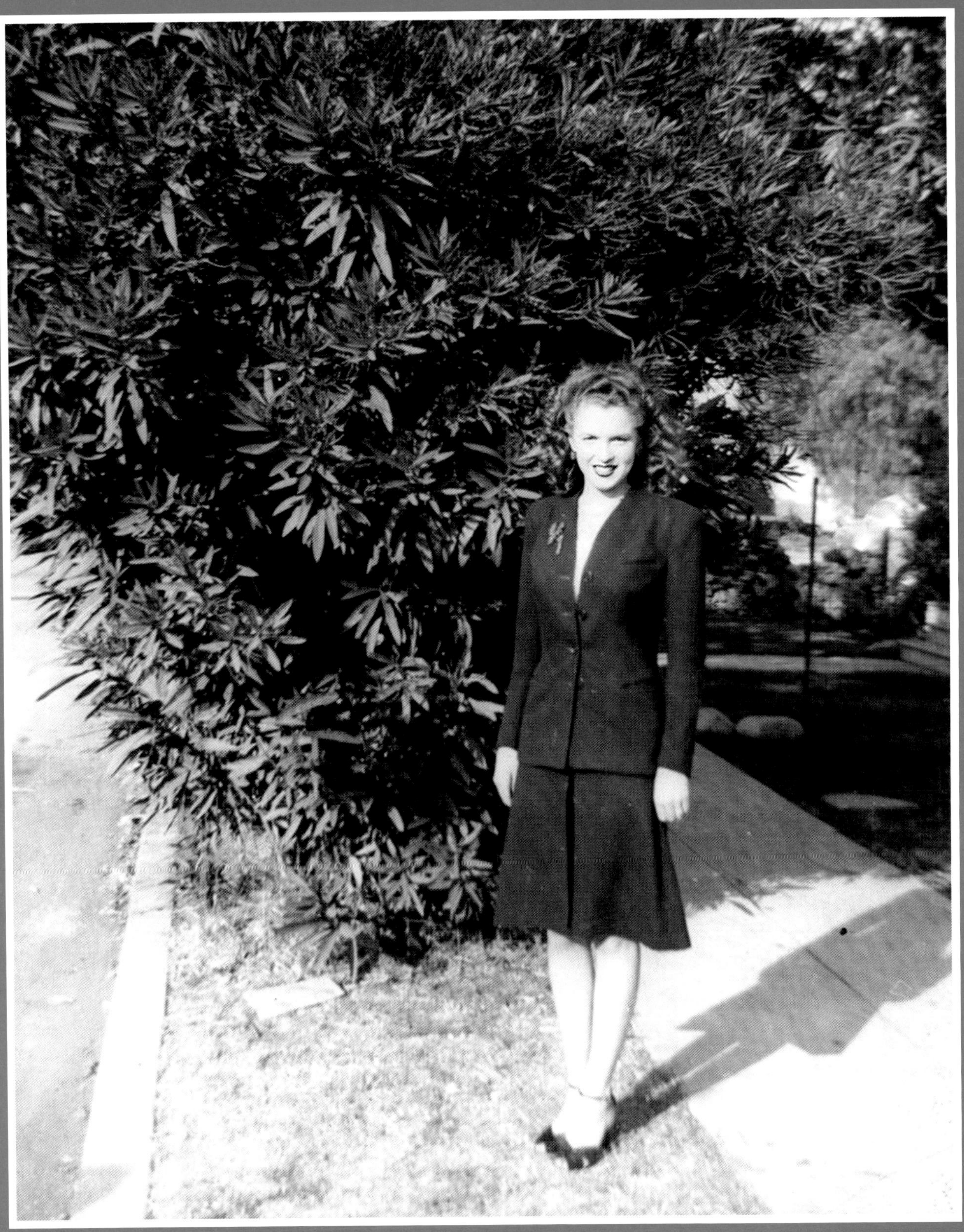

few clothes, and taking great care with the ones she did have. Monroe reveals the reality of her childhood in her unfinished biography *My Story* (1974), published posthumously: 'My own costume never varied. It consisted of a faded blue skirt and white waist. I had two of each, but since they were exactly alike everyone thought I wore the same outfit all the time. It was one of the things that annoyed people – my wearing the same clothes.'

In early adolescence, however, she discovered the impact clothing could have, recounting how 'one morning both my white blouses were torn, and I would be late for school if I stopped to fix them. I asked one of my "sisters" in the house if she could loan me something to wear. She was my age but smaller. She loaned me a sweater. I arrived at school [and] everybody stared at me as if I had suddenly grown two heads, which in a way I had. They were under my tight sweater' (1974). The clothes she wore, she was beginning to realise, were more than just clothes; they reflected who she was and who she wanted to be and could become.

Who she was, however, was dependent on circumstance and the moment. An image of her, aged 13 and sitting with her 'aunt' Ana Lower shows Norma Jeane Mortenson wearing a slightly balled, hand-knit, short-sleeve sweater with a basic skirt and a scarf tied loosely around her neck. A year later, a photo shows her sporting a boxy shoulder-padded tailored jacket, indicative of '40s practicality and worn over a useful button-up blue gingham shirt. During the 1940s, styling was often rather dreary, and Monroe's clothes reflect this in their unaffected and economical appearance. Simple print '40s tea-dresses, along with austere skirt and trouser suits, demonstrate the rationing imposed by Regulation L-85, a law that limited fabric and trim use at that time. According to the Law Library of Congress, 'hems and belts could not exceed two inches in width, garments could not have more than one pocket, and ornamental sleeves, hoods, and scarves were banned' (Goles, 2023). In contrast to the sultry luxury of clothes worn by Hollywood's female stars, the '30s and '40s are seen as a rather unglamorous period of fashion.

Yet, Yves Saint Laurent was infamously informed by this era for his 1971 *Libération/Quarante* collection, along with the looks that were being revived by his friend and muse Paloma Picasso, who thrifted original 1940s pieces from flea markets. The sensible shoes and fuss-free pieces that Monroe wore out of necessity became the source for St Laurent's scandalous couture show which had Parisians openly up in arms. To stylistically repeat a time of deprivation and dispossession felt immoral and for many it was a moment in fashion they'd rather forget. Yves, however, saw the beauty and caught the fashion significance and shape of those times, combining the sexuality of the silver screen with the austerity of day-to-day wear that Marilyn knew so well.

In a 2015 *AnOther Magazine* feature, Osman Ahmed discusses the show and how 'one of the models, a redhead called Annie Ferrari, was especially provocative in her braless and blowsy appearance. Guests cited her movements as sluggish, languorous, and lewd'. The article interviews one of Saint Laurent's closest friends, Loulou de la Falaise, who adds: 'Everything jiggled. She was very sexy. People were used to couture models who were very spiky; it was a shock to see a big sexual girl like that.' The fashion of the 1940s encompassed conflicting opposites: simple and functional through to glamorous and swish – paradigms which would go on to reflect the two different faces of Marilyn, one of the world's most captivating superstars.

In 1944, shooting for *Yank, the Army Weekly* magazine, David Conover took photos of Norma Jeane Dougherty (who had by this time married and taken her husband's name) as a contribution to the war effort at Radioplane munitions factory in Van Nuys, California. And it was clear that the young girl had *something*. Her simple, fitted work-shirt, tucked neatly into her side-button trousers, embodied what the working girl wore in the 1940s. It wasn't an unattractive look and there was a star behind the smile. In her memoir, Marilyn recalls that she 'wore overalls in the factory. I was surprised that they insisted on this. Putting a girl in overalls is like having her work in tights, particularly if a girl knows how to wear them' (Monroe, 1974).

A few months later in 1945, Bill Carroll would pay Norma Jeane her first modelling fee of $20. In an interview with *Canyon News*, he explains that 'she was a natural in front of the camera. She was doing what she thought was right. I just pressed the button. The pictures were her creations' (Anderson, 2010). Carroll took her to Malibu beach and remembered her as an 'agreeable, thoughtful girl. [...] I didn't want a model. I wanted a good-looking plain Jane, the kind of kid you'd like to live next to' (Fernandez, 2010).

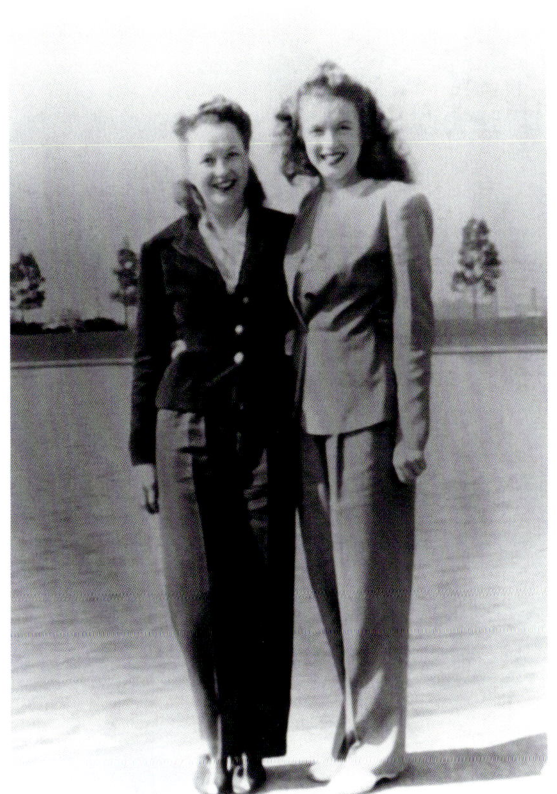

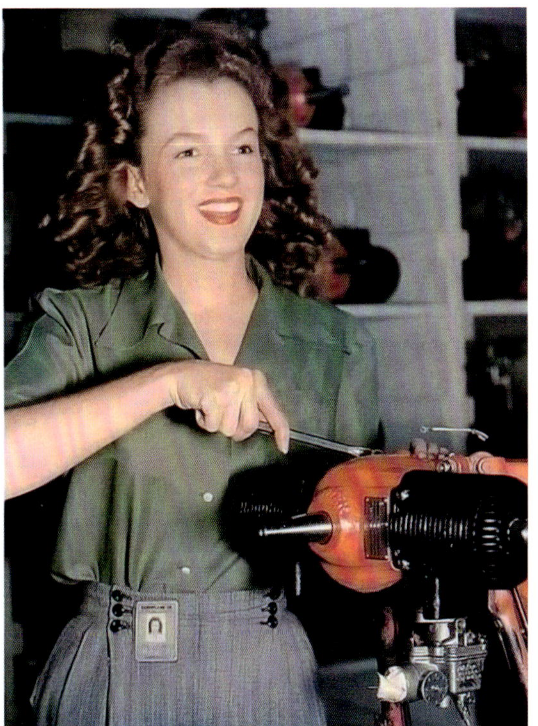

Norma Jeane with her half-sister Berenice Baker, wearing a relaxed trouser suit, 1944

Norma Jeane Dougherty (as she was then), posing for *Yank* magazine, 26 June 1945

The functional clothes Norma Jeane would wear daily were in tune with those that women throughout the country wore to take on jobs traditionally assigned to men. They were also in tune with the evolving 'American Style' of easy-to-wear classic sportswear that would become the calling card of designers, including Claire McCardell, whose influence was extolled in a recent *Vogue* feature: 'It is not an exaggeration to say that the concept of American fashion would not be what it is today without the designer Claire McCardell, who is credited with inventing the idea of American sportswear with her pragmatic approach to clothes in the 1940s and '50s' (Garcia-Furtado, 2022). Expediency was at the heart of Marilyn's wardrobe growing up, too, which was typical for a woman of the time. In her research paper on sportswear fashion during the 1930s, Rebecca Arnold (2007) explains how 'design details, pared-down, body-conscious forms and utilitarian fabrics would all enter the sphere of sportswear as it was to evolve during the Depression.'

A 1944 photograph of Monroe with her half-sister Berenice Baker shows her clad in a relaxed, low-key wide-leg trouser and jacket ensemble. The images Carroll took of Norma Jeane mark the clean lines and ease of mass-produced sportswear. She wears a white bibbed playsuit, teamed with simple striped jersey T-shirts and jumpers, peasant blouses with hair swept back in a scarf. The progression of American everyday fashion in the 1940s towards casual and uncomplicated silhouettes developed in contrast to the work of couture houses in Europe after the war. Professor Amy de La Haye (2020) points out that 'by February 1943, just 47 houses remained in business, and the following year the Nazis decreed that the bi-annual collections which had typically featured 100 models, be reduced to feature only 60'. Consequently, when the war was finally over, it was Christian Dior with his famous 'New Look' – which echoed the femininity of the Belle Époque and all its corseted finery – who was charged with revamping the French fashion economy by providing escapism and fantasy for a customer who had lived through rationing. Parisian houses depended on their trickle-down appeal across the world, and it was Dior's ultra-vogueish form that emerged as a foil to the unfussiness of the 'American look'.

As Marilyn took her first steps to stardom, she was living through a generation of cultural change; for women this meant returning to the household to look after their husbands as they returned from the war and took back the jobs that women had been doing while they were away. Alongside this came the expectation that women would discard their overalls and go back to wearing dresses. Yet women had a newfound assertion that comfort was key and wearing the trousers wasn't just for men. The paradoxes of fashion post-war indicated how flimsy women's rights were.

For Monroe, the early, dreamy draw of luxuriant '30s goddess-wear held firm – after all those years sitting in the cinema watching her favourite film actresses slink across the screen, it was embedded in her DNA. But at the same time, as she climbed the ladder to super-success, her sartorial choices did become pragmatic: outfits that fit her curves on camera and simple, American-line, laid-back separates when she was off-set. She would of course go on to wear some of the most high-profile designers and have outfits created for her by fashion houses such as Dior. However, the clothes she wore and saw growing up would, in many ways, mirror the clothes she would wear once she became a star; the yin and yang of dressing down and aspiring to dress up is at the core of Marilyn's fashion styling. She was a product of the Great Depression, the war and the Hollywood glitz and glamour of the movies, and her wardrobe announced this.

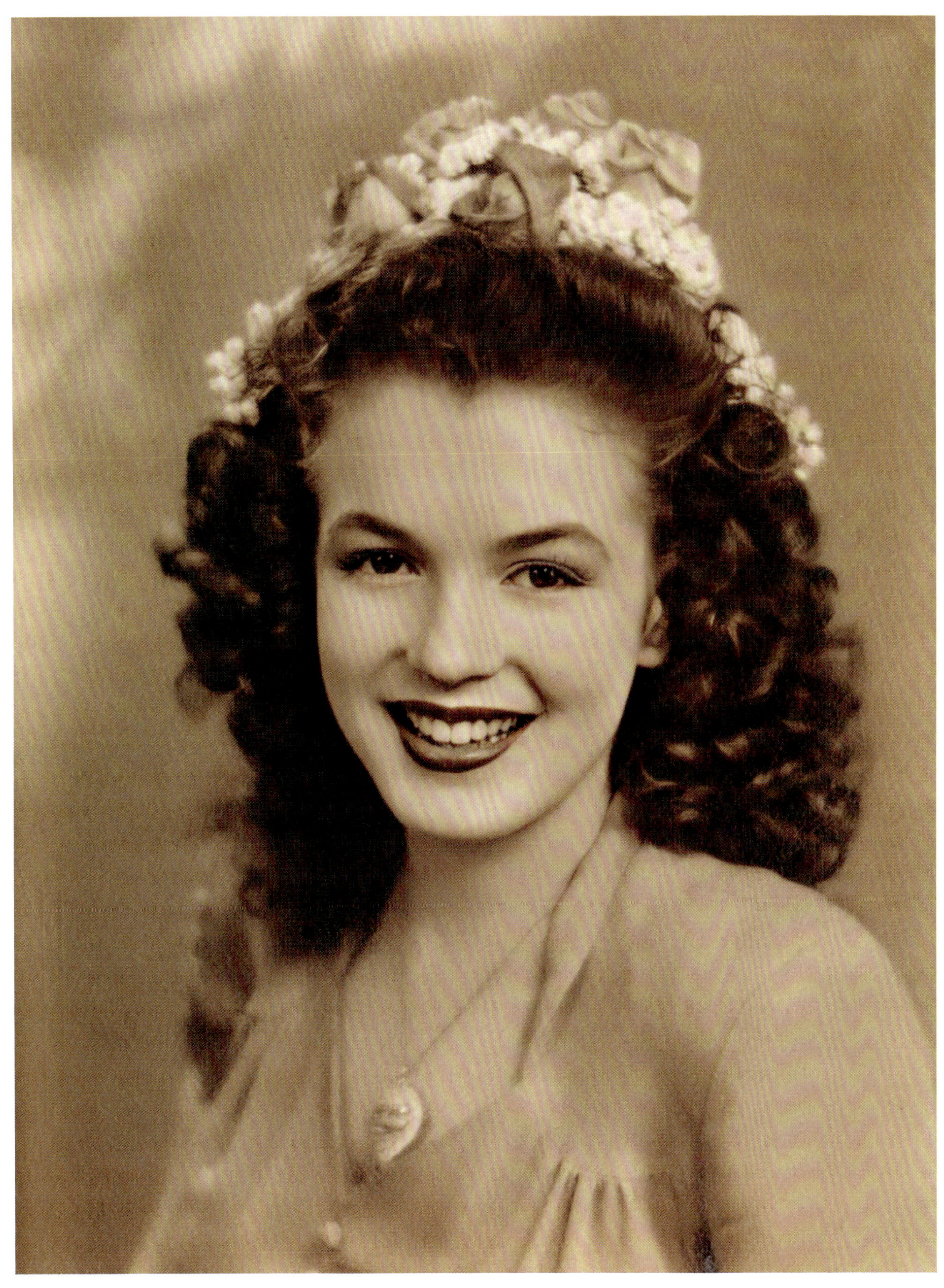

Norma Jeane posing for the Radioplane beauty contest, 1944

'IT WAS 1946 WHEN MRS SNIVELY
CALLED AND SAID, I HAVE A GIRL.
I THINK SHE MIGHT BE INTERESTING...
SHE WAS A VERY GOOD MODEL.
I HAD HER EASILY ON A HUNDRED
MAGAZINE COVERS. HER FACE AND
FIGURE WERE WELL KNOWN, LONG
BEFORE SHE BECAME MARILYN
MONROE... WHEN SHE SAW A
CAMERA, ANY CAMERA, SHE LIT UP.'

– László Willinger, *Marilyn Monroe:
Beyond the Legend*, 1987

A young Norma Jeane, starting out as a model, c.1945

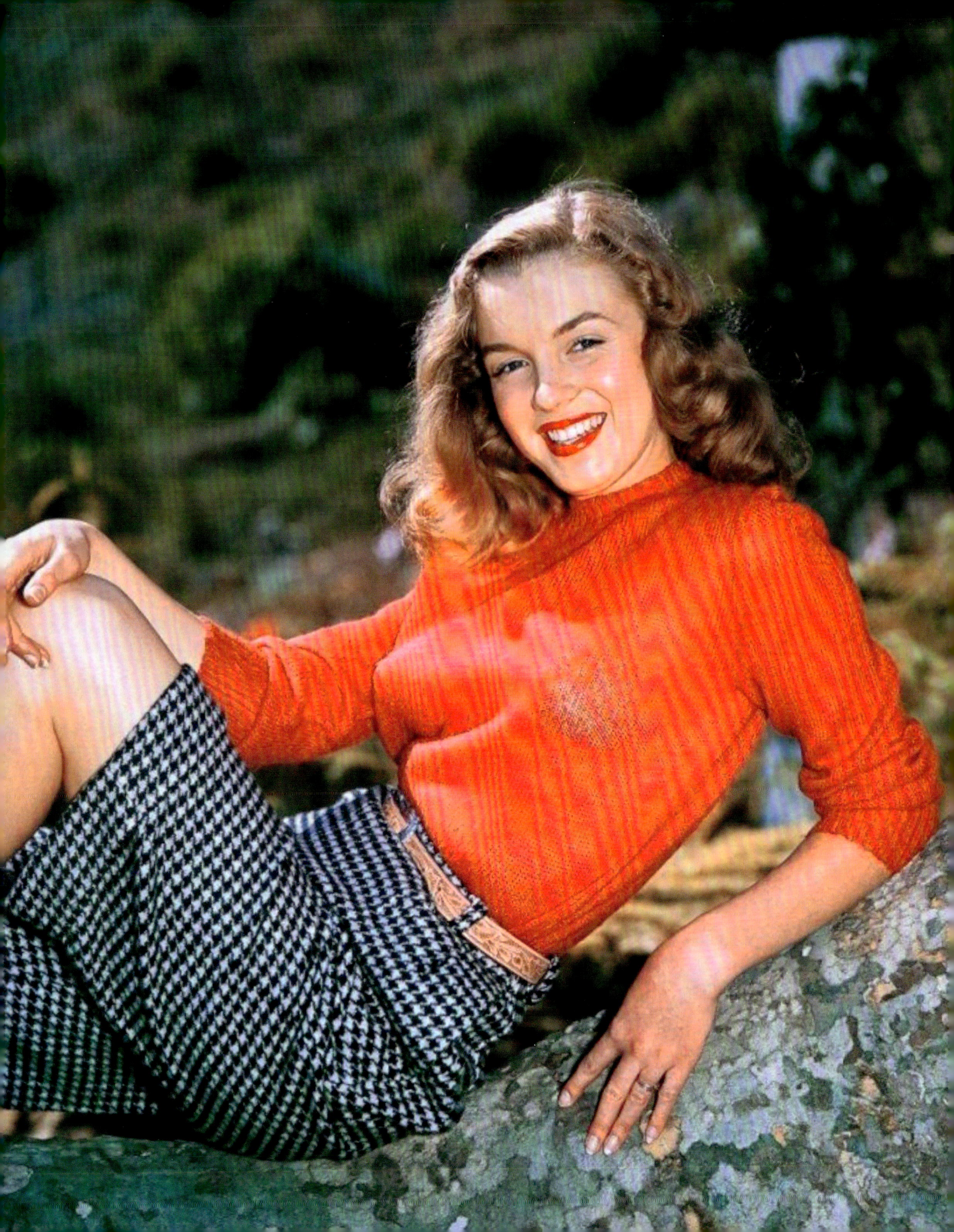

BECOMING
'THE GIRL'

In 1945, aged 19, Marilyn Monroe went to see the Emmeline Snively Blue Book Modeling Agency. In a 1962 interview, Snively describes how Marilyn arrived wearing 'a little white dress, not something you'd wear on a photographic shoot, and it was as clean and white and as ironed and shining as she was' (Marilyn Monroe History, 2023). The wholesome girl-next-door look that Marilyn manifested was something magazines and photographers sought to capture, and the resulting images of a conservative, idealised wife reflect this. But the clothes she wore for castings and campaigns are of a similar ilk, revealing how, post-war, gender equality was no longer encouraged. Factories were once again full of returning soldiers doing jobs that no longer existed for women. Instead, women were expected to return to the home and reconcile the strains of war and the Depression by way of their domestic prowess. Despite her clothes suggesting a certain conformity, Norma Jeane's home life was very different. She left her first husband in 1946, primarily because she wanted to work and had outgrown her marriage.

At the modelling agency, she was quickly in demand. Her first advertising job was for the *Douglas Airview* magazine, promoting their DC-6 aeroplane; the cover shows Norma Jeane enjoying its comforts while wearing an unassuming dark two-piece skirt-suit. The April 1946 issue of *The Family Circle,* shot by Hungarian photographer André de Dienes, features Monroe on the front page, barefoot, dressed in a puff-sleeved pinafore with a bow in her hair and holding a new-born lamb. That same year, Argo-Flex cameras featured her in their advertisement wearing gingham trousers and a tight jumper, with her curls pulled back in a bow. A 1945 shot of her by Dienes wearing a handmade fisherman's jumper would appear on the cover of the 13 December 1947 issue of the UK's *Picture Post*: it was a magazine that regularly attracted over one million readers. Dienes had taken the 19-year-old Norma Jeane on a five-week road trip when she first began modelling and, although he had originally wanted to shoot nudes, the shots he took portray Marilyn in technicolour health, posing in the hearty outdoors dressed in primary colours and cute sporty outfits.

Despite this initial success, the young Norma Jeane was deemed unpolished. German photographer László Willinger, who came to America in the late 1930s and would go on to portray some of Hollywood's most famous actresses, including Ava Gardner and Hedy Lamarr, remembers how 'she had one bad tooth at the front which I had fixed at my expense. Her hair was kinky which someone else fixed' (Marilyn Monroe: Beyond the Legend, 1987). The agency thought her hair was too curly and dark, so they lightened and straightened it, establishing a look that she would maintain throughout her career. By the end of 1946, she had her first contract at Twentieth Century Fox and began using her stage name 'Marilyn Monroe' (officially changing it in 1956). In 1949, Dienes and Monroe would drive to Malibu beach and create a set of pictures together for a book of poetry and philosophy. The resulting photographs show Marilyn wearing no make-up and wrapped in nothing but a black blanket; one of these pictures would go on to become the *Picture Post*'s March 1949 cover. These rare images show a young unadorned girl, eager for fame; a sneak preview of what she hoped to become.

Marilyn modelling shorts and crop top, California, 1953

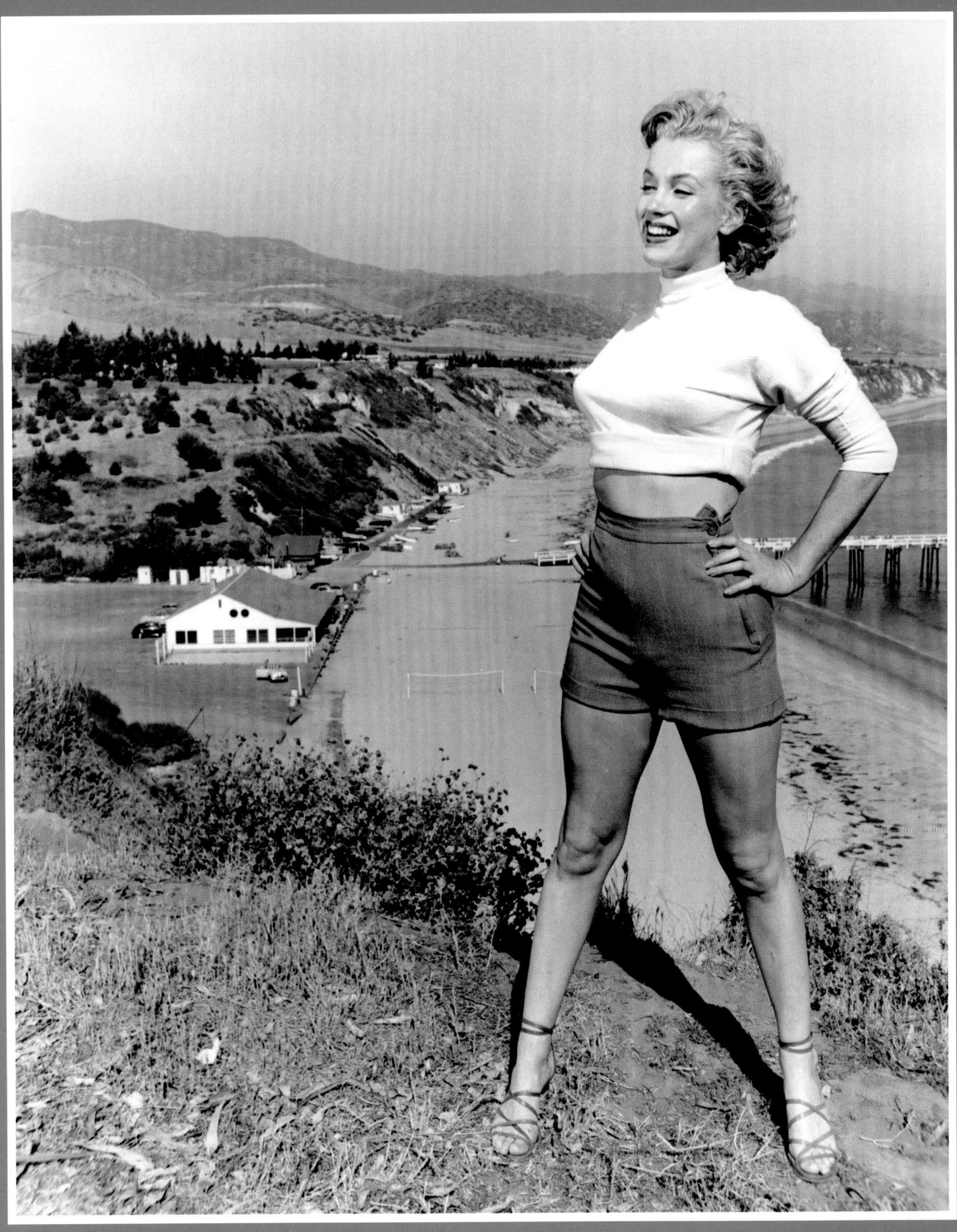

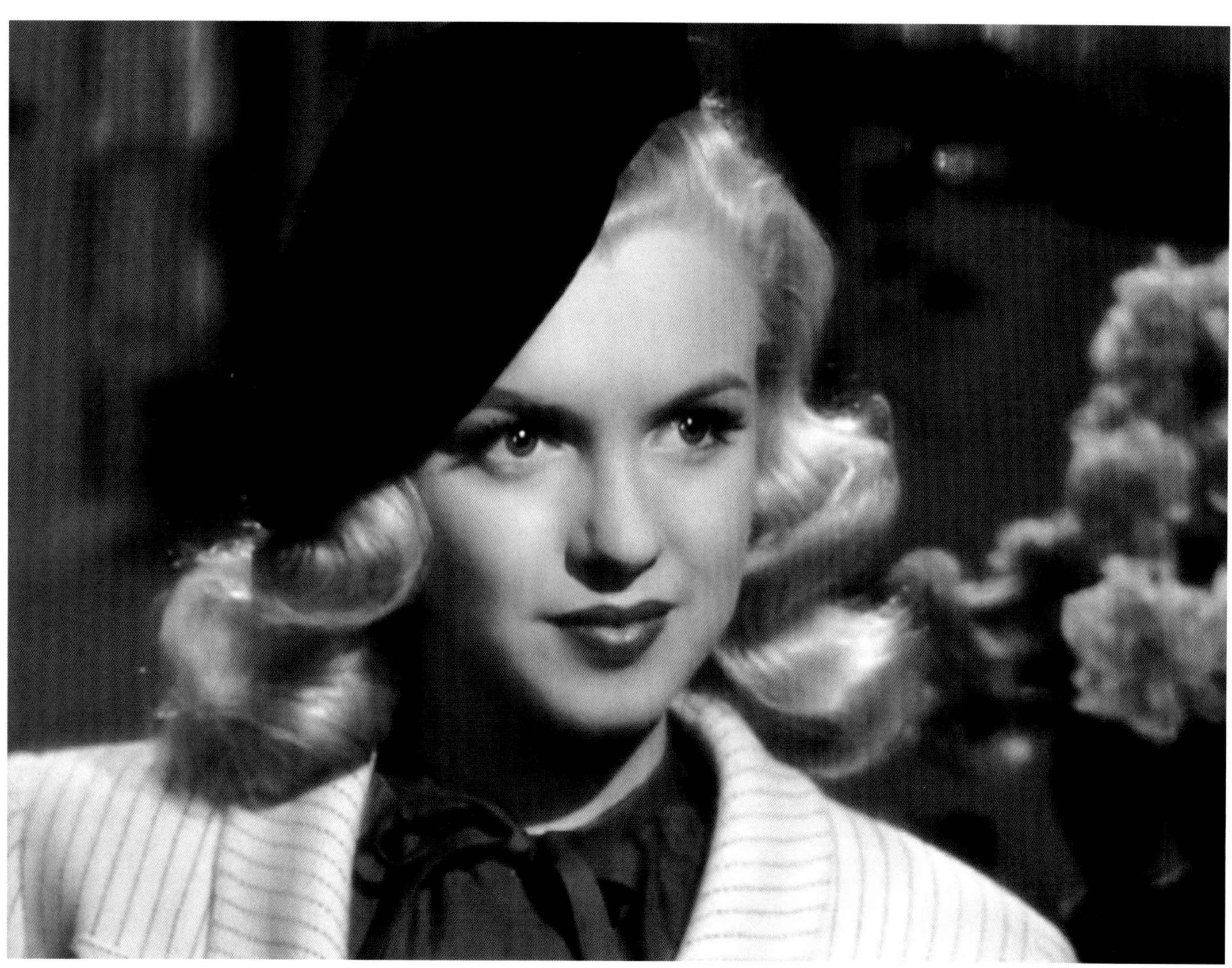

'AN ANGEL IN LACE,
 A FABULOUS FACE,
 THAT'S NO EXAGGERATION,
 THAT'S MY MARILYN.'

– 'Marilyn' by Ray Anthony, 1952

Above: *Ladies of the Chorus*, 1948

Right: Marilyn on the cover of *Picture Post* magazine, December 1947

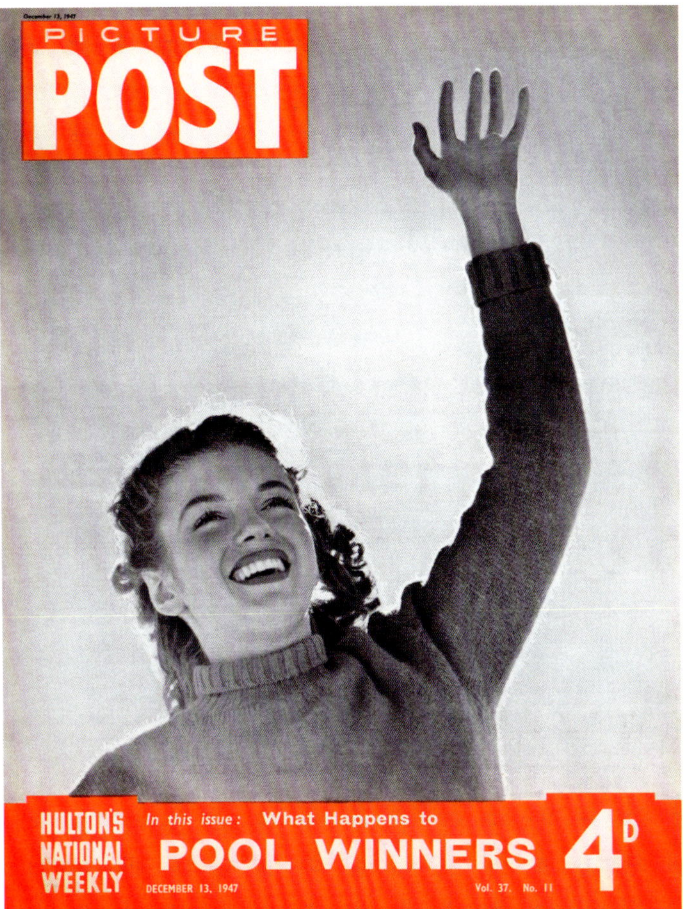

The Hollywood studio system was a hive of industry that moulded its contract actors and, if they were lucky, typecast and prepared them for a life in movies. They looked for young women who could generate publicity and were, as Sheree North discloses in the documentary *Marilyn Monroe: Beyond the Legend* (1987), 'highly saleable'. Although Marilyn had already been prepped and packaged at the Blue Book Modeling Agency, Emmeline Snively explains how she 'had no background. She'd only gone to the 10th grade, and she was so eager for training'. So, when she stepped foot onto the studio lot, she embraced all it had to offer. Snively continues, 'she signed up for every course they had to offer, which meant dancing, voice, ballet, tap […] she went whole hog in for the educational side of it because it had been neglected in her life' (Marilyn Monroe History, 2023).

Marilyn immediately set to work playing walk-on parts and can be glimpsed in her screen debut as Evie in *Dangerous Years* (1947), followed by Betty in *Scudda Hoo! Scudda Hay!*, released in March 1948. At that point, so near and yet so far from the inner sanctum of stars, Marilyn's didn't take her

clothes for granted. When she moved to Burbank, aged 21, she admitted, 'I owned one suit, two plain dresses, two pairs of shoes, some darned stockings, a little lingerie, and a bathrobe' (1974). Money was often tight and life as a fledgling actress always unstable. Despite her hard work, the hair and name change, Monroe's first contract with Fox lasted only until 1947, followed by less than a year at Columbia. She describes the way Fox fired her in her memoir:

> *'[…] it was the opinion of the studio that I was not photogenic […] "Mr. Zanuck feels that you may turn into an actress sometime," said the official "but that your type of looks is definitely against you." I went to my room and lay down in bed and cried […] I could learn, improve, and become an actress. But how could I ever change my looks? And I'd thought that was the part of me that couldn't miss!'* (Monroe, 1974)

The intense pressure on conforming to a studio type meant that looks and clothes were everything. Marilyn wasn't on the inside track yet and had much to learn. In around 1949, the year before she eventually returned to Fox, Marilyn met Joan Crawford at a dinner party held by Joe Schenck, a film studio executive. Crawford offered to help 'guide' Monroe's wardrobe after telling her that the white knitted dress she was wearing was 'utterly incorrect for a dinner of this kind'. She gave Marilyn advice, such as 'you mustn't come to church in flat heels and a gray suit with black trimming. If you wear gray you must wear different gray tones, but never black' and 'the main thing about dressing well […] is to see that everything you wear is just right—that your shoes, stockings, gloves and bag all fit the suit you're wearing' (Monroe, 1974). But Marilyn had only one good dress and one suit and was too ashamed to tell Miss Crawford so.

Fashion for a film star was prescriptive and careers were made and broken on the clothes you wore. Even as late as 1949, when she was cast in *Love Happy* alongside the Marx Brothers, she still had only the one suit. Despite this, glittering in a borrowed bandeau lurex evening gown and fur stole, she had impressed Groucho in the film. However, that dress had to be returned to the studio wardrobe and Monroe had few appropriate pieces of her own for the high-profile publicity tour that ensued. The director, Lester Cowan, gave her $75 to buy some new things but, lacking insight, she went out and bought three more suits, all in wool, that would be too heavyweight for New York, and a 'polka dot blue dress with a low-cut neckline that came with a red velvet belt [as] something more attractive to wear in the evening' (Monroe, 1974). By this point, Monroe was beginning to perfect her Monroe-isms. Marx later remarked that her walk was like 'Mae West, Theda Bara and Bo Peep all rolled into one,' (Monroe, 1974) and reportedly said that he fluffed his line because her dress in the film showed off her cleavage to such seductive advantage.

Marilyn already knew what made heads turn, whether she was wearing overalls in a factory or a younger girl's too tight sweater as an adolescent. She had caught the attention of super-agent Johnny Hyde at the end of 1948 and would later become his lover. Party pictures of the pair at the end of 1949 signal her evolution into 'Marilyn Monroe', with her blonde hair veering closer to silvery platinum, lips painted red and dresses that had become tighter. Even as she began to make a name for herself, the studio always had young women lining up to take her place, so she had to continually strive to keep her contract secure. While eager to learn and take classes, she was also adept at absorbing what worked visually onscreen. She knew that she had to follow Hollywood's sartorial rules if she was to keep her job, and she rose to the challenge, watching, learning, and surpassing those around her.

Monroe's superpower would become her clothes. When she was 'at work' at the studio, she began to understand how to dress, what to borrow, and what to wear to the right parties. Shelley Winters, her friend and housemate at The Studio Club in LA, where actresses lived, remembers this moment in time happily: 'we were blonde, Hollywood babies. But it wasn't sad when we began to get good roles, it was the most glorious and wonderful thing [...] It was exciting and wonderful, and she [Marilyn] got a used black Cadillac and drove people around and I had a new white Cadillac that Paramount got for me wholesale [...] And we really had fun' (Cliporama, 2018a). By 1952, dressing as the emerging film star she had become, Monroe was named 'Fastest Rising Star' by *Photoplay* magazine and 'Most Promising Female Newcomer' by *Look* magazine. The *Terre Haute Tribune* reported the sensation in its 13 March 1952 issue: 'The beautiful blonde now gets a fat paycheck every week from an excited 20th Century Fox studio. She's rated the most sensational sweater girl since Lana Turner. She lives in an expensive hotel room. She dines at Romanoffs.'

Equally, though, she would be recognised as much for what she didn't wear, following the 'Golden Dreams' pin-up calendar photograph that had been taken in May 1949 by Tom Kelley. It had been shot when Marilyn was between Columbia and Fox contracts and needed money for rent. But she is assertive and unapologetic about the photograph, choosing to be informed by her fans rather than the bosses at Fox. 'I was told I should deny I'd posed, but I'd rather be honest about it,' she said, 'I've gotten a lot of fan letters on it. The men like the picture and want copies' (Monroe quoted in Mosby, 1952). This self-determination was something the studio system encountered infrequently from its female roster, especially a supporting-role actress who had yet to break the box-office big time. The following year, however, wearing a red dress that would eclipse even her nude shots, Marilyn would take the world by storm in *Niagara* (1953).

'IT WAS THE CREATIVE PART THAT KEPT ME GOING, TRYING TO BE AN ACTRESS. I ENJOY ACTING WHEN YOU REALLY HIT IT RIGHT. AND I GUESS I'VE ALWAYS HAD TOO MUCH FANTASY TO BE ONLY A HOUSEWIFE [...] I WAS NEVER KEPT, TO BE BLUNT ABOUT IT; I ALWAYS KEPT MYSELF.'

– Marilyn Monroe, quoted in *Life* magazine, 1962

Marilyn with her agent, Johnny Hyde, c.1949

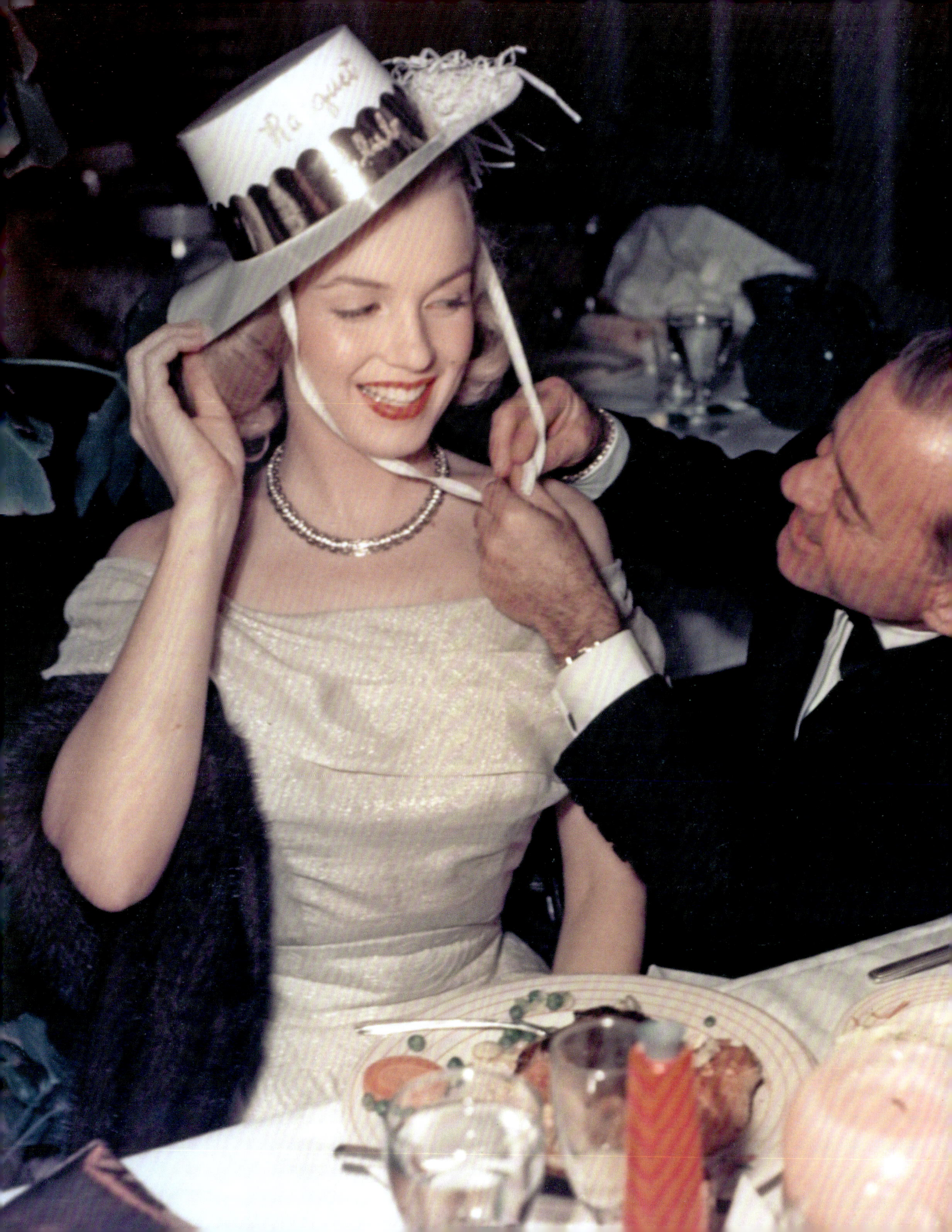

FILMS

Gentlemen Prefer Blondes, 1953

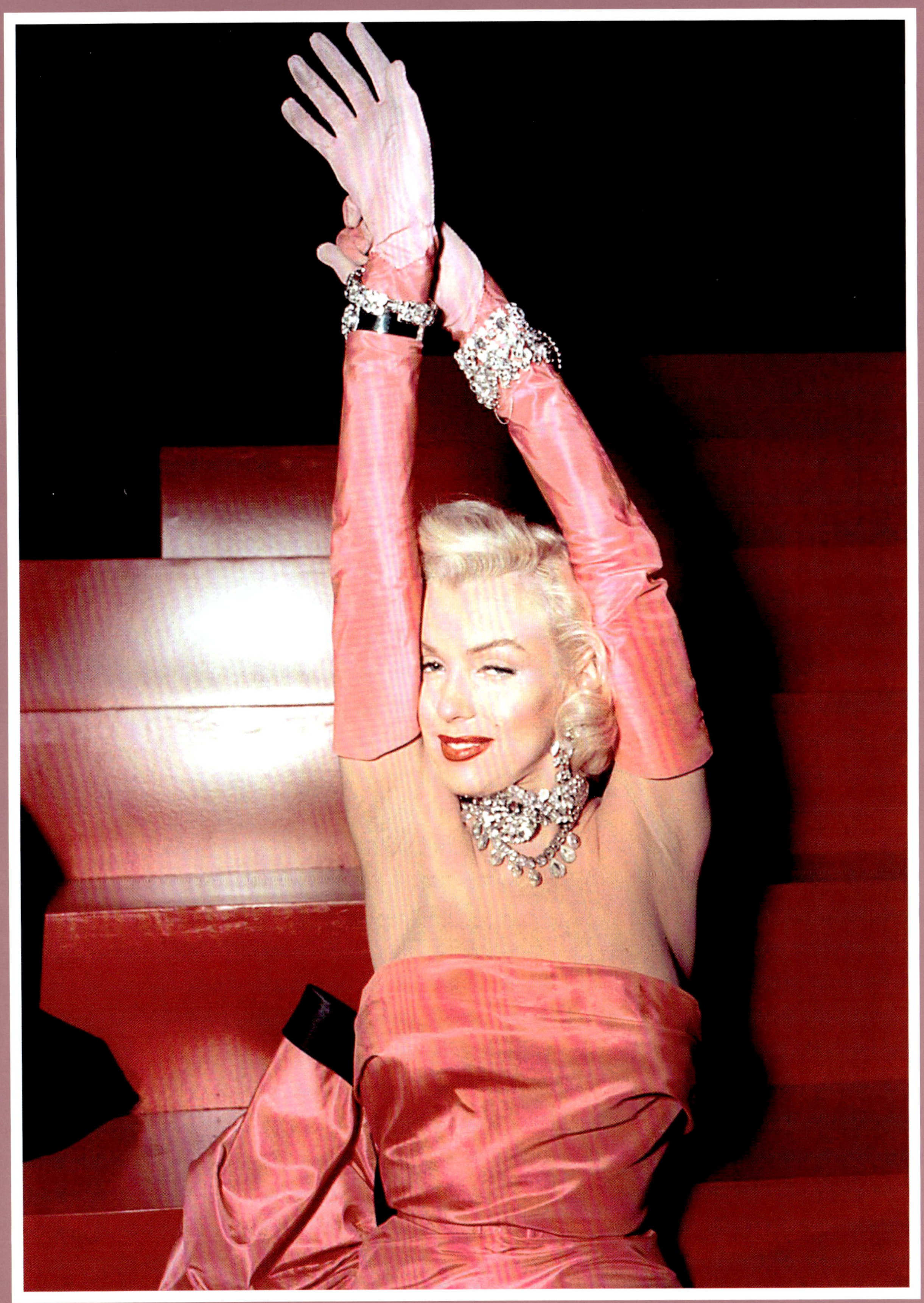

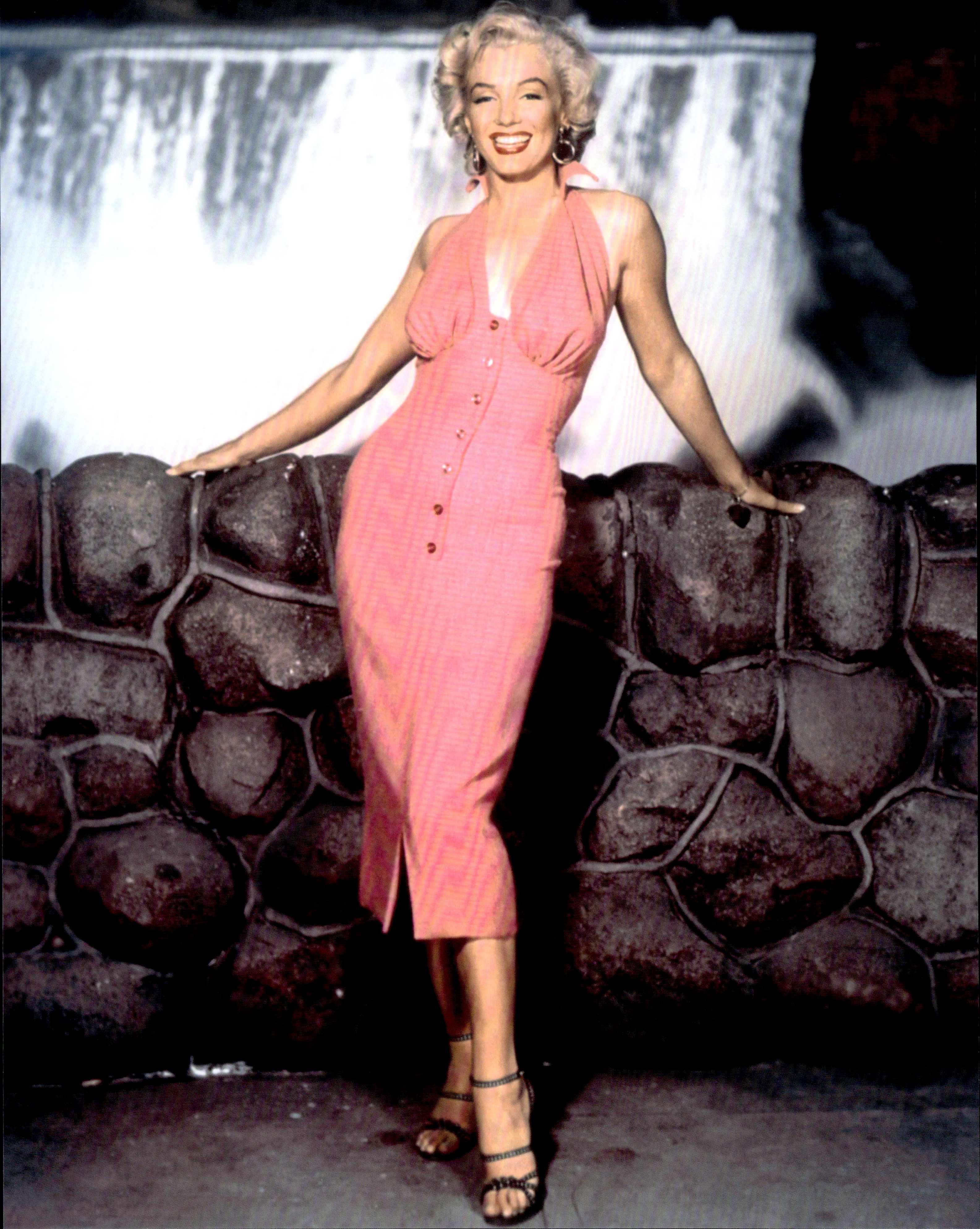

NIAGARA

The classic femme fatale silhouette is personified by Marilyn in her 1953 film *Niagara*, directed by Henry Hathaway. Driven by desire, her compelling character Rose Loomis tries to have her husband killed so she can escape with her lover. Dressed as a siren, Marilyn has a provocative allure that disrupts: she is both seductive and dissolute. While today the vamp has become a reductive cinematic stereotype, it can also be a source of empowerment, according to Minowa et al (2019), and Marilyn was canny enough to understand this, using her sexual attraction to her advantage. Just as a femme fatale is known to be magnetic and irresistible, creating a striking first impression and irresistibly drawing her audience to her, using her sexuality to get what she wants, so, too, does the public, professional Marilyn. She was a woman who knew exactly what she wanted, and how to get it. In contrast to the manipulative character that Marilyn plays, however, the private Marilyn couldn't be more different. According to the writer Fred Woodress, who interviewed Monroe on set, 'She was a warm, wonderful person who gave me full attention [...] Some stars talk to you while looking over your shoulder for someone more important. Not Marilyn' (quoted in Durrer, 2005).

With the help of her make-up artist, Allan 'Whitey' Snyder, and the Oscar-winning costume designer Dorothy Jeakins, who created a wardrobe for Monroe that got under the skin of her role, Marilyn presented a refined appearance that accentuated her character's swaying sexuality and embodied the full force of her mesmerising charm. As Laura Mulvey points out in her essay on the actress, in relation to the history of Hollywood, Monroe had 'evolved and defined the characteristic "Marilyn" look and there is no doubt that she realized that she had to construct, even exploit, herself for the "male gaze" to establish her Hollywood career' (2017).

Marilyn wearing one of Dorothy Jeakins' creations for *Niagara*, 1953

Clothes were central to all Marilyn's performances and her wardrobe in *Niagara* is a great example of how an outfit can so effectively reveal what sort of a character Monroe is playing before she has uttered her first line. Although the film is shot in technicolour, the sartorial language speaks of a film noir, with Monroe following in the tradition of irresistible vamps played by Hollywood doyennes such as Joan Crawford in *Mildred Pierce* (1945), Ava Gardner in *The Killers* (1946) and Veronica Lake in *The Blue Dahlia* (1946). Marilyn more than matches their sultry deviousness, having already played a similar role as Angela Phinlay in the 1950 film *The Asphalt Jungle*. However, the biggest hit in *Niagara* is, without doubt, the now-iconic pink dress that Monroe wears for the hotel party scene, where she sings 'Kiss' by Haven Gillespie and Lionel Newman. Her husband, George Loomis, played by Joseph Cotten, thinks she's a 'tramp', remarking that her dress is 'cut so low in front you can see her kneecaps'. Some churches even banned the film when it came out because of its alleged indecency. Nonetheless, the clothes Monroe wears in the film went on to help define her signature 'seductive style' when she was 'being Marilyn'.

Jeakins created two versions of the bosom-hugging frock, one in hot red and the other – used in the film – in a more flirtatious fuchsia. Pictures by sound engineer Lani Carlson, an amateur photographer, show how Monroe borrowed the showpiece in August 1952 to wear to a party thrown by big band maestro Ray Anthony in tribute to the rising star and to celebrate his song 'Marilyn'. The director, Hathaway, would eventually gift the dress to Marilyn, cognisant of the very few clothes she owned. Monroe would often use the studio wardrobe for special events, not just because she didn't have many outfits herself, but because it connected her cinematic identity with her public one – which ultimately is why the clothes she chose to buy for herself are so fascinating to examine because they offer a glimpse of the other Marilyn behind the scenes, the one who wasn't performing. The famous off-the-shoulder hot-pink frock was not the only style success of the film. Monroe slips into chic wiggle-tight pencil-skirt suits that, while figure-hugging, have an edge of propriety. In a pure white, marabou-trimmed housecoat, Marilyn's Rose Loomis looks ravishingly vampy and is darkly assured of her charms.

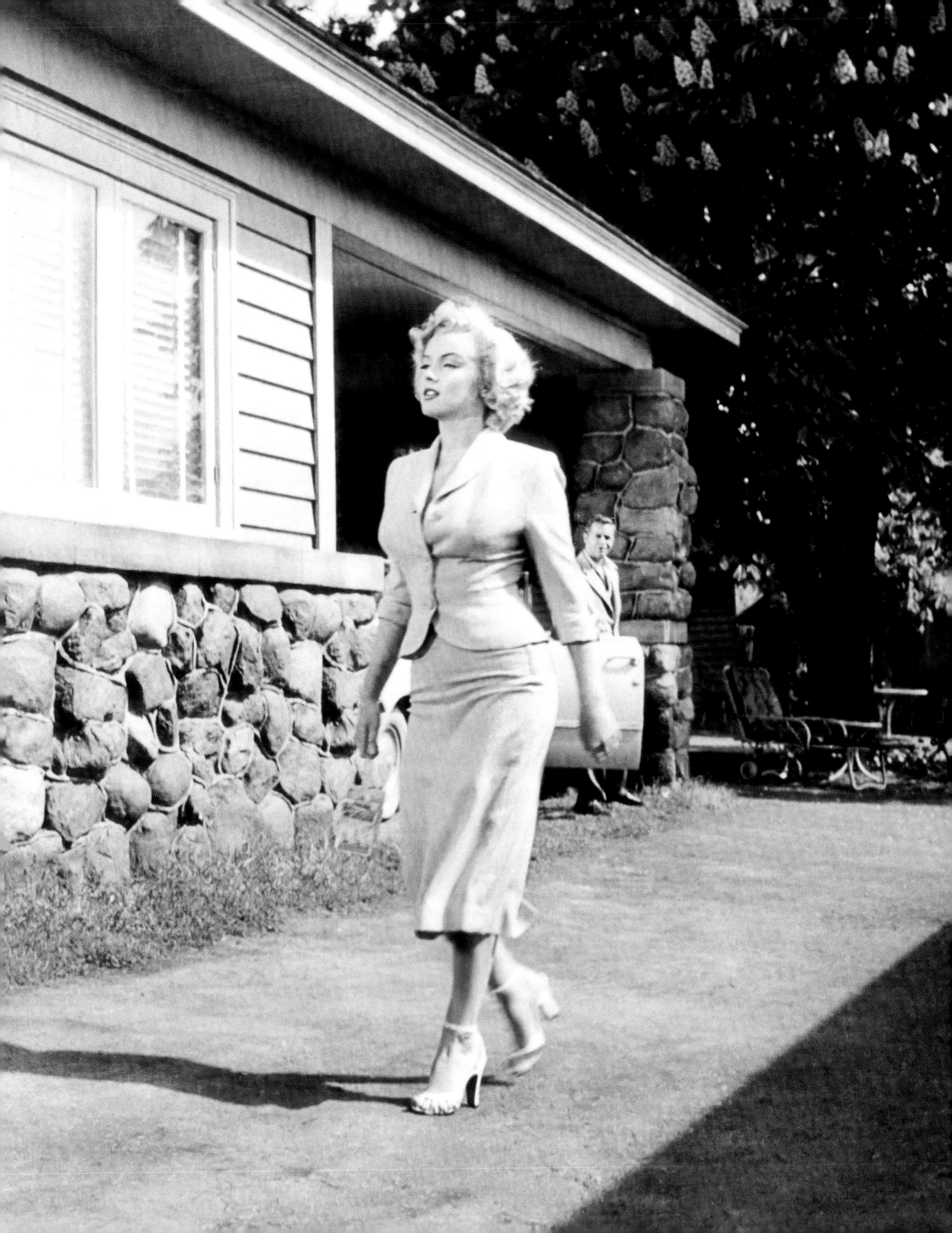

Fashion worn on the big screen is a powerful influence and to this day designers find inspiration in the dress sensibilities of *Niagara*'s Rose Loomis. In 2022, Donatella Versace sent Gigi Hadid down the catwalk in a skilfully fitted skirt suit and a plunge-necked dress, seamlessly inspired by the killer pieces Jeakins produced for Monroe. But although Monroe clearly prized Jeakins, who would be commissioned to create the wardrobe for Marilyn's role as Amanda Dell in her 1960 film *Let's Make Love*, she was openly critical of some of the silhouettes. The film wardrobe was pivotal to Marilyn's success and if she wasn't sure of a look, it had to go. Later, dressing Marilyn as Roslyn in her 1961 Western, *The Misfits*, the wardrobe designer would be unceremoniously dismissed by the star. A May 1960 letter from Jeakins to Monroe, says, 'I am sorry I have displeased you. I feel quite defeated—like a misfit, in fact. But I must, above everything, continue to work (and live) in terms of my own honesty, pride, and good taste' (Julien's Auctions, 2016a). The privilege would instead go to Jean Louis, one of Hollywood's most famous designers. Monroe would rely on him again to create outfits for the unfinished film *Something's Got to Give* (1962), wearing his designs when she needed to impress the most, such as singing to John F. Kennedy that same year at Madison Square Garden in New York.

'MARILYN MONROE, WHO IS AN INEXPERT ACTRESS BUT A TALENTED WOMAN. SHE IS A SAUCY, HIP-SWINGING 5FT. 5½-IN. PERSONALITY WHO HAS BROUGHT BACK TO THE MOVIES THE KIND OF UNBRIDLED SEX APPEAL THAT HAS BEEN MISSING SINCE THE DAYS OF CLARA BOW AND JEAN HARLOW. THE TRADEMARKS OF MARILYN'S BLONDE ALLURE (BUST 37 IN. HIPS 37 IN. WAIST 24 IN.) ARE HER MOIST, HALF-CLOSED EYES AND MOIST, HALF-OPENED MOUTH. SHE IS A MOVIE PRESS AGENT'S DREAM.'

– *Time* magazine, 11 August 1952

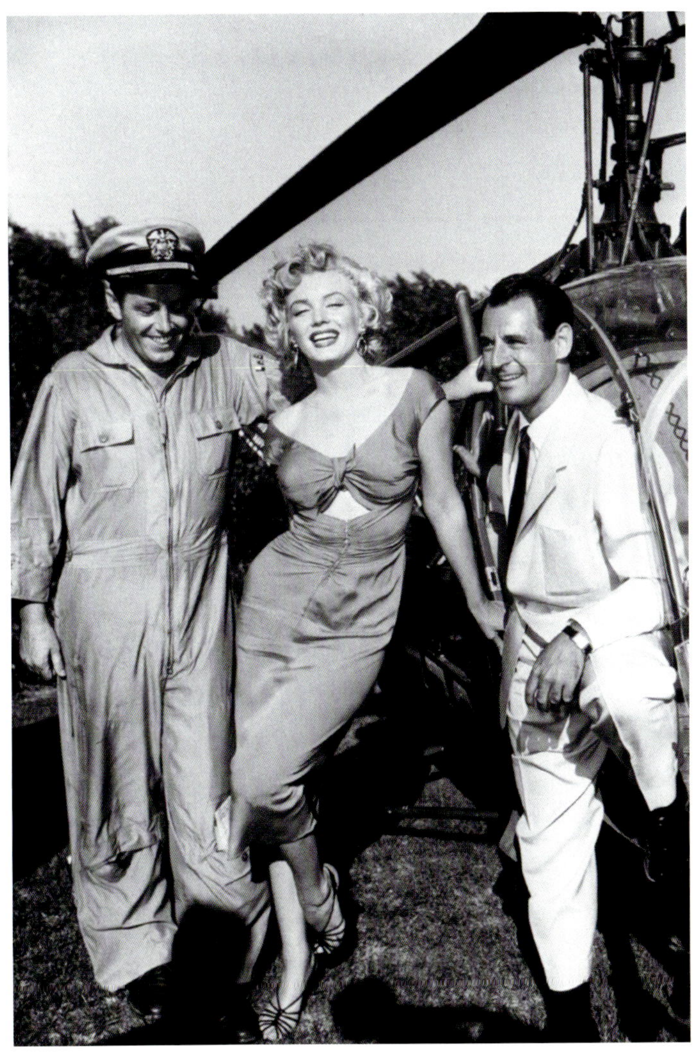

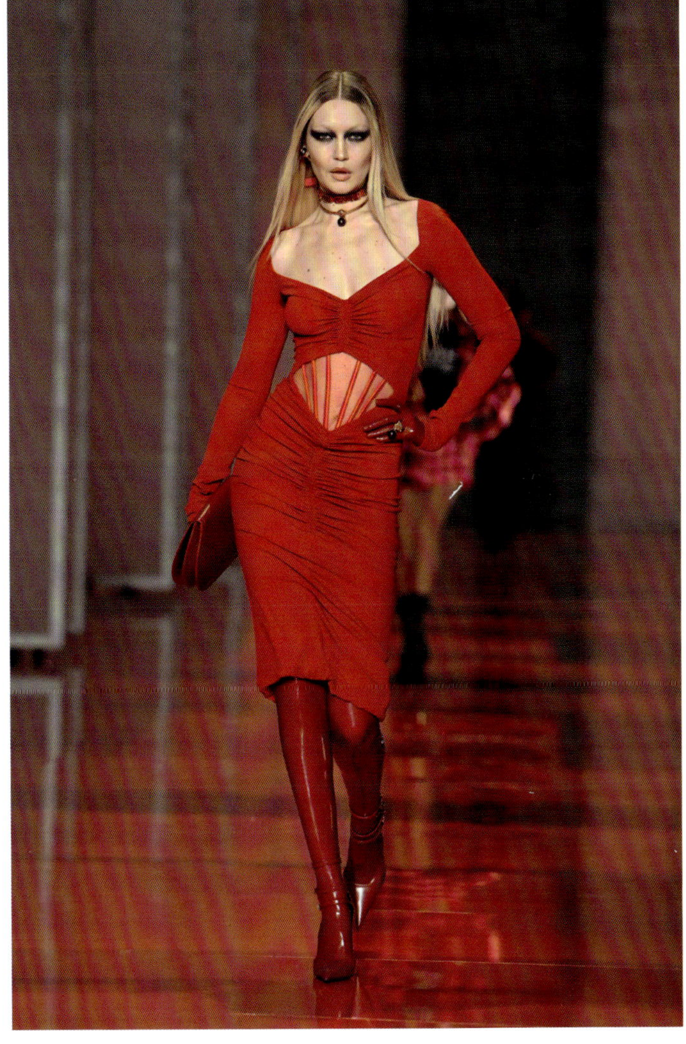

Marilyn posing with bandleader Ray Anthony at his party, wearing *the* pink dress, 1952

Gigi Hadid walks the catwalk for Versace 2022 wearing a Marilyn-inspired dress

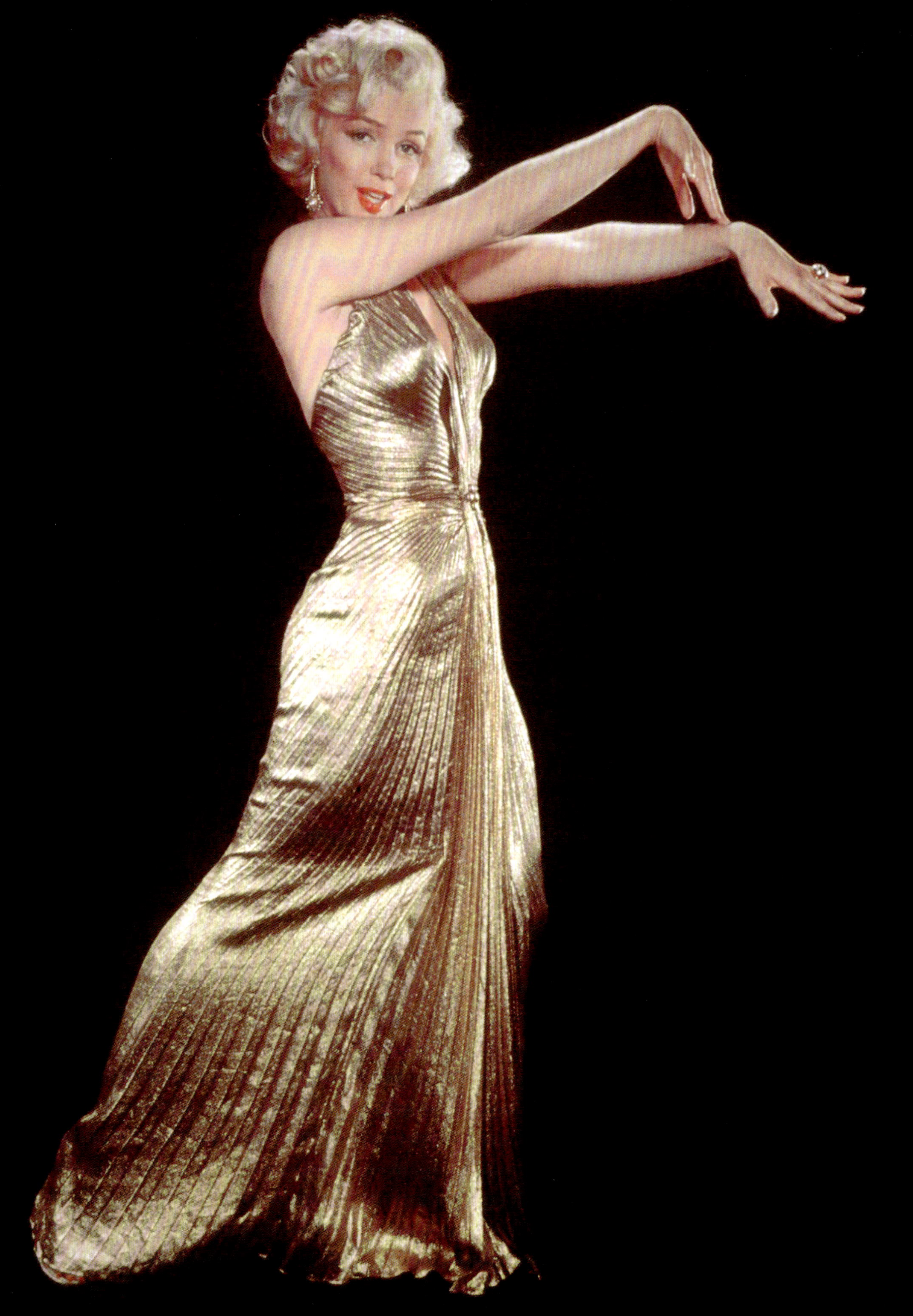

GENTLEMEN
PREFER BLONDES

Gentlemen Prefer Blondes (1953), an adaptation of Anita Loos' 1926 book of the same title, directed by Howard Hawks, is every bit as funny, clever and satirical. Showcasing Monroe as an arch blonde bombshell who is played for conscious laughs, it's also one of her most stylish films. Twentieth Century Fox recreate an impressive panoramic of Maison Schiaparelli, Lucien Lelong and Dior, spotlit during Lorelei Lee and Dorothy Shaw's shopping scene when the girls hit the heights of Parisian couture and go on a spree. It's the film that platforms the artistry of designer William Travilla.

Travilla graduated from Woodbury University in Burbank, California, in 1941 and initially worked at Western Costume, where Hollywood studios would go to outfit their actors. He was later enlisted by Warner Bros. for five years, where he created wardrobes for one of his earliest champions, the actress Ann Sheridan, and won an Oscar for dressing Errol Flynn in the 1948 *Adventures of Don Juan*. Over the course of his career, Travilla worked with luminaries including Sharon Tate, Joanne Woodward and Diahann Carroll, as well as launching his own label, Travilla. It is his collaborations with Marilyn Monroe, however, that are forever crystallised in fashion history, and which continue to inspire clothes designers today.

The famous pink dress he made for her in *Gentlemen Prefer Blondes* has frequently been recreated, most famously in Madonna's 1985 video for 'Material Girl', her second single from the album *Like a Virgin* (1984). In a 1987 *New York Daily News* interview, Madonna explains what drew her to wear Monroe's dress:

Marilyn wearing the gold lamé Travilla dress, 1953

'[W]ell, my favorite scene in all of Monroe's movies is when she does that dance sequence for "Diamonds Are a Girl's Best Friend." And when it came time to do the video for the song ['Material Girl'], I said, "I can just redo that whole scene and it will be perfect." [...] Marilyn was made into something not human in a way, and I can relate to that. Her sexuality was something everyone was obsessed with, and that I can relate to. And there were certain things about her vulnerability that I'm curious about and attracted to.' (Quoted in Thakur, 2010)

The dress almost never existed, though, and came about only because of the 1952 'Golden Dreams' calendar that Monroe posed nude for in 1949. Fox decided that, following the response to the naked shots, the original design Travilla had conceived – a showgirl fishnet bodystocking with strategically placed crystals, reportedly costing $4,000 – was far too risqué and could generate a backlash or even cause the film's backers to abandon the project. Instead, it was replaced by the floor-length, heavy silk bustier gown that is now part of Marilyn's style iconography. The dress was boned to stop breasts jiggling and, although strapless, is an elegant evening dress that largely covers the body. Accessorised with matching opera gloves, the dress would not look out of place in the couture salons of Balenciaga and Balmain at the time. In a 2014 interview, Kimberley Ashley, founder of the Ashley-Travilla Fashion Foundation, explained the relationship between Monroe and the designer:

'Marilyn recognized the brilliant psychology [of] Billy [...] as a costume designer. Although she may have blurred the lines of using costumes in real life, as an actress, she realized [...] they are first and foremost tools to tell the audience about the personality of that role. Marilyn trusted Billy's brilliance implicitly. Billy's strategy on all of Marilyn's films was to make her believable in that role, and yet, show her beauty. Fortunately for Billy, many of Marilyn's roles required glamour as they were that of a woman using her appearance to "catch a man." Which, of course, was a very common theme in the 1950s.' (Truhler, 2014)

Marilyn wearing a white version of the famous pink dress she wore in *Gentlemen Prefer Blondes*, March 1953, Los Angeles

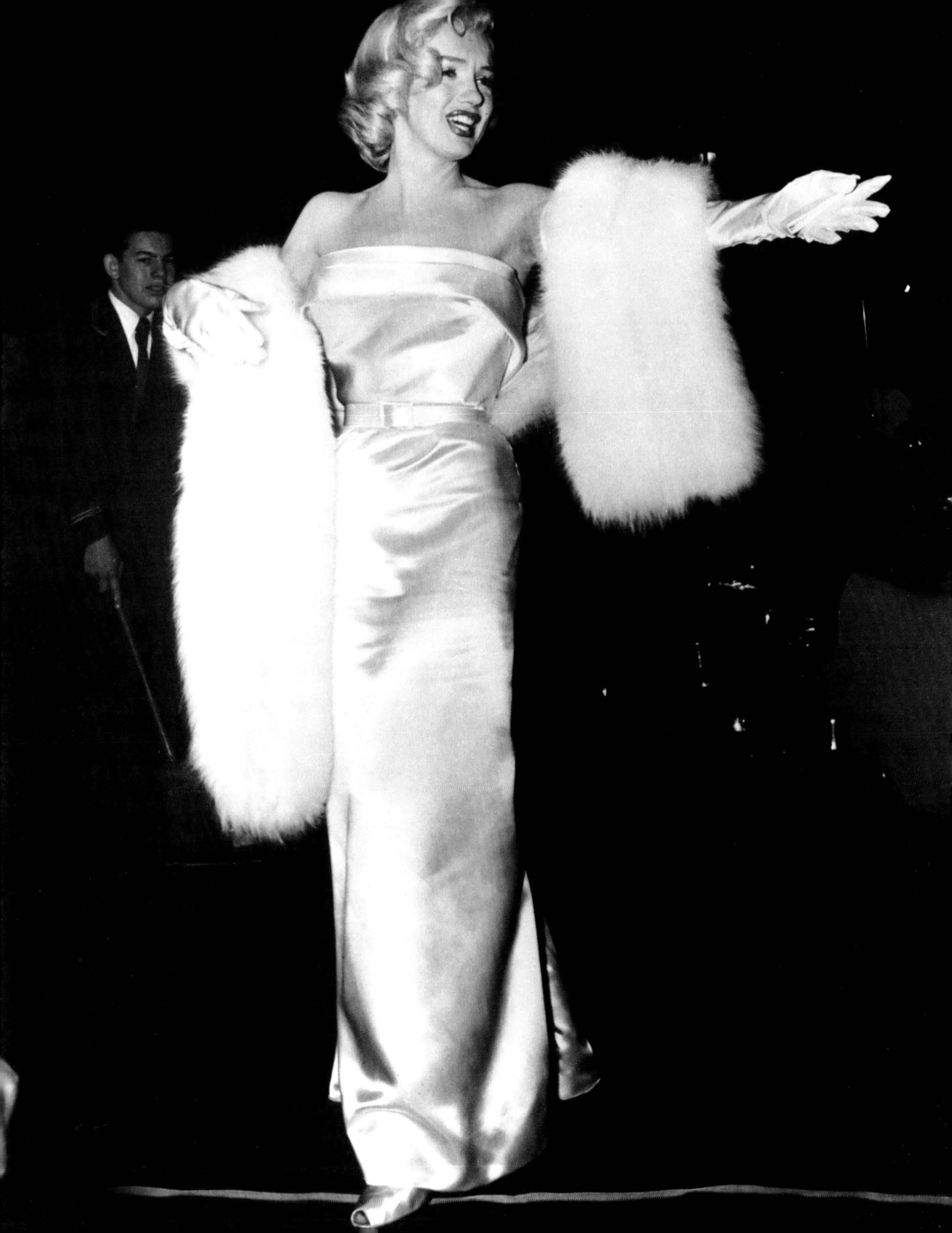

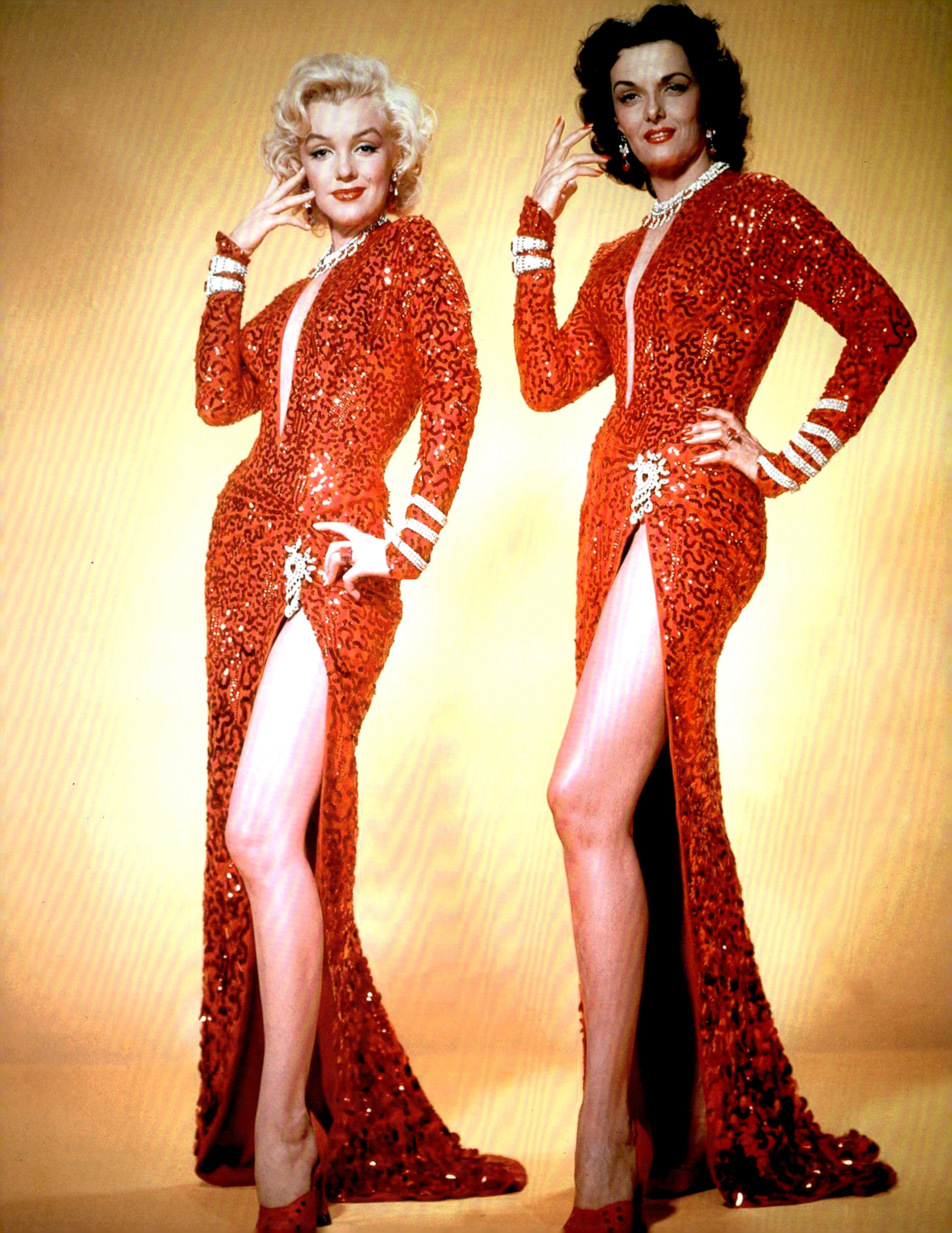

Marilyn adored the pink dress and insisted Travilla create a specially
made white version of it to wear in 1953 to the film premiere of *Call
Me Madam*. She looked divine, matching it with a snowy fur wrap. The
equally iconic gold sunray-pleat halterneck frock that Monroe dances
in, in *Gentlemen Prefer Blondes*, was another outfit she was utterly
charmed by. She borrowed and triumphantly wore the dress to the
Photoplay Awards ceremony in 1953, where she took home the 'Rising
Star' trophy. Travilla had been concerned and felt it was 'too flashy'
to sport outside of the film, but *Daily Mirror* journalist Florabel Muir
reported on the dress's wild success, saying, 'with one little twist of
her derriere, Marilyn Monroe stole the show… The assembled guests
broke into wild applause, [while] two other screen stars, Joan Crawford,
and Lana Turner, got only casual attention. After Marilyn, every other
girl appeared dull by contrast' (quoted in Robinson, 2017).

The super-sexuality of the clothes designed by Travilla for *Gentlemen
Prefer Blondes* exemplify the marked public identity Monroe was
building. At this time, she was still a fledgling star and the clothes she
wore for events off-screen were in many ways parallel to the clothes
worn by the characters she played. In her study on Hollywood film
aesthetics, Anna Cooper perfectly describes Monroe and Jane
Russell's red sequin frocks which were the opening outfits in the
film: 'split up to the hip and with necklines that plunge down to their
waists, these form-hugging gowns show off the women's ample
curves, transforming their bodies into a dazzlingly compelling
spectacle accessorized with copious rhinestones and excessive
feather headdresses. Their look is an immediately recognizable image
of bombshell glamour' (Cooper, 2023).

Monroe is most well-known for personifying the bombshell look, which
was an aesthetic to propel her into the limelight and facilitate her rise
to stardom. She had learned young that the way you look will get you
noticed. As she recalls in her memoir (1974), 'the world opened up
and started becoming friendly' when she had worn a friend's too-tight
sweater to school. Years later, the world was now responding en masse
and the formula that had worked when she was an adolescent worked
even better now that she had access to the stylish support of her friend
Billy Travilla.

Marilyn and Jane Russell posing for a publicity shot, 1953

'MY CLOTHES FOR MARILYN WERE AN ACT
OF LOVE, I ADORED HER.'

– William Travilla, quoted in Hansford & Homer, 2011

William Travilla fitting Marilyn with one of his designs, 1953

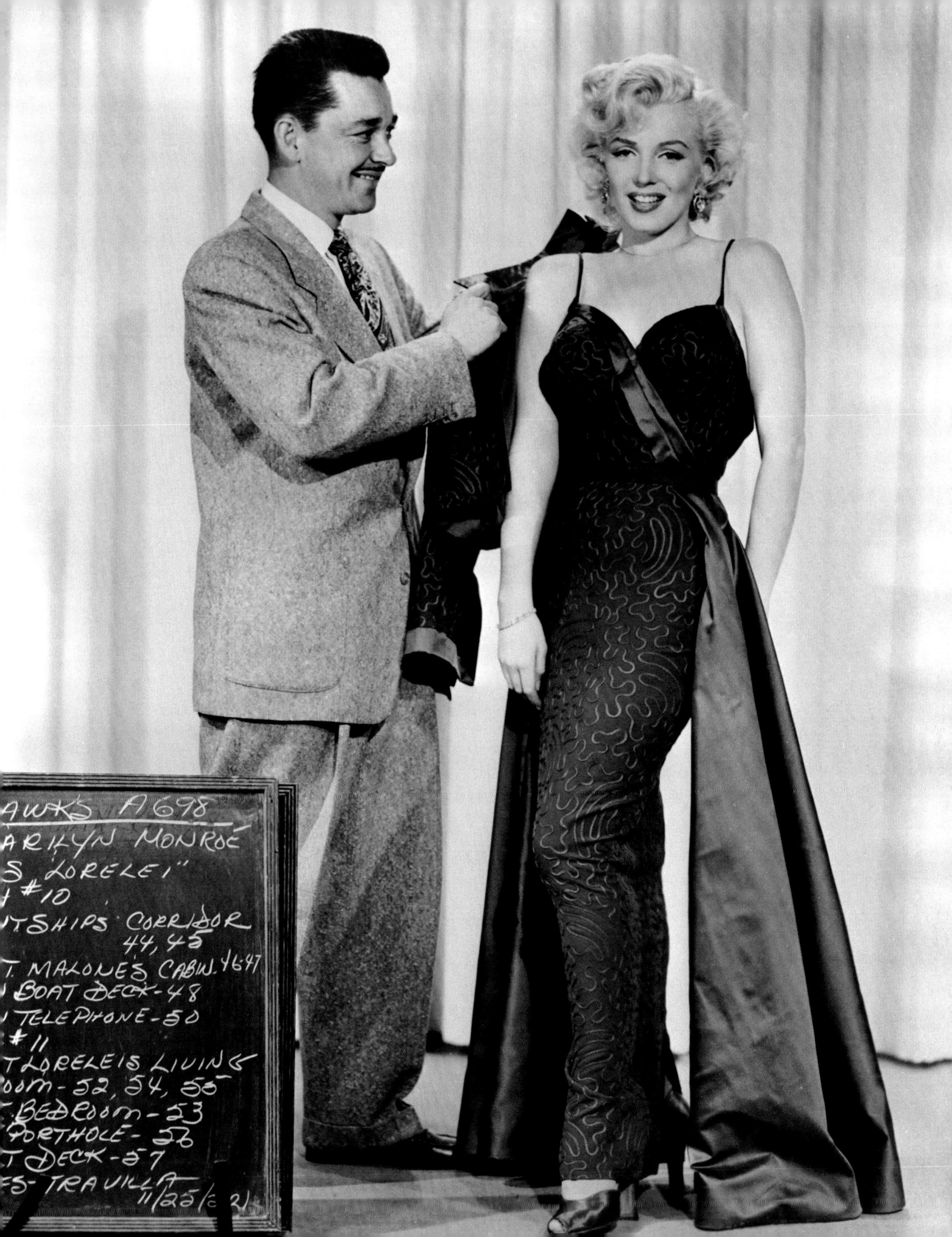
AWKS A 698
ARILYN MONROE
S "LORELEI"
#10
TSHIPS CORRIDOR
44, 45
T. MALONES CABIN. 46-47
BOAT DECK-48
TELEPHONE-50
#11
T LORELEIS LIVING
OOM-52, 54, 55
BEDROOM-53
PORTHOLE-56
T DECK-57
S-TRAVILLA
11/25/52

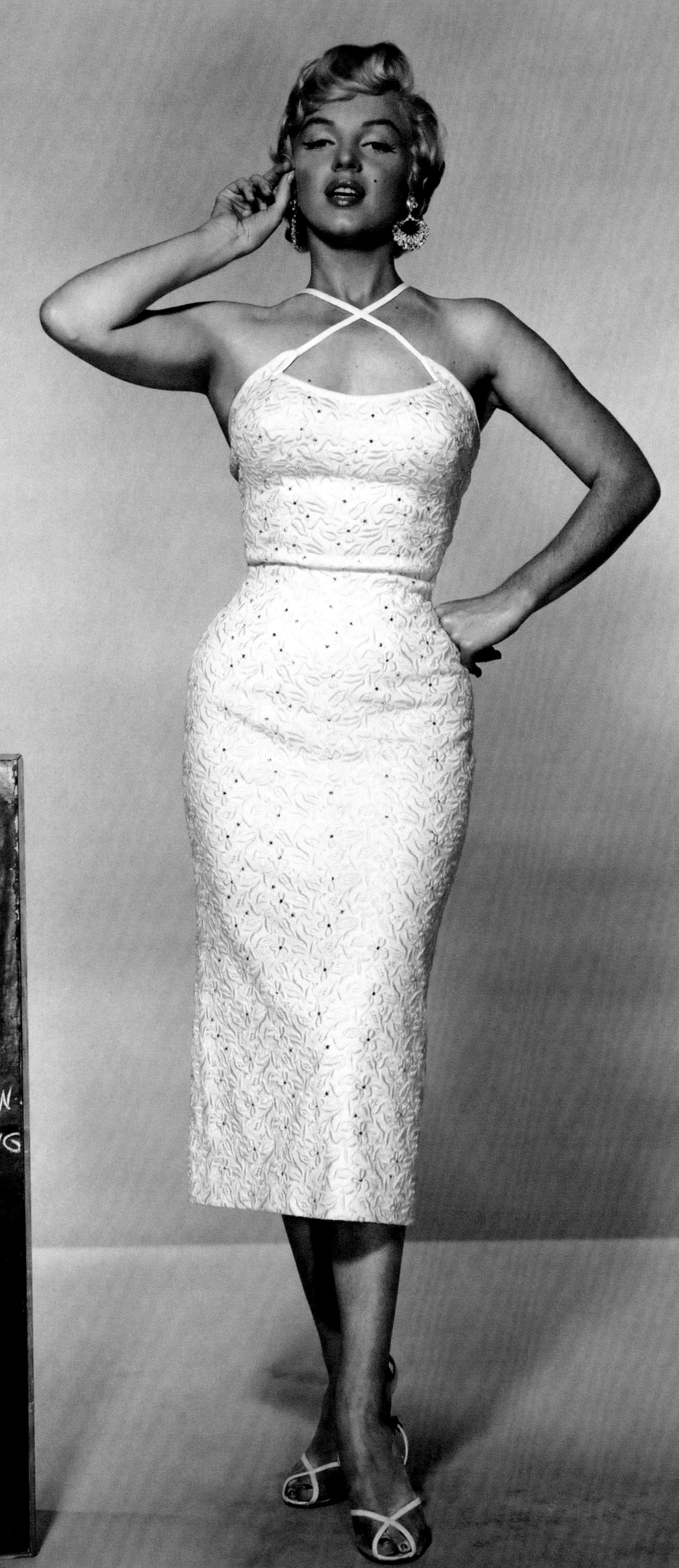
A-134
WILDER
M.MONROE
AS
THE GIRL
EXT. APT Window
EVENING
Sc. 55
CHG #7
DES. TRAVILLA
8/28/54

THE SEVEN
YEAR ITCH

'SHE WAS A FULL-SIZED WOMAN, BUT SHE HAD A TINY WAIST.
SHE COULD WEAR THE MOST OUTRAGEOUS LOOKING CLOTHES
WITHOUT EVER LOOKING VULGAR.'

– William Travilla, quoted in *Classic Hollywood Style*, 2012

Marilyn's wardrobe in *The Seven Year Itch* (1955) is a masterclass in 'Travilla wear': a satin, 'tiger' zigzag column gown and a wiggle dress with a criss-cross neckline, both fitting her like a glove. However, it is the stunning bone-white, rayon acetate, fit-and-flair halterneck dress that the designer created for Marilyn's character, 'The Girl', which shows his mastery of pleat work. It was the seventh film he had dressed her for: 'I wondered, what could I do with this most beautiful girl that Marilyn was to play to make her look clean, talcum-powdered, and adorable?' (quoted in Hansford, 2017). Travilla knew and loved Marilyn and worked hard to create something that she would approve of, but also something that respected her. He once quipped, 'When I die, I don't want to be buried or cremated, just pleat me' (quoted in Jorgensen & Scoggins, 2015). His signature design feature was used to incomparable effect for Monroe's *The Seven Year Itch* dress, its sunray crimping working to its very best advantage for the famous moment in the fim when she stands above the subway grating. Travilla was an engineer of fabric, and the intricate folds and tucks he used to form Marilyn's most famous dress go unnoticed, with the point of focus becoming Marilyn's underwear as the dress flies up. By then, she was married to baseball star Joe DiMaggio and, although she wore two pairs of knickers that day to appease her then husband, he loathed the dress and the attention it brought to his wife. Shots of the scene reveal a throng of over 100 photographers surrounding Monroe during filming in September 1954, with over 1,000 onlookers in the background. It was after midnight before shooting finally finished. Film director Billy Wilder repeated the spectacle 14 times but had to reshoot again back at the Fox lot because of the noise from the crowd.

Marilyn wearing a Travilla wiggle dress, 1954

Though Travilla famously described the gown as 'that silly dress',
it has become the most singular silhouette of Marilyn's career. The dress
has resoundingly become an essential element of Monroe's fashion
iconography but is also symbolic of the character Marilyn played – an
unnamed woman simply called 'The Girl', who represented the fantasies
of Richard Sherman (played by Tom Ewell), a middle-aged man whose
wife is out of town. The feverish heat of New York in the summertime
adds to the dream-like meta-sequences where Sherman floats in and
out of reality. At one point, when asked about the attractive girl who's in
his kitchen, he declares: 'Maybe it's Marilyn Monroe!'

Astonishingly, the dress was first sold for just $200 in 1971 in a
wardrobe studio sale to the actress Debbie Reynolds, who had a
plan to use it as a star piece in a dedicated museum of Hollywood
ephemera she wanted to set up. It never happened and instead the
gown was sold again in 2011, with Reuters reporting at the time that
it fetched $5.6 million after taxes and fees.

By this point in Monroe's career, she had a desire to challenge herself
and break out of the stereotype the studio had created for her and
that she had inhabited so exhaustively. In January 1954 she had walked
out on Fox, something unheard of at that time. *The New York Times*
reported the scandal:

> *'Marilyn Monroe failed to report at Twentieth Century-
> Fox for work this morning and the studio announced
> this afternoon that the star had been suspended from
> salary. Miss Monroe, crowned as the box office queen
> in* The Motion Picture Herald's *1953 poll of the ten top
> money-making stars, was to have joined Dan Dailey
> and Frank Sinatra in rehearsals for the musical "Pink
> Tights."'* (Pryor, 1954)

She had been offered her usual salary of $1,500 as opposed to Frank
Sinatra's $5,000 per week, and she wanted to renegotiate her contract.
In the end, the film was cancelled and Marilyn agreed to return to work
on the proviso that she could play 'The Girl' in *The Seven Year Itch*, a
part that, while stereotypical, has critical nuance. Her self-referential
performance resulted in great reviews, with Marilyn playing a woman

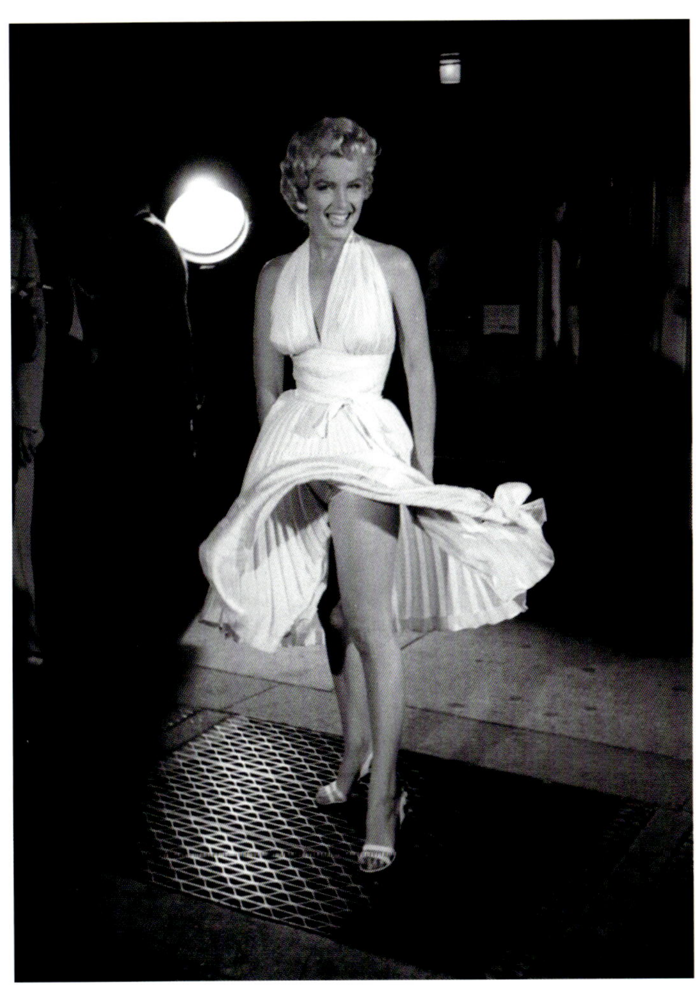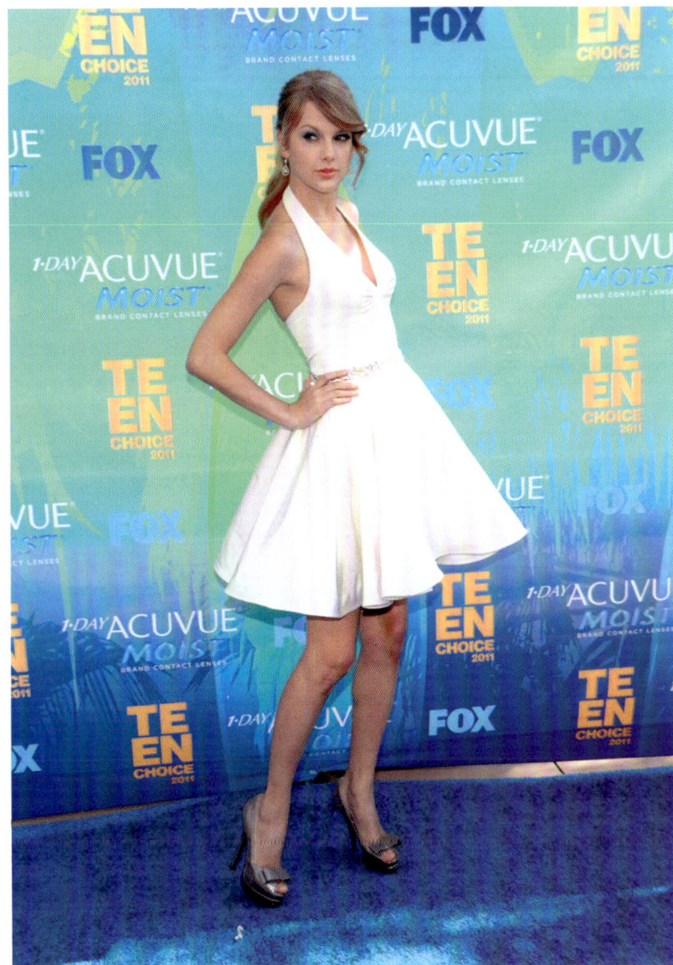

Marilyn wearing the Travilla halterneck dress in the famous subway-grating scene, 1954

Taylor Swift wearing a Marilyn-inspired dress at the Teen Choice Awards in Universal City, California, 2011

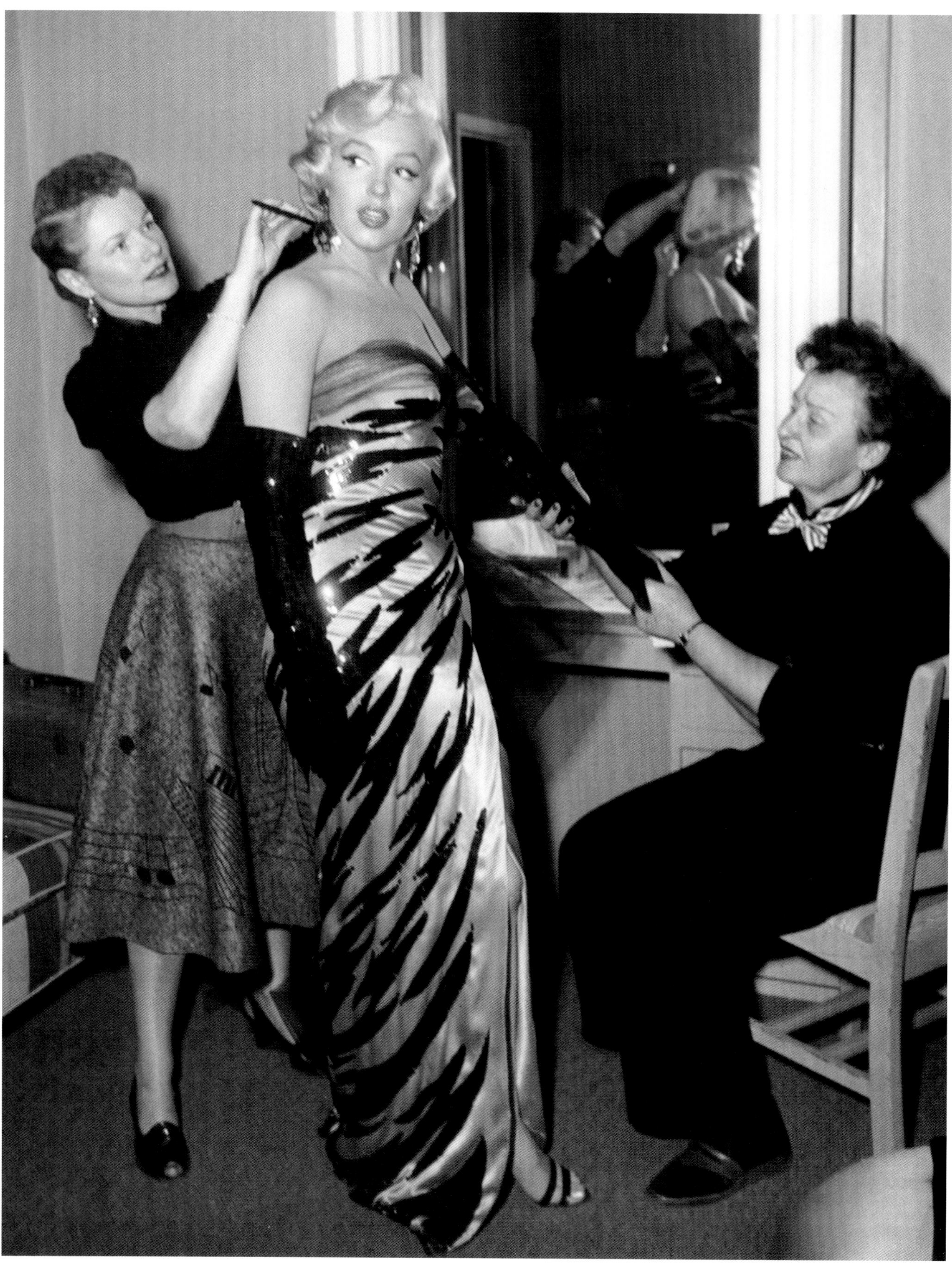

Wardrobe mistress Ann Landers (left) readies Marilyn for a scene wearing
another Travilla creation, 1954

who is sure of herself, her sexuality, and is in control. It's a surreal comedy that moves away from the earlier sexy pin-up typecast roles she was becoming tired of. It was the beginning of a new era, and she began to craft her career with even more determination. When the film came out in June 1955, she had left Fox, set up MMP (Marilyn Monroe Productions) – a production company with her friend Milton Greene – and had started taking classes at Lee Strasberg's celebrated Actors Studio in New York. It is telling that, although most of the wardrobe for the film serves to support Marilyn as 'The Girl' she had become, one of the studio publicity stills features her unadorned, wearing what would become remembered as one of her most favourite outfits: a white towelling robe.

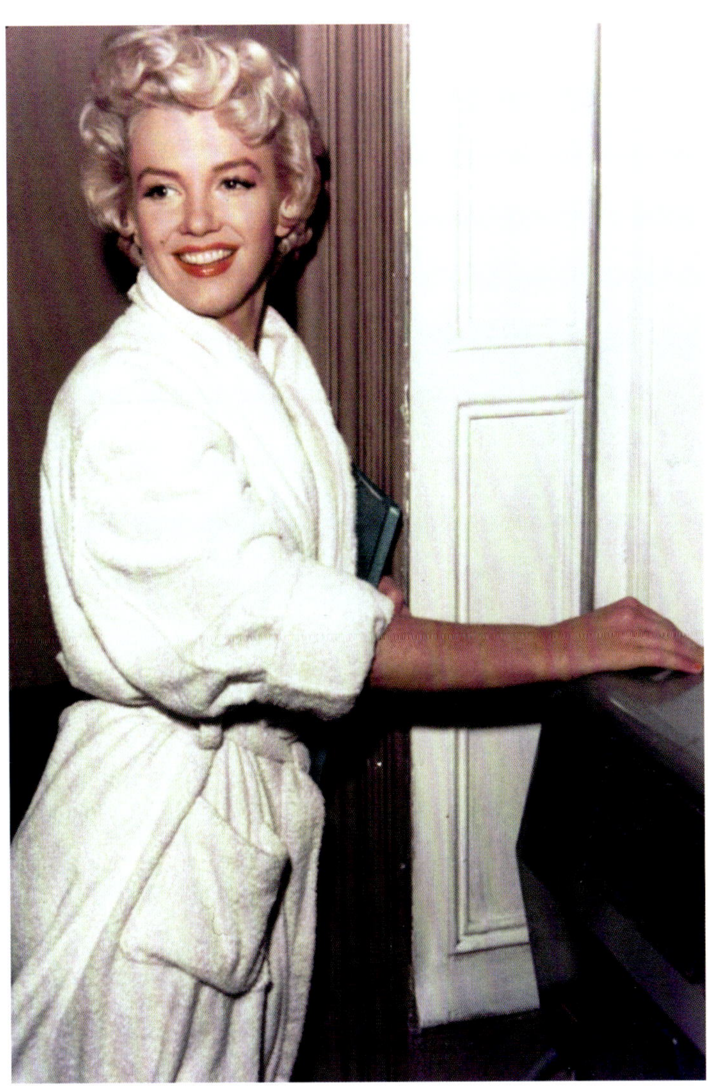

June 1955, on the set of *The Seven Year Itch*

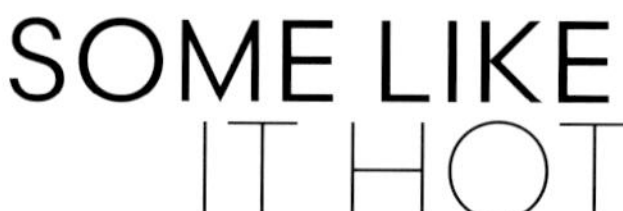

SOME LIKE
IT HOT

Born in Kiama, New South Wales, Australian designer Orry-Kelly (born Orry George Kelly) worked on almost 300 Hollywood films and was posthumously inducted into the Costume Designers Hall of Fame in 2000. In 2015, Melbourne's ACMI (Australian Centre for the Moving Image) celebrated his glittering career with an exhibition, 'Orry-Kelly: Dressing Hollywood'. He won Academy Awards for the 1951 Gershwin musical *An American in Paris* and the 1957 Cole Porter comedy *Les Girls*, before taking an Oscar for the 1959 Monroe film *Some Like It Hot*. Thus, he was already established by the time he dressed Marilyn in one of her most significant roles as Sugar Kane, a member of Sweet Sue's Society Syncopators, who sang and played the ukulele.

Orry-Kelly's appreciation of fabric was second to none and, alongside the biggest Hollywood stars, cinema fans wanted to wear his outfits, too. In 1933, for that year only, Butterick began making paper patterns of outfits worn by the Hollywood stars (Emery, 2014). In their *Delineator* magazine each month, they produced a Butterick Starred Pattern, of which the June issue included Orry-Kelly's designs for the dress and swimsuit that Bette Davis wore in *The Working Man* (1933). Talking about Orry-Kelly in her 2015 documentary, *Women He's Undressed*, director Gillian Armstrong reflects on his prowess:

> *'This man really knows what he's doing. He was a master of shape, silhouette and colour. Amongst the many articles that we found was one where he was talking about fashion, he said a costume designer can't be following fashion, we have to be ahead of fashion, because it's six months before the film comes out. He always saw the costume from the story point of view and the actor's point of view.'*

On the set of *Some Like It Hot* on Coronado Beach, California, 1958

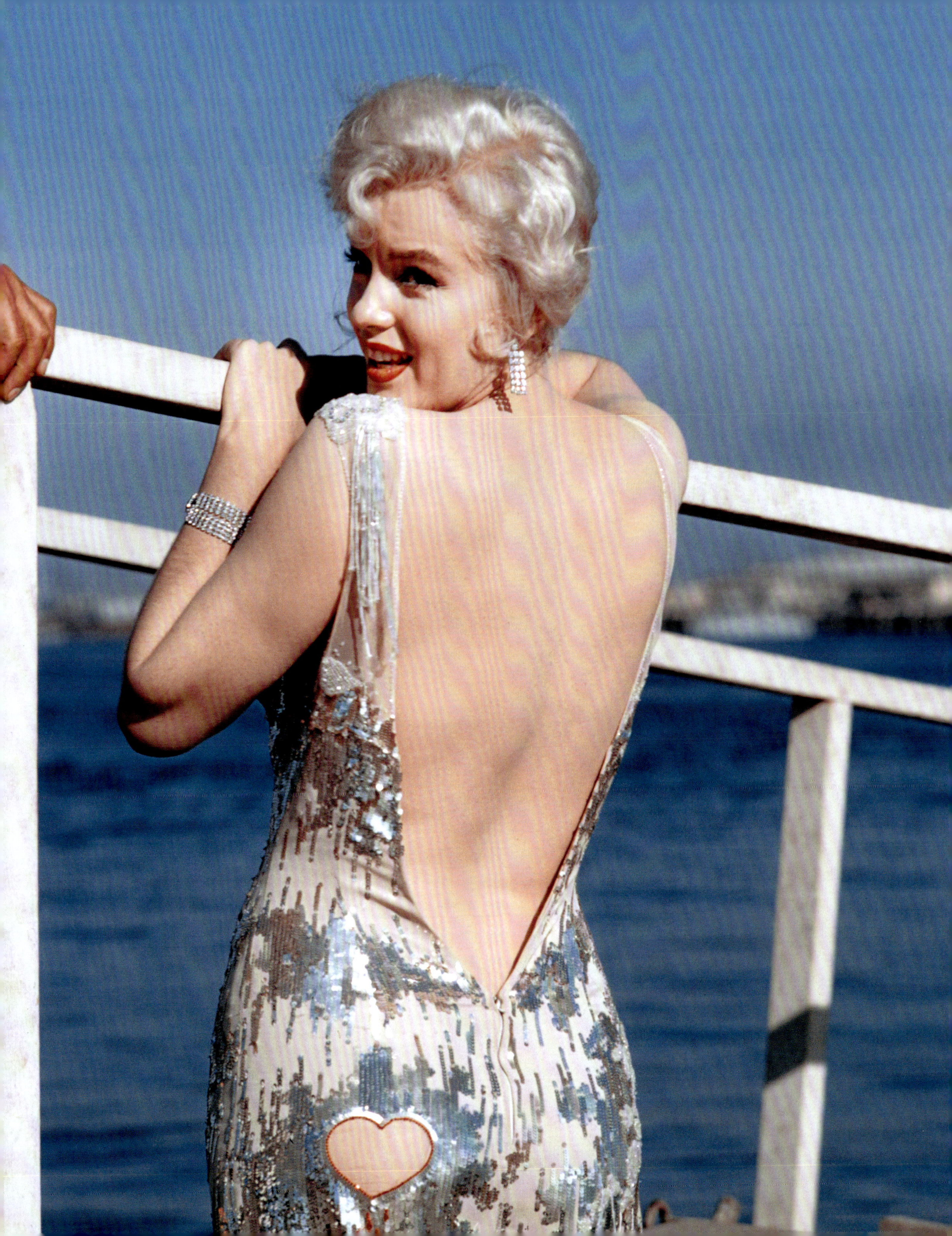

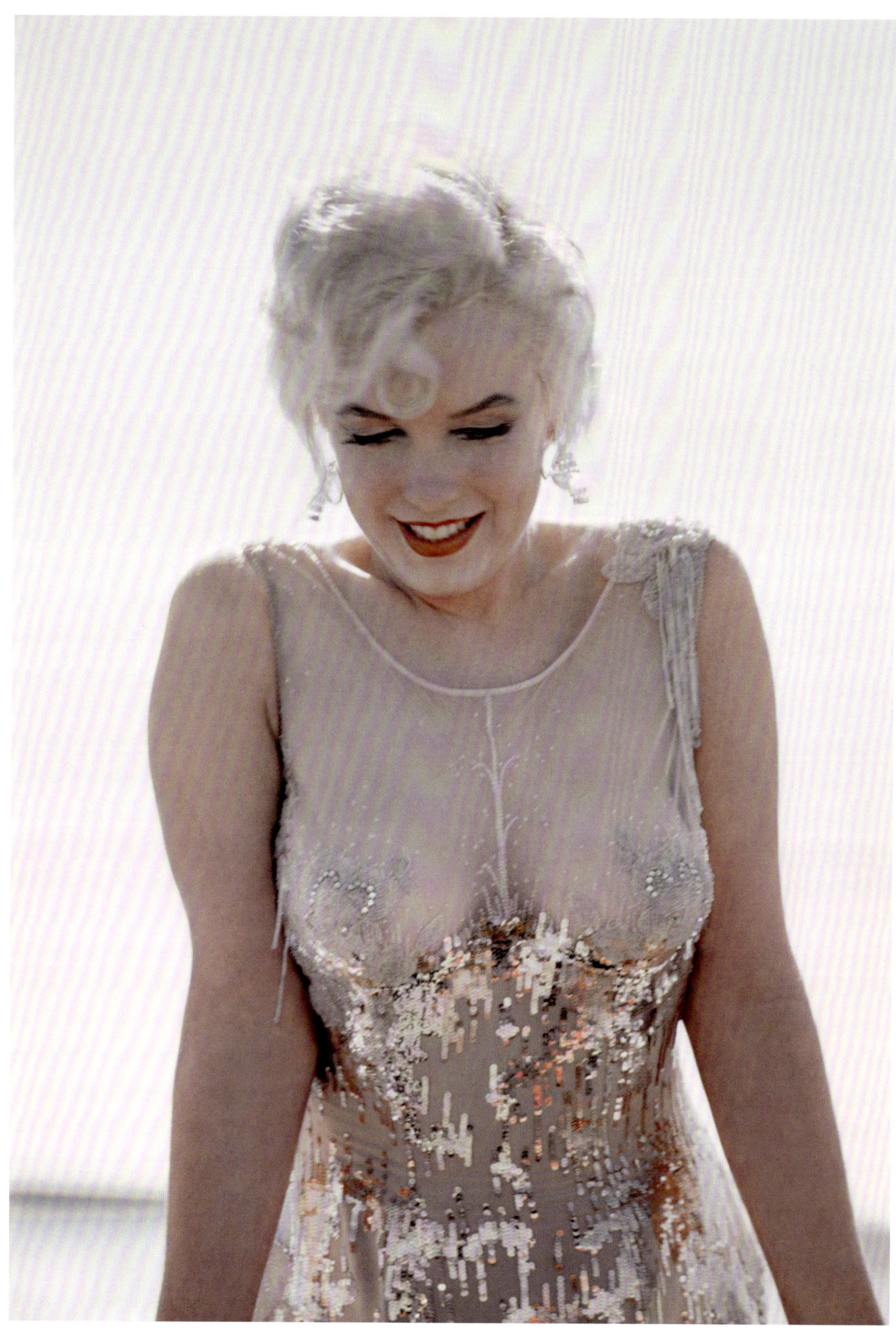

On the set of *Some Like It Hot* on Coronado Beach, California, 1958

Orry-Kelly, known as Jack, had lived a somewhat chaotic life; he wanted to become an artist, but won acclaim dressing stars instead. He was a fine-art painter and interior stylist who created nightclub murals along with cushions and decorative shawls for friends. But he also suffered from alcoholism and could be snappish and difficult to deal with. When he died in 1964 at the age of 66, Cary Grant was his pallbearer, along with *Some Like It Hot* family members Billy Wilder and Tony Curtis.

For the Best Costume Design nominations at the 1959 Oscar awards ceremony, Orry-Kelly's strategically transparent, crystal-beaded, silver-sequinned nude soufflé dress, designed for Monroe's *Some Like It Hot* character Sugar, was modelled on stage before the winner was announced. It was the penultimate piece to be presented and its sheer translucence was in direct contrast to the other nominees, which included the evocative clothing from *The Diary of Anne Frank* and the chic glamour of Edith Head's outfits for the film *Career*. The audience's whoops for Orry-Kelly's gown was an astonishing moment when the context of his work's impact was truly felt, the frock daring and outrageous but absolutely spot on for Marilyn's portrayal of Sugar's famous scene singing 'I Wanna Be Loved by You'. It felt so right that Orry-Kelly also made a version in black, with butterfly appliqués, for her to wear at the end of the film, too. Monroe instinctively grasped her value as a visual performer and understood how to bring a role to life. Together, Monroe and Orry-Kelly were unbeatable: the designer was aware she wanted to show off her body and equipped her with the wardrobe to do so. The film is set in the 1920s, and the first glimpse audiences catch of Sugar is when she is walking along the Chicago railway platform wearing a flapper hat, heels, tight skirt and fur-collared coat; smoke from the train swirls around her and, for a moment, keen

'ALL HIS [ORRY-KELLY'S] GENIUS WAS
ON DISPLAY IN *SOME LIKE IT HOT*.
YOU COULD NOT TAKE YOUR EYES
OFF HER [MONROE'S] BREASTS.'

– Jane Fonda, *Women He's Undressed*, 2015

viewers are reminded of her previous iconic film, *The Seven Year Itch,* and The Girl's famous white dress in the scene when she is standing over the subway grating.

Monroe's co-stars in *Some Like it Hot*, Tony Curtis and Jack Lemmon, who play their alter egos Josephine and Jerry, wear equally exquisite womenswear created by Orry-Kelly. This film is today widely recognised to be Monroe's finest. A *Variety* magazine online feature on Marilyn's performance professes that 'Sugar "Kane" Kowalczyk, the emotionally bruised, gin-swilling singer and ukulele player, remains her most accomplished performance. In it, Monroe is alternately hilarious and heart-breaking' (Lang, 2021). The film is indeed a poignant legacy.

By the time Monroe picked up the phone to Billy Wilder, the director of *The Seven Year Itch*, saying she was keen to work with him again, she was married to playwright Arthur Miller, her relationship with Joe DiMaggio having ended in 1954, after just nine months. In *My Story*, Marilyn reveals: '[M]y illusions didn't have anything to do with being a fine actress. I knew how third rate I was. I could actually feel my lack of talent, as if it were cheap clothing I was wearing inside. But, my God, how I wanted to learn!' (1974). She was determined to craft her art as an actress and she arrived on set for *Some Like It Hot* with Paula Strasberg, her acting coach and the second wife of Actors Studio founder Lee Strasberg. In a letter to Lee, Monroe writes about this relationship and her fearful ambition:

> '[A]s soon as I walk into a scene I lose my mental relaxation for some reason, which is my concentration. My will is weak, but I can't stand anything. I sound crazy but I think I'm going crazy. Thanks for letting me have Paula help me on the picture. She's the only really warm woman I've known. It's just that I get before camera and my concentration and everything I'm trying to learn leaves me. Then I feel like I'm not existing in the human race at all.' (Quoted in Ogilvie, 2013)

After *Some Like It Hot* wrapped, director Billy Wilder felt the angst had been worth it. He knew she was a serious star and recollected his time with Marilyn in his book *Conversations with Wilder*:

(Wilder & Crowe, 1999)

And it wasn't just Wilder that thought she had excelled; in 1960, she
won the Golden Globe for 'Best Actress in a Leading Role – Musical
or Comedy' for her part in the film.

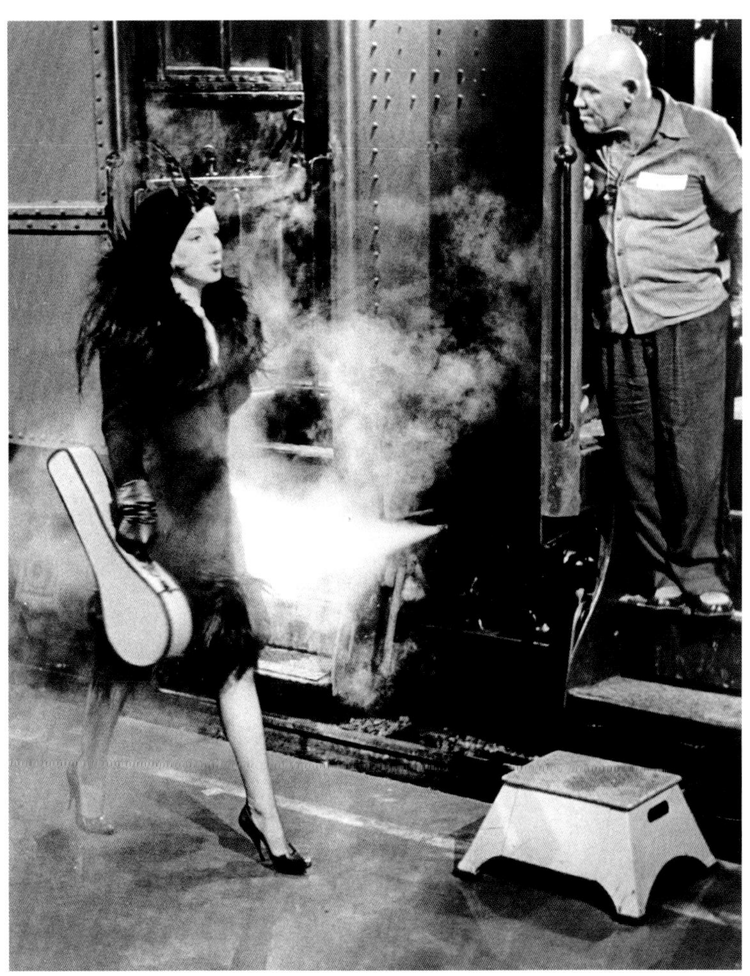

Marilyn in *Some Like It Hot* in 1959, wearing a dress by Orry-Kelly

'MY CONCEPT IS THAT CLOTHES HAVE TO WRAP
AROUND THE BODY LIKE SMOKE, AND IF YOU DO
THAT YOU WILL BE AHEAD OF YOUR TIME.'

– Orry-Kelly, quoted in Armstrong, 2015

Marilyn as 'Sugar' in *Some Like It Hot* in 1959

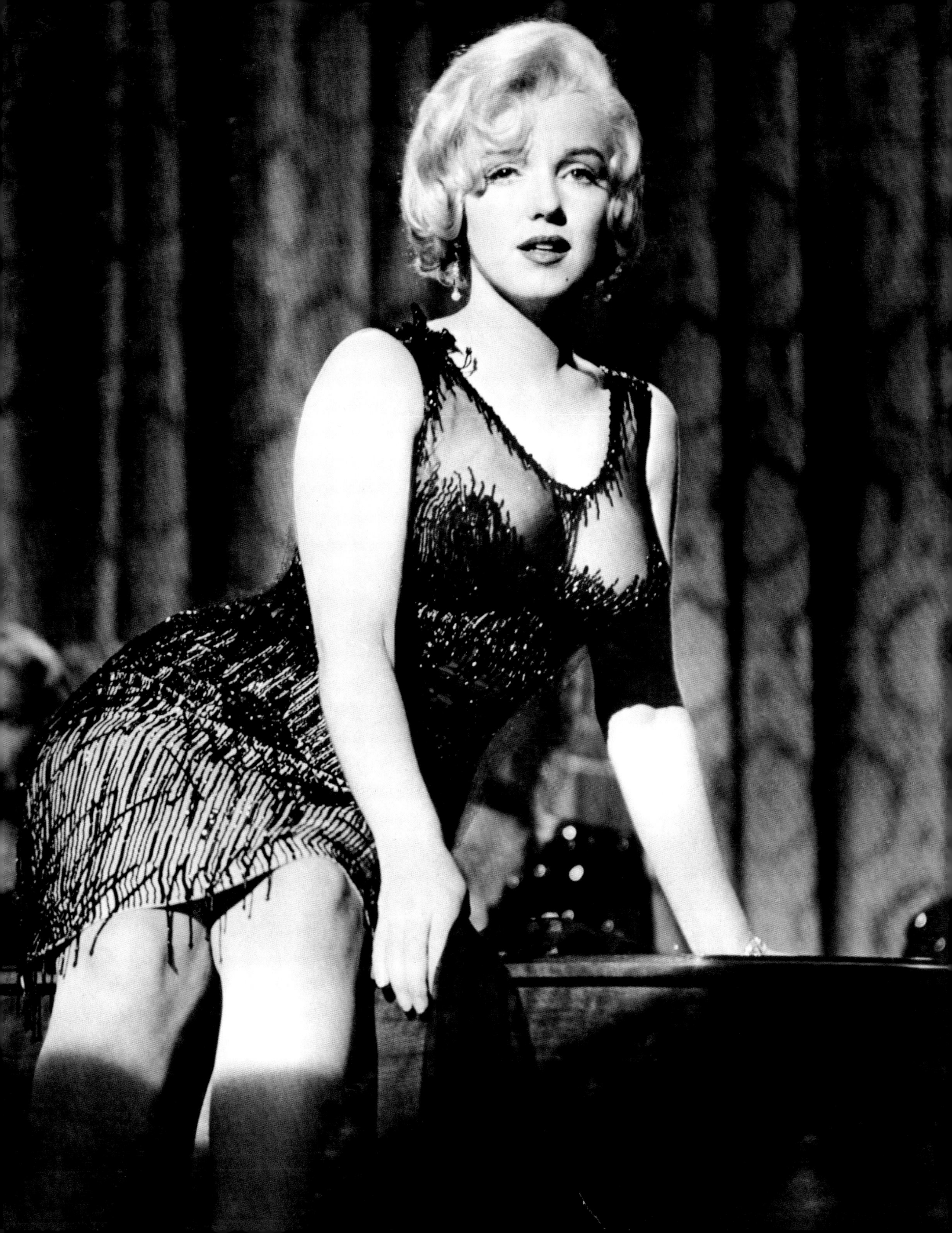

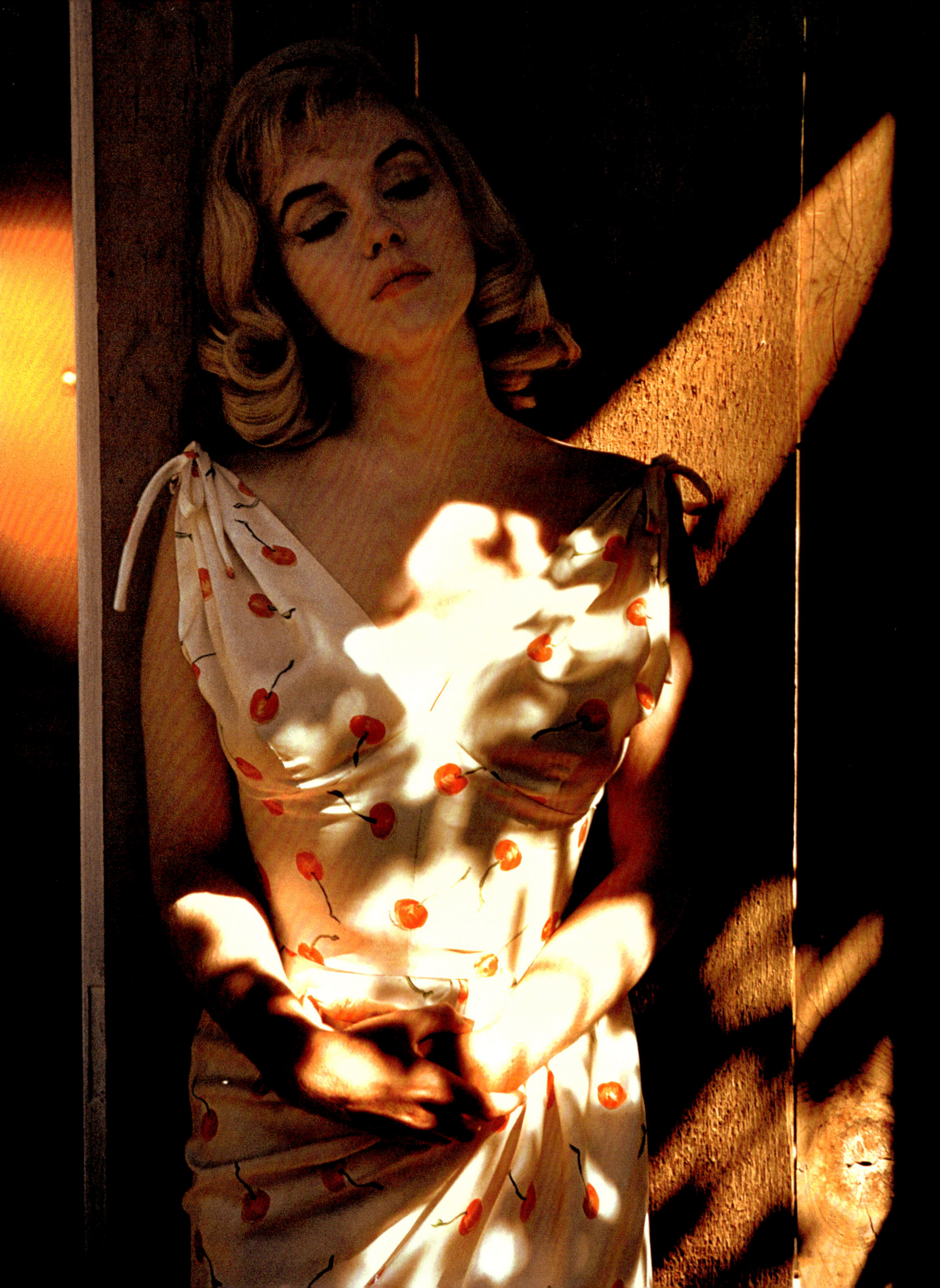

THE MISFITS

– Eve Arnold, 1960

French designer Jean Louis Berthault moved to New York in 1935, where he worked with the iconic fashion businesswoman Hattie Carnegie, before going to Hollywood to create costumes for Columbia Pictures. He first met Marilyn Monroe when she was cast in her 1948 film *Ladies of the Chorus,* dressing her for the part of Peggy Martin in a series of shimmering sparkly gowns. Glamour was Jean Louis' signature but when Monroe requested his help for her 1961 film, *The Misfits,* the wardrobe he created shifted from his usual theme and instead revamped her familiar onscreen wear beyond its customary sex-kitten silhouette to mirror the multifaceted role of Roslyn Taber that she played. The screenplay had been written especially for Monroe by her husband Arthur Miller, to help validate her credentials as a serious actress. He cast her as a plaintive divorcee who meets up with three other outsiders in the Nevada desert and falls in love with an older cowboy, Gay, performcd by Clarke Gable.

As Eli Wallach, who plays the Second World War pilot Guido Racanelli, explains in a documentary on the making of the film: '"Misfit" means you don't fit into the form or structure of a society, so the three of those men, the Monty Clift character, the Clarke Gable character, and the Guido character, each one has their area of pain, and they are all explaining their pain to this woman who is in pain too' (Making 'The Misfits', 2002). During filming, Monroe's own marriage to Miller would disintegrate and the film, which reflects on Roslyn's self-doubting search for love, is at times emblematic of her real-life narrative.

Marilyn wearing a Jean Louis dress on the set of *The Misfits*, 1960

The most celebrated frock in the film is a white, cherry-print dress which, set against the backdrop of the scorching desert, resonates with the sweet frailty of Monroe-as-Taber. But, equally, wearing the cotton Jean Louis dress shows off her intrinsic allure, as demonstrated in the Odeon Salon in Dayton scene when she is surrounded by cheering cowboys and breaks a paddle-ball record – a scene Miller wrote for his wife when he found out she was an expert player. Jean Louis' wardrobe carefully follows the character Miller created and Monroe builds. At the beginning of the film, she wears a lace-trimmed satin slip, while getting ready to secure her divorce. She pulls on a silk crepe dress with a short bolero jacket that she loved so much, the designer created a duplicate for her to take home. While form-fitting and flattering, the outfit was cut simply and chicly – far from the showgirl glitz of Marilyn's early onscreen ensembles and more akin to the smart-casual outfits she wore off-duty but with somewhere to go.

Manifesting a role that didn't, as Miller pointed out, 'end in a wise crack' meant that Monroe's wardrobe in the film could equally be more complex. As the film progresses, her clothes become more basic and minimalist. A white shirt is one of her key pieces and it becomes part of the appeal of a series of images shot by Magnum photographer Eve Arnold during filming. The pictures she takes feel like a behind-doors glimpse of the 'real' Marilyn: unadorned by the ostentation of her usual working wardrobe, she is revealed by the plain language of the white blouse. Nine photographers from Magnum had been given the task of documenting the film, including Inge Morath, who would go on to marry Miller in February 1962. Miller recalled: 'Inge took comparatively few pictures. When she pointed the camera, she felt a certain responsibility for what it was looking at. Her pictures of Marilyn are particularly empathetic and touching as she caught Marilyn's anguish beneath her celebrity, the pain as well as her joy in life.' (Morath, 2001).

For many, the film has a metanarrative: Marilyn's marriage was falling apart and her unhappiness fed her role, causing her to begin to unravel on set. Meanwhile, the clothes she wears, all approved by herself, move very distinctly away from the stereotype on which she had built her career. The film was a high-profile statement crafted around Marilyn. She had always constructed a single-note, audience-pleasing

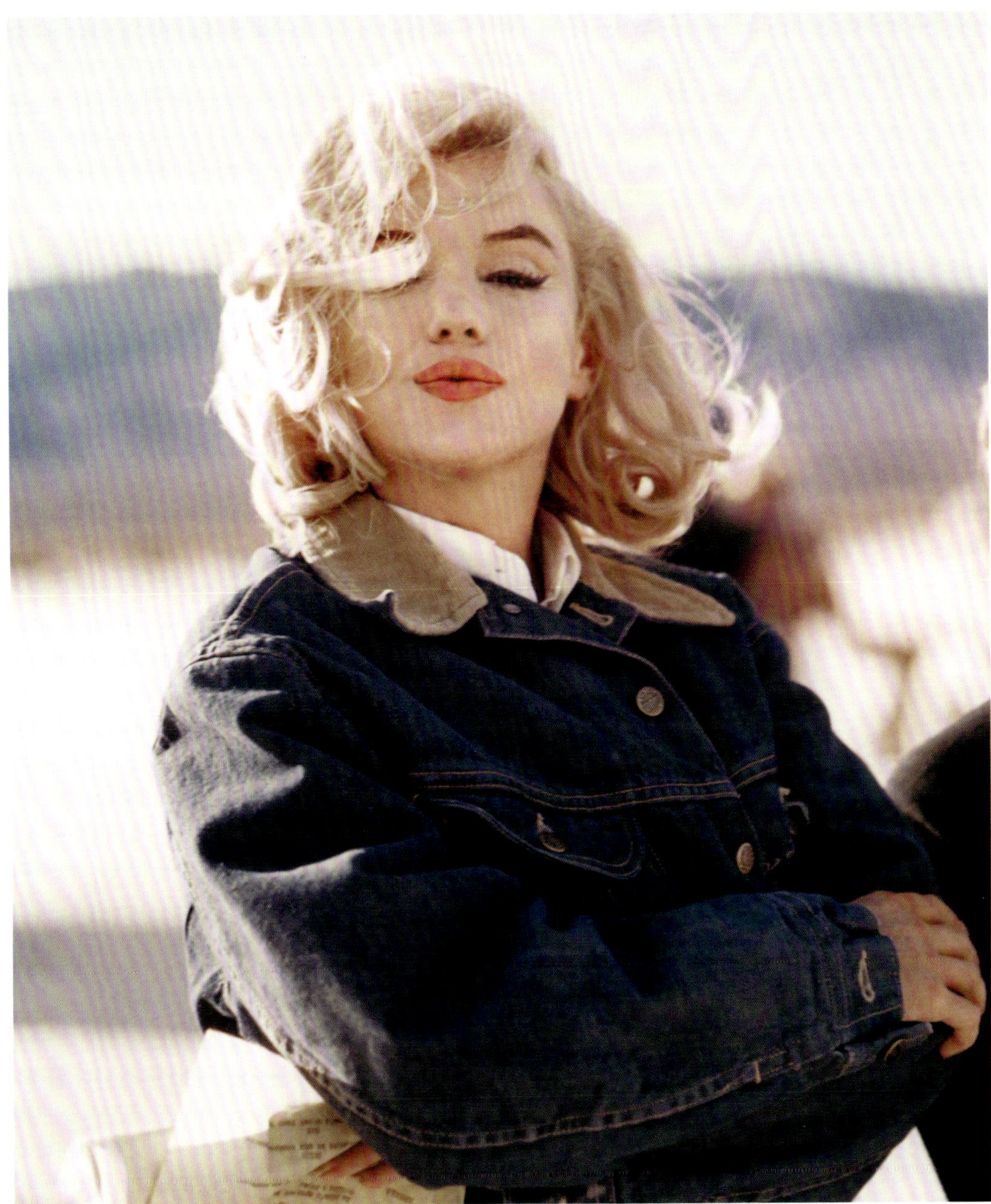

persona through big-screen outfits, which she often wore to parties and premieres, tangling the role she was performing with the person she was. But in this final (completed) Hollywood movie, her clothes express the deeper layers of Marilyn; they are no longer one-note and instead are used to create a more intricate character.

In the second half of the film, she wears a man's blanket-lined, corduroy collared Lee Storm Rider jacket, a size and a half too big, along with a pair of Levi's jeans and Hyer cowboy boots. It's not the

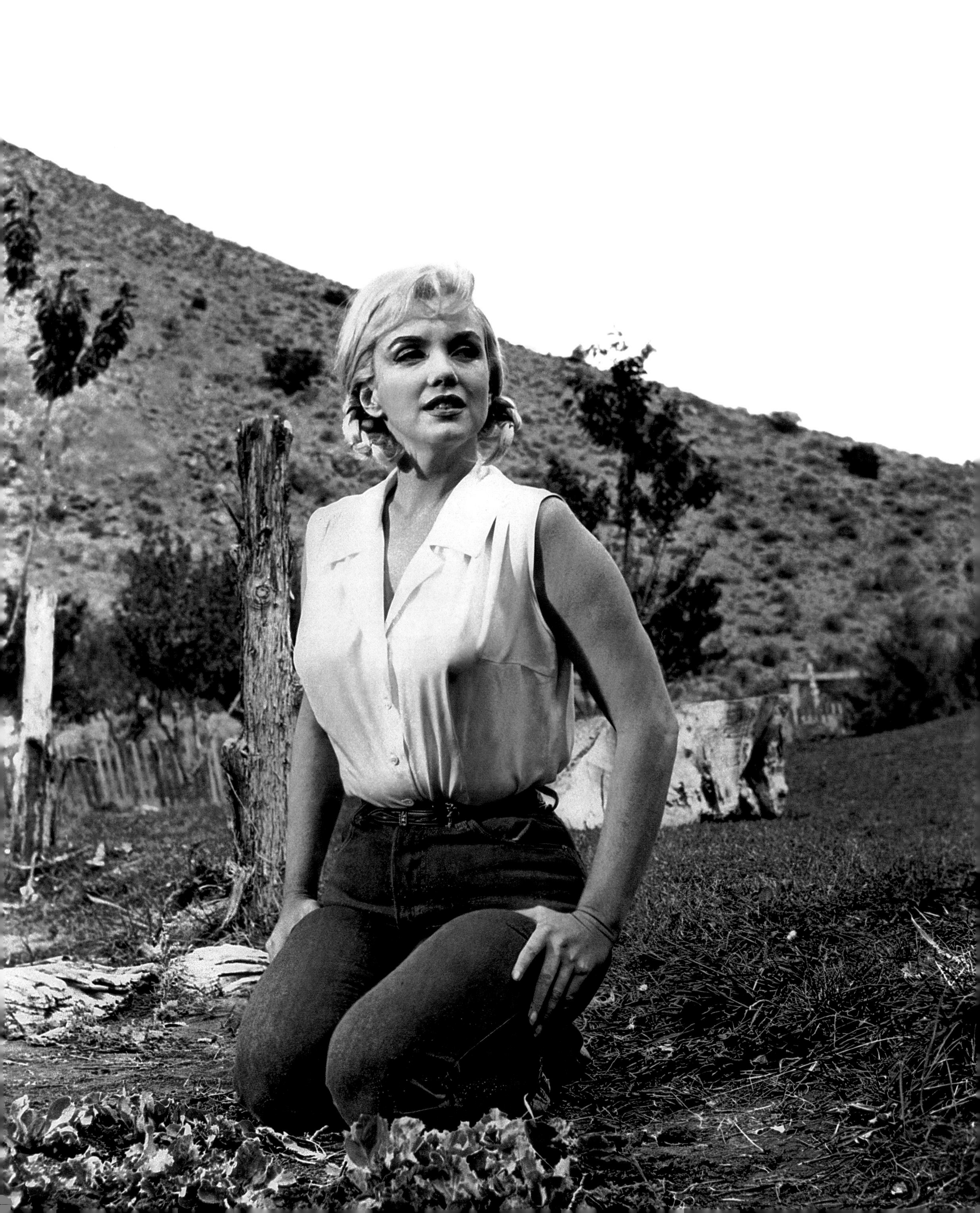

first time Marilyn's audience had seen her in jeans on camera, but it is an authentic, designed-to-get-dusty, down-to-earth outfit. Hyer was originally a cobblers, founded in Kansas in 1875, and is a heritage brand that invented the cowboy boot after responding to a customer who needed sturdy footwear strong enough for the daily cattle drive. They asked for 'a toe shape that would slide into the stirrup, a raised heel that would hold the stirrup and a scalloped top so he could slide his foot in and out of the boot more easily' (Hyer, 2024), and the cobbler went on to make the same for the likes of Buffalo Bill and exactly the model Marilyn wears in the film.

The denim jeans Marilyn puts on are Lady Levi's, first created in 1934 to fit the female form more practically. On set, she was often to be found wearing easy slacks and halternecks. When she arrived at the airport before filming began, to be greeted by her usual crowds, she wore a Rosalyn-like white blouse and unfussy pale slacks. Her clothes were less attention-grabbing and more about comfort: a reflection of the wardrobe she chose to wear when the publicity spotlight wasn't glaring. The transition towards new horizons linked to the low-key pieces she was choosing to wear more often, although of course, Jean Louis was still a firm favourite. He went on to dress Monroe for her final, unfinished film, *Something's Got to Give* in 1962, as well as to create the showstopping dress she wore to sing to President Kennedy that same year. This piece reverted back to the typical 'Marilyn' type, expedient for the occasion but something she was beginning to question. In an extended interview with the journalist W.J. Weatherby on *The Misfits* set, Monroe reveals:

> *'Marilyn Monroe became an albatross […] people expected so much of me […] it was too much of a strain. I still feel that way. Marilyn Monroe has to look a certain way – be beautiful – and act a certain way, be talented. There were times on* The Misfits, *in those emotional scenes, when I had a feeling I'd fail, however hard I'd try, and I didn't want to go to set in the morning.'* (Weatherby, 1989)

Marilyn as Roslyn Tabor, on the set of *The Misfits*, 1960

'MARILYN WAS FASCINATING TO WATCH.
THE WAY SHE MOVED, HER EXPRESSIONS;
SHE JUST WAS EXTRAORDINARY.
THERE WAS SUCH STRENGTH AND ENERGY
COMBINED WITH THIS FRAGILITY.'

– Inge Morath, 2001

Marilyn is greeted by the daughter of the Nevada Governor as she arrives at the airport
to begin work on *The Misfits*, 20 July 1960

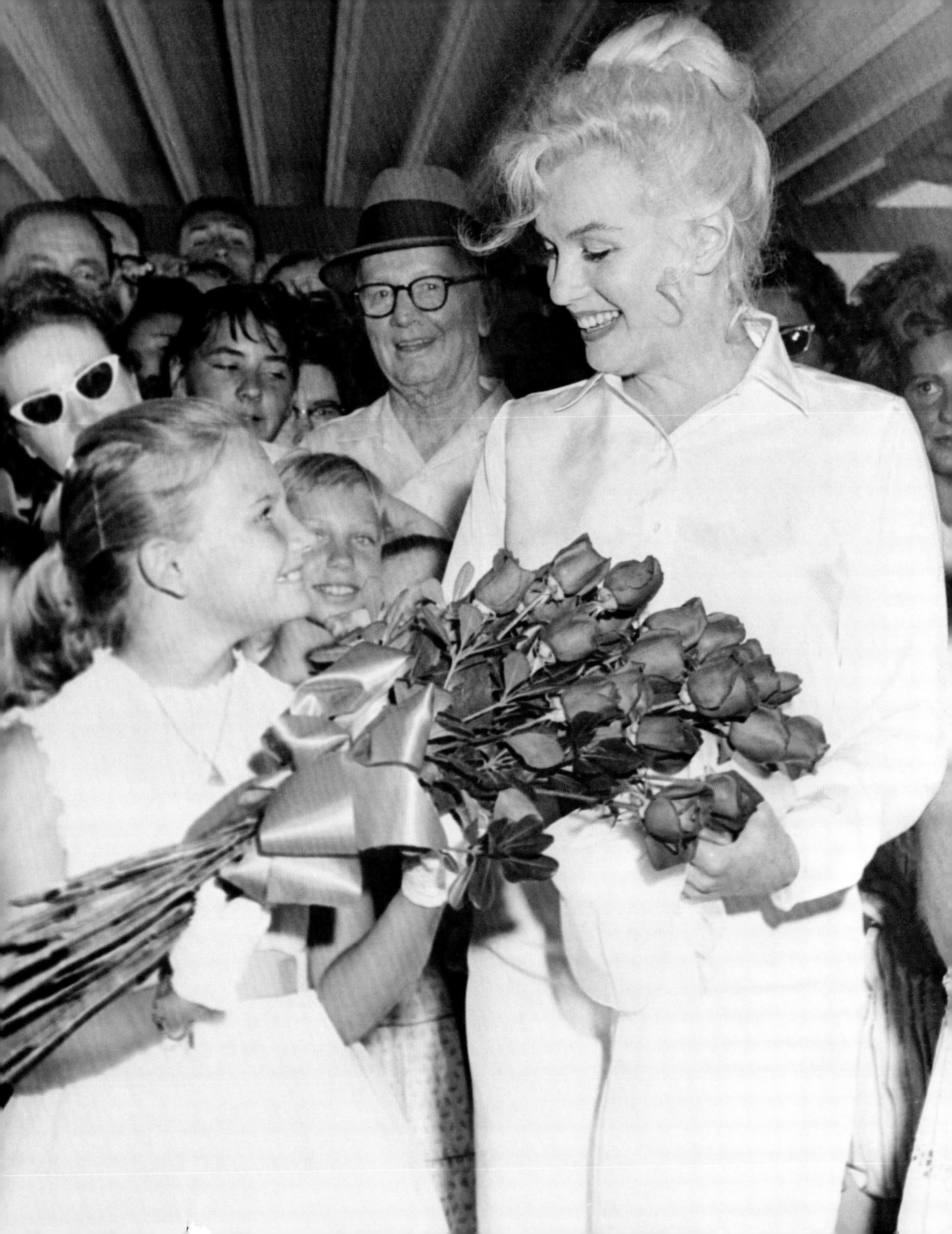

CLOTHES

Marilyn arrives at the premiere for *There's No Business Like Showbusiness*, New York City, 1954

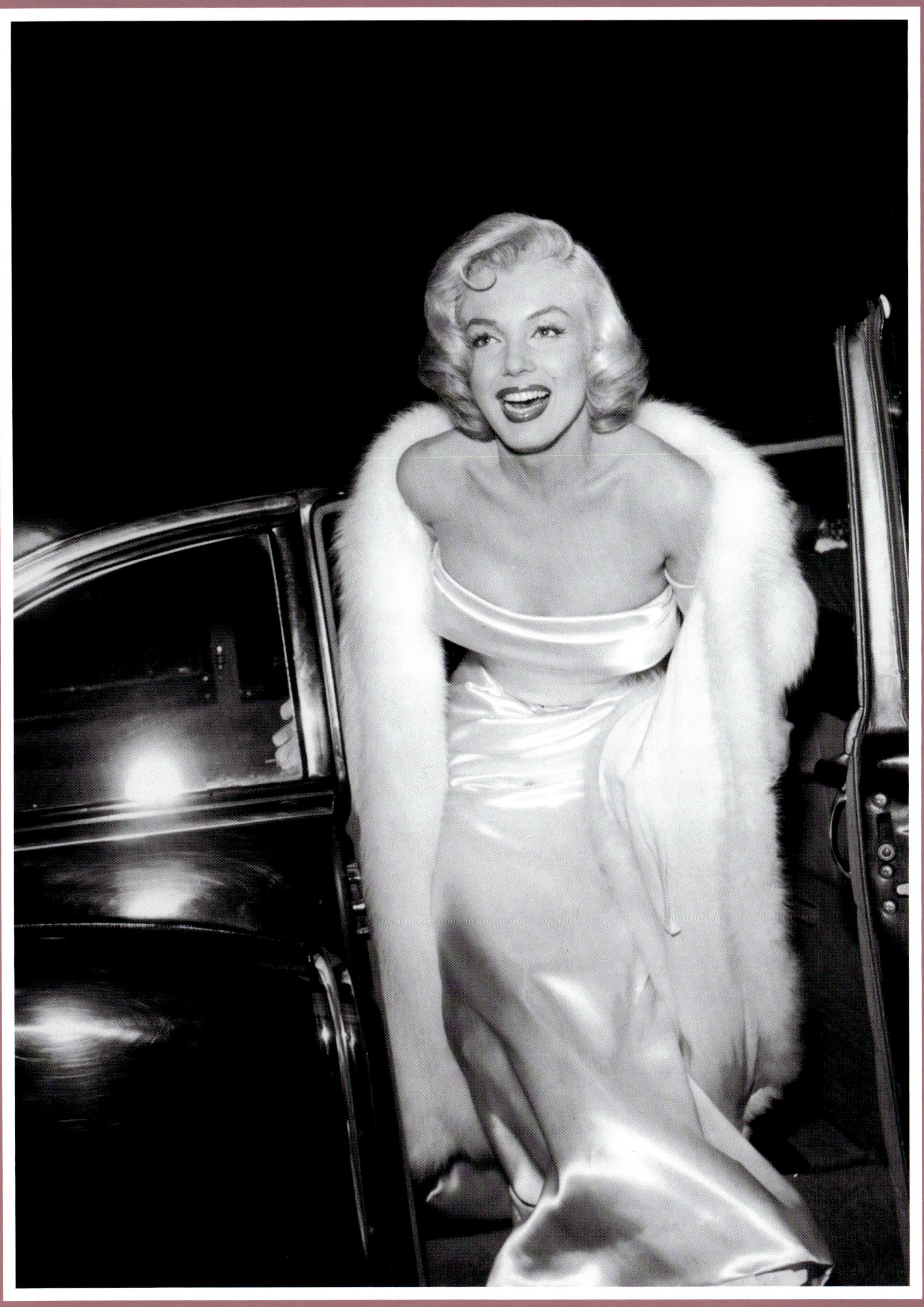

DENIM

'MY FAVOURITE CLOTHES ARE
SOMETHING STAND-OUT SLINKY
OR ELSE JUST PLAIN BLUE JEANS.'

– Marilyn Monroe, *Photoplay Magazine*, 1952

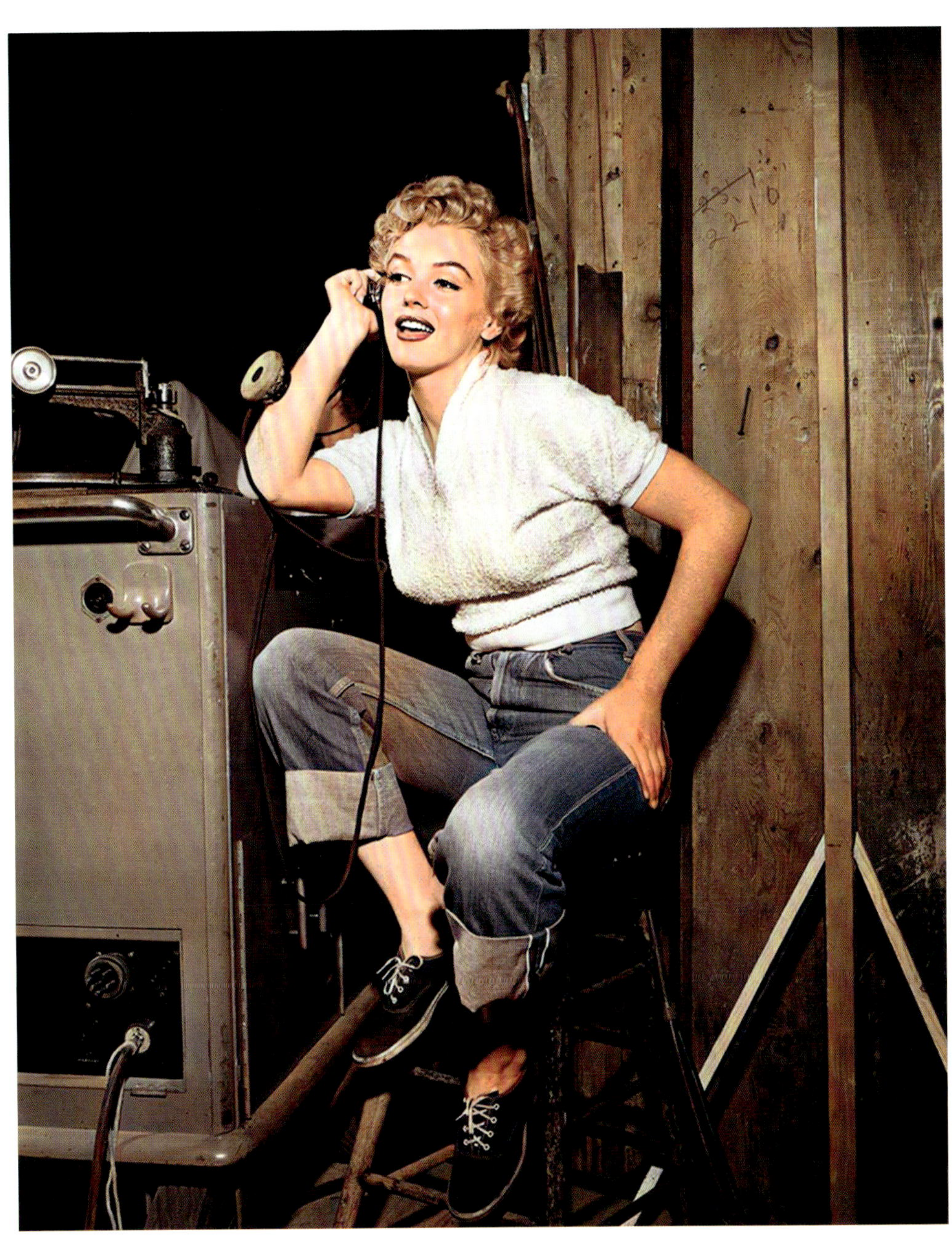

Marilyn in blue jeans on the set of *Clash by Night*, 1952

When Marilyn was cast as Peggy in director Fritz Lang's film *Clash by Night* (1952), she researched her role as a fish factory girl with keen attention. She took an overnight bus to Monterey to a canning factory where she could observe the workers cutting up fish and learn how to behave in a 'working class' fashion (Banner, 2012). It was a role she coveted and, unusually, she succeeded in getting permission to leave Fox, where she was contracted, and work for RKO to fulfil the part. It was a world away from the office-girl blondes and showgirls she had been playing until then, and her onscreen wardrobe reflected this. She wore Keds plimsoles and JCPenney selvedge jeans – an outfit that underlined the fashion gap between generations which was emerging after the Second World War.

Jeans began as a practical workwear solution, according to Levi's historian, Lyn Downey. Born in Bavaria in 1829, 'Loeb' Strauss travelled to San Francisco in 1853, changing his name to 'Levi' upon arrival. He went on to patent 'Improvement in Fastening Pocket-Openings' with the tailor Jacob Davies, who worked in Reno making copper-riveted overalls. Downey (2016) notes that in 1934 the company would launch their 'Lady Levi's' for female

ranchers, which were also bought by the growing number of female tourists vacationing on farms. To cater to this consumer, select stores in New York began selling the new range and their popularity spread. Over the years, denim jeans have become emblematic of the American West and an integral part of its history. Yet, Downey points out that it wasn't until the 1950s that Levi Strauss & Co. began selling its products nationally for the first time and that 'Easterners and Midwesterners finally got the chance to wear real Levi's jeans'.

It wouldn't be until 1953 that Marlon Brando would appear in The Wild One wearing jeans and making a rebellious biker-fashion statement as a member of the Black Rebels Motorcycle Club, teaming his Levi's with a leather jacket and heavy boots. Monroe wearing androgynous jeans on camera a year earlier might feel a pale win in comparison, but during the early '50s, when gender roles were sharply drawn, jeans worn by women signified a move towards equality. Countercultural styling meant young people didn't want to look like their parents and *Clash by Night* (1952) is one of the only films Monroe shot where she dresses more casually, like a typical young person of the time. Three pairs of the JCPenney jeans she

wore on set were sold in Christie's' 1999 'Personal Property of Marilyn Monroe' auction to the designer Tommy Hilfiger, who gave a pair each to popstar Britney Spears and the model Naomi Campbell. The last was sold with a percentage of the profits going to Hilfiger's favoured charity, Autism Speaks, in 2017.

They are seen as part of Monroe's visual legacy because of their starring role in the film, but jeans were very much part of Marilyn's behind-camera wardrobe, too. In her 1952 interview for *Movieland Magazine*, she admits she wore boys' jeans for their fit. Monroe has been well documented wearing jeans; the series of images taken by André de Dienes in 1945, when she was just 19 years old, show her with her natural darker hair, teaming indigo jeans and crisp boyish shirts. She wore them to relax in and later, as an actress, she wore them on set to rehearse.

In her 1986 autobiography, Jane Russell relates how, during the run-throughs for the 1953 film *Gentlemen Prefer Blondes*, Marilyn would always wear jeans, no make-up and 'tangled' hair. Photographs of Monroe behind the scenes during the filming of *There's No Business Like Showbusiness* (1954) and the following year's *The Seven Year Itch* pay testimony

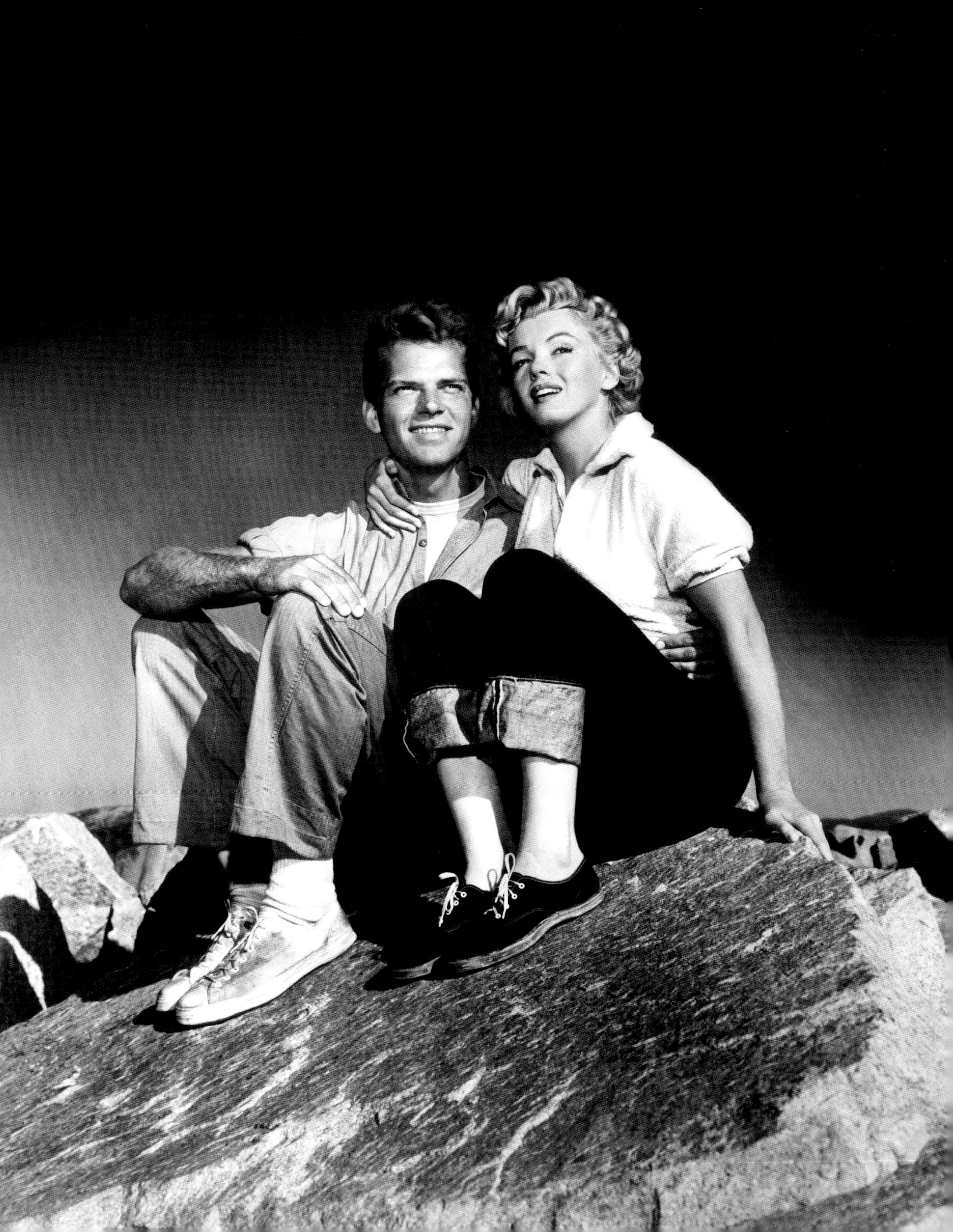

to how essential a staple jeans were for her. A starlet in jeans, however, was ripe gossip for a magazine.

In 1952, a *Photoplay* feature, 'Inside Stuff; Cal York's Gossip of Hollywood', reported on the scandal of Monroe's casual choice of daywear, quoting customers in one of Beverly Hills' smart shops saying: 'That can't be a movie star!' and 'They're supposed to be super-sexy Hollywood beauties.' The girl they were referring to wore old, wrinkled dungarees and Indian moccasins, with the remains of her studio make-up still on her face and mussed-up hair. Several nights later, that same girl walked into *Photoplay*'s Gold Medal Award dinner, her face surrounded with a halo of golden curls. Marilyn wore a figure-hugging red taffeta gown covered with black lace. She was poised, charming, and all but stole the show.

Monroe's 'working wardrobe' was regalia she inhabited when she needed to be a bombshell. The year before, she had been awarded trophies for 'Miss Cheesecake of the Year' in 1951 and 'Cheesecake Queen of 1952' by *Stars and Stripes* newspaper. For the photoshoot, she wore only a white bustier, high heels, a taffeta apron and cartoon chef's hat – a 360-degree contrast to the asexual jeans she opted for when off-camera. Monroe would don jeans once again, this time in character for *River of No Return* (1954), a film she reportedly hated, saying: 'I think I deserve a better deal than a Grade Z cowboy movie in which acting finished second to the scenery and the CinemaScope process' (quoted in O'Hara, 2015). At first, Marilyn refused the script, which came after her blockbuster 1953 comedies *Gentlemen Prefer Blondes* and *How to Marry a Millionaire*, which had pulled in millions of dollars for the studio, while Monroe was paid the standard contract rate.

Eventually she played the part of Kay, a Gold Rush era saloon chanteuse, but after filming finished, she walked out on Fox and began a campaign for a fair contract and more control. Her frustration hadn't come about overnight. In 1953, she was already declaring: 'I'm really eager to do something else. Squeezing yourself to ooze out the last ounce of sex allure is terribly hard. I'd like to do roles like Julia in *Bury the Dead*, Gretchen in *Faust*, and Teresa in *Cradle Song*. I don't want to be a comedienne forever' (quoted in Spoto, 1993). In 1961, Marilyn would be offered the chance when given the contemplative part of Roslyn in Arthur Miller's screenplay, *The Misfits*. Written for Monroe, it offered her the breadth and scope she had dreamt of and, fittingly enough, the character of her career was largely played with her wearing a pair of reassuring Levi's blue jeans.

'IF THE ARTIFICIALITY, THE ROLE, THE STEREOTYPE, THE SEX GODDESS IS WHAT YOU ARE MOSTLY REWARDED FOR, IT'S EXTREMELY DIFFICULT TO LET IT GO. YOU HAVE VERY LITTLE ASSURANCE THAT YOU ARE GOING TO BE LOVED AND SALARIED AS YOUR REAL SELF, AS YOUR UNIQUE, UNDERNEATH SELF. THERE ISN'T, EVEN NOW, VERY MUCH EVIDENCE OF FEMALE HUMAN BEINGS BEING REWARDED FOR THAT, THOUGH. THERE IS LOTS MORE, BUT THERE WAS MUCH LESS IN THE '50S THAT FORMED MARILYN.'

– Gloria Steinham, American Masters Digital Archive, 2006

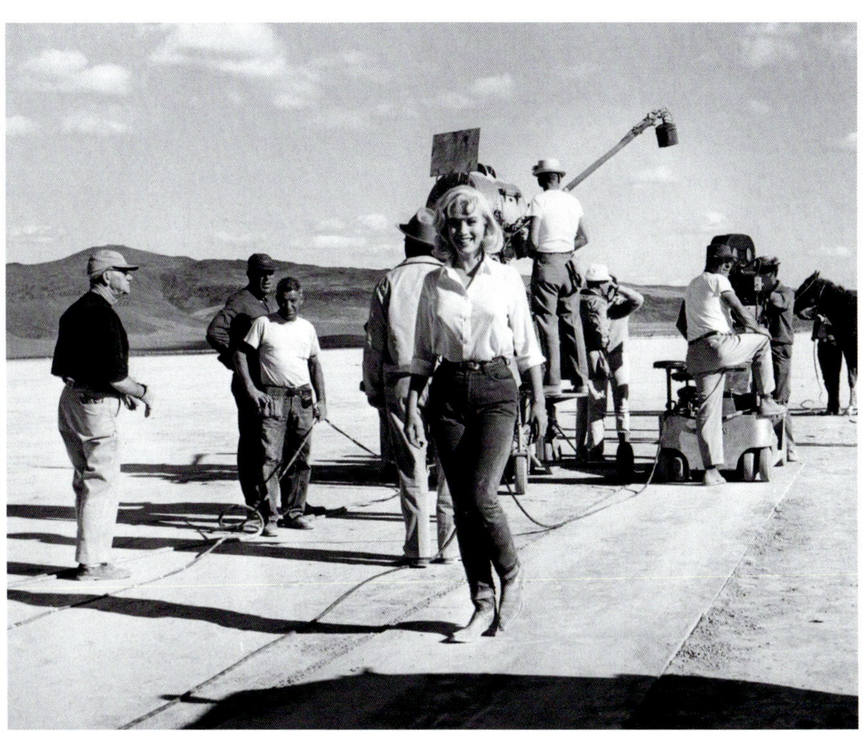

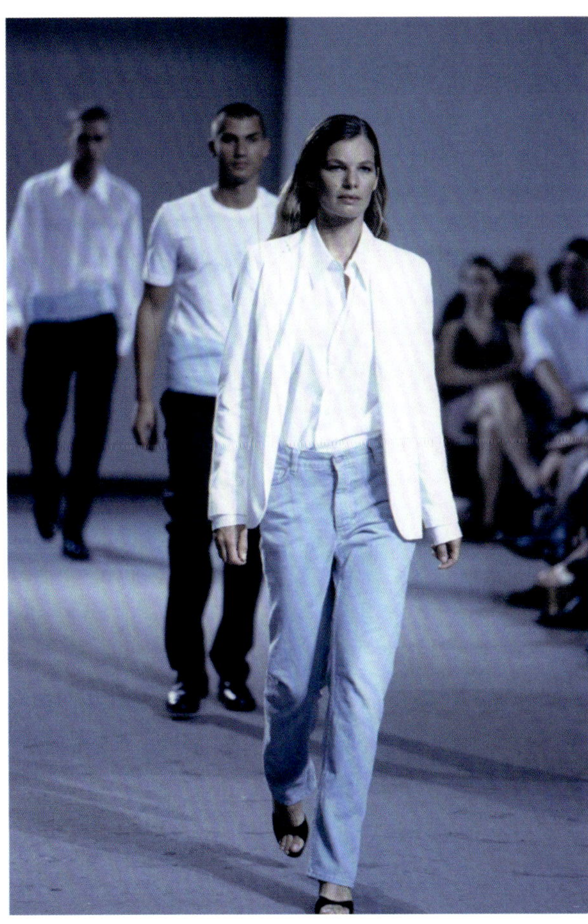

Above: The white shirt and jeans combination has become a firm favourite of designers, as seen here in the Helmut Lang Spring/Summer 1998 show in Paris

Top: Marilyn wearing her favourite jeans, behind the scenes on the set of *The Misfits*, 1960

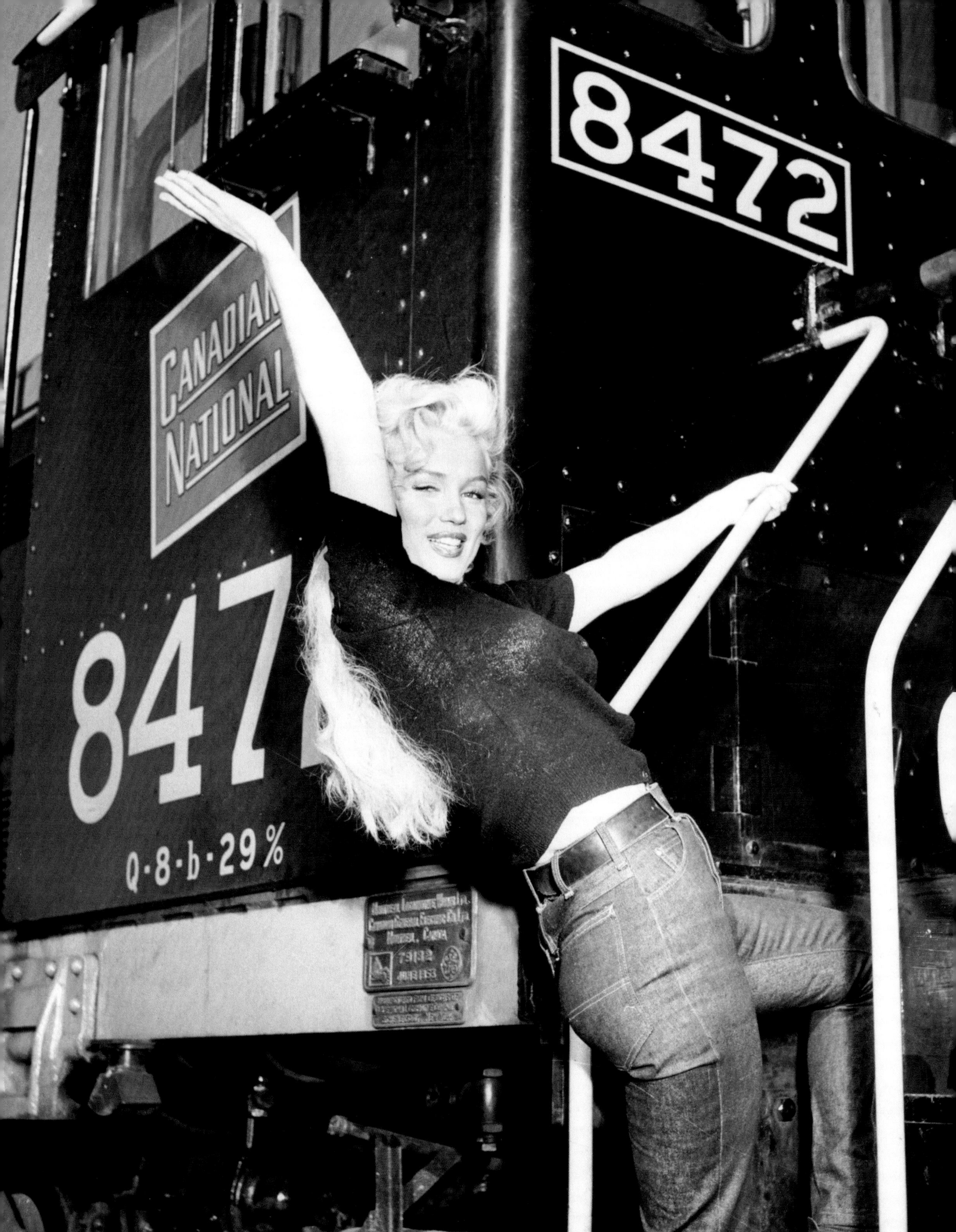

8472
CANADIAN NATIONAL
847
Q·8·b·29%

'YOU CAN BE FEMININE EVEN IN JEANS,
BUT EVEN MY JEANS FIT! I BUY BOYS' JEANS,
BECAUSE THEY ARE LONG WAISTED LIKE ME;
AND BOYS' SHIRTS TO GO WITH THEM.'

– Marilyn Monroe, *Movieland Magazine*, 1952

Left: Marlilyn on location for *River of No Return*, summer 1953

Overleaf: Marilyn backstage with Dan Dailey while filming *There's No Business Like Showbusiness*, c.1954

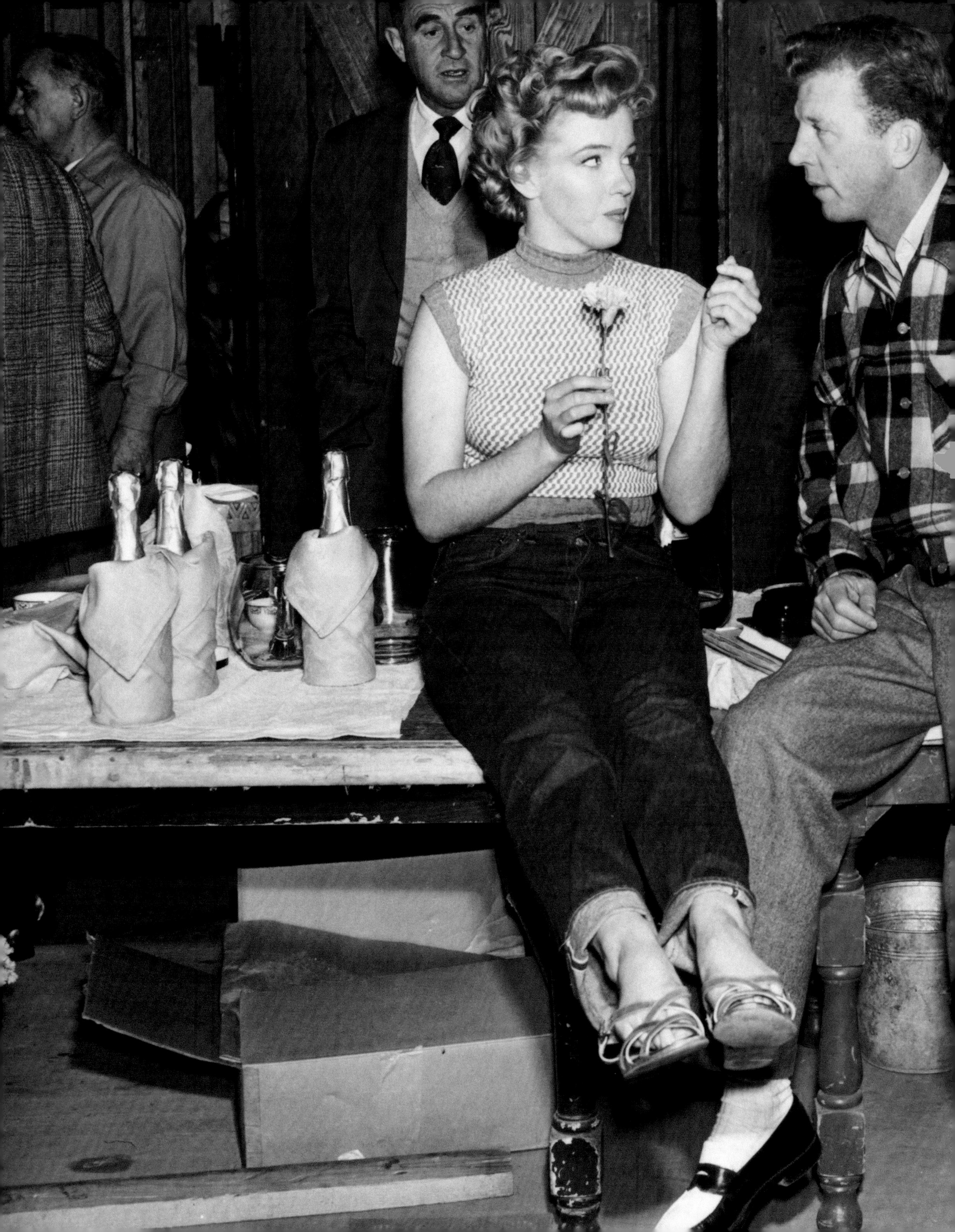

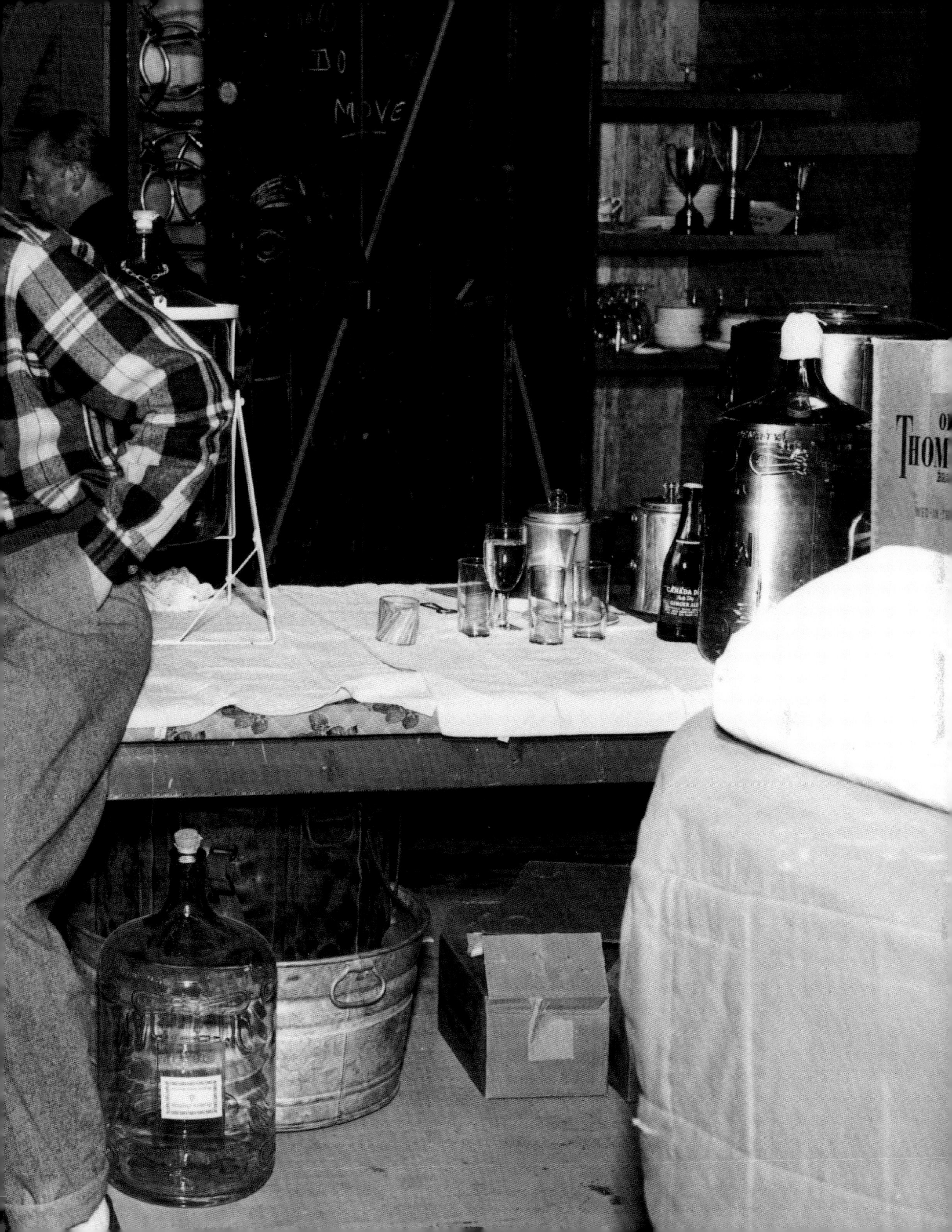
DO
MOVE
THOM
GINGER ALE
CANADA DRY

SWIMWEAR

'I KNEW I BELONGED TO THE PUBLIC
AND TO THE WORLD, NOT BECAUSE
I WAS TALENTED OR EVEN BEAUTIFUL
BUT BECAUSE I HAD NEVER BELONGED
TO ANYTHING OR ANYONE ELSE.'

– Marilyn Monroe (quoted in Steinem, 2014)

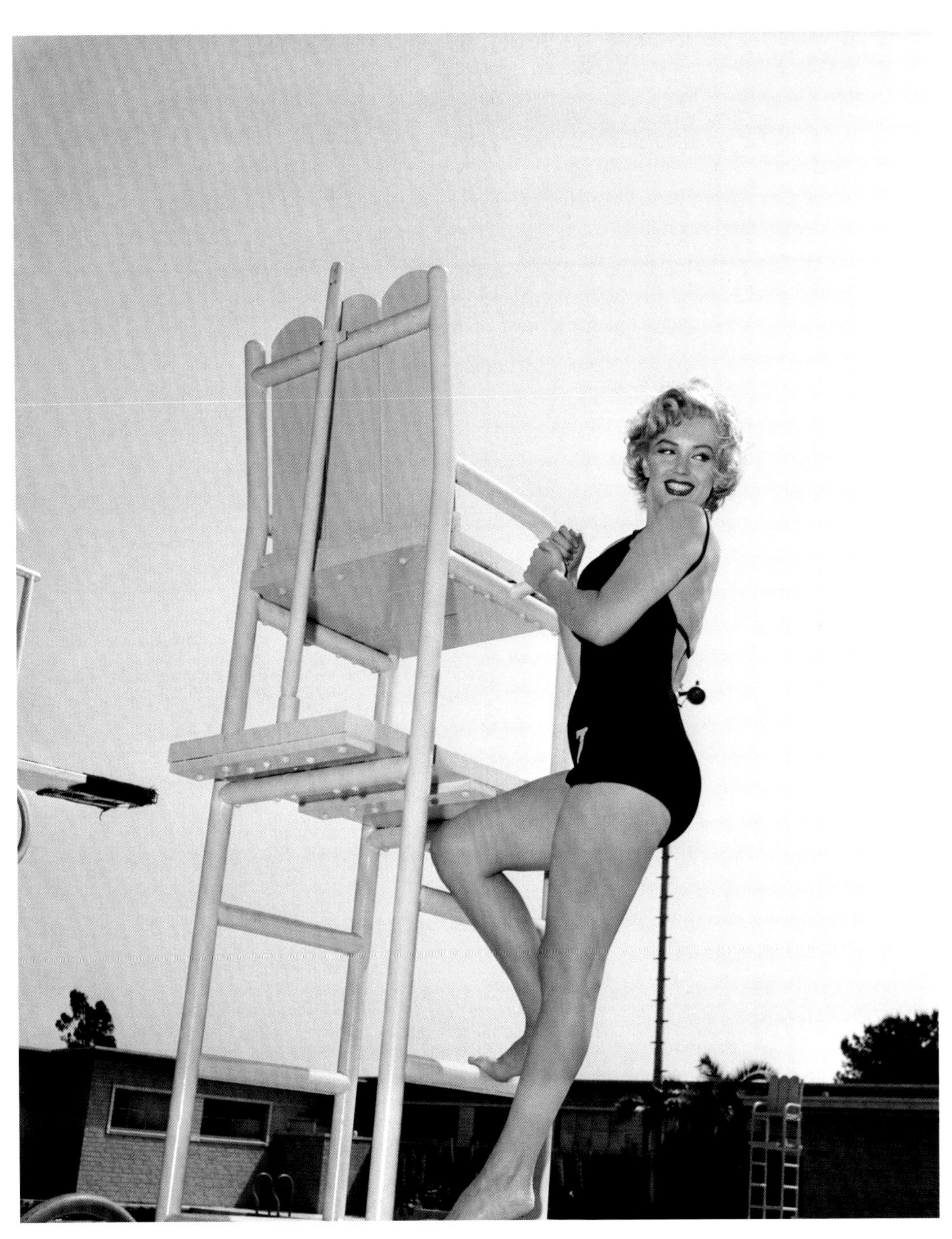

Marilyn during filming of *Monkey Business*, 1952

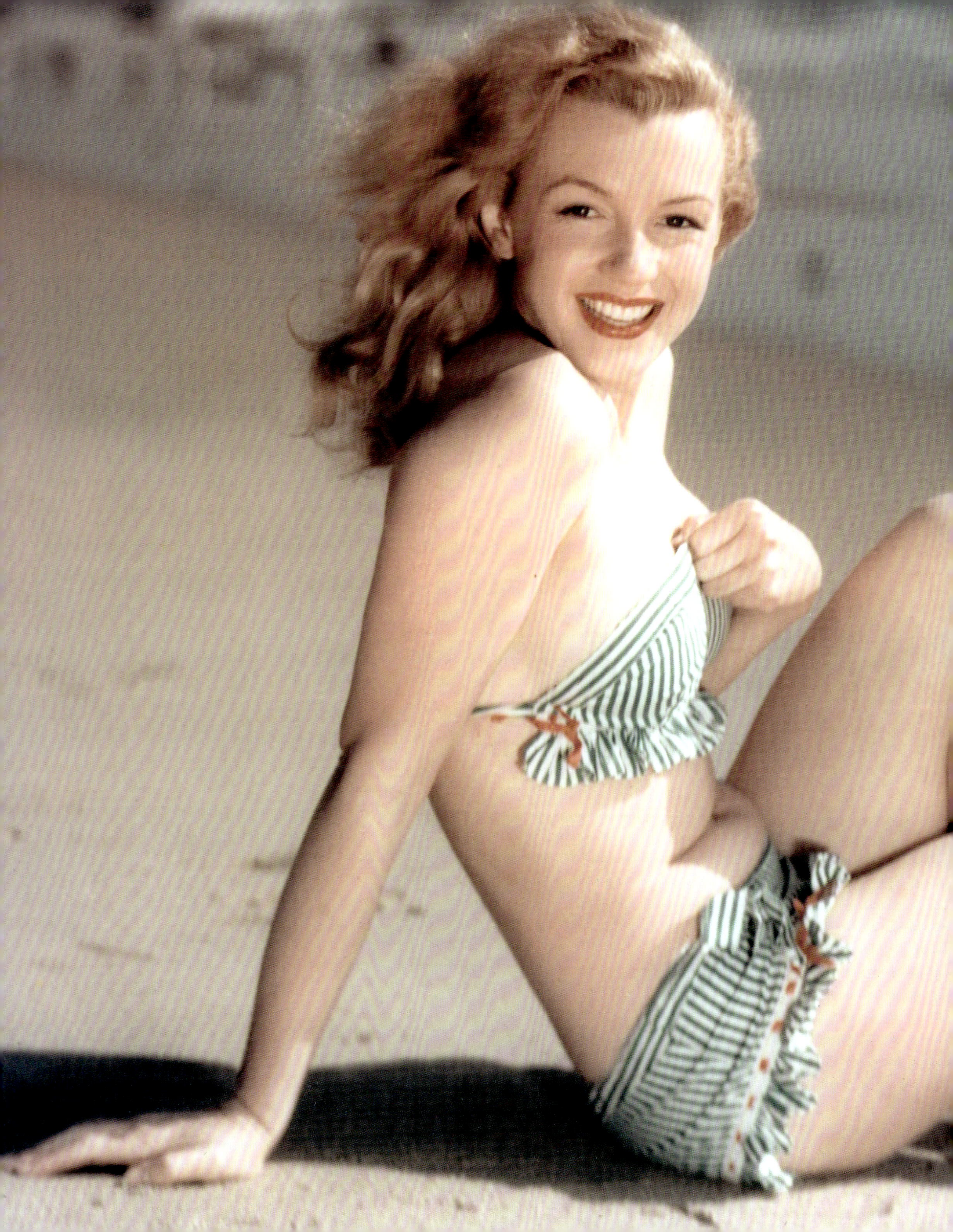

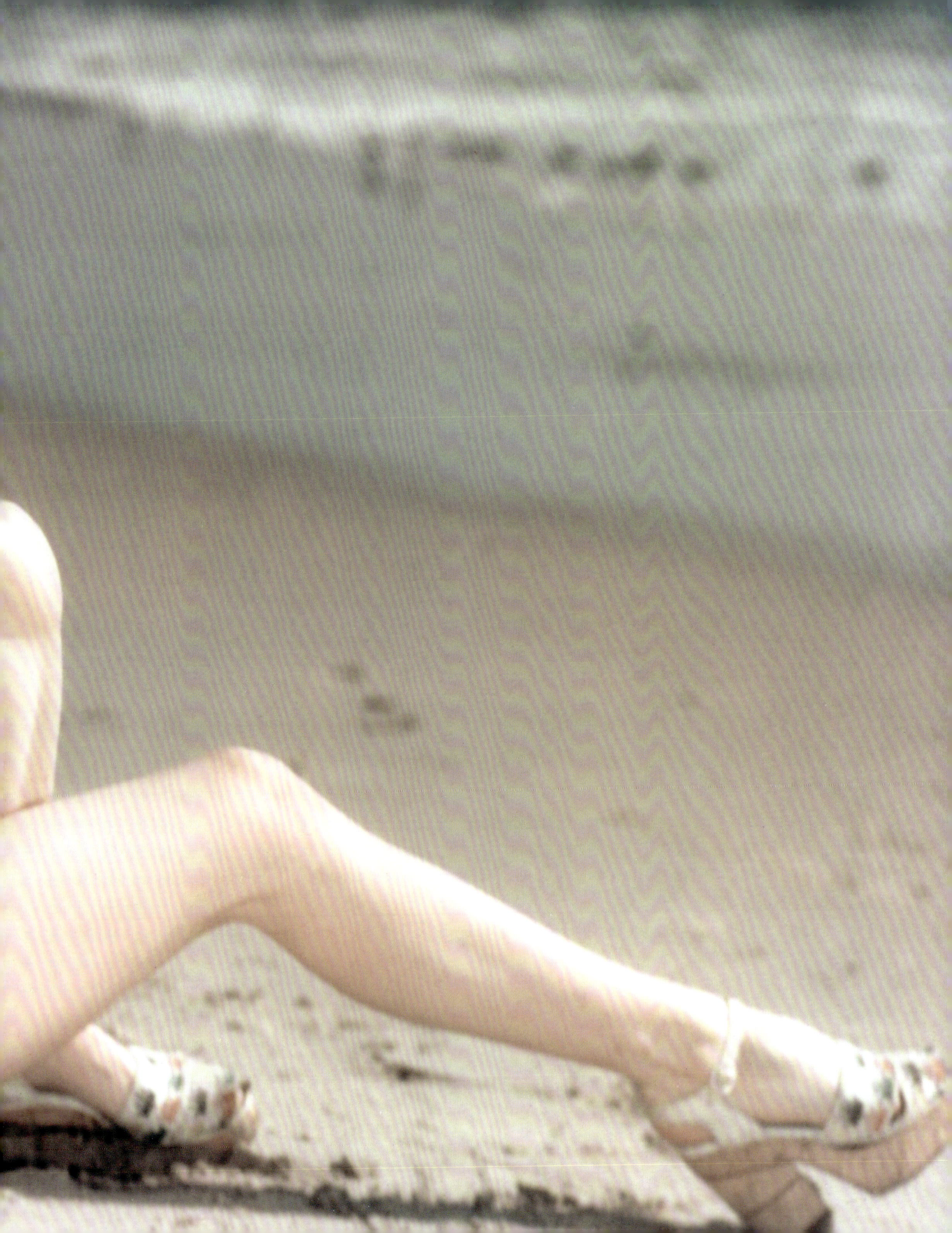

AT THE AGE OF 15, Marilyn was gifted her very own swimsuits by the Howell family, who were friends of her guardian, Grace Goddard. A home movie exists of her wearing a white bikini and another sporting a red two-piece and white swimming cap, playing with Howell's daughters at a beach in Santa Monica. Marilyn turns cartwheels and waves at the camera, and although there is a nascent glimpse of the successful model and actress she would become, she looks and behaves like a child. A year later, just 16, she would marry her first husband, James Dougherty, moving to Catalina Island in 1943, where he was stationed to teach marine ocean safety. A picture of the young bride on the beach at Avalon shows her dressed in a printed-cotton, square-necked, cropped top and tiered bathing skirt, which is hugely reminiscent of the fashionable styles of the time.

Swimwear in the 1930s and early '40s had evolved to become charming fashion statements and was a far cry from the bathing suits women had worn at the turn of the century. A June 1928 *Vogue* feature, 'Chic at High Tide: New Costumes for Sand and Sea', recalls: 'We all remember the old-fashioned bathing girl as a ridiculous figure, with her bunchy bloomers and her long-sleeved high-necked blouse and we poke fun at her at every occasion in a thoroughly ungrateful manner.' Instead, the magazine champions fluid lines from the Parisian fashion houses of Jean Patou and Lucien Lelong, spotlighting their androgynous maillot costumes, designed to show off a lean, athletic body that was in style after the First World War when flappers aspired to string-bean shaped bodies.

By the 1930s, swimwear worn by film stars such as Dolores del Rio, most famously in her 1932 film *Bird of Paradise*, was often strikingly glamorous, and in the days before the Hays Code (Motion Picture Production Code – the industry censorship guidelines) allowed navels to be shown. One of the most celebrated bathing costume makers, Catalina, originally a knitwear company, was well known for their fabric technology and the silhouettes used in their chic 'styled for the stars of Hollywood' beach range. Marilyn's later dresser, Orry-Kelly, designed for the company during the 1930s, and Monroe would be one of the biggest stars to wear their collection in their advertising campaigns of the early 1950s. From the start of her career at the Blue Book

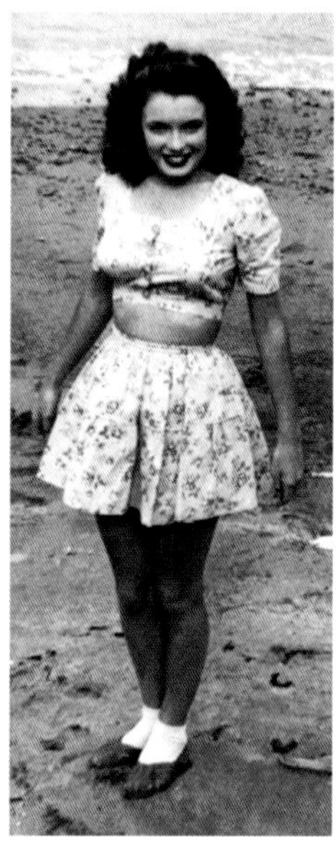

Modeling Agency, she would constantly model swimsuits which, in turn, boosted her burgeoning bombshell appeal. It set her on track as an actress whose looks, first and foremost, were her calling card and, at the time, if you wanted success, there was no other option but to conform to the beauty-queen stereotype: it was what the studios were looking for in their contract players.

Monroe had a bit part in her first film, *Scudda Hoo! Scudda Hay!*, which hit cinemas in 1948, with her character Betty appearing onscreen for only a second. Still images from the film,

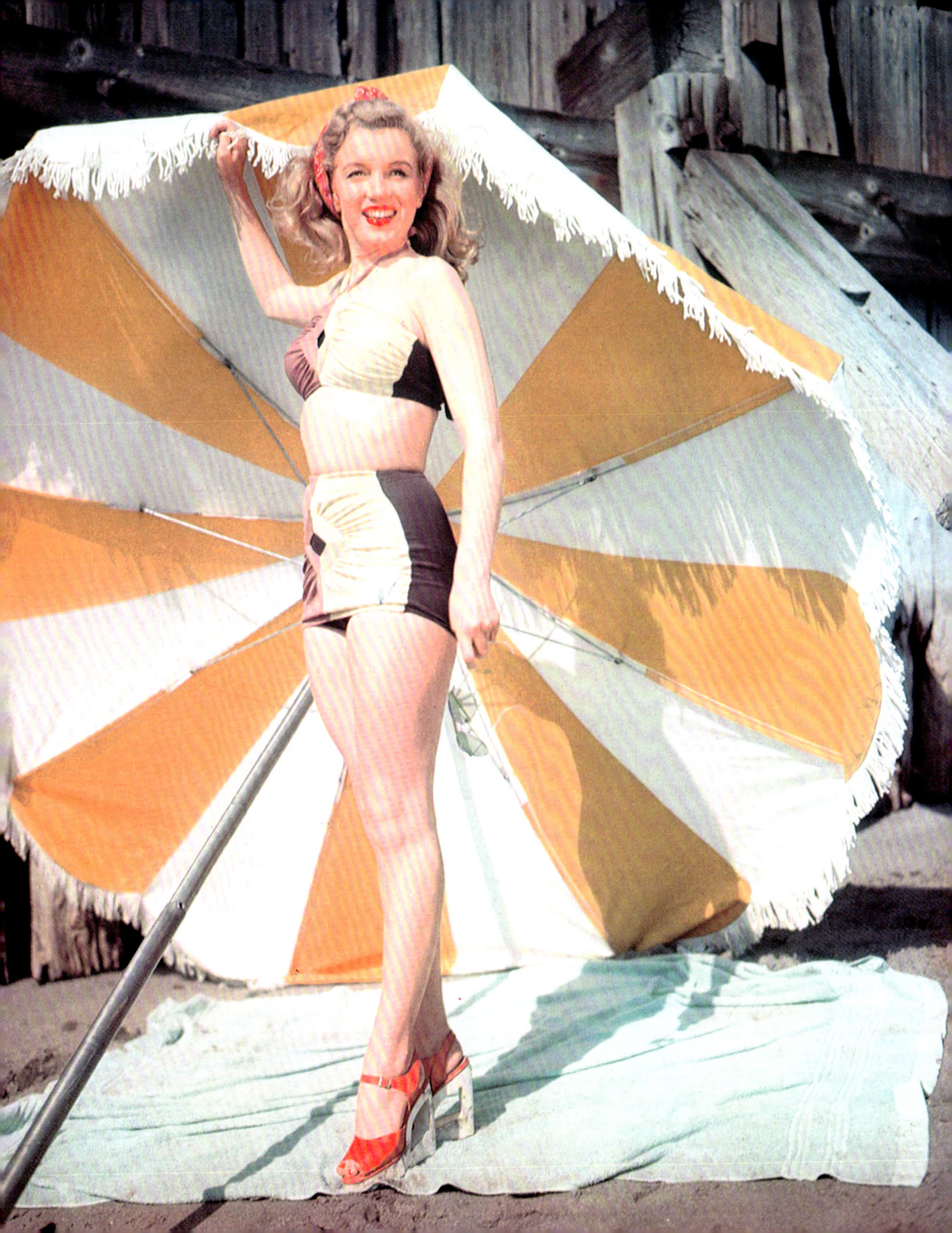

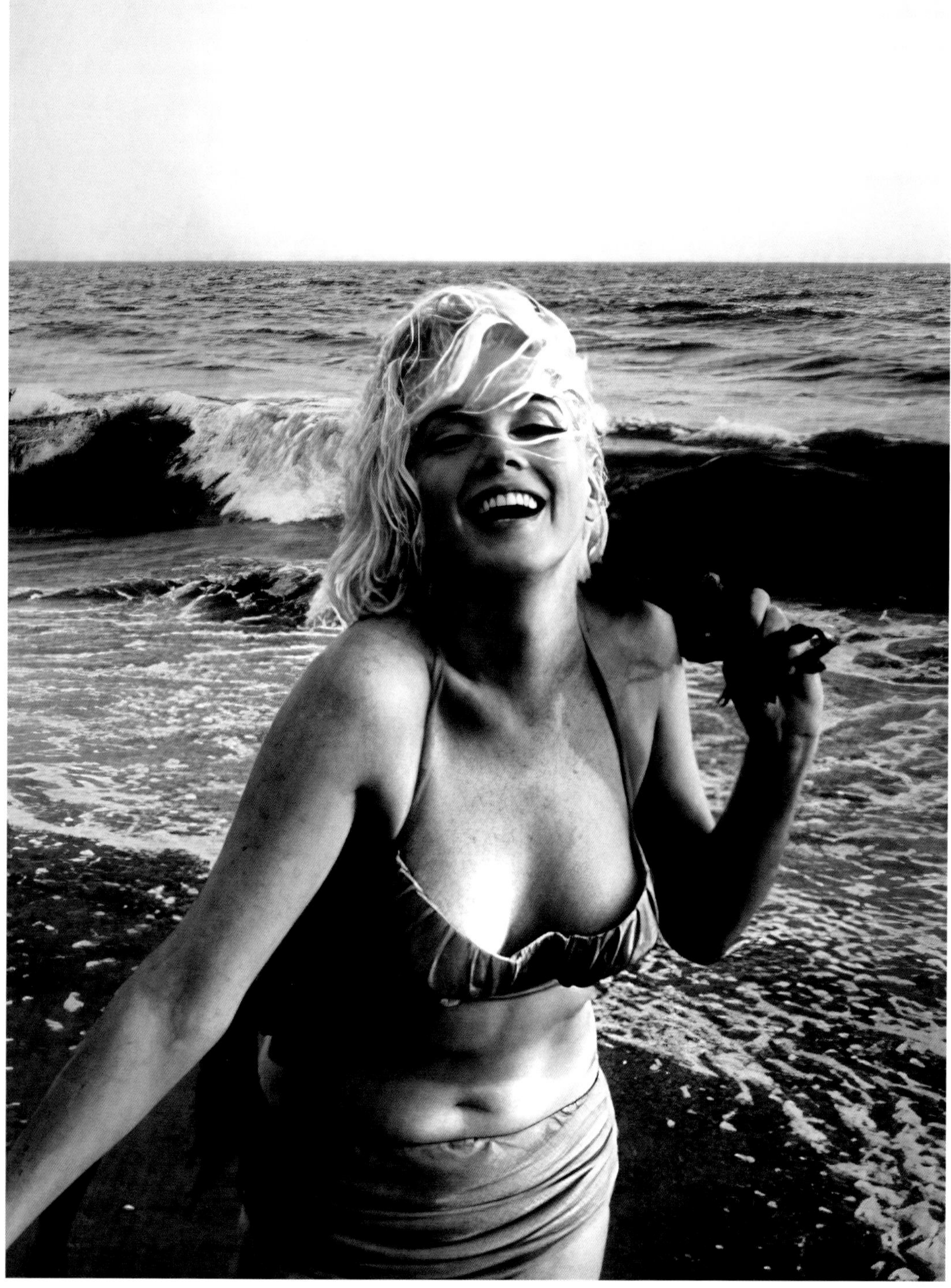

'I DON'T WANT TO BE BONE THIN,
AND I MAKE IT A POINT TO STAY
THE WAY I WANT TO BE.'

– Marilyn Monroe, *Movieland Magazine*, 1952

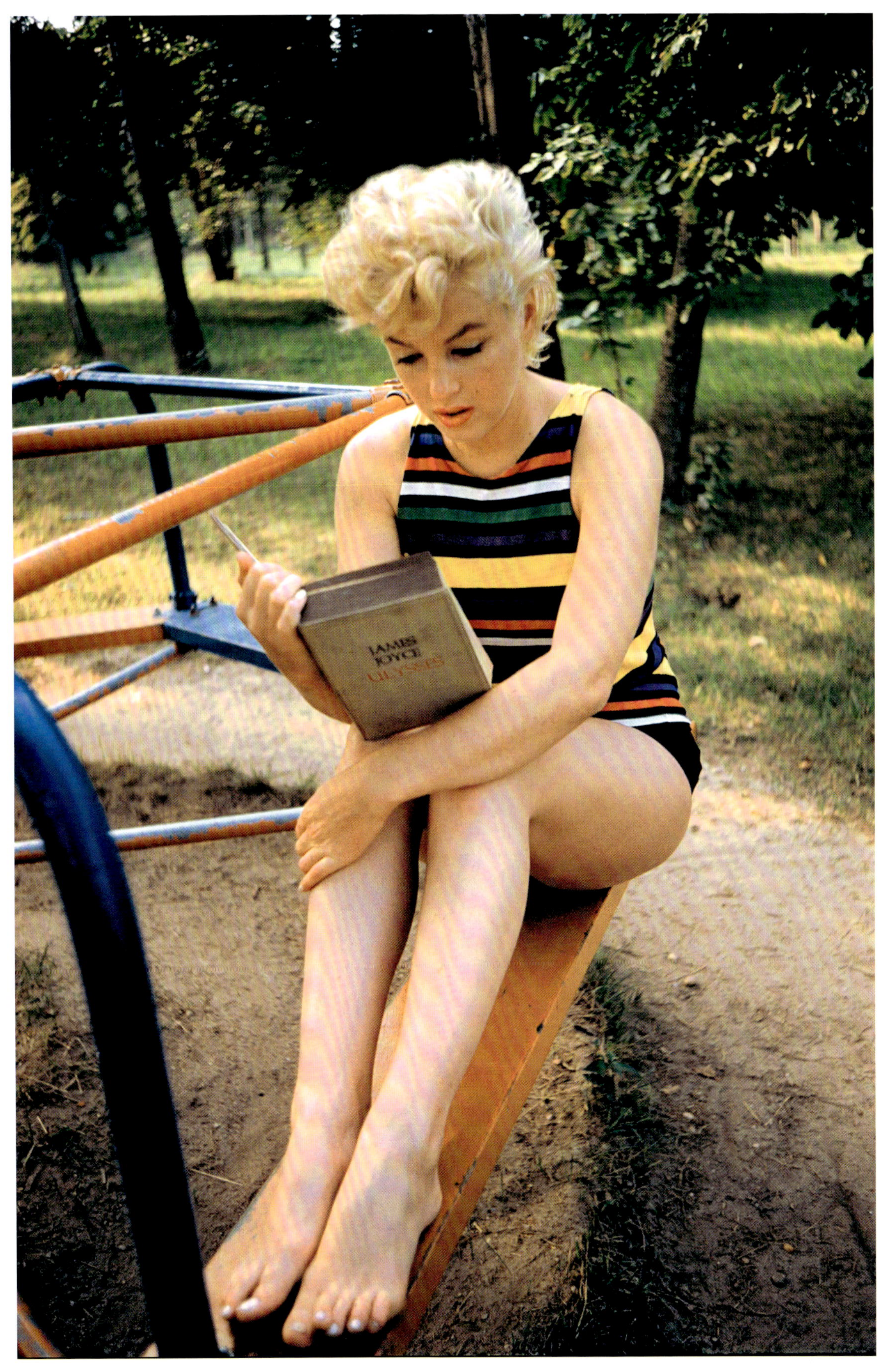

Marilyn on a photoshoot with Eve Arnold, Long Island, New York, 1952

however, show a rowing boat scene with her wearing a scoop-necked one-piece swimming costume. In 1934, the Hays Code implemented, among other restrictions, a 'no suggestive nudity' clause. This meant that from then until 1968, swimsuits had to hide the stomach and therefore only the bathing suit was deemed suitably wholesome. In the 1950s, these restrictions were somewhat stretched by the increasing sexuality on show in films produced by the big studios. In *Love Nest* (1951), Monroe plays Roberta Stevens, a sexy former WAC who wears a series of seductive outfits, including a corseted, black-lace girdled suit with matching strappy Perspex heels, and a pretty polka-dot bikini, clearly showing her midriff. The same year she plays Joyce Mannering in *Let's Make It Legal* (1951) wearing a glitzy, gathered, sweetheart swimsuit, which may cover her up but is considerably incompatible with any water sports. The film's publicity poster declared: 'Who cares if it's legal as long as it's fun!'

After a stint of wearing jeans in *Clash by Night* (1952), her following film *We're Not Married* (1952) was written to ensure Monroe was back wearing a swimming costume. Then in *Monkey Business* (1952), her character, Lois Laurel, puts on the requisite swimwear once more; this time, however, she dons a far more utility-wise, simple, black one-piece. Monroe's final film of 1953, *How to Marry a Millionaire*, sees her wearing the ultimate bathing suit: hot-red, diamanté-decorated and designed by wardrobe maestro William Travilla. Fittingly shown off during the film's fashion show scene, it is a high point of Monroe's pin-up styling. Playing the part of Pola Debevoise, she completely inhabits the blonde

goddess role she had created for herself, and she is a sensation.

It wasn't until 1959 in *Some Like It Hot*, however, that audiences would again see Monroe wearing a swimsuit onscreen: a reproduction vintage 1920s maillot created by Orry-Kelly. In her unreleased 1962 film, *Something's Got to Give*, the bikini she wears is fully contemporary, with its tiny, triangle-shaped bra and side-tie briefs reflective of the era's fashion-forward, scanty silhouette that wouldn't look out of place today. One of the first bikinis had been shown off back in 1946, when a version created by Louis Réard was modelled at the Piscine Molitor in Paris by Micheline Bernardini, a little after the United States had performed atomic bomb testing at the Bikini Atoll in the Pacific Islands. It's an astonishing sign of the times that the impact of a daring two-piece was compared to the impact of a bomb that rendered the island unfit for habitation and forced its inhabitants to permanently relocate.

Nevertheless, the swimwear and its name took off. By 1947, fashion editors had picked up on it and were featuring the bikini on the pages of their magazines, with celebrated style-monger Diana Vreeland calling it 'the swoonsuit'. Swimsuits became synonymous with Marilyn, and the examples she wore in her films and possessed at home illustrate a timeline of this item's fashionable silhouette. Monroe's own wardrobe of beachwear included a large variety of styles that were reflective of the 1950s, in particular. A baby blue, chequered outfit of frilled knickers, matching hat with a velvet bow, cropped frilled tank top, capri pants and a dirndl skirt, all in matching prints, was

sold during the auction of her property in 1999, along with swim-pants in both orange-and-yellow and blue-and-purple polka dots.

Tops are mostly styled with her favourite signature halterneck detailing. She was shot in 1955 by Magnum photographer Eve Arnold in a celebrated series of images taken at a children's playground. In one, she is wearing a geometric monochrome halter-neck top and bathing pants, reading her copy of James Joyce's *Ulysses* (1922). It's a moment that shows off Monroe's rarely seen reflective side to the public. Arnold was a photographer she trusted and, in 1961, Arnold captured her again on the set of *The Misfits* wearing the halterneck she loved so much. Candid, windswept and naturally beautiful: a million miles away from the pin-up swimwear shots she built her career on.

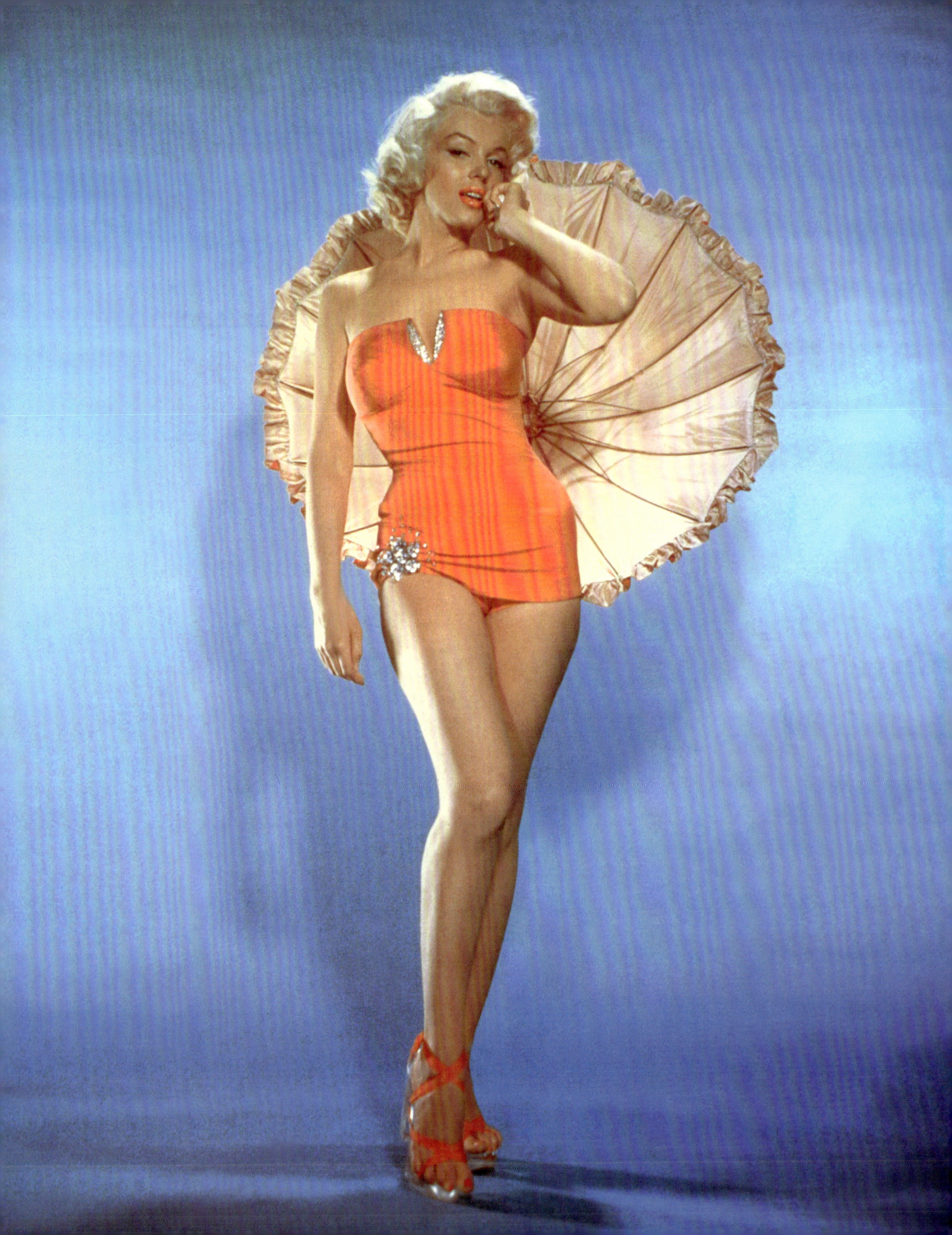

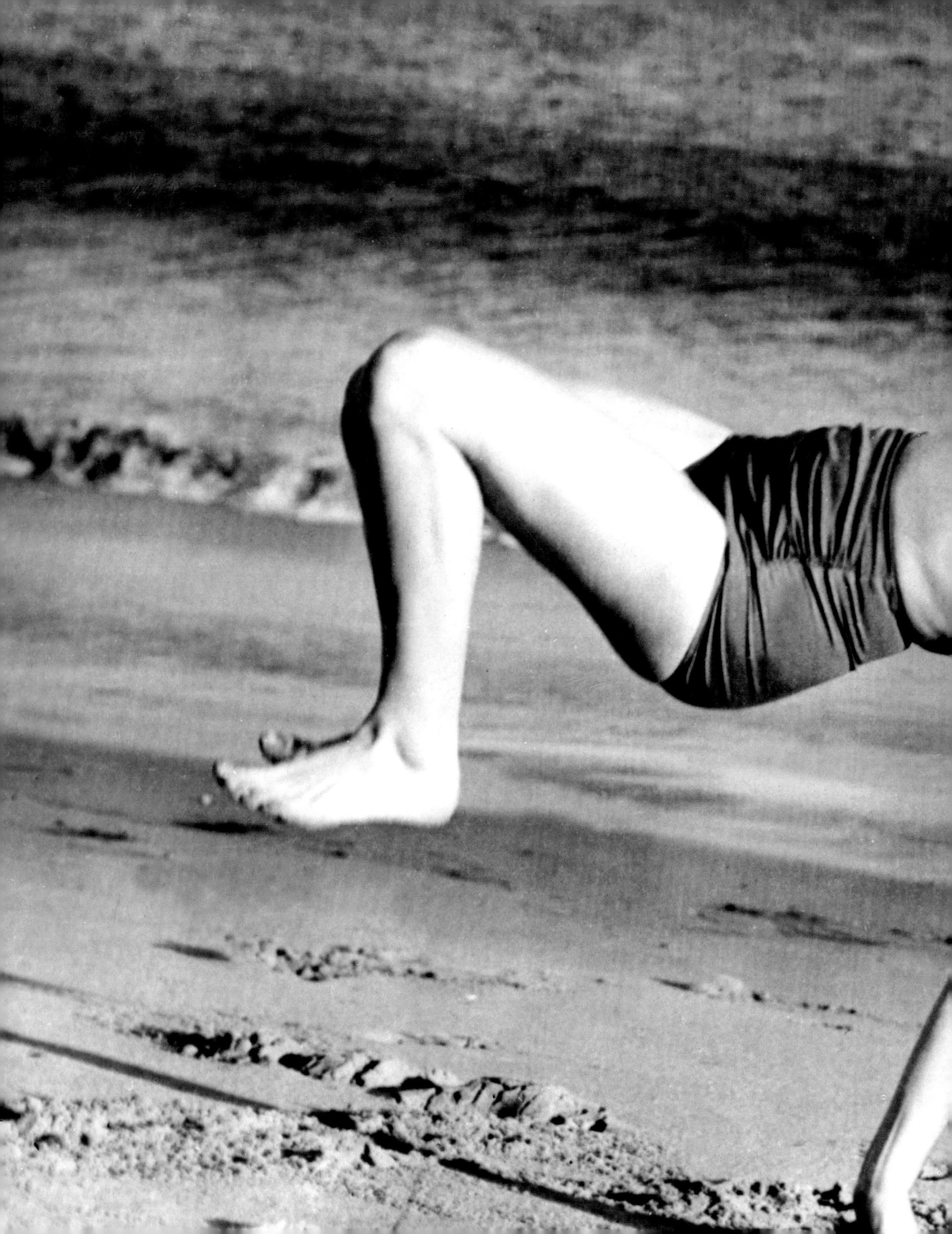

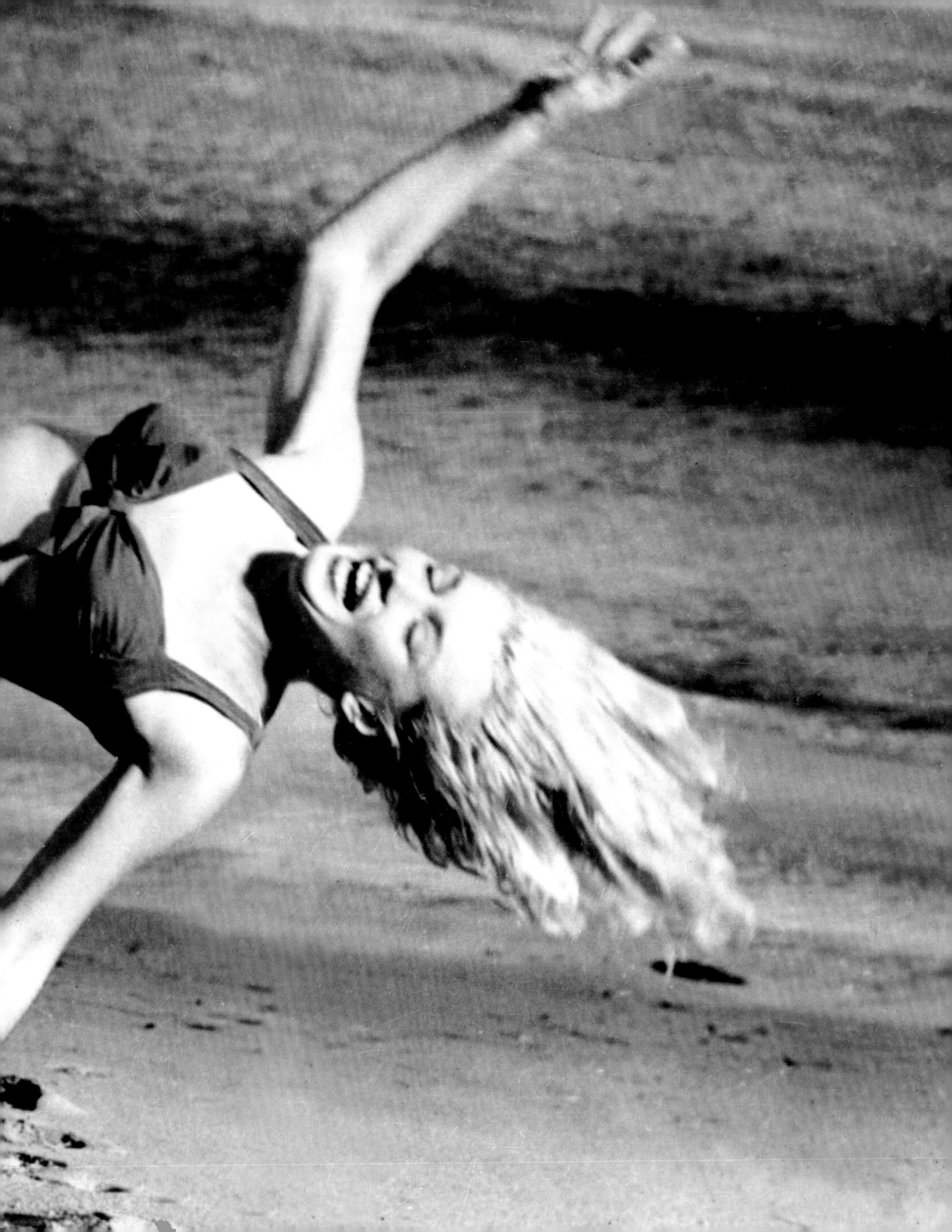

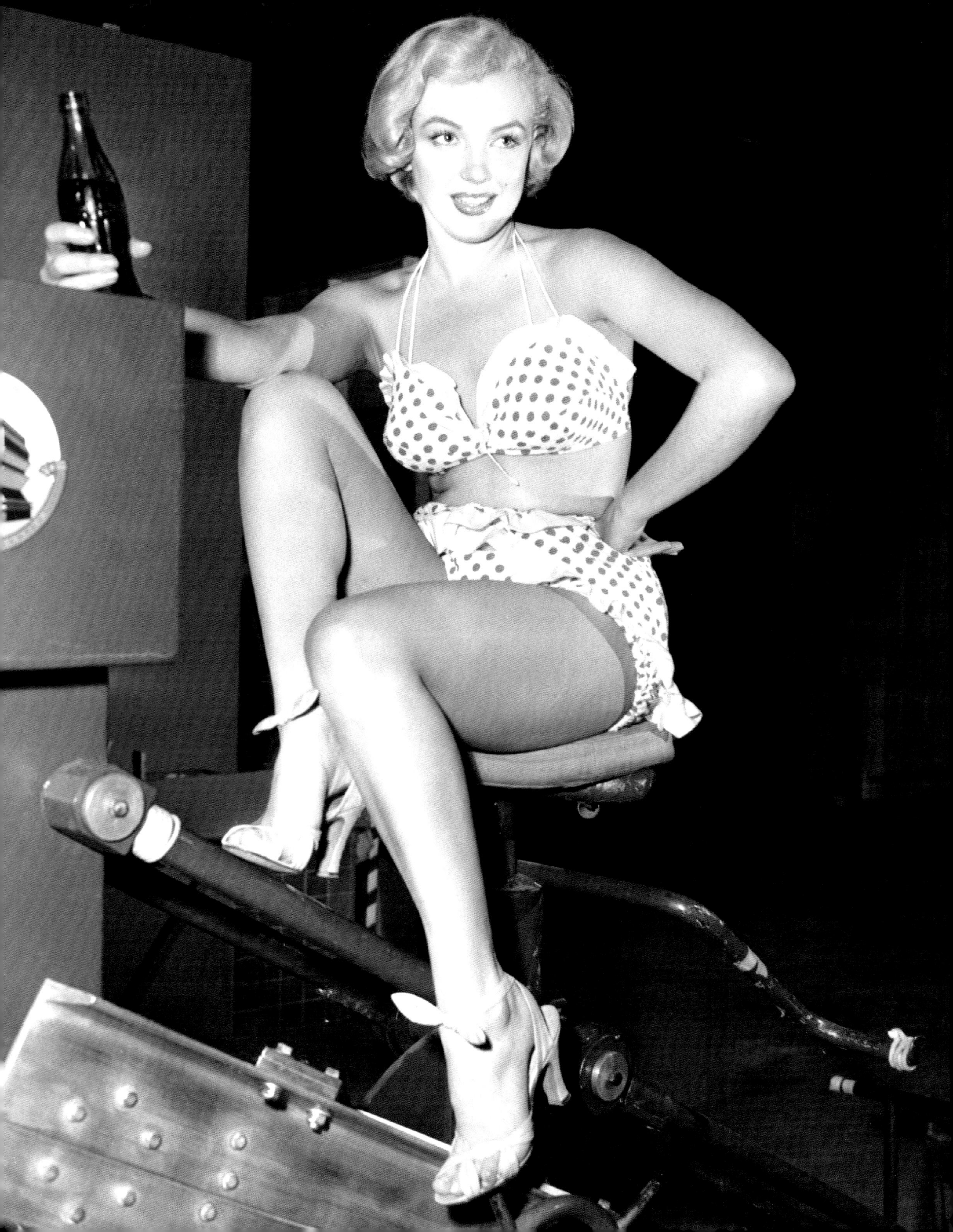

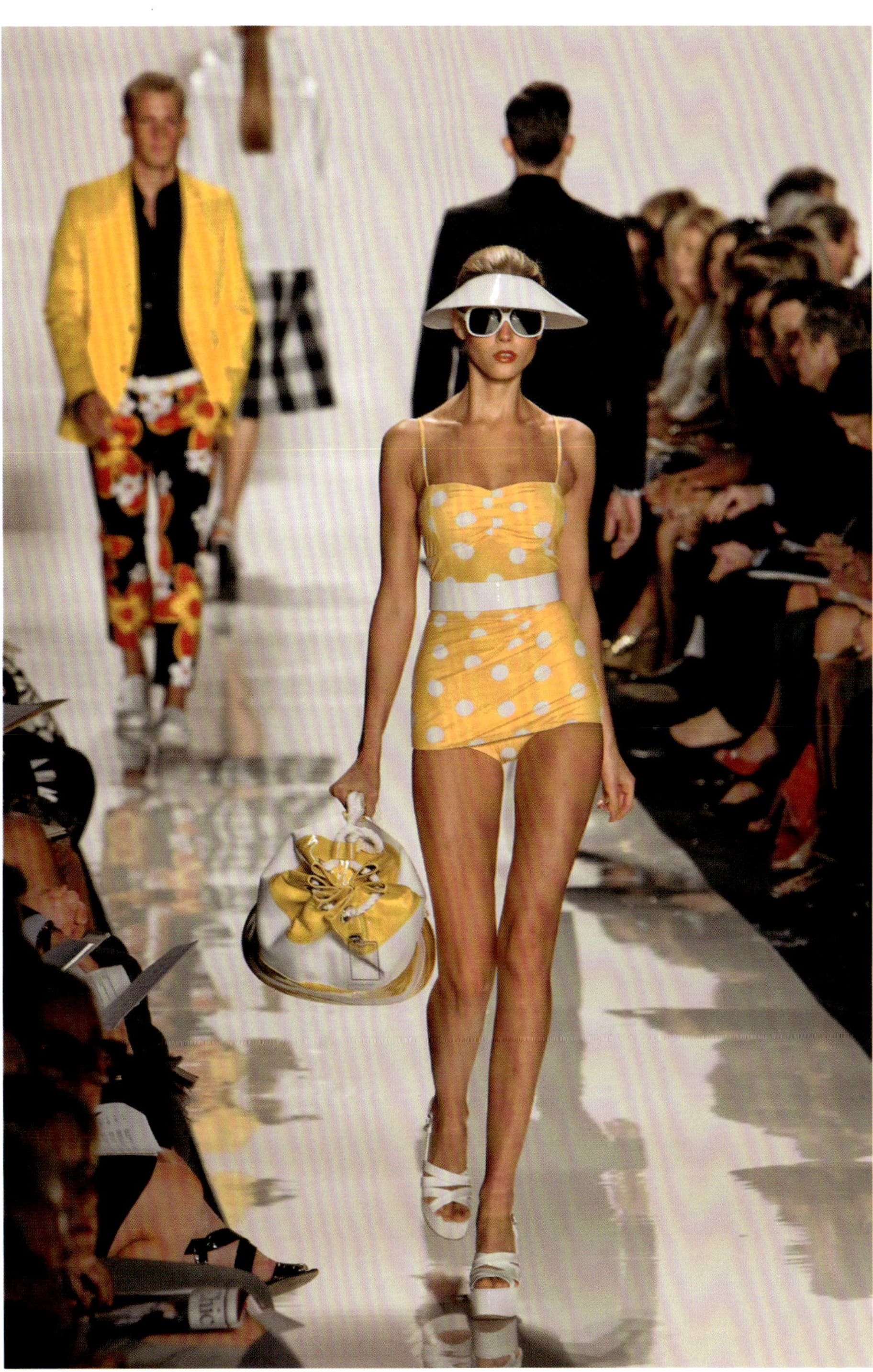

Left: Marilyn on the set of *Love Nest*, 1951

Above: Marilyn's spotty swimwear makes a comeback on the
catwalk in Michael Kors Spring/Summer collection, New York, 2008

'I LIKE TO BE REALLY DRESSED UP OR
REALLY UNDRESSED – I DON'T BOTHER
WITH ANYTHING IN BETWEEN.'

– Marilyn Monroe, 1954 (quoted in Church Gibson, 2015)

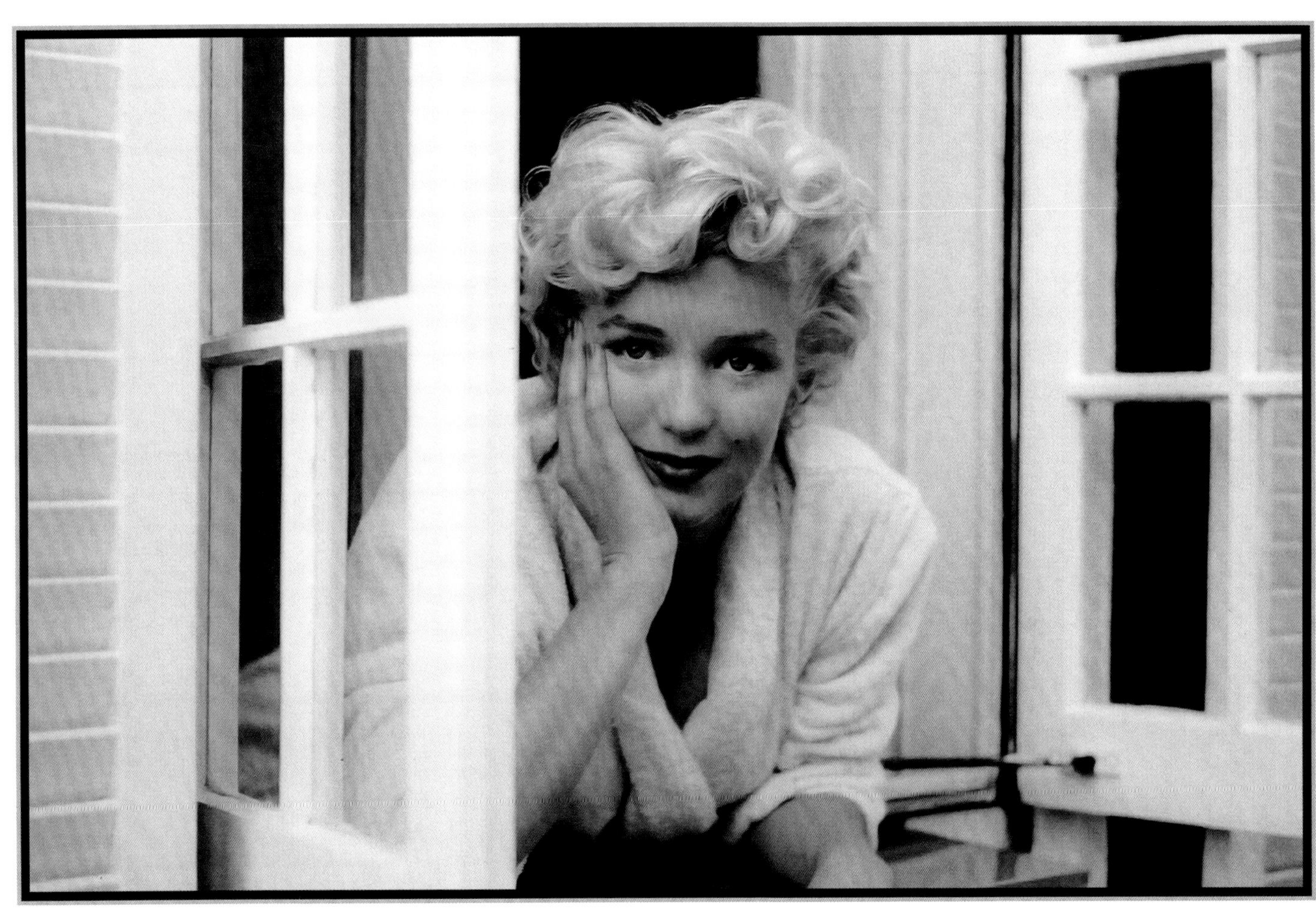

Hollywood, 1960s

MARILYN MONROE'S

ability to model and look great in front of the camera were skills she cannily used to her advantage in order to build a successful career. She knew how to make any outfit look attractive and that included the famous terry towelling bathrobes she loved to wear. She made something cheap, cheerful, frumpy and informal look like a white mink coat wrapped around her. A celebrated series of images taken by Milton Greene in March 1955 show the intimate and trusting rapport between the film star and the photographer.

The remarkable collection of pictures shows Monroe as assured and relaxed, wearing a beloved robe. Her playful energy is wholly evident as she reveals herself not quite in full-actress mode. Apart from red lipstick, powder and coiffured hair, she wears no fashionable armour to protect her, but simply sits cross-legged and laughs.

Bathrobes can be about an in-between moment, worn when you are either getting ready for the day or getting ready for bath and bed. Marilyn often wore them just to hang out; her love of this casual, throw-it-on attire reflected a makeshift moment when she wasn't existing as a glamorous onscreen star and had yet to turn on the full-beam light of her stardom.

Wearing a robe is also emblematic of becoming someone – something to be worn before morphing into a more glamorous version of yourself. As the young orphan who became the biggest film star ever, Marilyn had a persona that echoed the American Dream – wherever you came from, you could still become a success. Her generation's dream, however, was tempered by Cold War paranoia, and this edgy dichotomy runs in parallel to Monroe's own story: growing up, watching the movies, and dreaming the American Dream alongside the eventual disillusion with the parts she was being given.

Stars were required to play their parts onscreen and inhabit these personas off-set, too. Marilyn wasn't Marilyn unless she was wearing a bombshell wardrobe. When we see her in her favourite bathrobes, she is, in part, connecting with her unaffected self. They were easy and reliable things to wear.

Her closet, especially in the early days, was always small. In 1950, after *The Asphalt Jungle* opened, she moved into a friend's house in Burbank in Los Angeles to save rent while they were away for a couple of months. She remembers how 'moving wasn't hard' because she had so few clothes (Monroe, 1974). But the one essential she packed was her white bathrobe.

She wore robes all her life, including for André de Dienes' celebrated 1949 images of her on Long Island's Tobay Beach. In 2009, Julien's Auction House in Beverley Hills sold the one she wore in spontaneous and candid pictures taken by George Barris in 1962 on Santa Monica Beach. They became the very last images taken of Marilyn before she died, and the bathrobe she was wearing – a hooded 'Catalina Beach-Blotter' – fetched $125,000.

From time to time, the white terry towelling wrap would make an appearance in Monroe's films. In her 1953 film *How to Marry a Millionaire*, as Pola Debevoise, a model on the hunt for a rich husband, she dressed in an elegant, floor-length version featuring a waist-cinching belt, accessorised with a towelling turban and

The Seven Year Itch, 1955

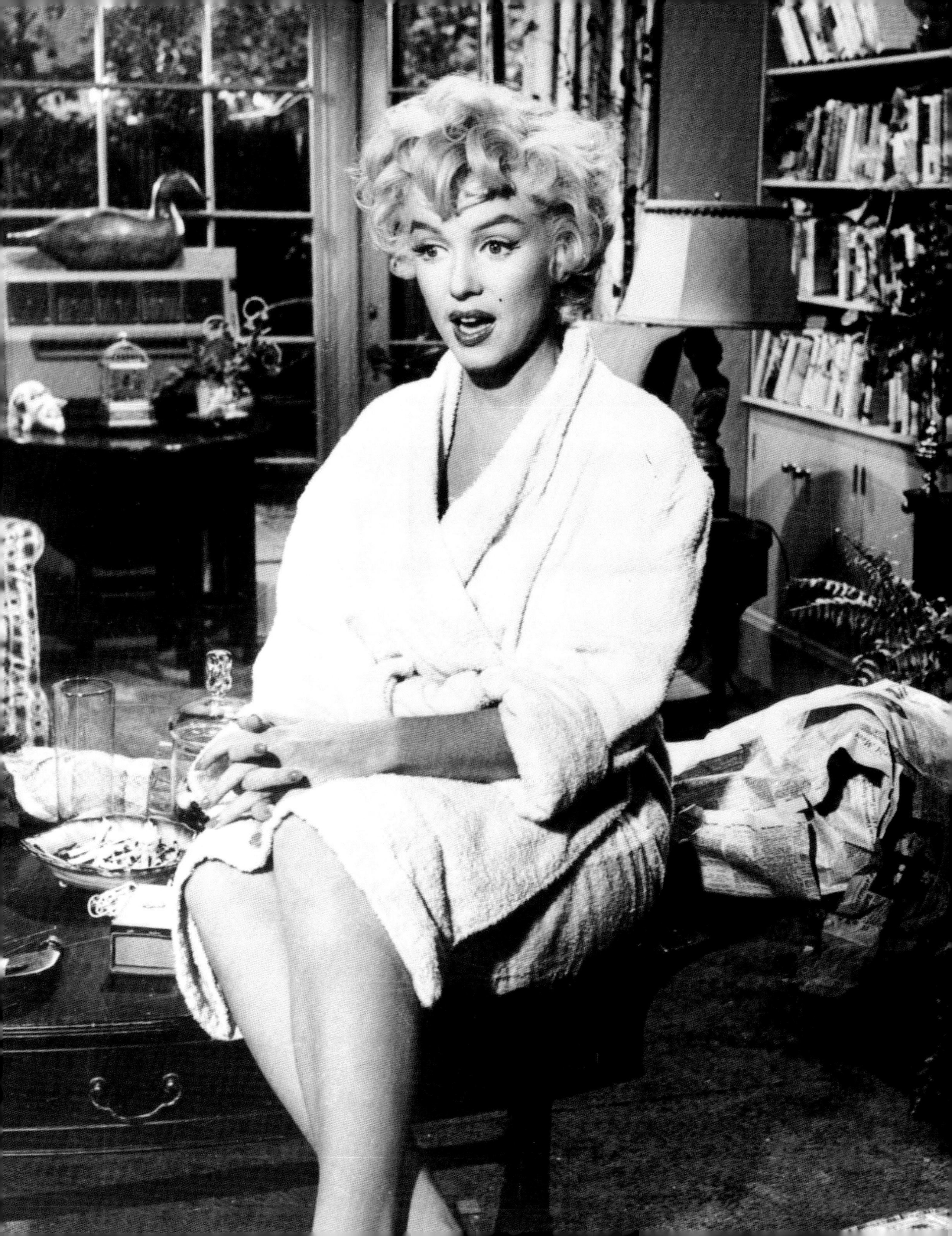

comedy cat's-eye glasses. For *The Seven Year Itch*, Monroe, as 'The Girl', wears a less stylised, simpler robe to kiss her co-star, Tom Ewell, playing Richard Sherman, goodbye. Off-camera shots of Marilyn, on the sets of *Some Like It Hot* and *The Misfits*, show the white robe as the cover-up she reaches for between takes. For her last and unfinished film in 1962, *Something's Got to Give*, she is seen clad in a '60s-fashion, short floral towelling robe and, in images taken by Lawrence Schiller, she is swathed in a cornflower-blue towelling dressing gown, after completing the famous scene where she swims nude in a pool.

In fashion history, the designs of beach robes are not all so simple. Christian 'Bébé' Bérard, the idiosyncratic artist and creative who worked with Christian Dior, designed a range of couture-like beach dressing gowns for the American department store Bonwit Teller in 1936. A *Vogue* feature at the time pitches the bathrobe as an ultra-modish, unpretentious cover up: 'Bérard would send you forth to compete with the brilliance of the sun and water. Every artifice is fair game as long as you're made dazzling. Dress for the beach with all the elegance of the evening […] Have your most dramatic, long, evening coat copied in towelling and wear it wrapped tightly around you.' Equally, many years later the bathrobe was featured on Gianfranco Ferré's Spring/Summer 1991 womenswear collection for Christian Dior, where models wore oversized versions on the catwalk.

Style-wise, the bathrobe is a near relation of the more seductive négligée, which Monroe would regularly sport in studio publicity shots and onscreen. From as early as 1948, in her film *Ladies of the Chorus*, she can be seen wearing a white satin and shoulder-padded version, while

in 1959's *Some Like It Hot*, she wears a comically seductive, see-through, marabou-trimmed type. As Simone de Beauvoir famously bemoaned, 'society even requires woman to make herself an erotic object,' while men's clothes are created with only comfort in mind (Beauvoir, 1946). Monroe's oscillation between the security of her beloved bathrobe and the *peignoir* of the sex kitten is a juxtaposition of her reality; when she wasn't required to be 'an erotic object', she would elect to wear clothes that were relaxed and laid-back, representing the Marilyn with nothing to prove and no one to impress.

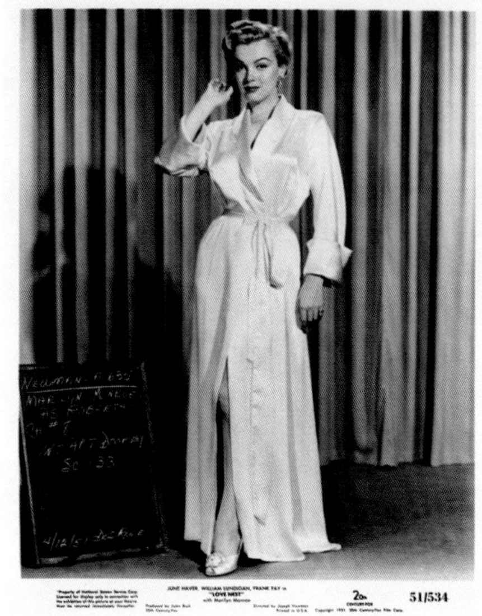

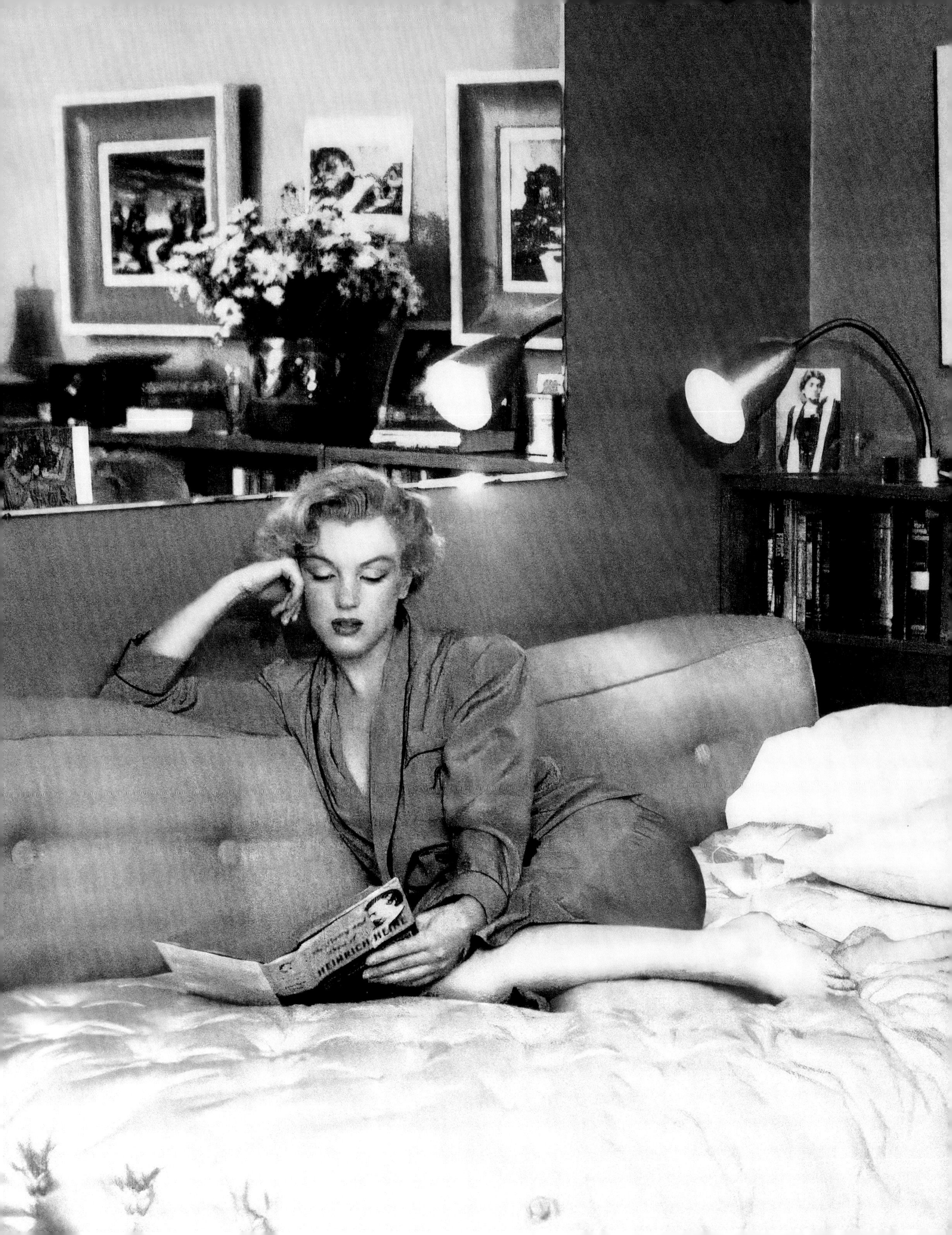

'I DON'T MIND IF PEOPLE THINK I AM
A DUMB BLONDE, BUT I DREAD THE
THOUGHT OF BEING A DUMB BLONDE.'

– Marilyn Monroe, *Screenland*, August 1952

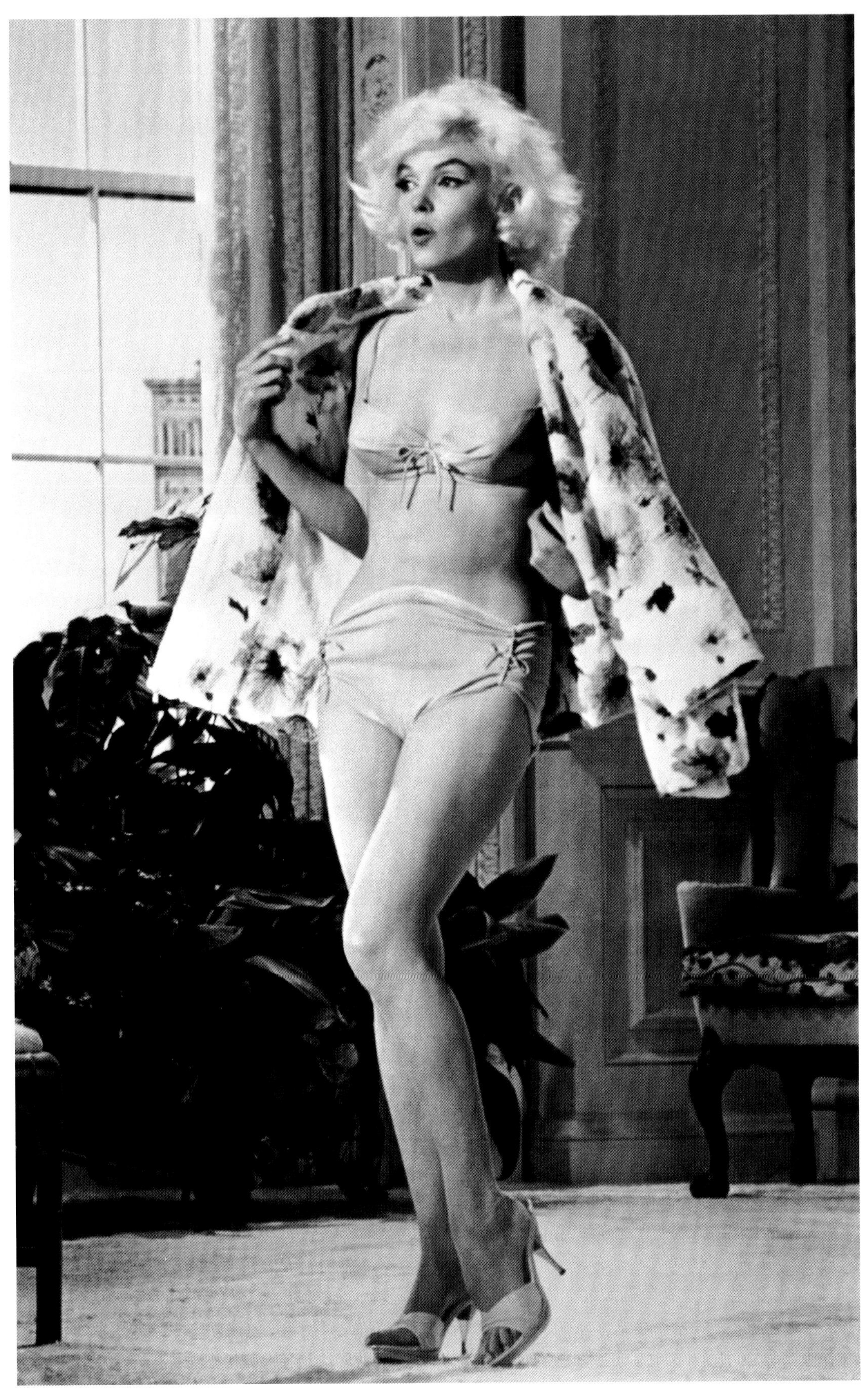

Marilyn on the set of *Something's Got to Give*, 1962

SWEATERS

'YOU FELLOWS DOWN THERE ARE ALWAYS
WHISTLING AT SWEATER GIRLS.
WELL, TAKE AWAY THEIR SWEATERS
AND WHAT HAVE YOU GOT?'

– Marilyn Monroe, *Saturday Evening Post*, May 1956

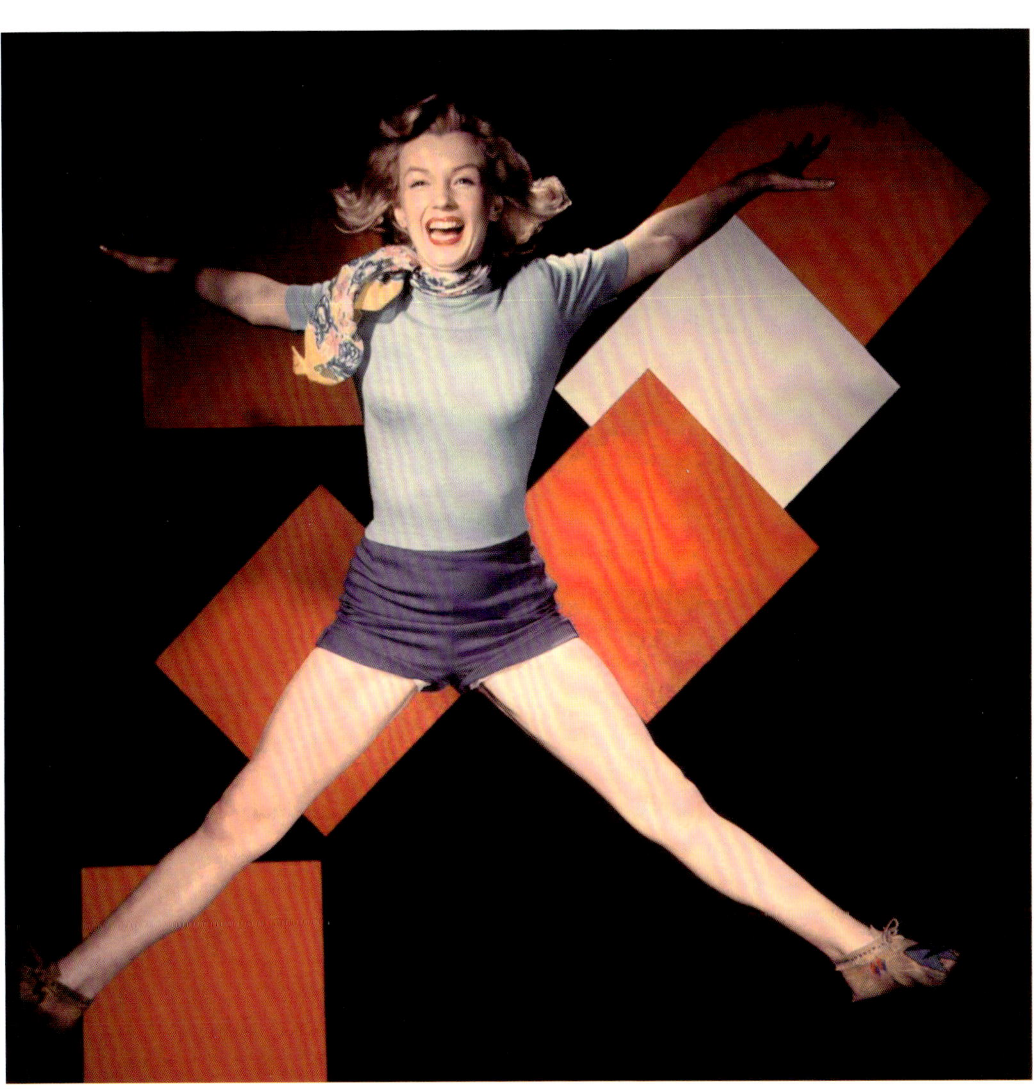

A young Marilyn posing for photographer László Willinger in 1949

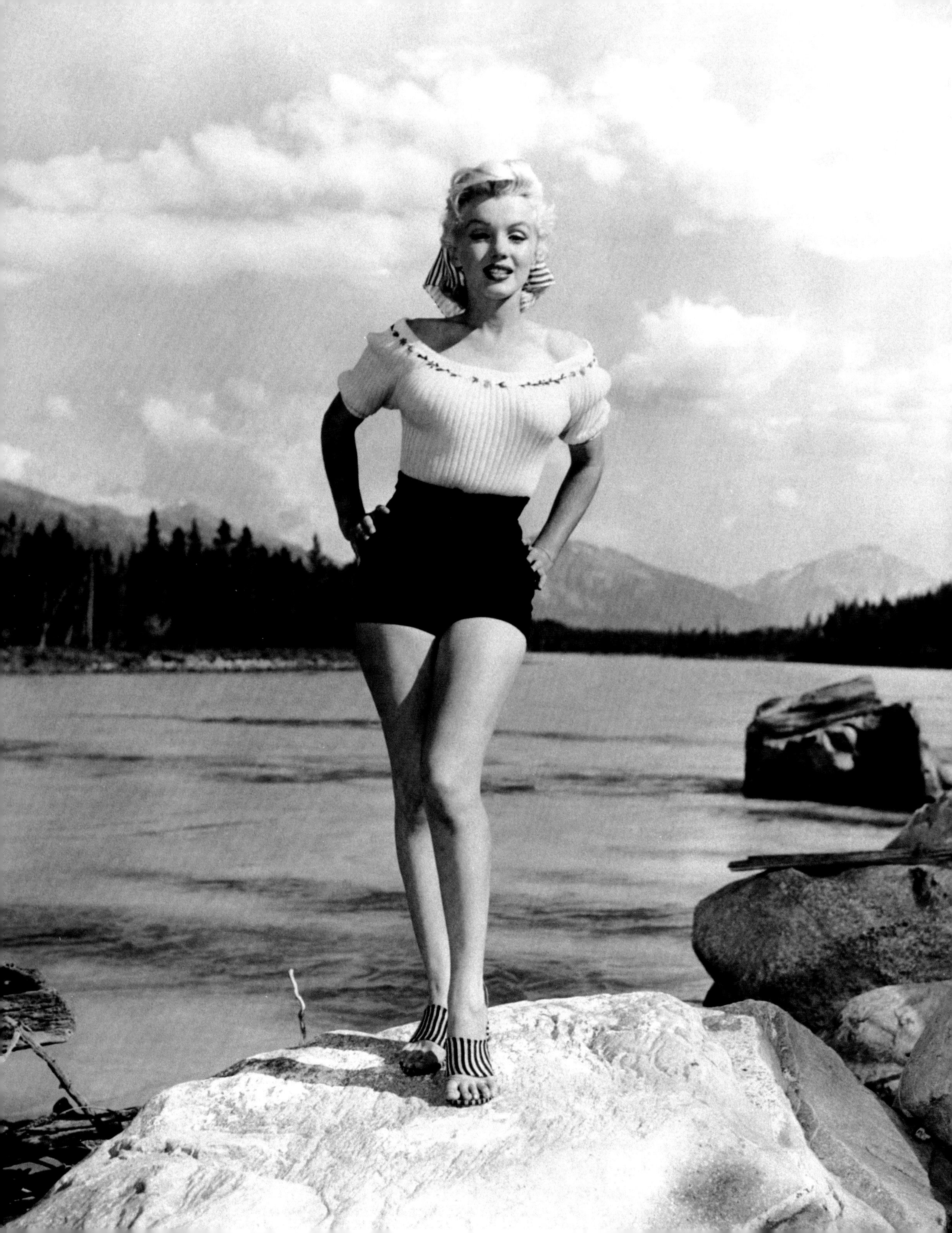

MARILYN WAS ONLY 11

years old when Lana Turner wore a tight sweater and a beret during her 1937 film *They Won't Forget*. Turner was onscreen for less than 15 minutes, but her outfit caused a stir because of its figure-hugging fit. She heralded the arrival of the sassy 'Sweater Girl' trend, though fashion-forward knitwear had been a wardrobe staple for some years prior. In the 1920s, Chanel pioneered a fresh aesthetic for women, designing boyish cardigans made of jersey, which became a signature of the Parisian house. At around the same time, Jean Patou made sporty woollen separates; his creations were functional but chic, so could be worn for more than just playing tennis.

Hand-knitting at home was a useful and efficient way of reworking second-hand or outgrown pullovers, and during the American Depression and again when the Second World War raged, it became essential. Body shape follows the fashion sweater. In the '20s, a slim, androgynous figure echoed the fluid knitwear featured on magazines' style pages. In the '30s and '40s, a more curvaceous silhouette was desirable. In August 1944, *Vogue* declared:

> '*It's a smart girl who does not [...] even this year, play traitor to the sweater. Only now, the sweater fits, it defines, often emphasises the girl inside. It's pulled snug over the hips, exclamation-pointed at the waist [...] in it she looks and feels like the all-American pin-up girl, only better.*'

Lingerie manufacturers' brassieres at the time, including Maidenform's bullet bra and Perma-Lift's 'lift that never lets you down' designs, took the sweater girl to almost cartoonish levels, and starlets including Marilyn and Jane Russell would use the look to their best advantage. Monroe's earliest modelling tests with André de Dienes in 1945, when she was 19, feature her wearing versions of the sharp sweater-girl silhouette. She reportedly had the habit of sewing buttons into her sweaters to create the favoured erect-nipple shape. Later, this ultra-pointy profile evolved into a softer 'cone' contour, but the bust was still a key erogenous zone and the fashion sweater a versatile, core closet essential for stylish women. Marilyn's 1948 film, *Ladies of the Chorus*, features her as Peggy, who wears an elegant, black knitted top with plunging neckline, designed to show off her figure.

Her supporting role as the secretary, Iris Martin, in *Home Town Story* (1951) sees Marilyn wear a stylish two-tone jumper adorned with a brooch at the neck. She had worn the same a year before in *The Fireball* (1950) – a sweater that likely came from her own wardrobe, as it was well known for contract actresses to supplement their onscreen looks with their own clothes. A June 1953 *Vogue* editorial championed the options available and features the myriad styles of sweaters from pillbox, halter, blazer, city, and even beach and bathing: 'the better half of a summer wardrobe could be built on the summer sweater.'

Marilyn posing in Jasper National Park, Alberta, Canada, 1953

Evening woollens, embellished with sequins, beading and embroidery, echoed the ultra-feminine style sensibilities of the 1950s, often inspired by the red-carpet glamour of Hollywood. Unlike today, women of this era were essentially seen as wives and mothers, and their closets represented their decorative, rather than professional, roles. Many of Monroe's most iconic jumper moments reflect fashions of the time. In her 1960 film *Let's Make Love*, the boat-neck Aran jumper she wears with tights is more in tune with a looser, beatnik styling rather than the sweater girl of the '40s and '50s. Dorothy Jeakins, Monroe's dresser for the film, sourced the classic fisherman jumpers from traditional knit company Cleo, based in Dublin, Ireland. Marilyn's publicist, Rupert Allan, revealed the inside story of the sweater:

> *'She rehearsed in it and every time she wore it, it got another inch longer. The wardrobe department made the mistake of ordering only one sweater, and [George] Cukor had to shoot other scenes while a replacement was knitted in western Ireland. Fox eventually air-expressed four extra sweaters to the wardrobe department'* (quoted in Vitacco-Robles, 2014)

One of the originals was subsequently bought by designer Gerard Darel, who later recreated a version of the chunky cable knit in collaboration with The Marilyn Monroe Estate in 2010. When Marilyn found something she felt was useful, she would often buy it in multiples. This habit of wearing the same thing over and over was something she had done when she was much younger.

In the 1999 Christie's sale of her property, there are 'three identically designed sweaters in white, black, and beige wool; all with rounded lapels, two front pockets and seven-button front closures' listed. The label shows they are made by Geist & Geist, who manufactured women's knitwear and was based in New York's garment district. They are designed to be cosy and, as photographed in the auction catalogue, are well worn – clearly part of Marilyn's off-screen attire. Equally, the celebrated 1962 series of images by photographer George Barris, shot on Santa Monica Beach, shows her wearing a handmade Cowichan-style cardigan that she reportedly bought in Mexico and loved for its warmth and cosiness, rather than its body-hugging allure.

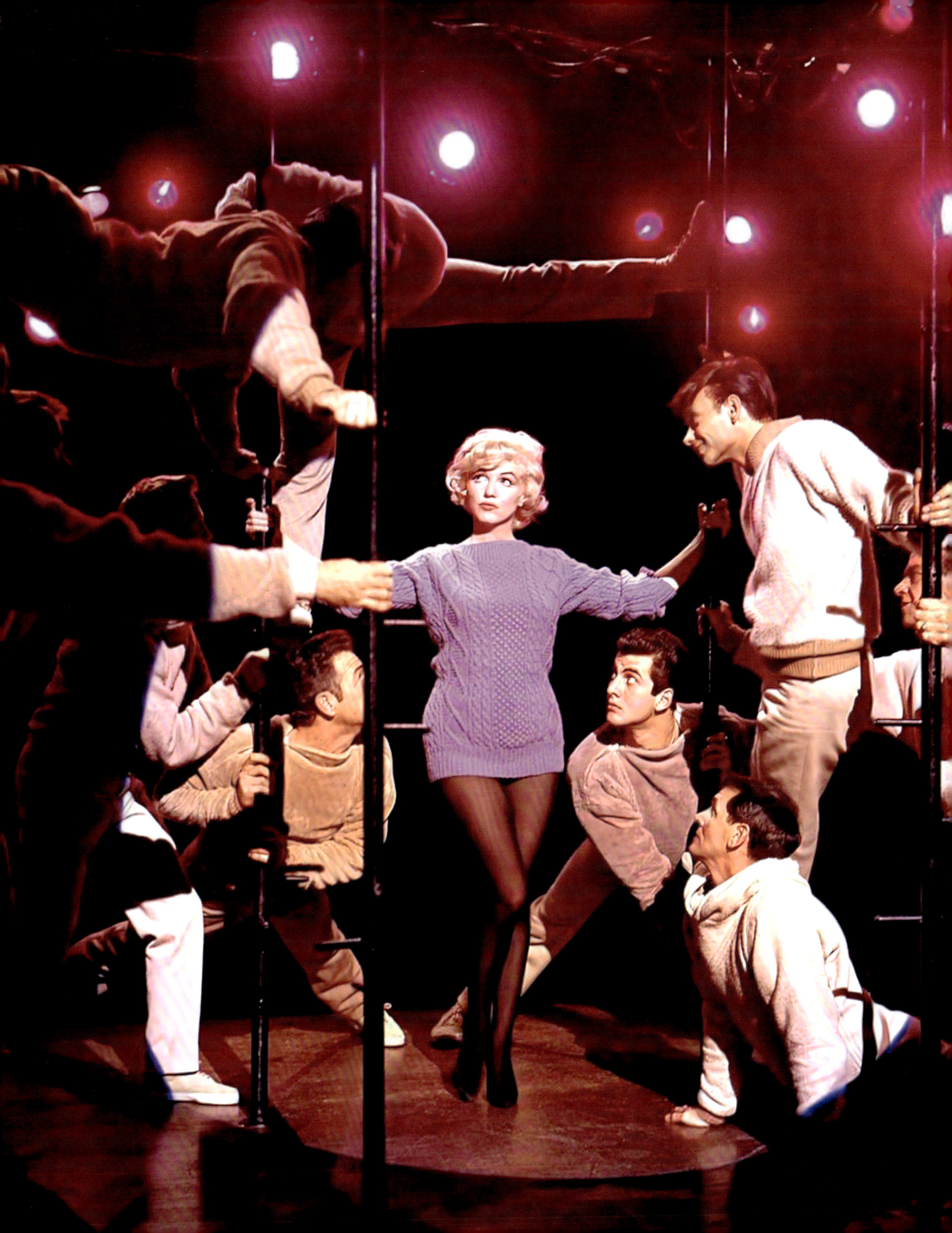

'IN SCHOOL THE PUPILS [...] MADE FUN OF
MY ORPHAN'S OUTFIT [...] ONE MORNING
BOTH MY WHITE BLOUSES WERE TORN, AND
I WOULD BE LATE FOR SCHOOL IF I STOPPED
TO FIX THEM. I ASKED ONE OF MY "SISTERS"
IN THE HOUSE IF SHE COULD LOAN ME
SOMETHING TO WEAR. SHE WAS MY AGE
BUT SMALLER. SHE LOANED ME A SWEATER.
I ARRIVED AT SCHOOL [...] EVERYBODY STARED
AT ME AS IF I HAD SUDDENLY GROWN TWO
HEADS, WHICH IN A WAY I HAD. THEY WERE
UNDER MY TIGHT SWEATER.'

– Marilyn Monroe, *My Story*, 1974

Marilyn in *Home Town Story*, 1951

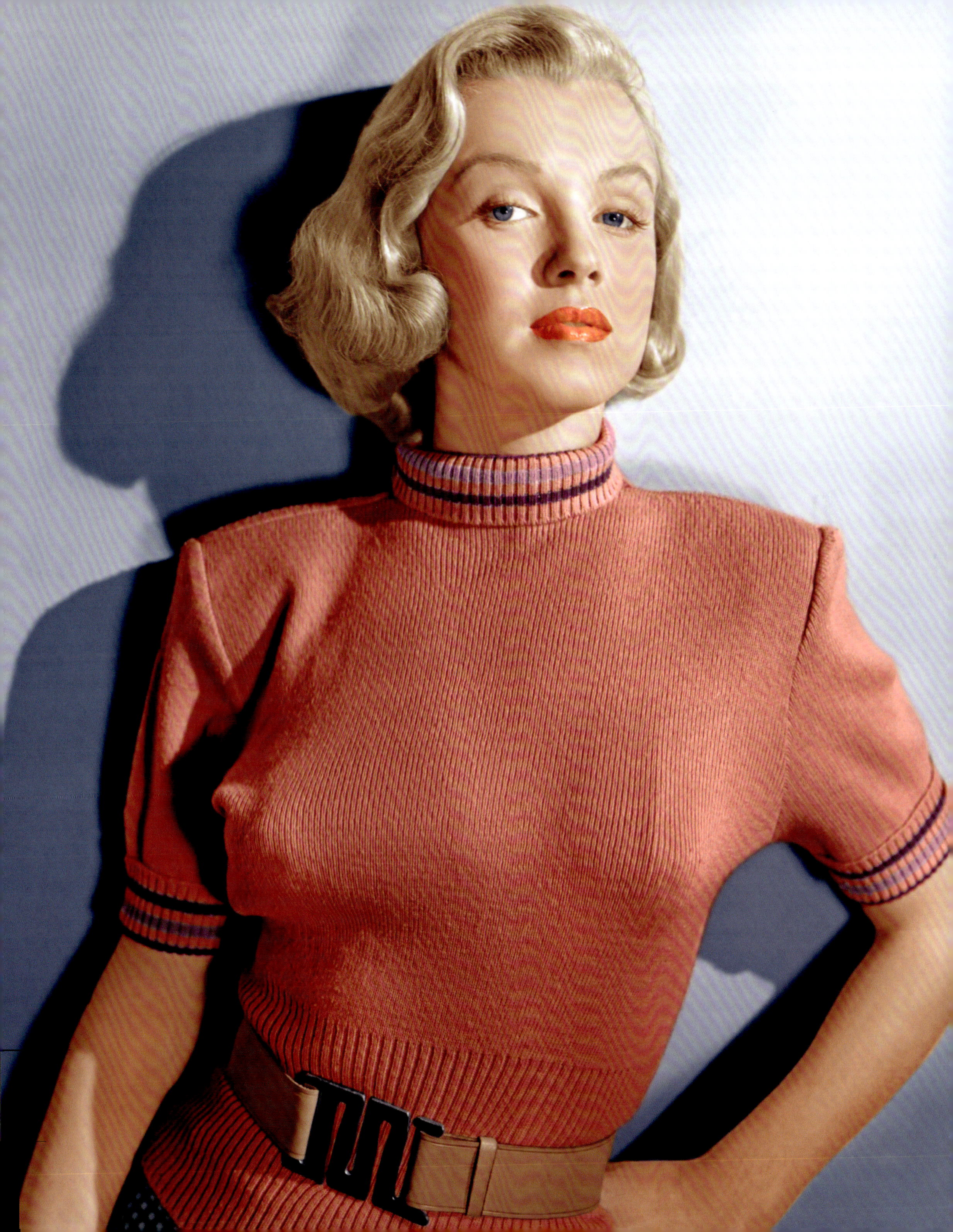

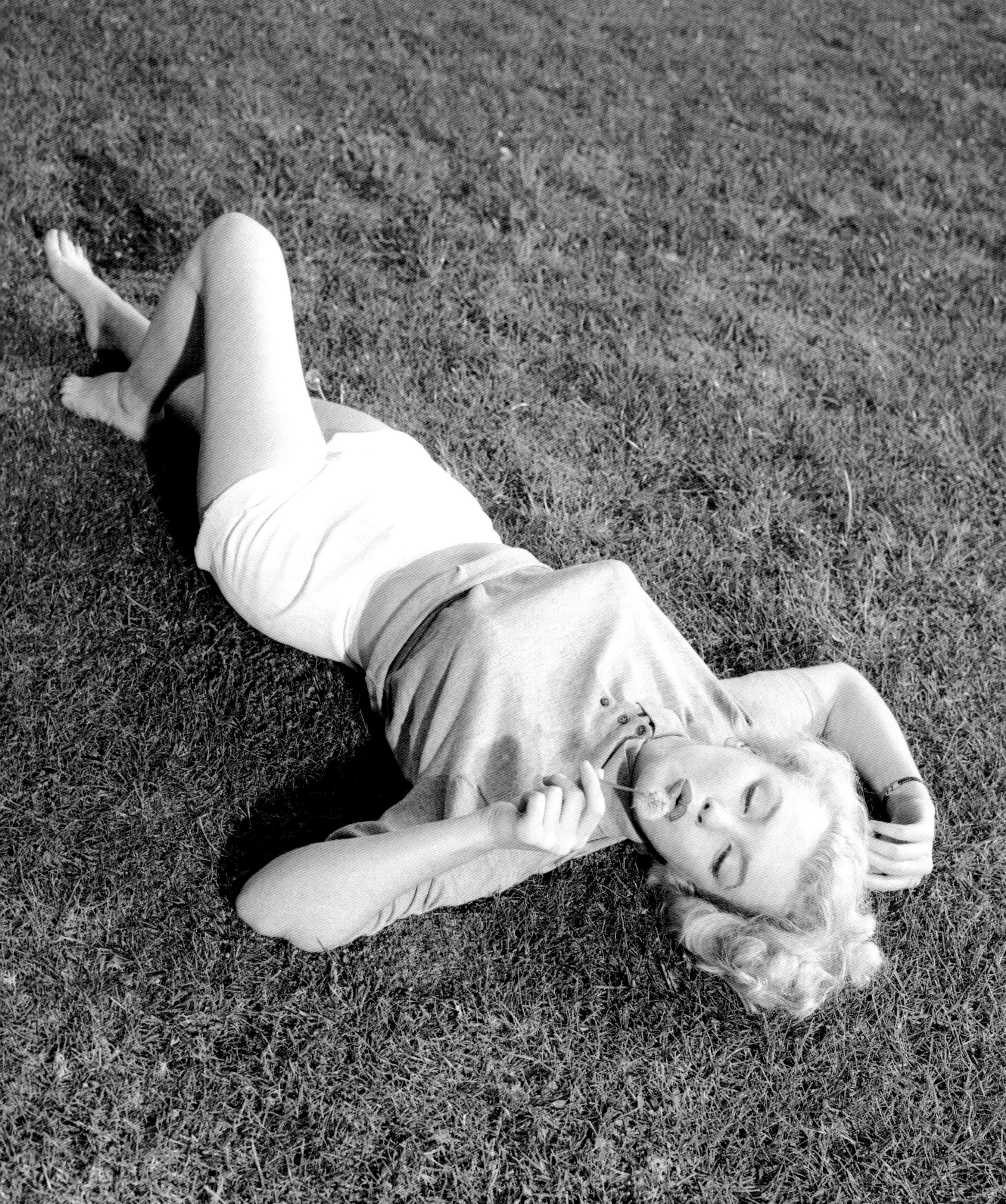

Marilyn, February 1951

'I FOUND A WONDERFUL PHOTO OF
HER TAKEN DURING THE TIME THE FILM
MY WEEK WITH MARILYN (2011) IS SET,
CYCLING IN THE ENGLISH COUNTRYSIDE.
SHE IS WEARING CAPRI PANTS, FLAT
LOAFERS AND A CHUNKY NAVY
CARDIGAN. SHE HAD A VERY NATURAL,
UNDERSTATED WAY OF DRESSING. I THINK
SHE WAS RATHER AHEAD OF HER TIME,
IN FACT.'

– Michelle Williams, quoted in *The Guardian*, 2011

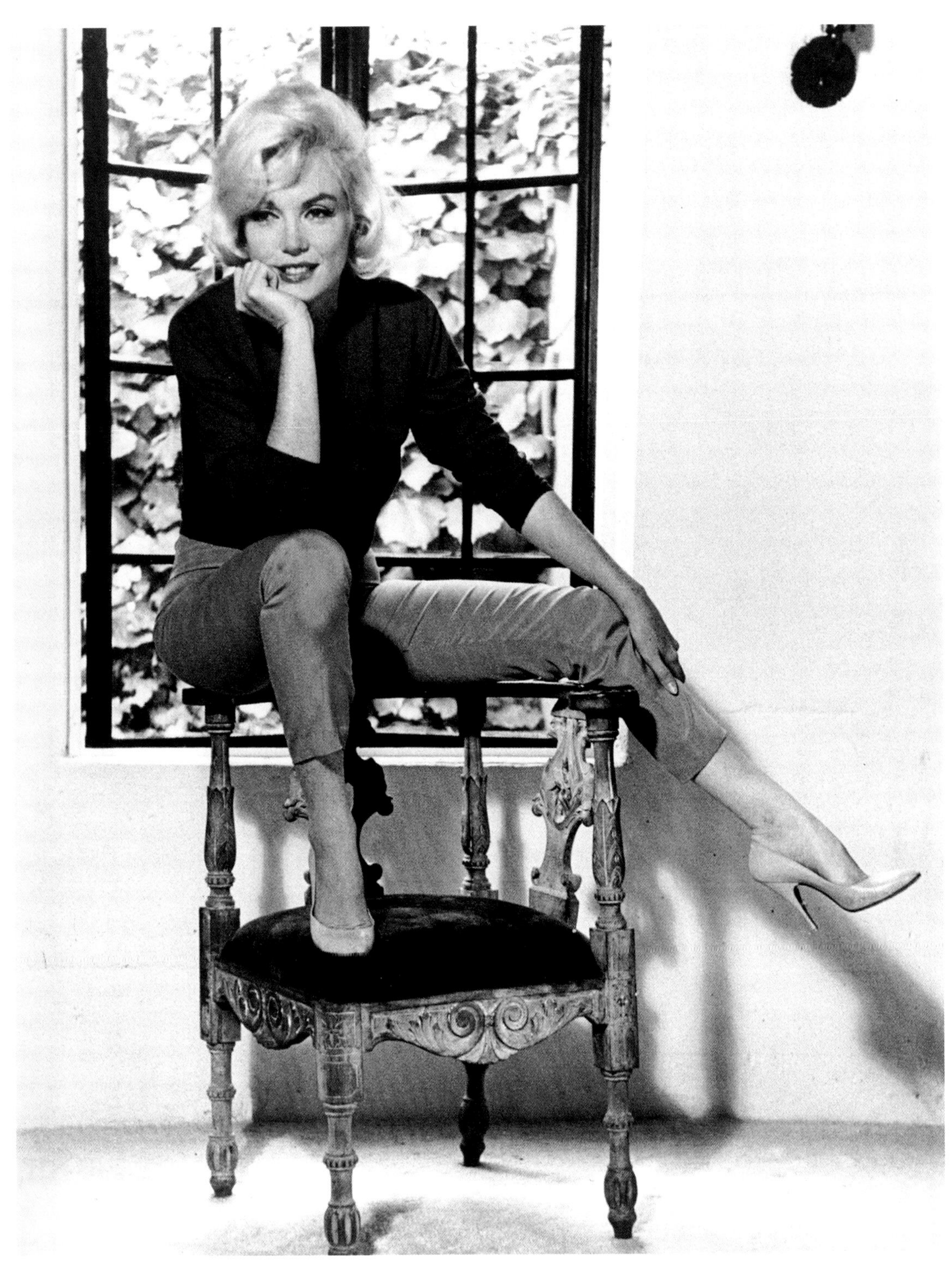

Marilyn at her home in Los Angeles, 1962

 Milton Berle met
Marilyn in 1948 when she was just 22 and
playing Peggy Martin in her third film,
Ladies of the Chorus. Over a decade
later, they would go on to star together
in Marilyn's penultimate film, *Let's
Make Love* (1960). Marilyn's vivacious
onscreen persona was already taking
shape when they met, but when Berle
took her driving around Hollywood,
he reflected how 'she liked to dress in
slacks, no makeup or anything. She
wasn't that glamorous' (quoted in
Marilyn Monroe History, 2013a).

In stills of the *Ladies of the Chorus*
(1948) backstage show, Monroe wears
wide-legged trousers while applying
her make-up to become the burlesque
dancer. Fashion has a transformative
quality and Monroe understood how
the bombshell uniform she assembled
enabled her rise to superstardom. It
changed her from a lonely orphan to an
actress with her name in lights. As Berle
points out in his autobiography, there
was more to Marilyn than just her look,
however: 'Marilyn was on the climb in
Hollywood, but there was nothing cheap
about her. She wasn't one of the starlets
around town that you put one meal into
and threw into the sack. Maybe she
didn't know exactly who she was, but
she knew she was worth something. She
had respect for herself. Marilyn was a
lady' (Berle, 1974).

She was a lady who liked trousers, and
in a series of images taken by André de
Dienes in 1945, she can be seen wearing
a favourite gingham pair, rolled up to the
knee, on Paradise Cove Beach in Malibu.
They are the same pair she wears in
1952, as she applies make-up, sitting
cross-legged; then again while reading
a script as she sits in an armchair at the
Hotel Bel-Air, Los Angeles, in 1953; and
once more, rolled up, barefoot at home
in 1955. Photographs of her wearing the
straight-legged trousers are testimony
to the fact that when Monroe found
clothes she liked, she would wear them
on repeat and buy them again and again.

She made a beeline for trousers made
by Jax, too, and would buy their slim-
fitting cropped ones in all colours. In a
March 1977 feature, *The New York Times*
called the original 1950s Jax Boutique
'the place where society women—
not the kind who go to parties and
committee meetings, but the kind who
ride and swim and ski—went for sports
clothes' (Morris, 1977). It became the
shop to be seen in and its designs, sleek,
minimal and in tune with the modish
simplicity of the incoming '60s, were the
ones to be seen wearing. Jax's founder,
Jack Hanson, spoke to *Sports Illustrated*
in 1967, saying, 'if any one person made
us, it was Marilyn. She wore our things
constantly, everywhere, and was always

Marilyn on the set of *Clash by Night*, 1952

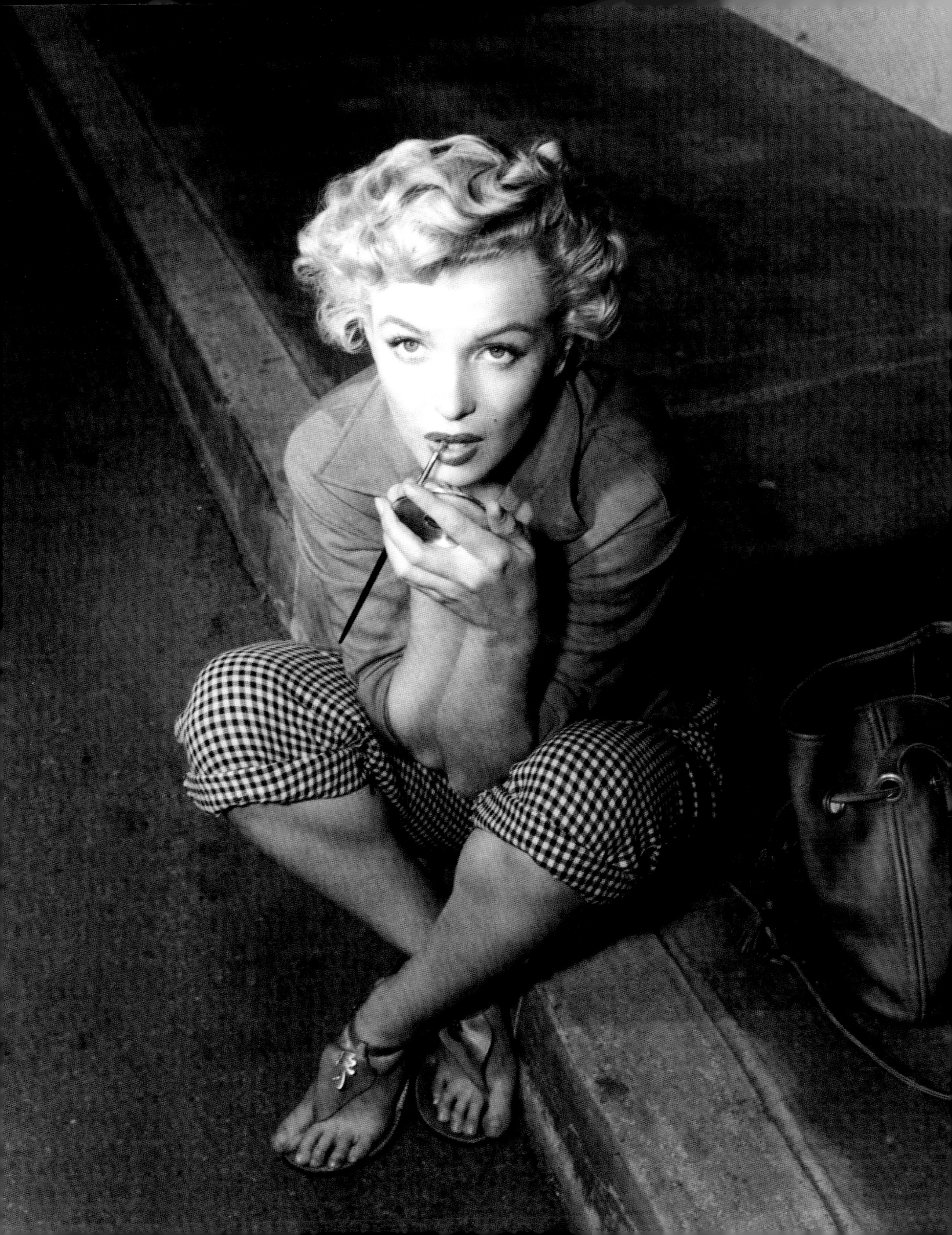

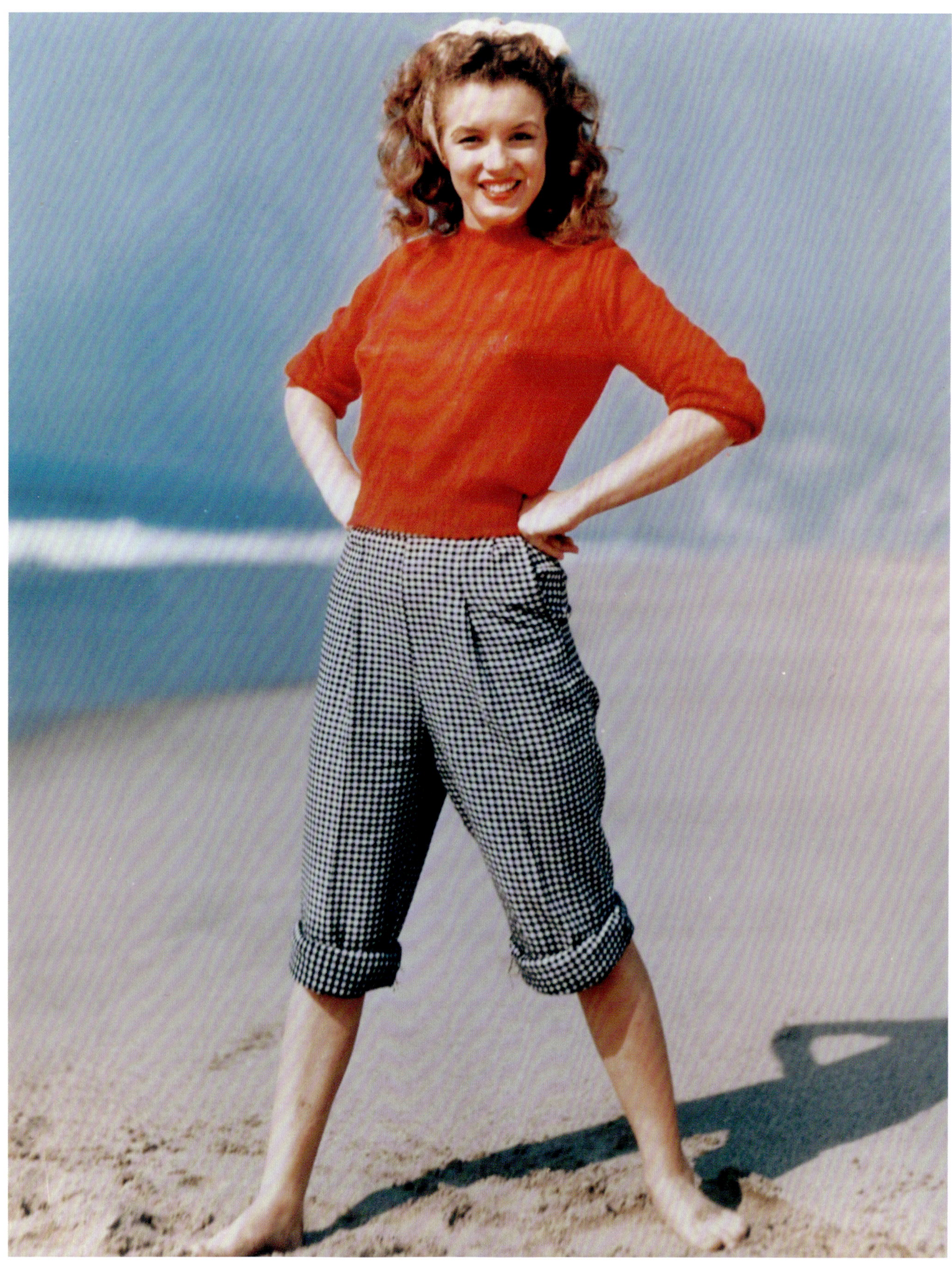

Norma Jeane posing for André de Dienes in Malibu, California, 1945

in the shop. We designed a lot of things especially with her in mind' (Jenkins, 1967). The first store opened in Balboa, California, in the early 1950s and more shops quickly launched in Beverly Hills and later New York – conveniently close to where Marilyn would go to live in December 1954.

The night Marilyn left LA for her new life in New York to launch Marilyn Monroe Productions with her friend, the photographer Milton Greene, she wore 'no makeup, a man's oxford shirt, and Jax cigarette trousers under a full-length black mink' (Winder, 2017). Jax trousers were simple but effective; they flatteringly featured a zip at the back and no pockets and Monroe frequently wore them with either stilettoes or pumps. A luxe black satin pair of Jax trousers was sold at Julien's Auctions in 2010. Their provenance was from the Estate of Dr Ralph Greenson, and the auctioneers reported at the time that they had been given to Greenson's daughter 'in 1962 because Monroe felt they were too large for her' (Julien's Auctions, 2010). Jax slacks had to fit just right.

Monroe felt relaxed in trousers, but also knew she made them look good. In February 1954 she flew to South Korea and played 10 shows for the US troops there who were fighting in the Korean War. She wore a military bomber jacket, boots and regulation parachute trousers when she was on stage entertaining. From time to time, Monroe would also don trousers as part of her film roles. William Travilla designed a pair of chic black slacks for her to wear with a jewel-green blouse in the 1953 film *Gentlemen Prefer Blondes*. A year later, Travilla would put her in capri-style trousers as 'The Girl' in *The Seven Year Itch*.

It wouldn't be the most famous outfit of the film – that would of course go to the sunray-pleat halterneck dress – but it was a memorable and chic trouser look, nevertheless.

By the early '60s, Monroe's casual fashion sense no longer felt underdressed and although she would still dazzle in slinky frocks for big occasions, she would equally wear designer blouses by Pucci more often in public. She typically had favourites and wore white Jax trousers as a matter of course, with photographs dating from 1962 showing her wearing them on the way home from a week in Mexico, and when having drinks with the rest of the cast of *Something's Got to Give*. Milton Greene, who was trusted implicitly by her, took some of his most celebrated casual images of Marilyn wearing trousers – images that have been referred to as those of the 'real' Marilyn behind the lens (Kotsilibas-Davis, 1994).

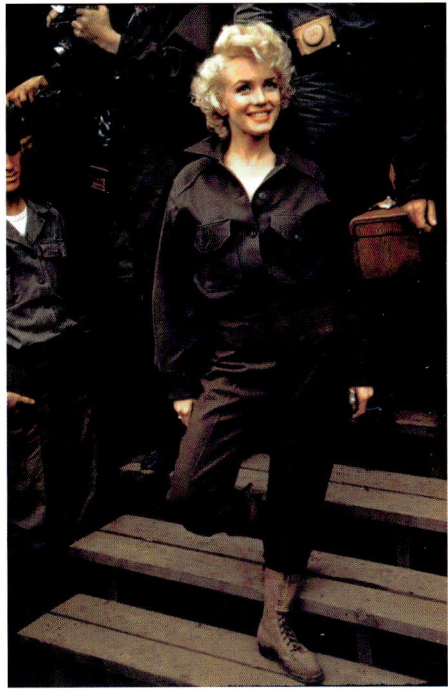

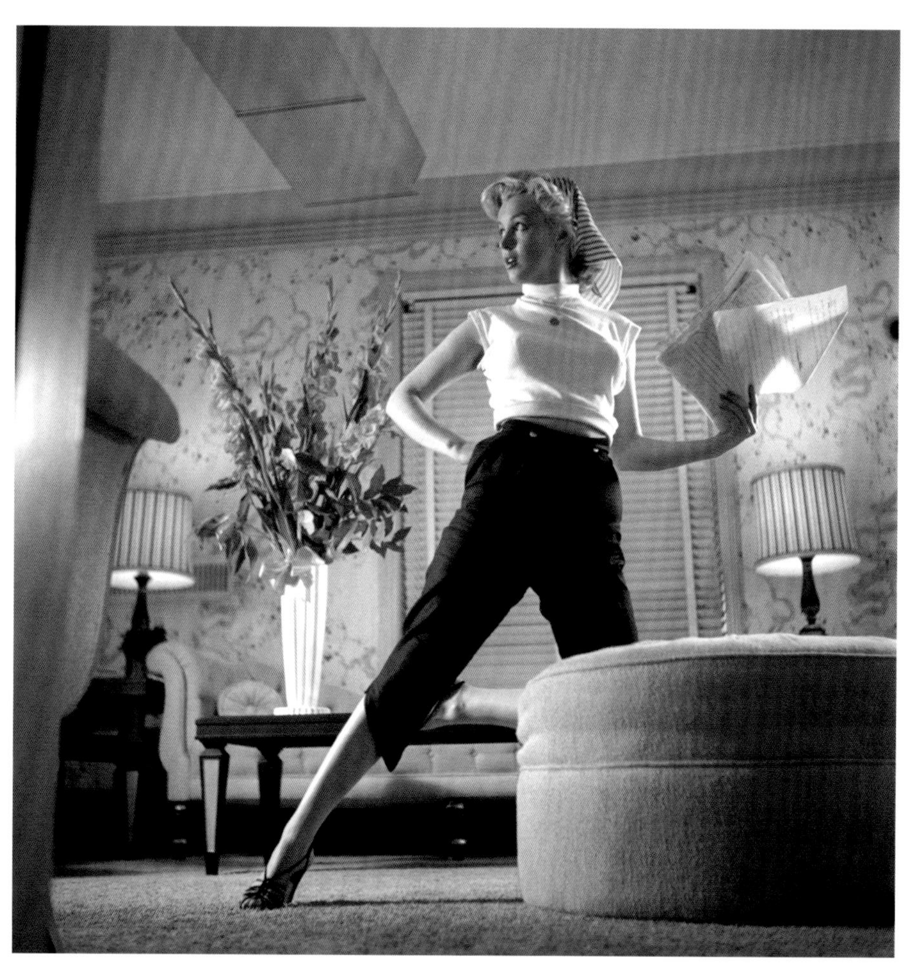

Marilyn wears a pair of stylish black three-quarter-length
trousers for a portrait in her dressing room, Los Angeles, 1952

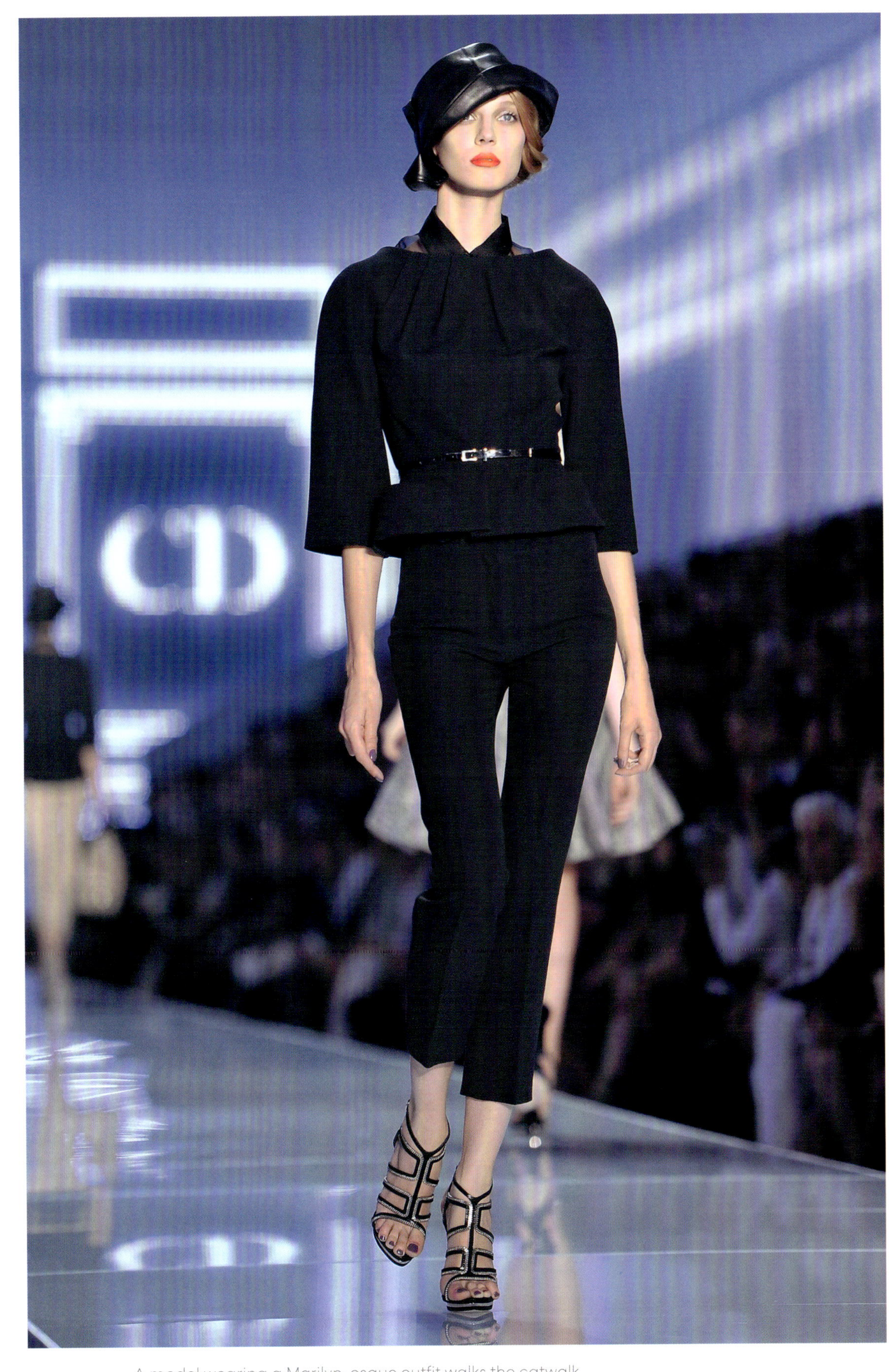

A model wearing a Marilyn-esque outfit walks the catwalk
at the Christian Dior Spring/Summer 2012 show in Paris

SIMPLE CASUAL & CHIC

'IF YOU ASK ME WHAT I'D MOST LIKE TO HAVE INVENTED IN FASHION, I'D SAY THE WHITE SHIRT. FOR ME, THE WHITE SHIRT IS THE BASIS OF EVERYTHING. EVERYTHING ELSE COMES AFTER.'

– Karl Lagerfeld (quoted in de Klerk, 2019)

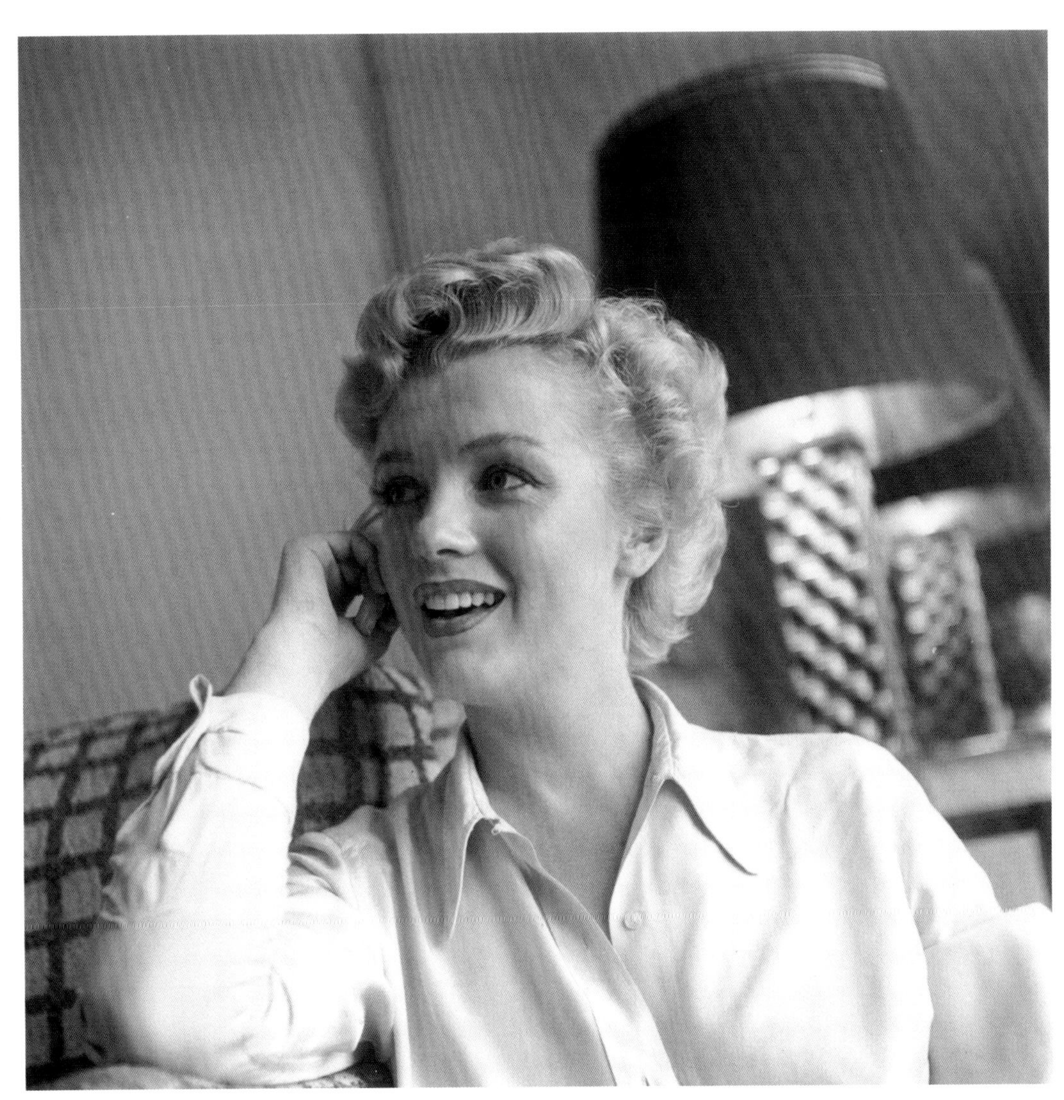

Marilyn wearing a favourite white shirt, c.1952

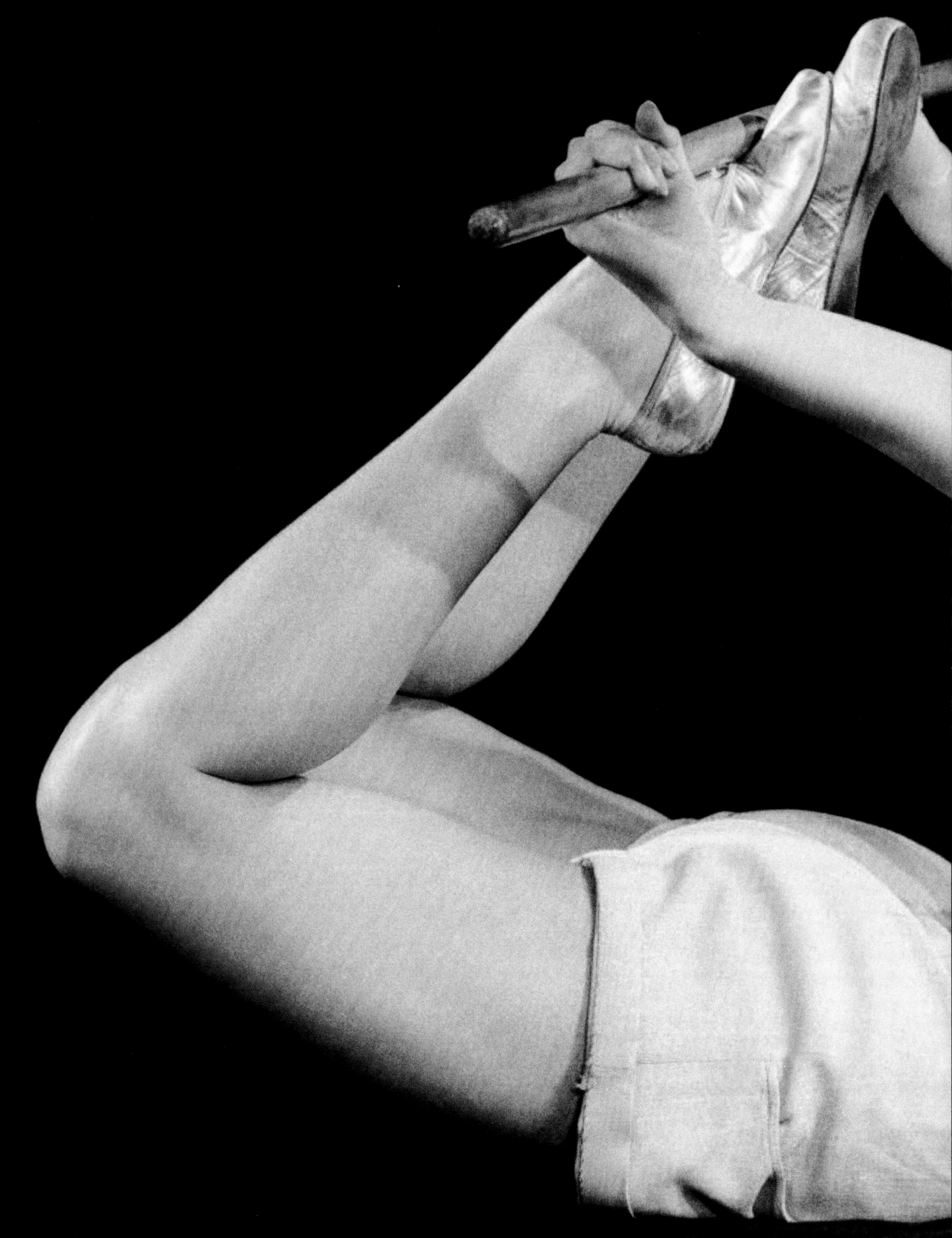

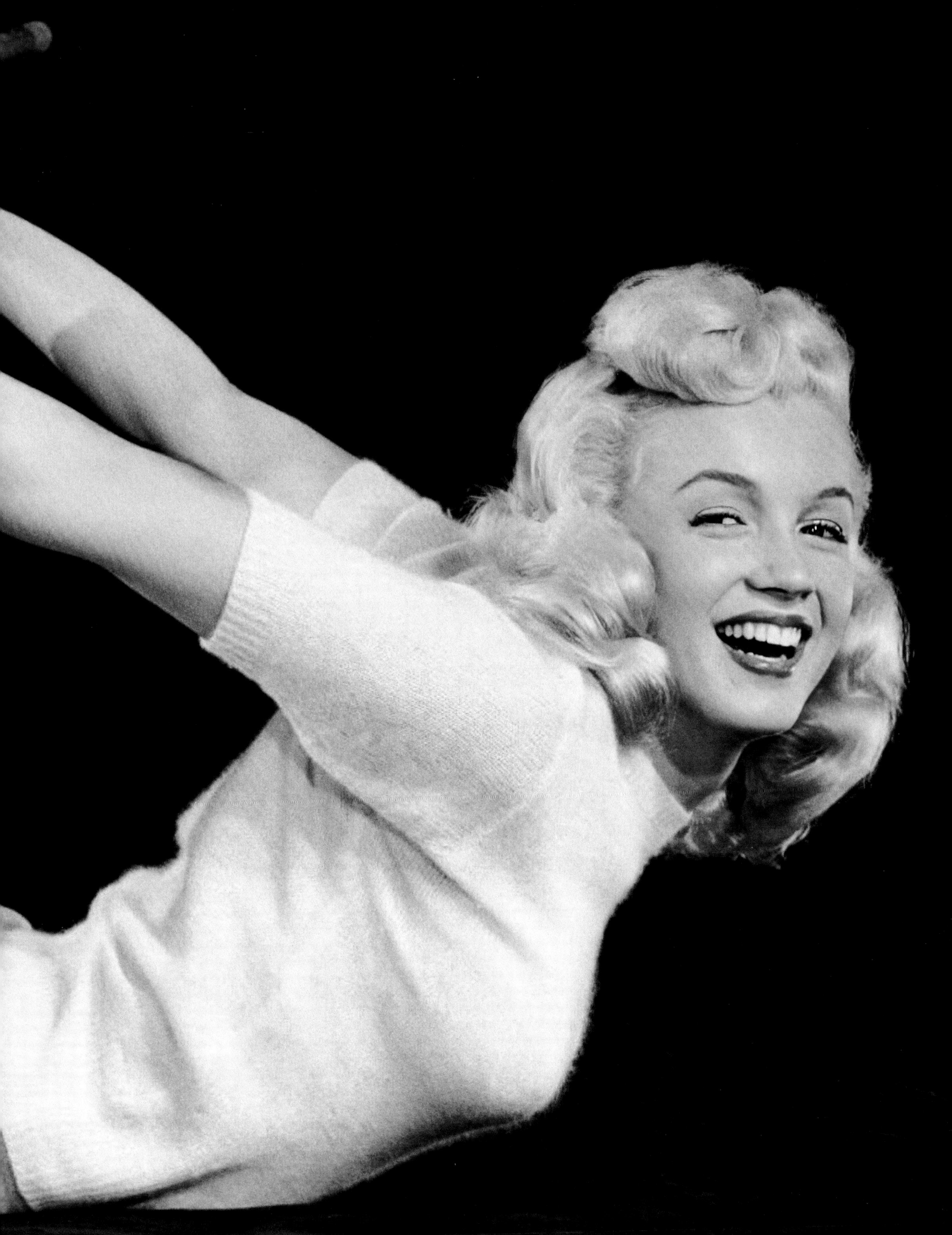

WHEN MARILYN slipped into the Prada-like simplicity of an everyday pencil skirt and blouse, it was usually her downtime and a moment of respite when she preferred the effortlessness and ease of classic American preppy casualwear. When she lived in Connecticut with husband Arthur Miller in 1956, her wardrobe was full of these slightly prim, librarian-chic statements – a world apart from the drama of her work wardrobe. The optional silhouettes of the 1950s were either a narrow cut or a loosely gathered dirndl shape, with Monroe largely favouring the former. In a pencil skirt she could still wiggle, but it also had a no-nonsense nuance. Author Colin McDowell talks about the legacy of Christian Dior's ultra-feminised, corseted and petticoated 1947 New Look in his book *Forties Fashion* (1997), explaining that fashion during the fifties was a 'fight […] over sex appeal, and what form it should take. […] Practicality and ease versus romanticism and glamour; the old world versus the new; the male designer versus the female […] and it was a conflict – of fundamental ideology as well as social balance.'

When Marilyn was playing Marilyn onscreen and on the red carpet, she was in the sex-appeal camp; when she was at home, she aimed for functional and low-key, wearing designers such as Claire McCardell. American fashion, as it emerged during and after the Second World War, defined itself with designers such as McCardell, who helped to pioneer ready-to-wear clothing and a pragmatic approach to clothes, and who has been described as 'the founder of democratic American fashion' (quoted in White, 1998). In a 1955 *Time* magazine interview, McCardell explains her creative aesthetic saying: 'I've always designed things I needed myself. It just turns out that other people need them too. Monroe's behind-the-scenes wardrobe was one worn by women who dressed for themselves, not for the men in their lives. Monroe looked for practical and useful creations, and McCardell provided them.

Inspired by dancewear, McCardell introduced ballet slipper-style shoes and the leotard as a simple separate. When Monroe wasn't wearing stilettoes, she reached for pumps and owned a classic Capezio leotard, cut with a boyish body but with a ribbon belt. On set during *Let's Make Love* (1960), she looks chic in a shirt and dancewear.

Marilyn loved the minimal sartorial look, favouring mix-and-match neutrals – cream, beige and black blouses. McCardell reflects: 'most of my ideas seem startlingly self-evident. I wonder why I didn't think of them before' (1956). Marilyn's easy approach to dressing was far more forward-looking in many respects than the glamorous frocks in which she dressed to impress, and in fact, heralded the more informal fashion statements of the modish 1960s to come.

Freedom was at the heart of Monroe's laid-back look. In 1954, the photographer Baron (Sterling Henry Nahum) took a classic series of Monroe images wearing a monochrome-striped, sleeveless dress by American manufacturer, Walter Bass. Bass employed the avant-garde designer and ex-dancer Rudi Gernreich during the 1950s and it is likely he

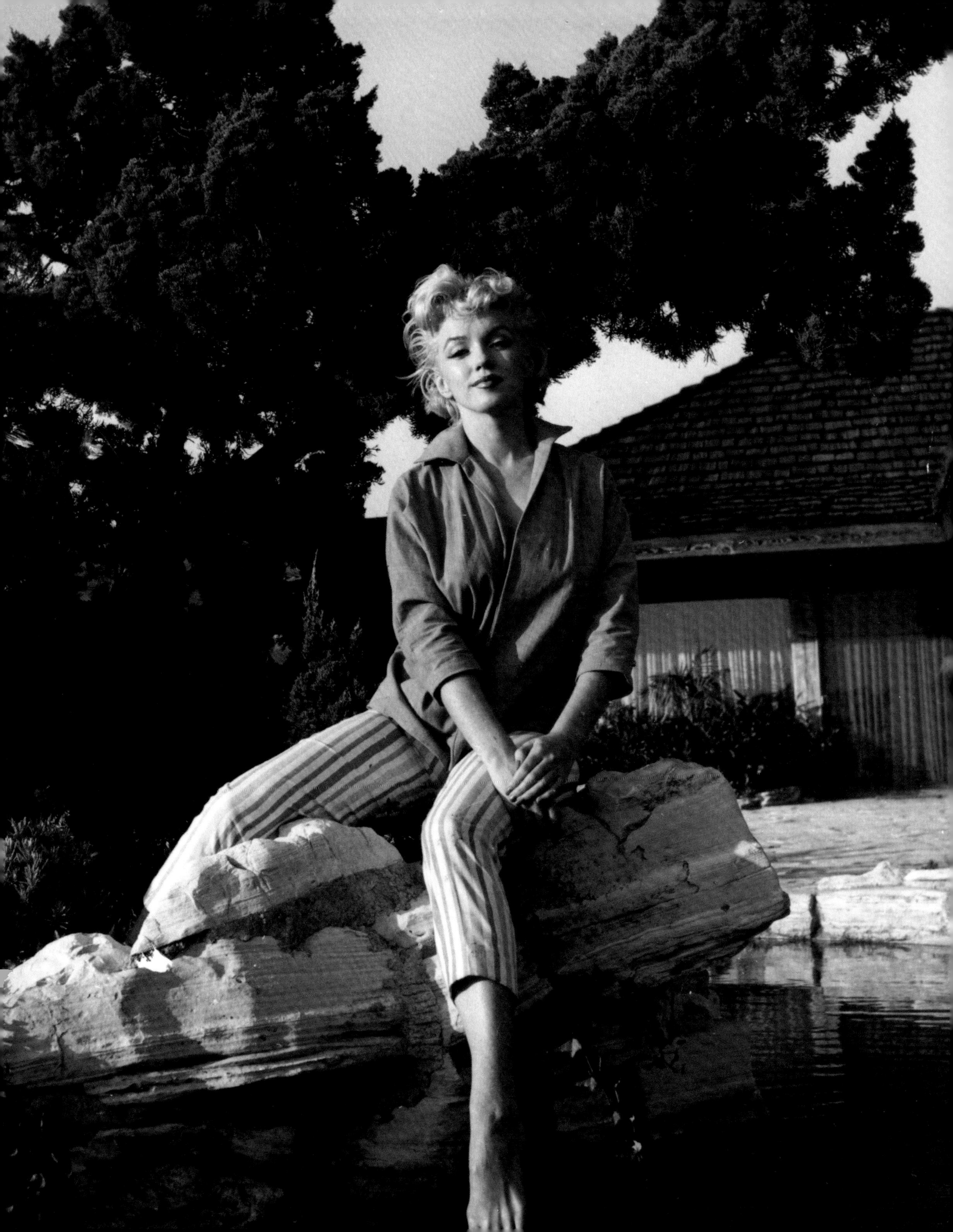

'MEN LIKE SIMPLICITY IN CLOTHES, AND SO DO I.
THERE'S NOTHING SO STARTLING ABOUT THAT.
MANY FAMOUS WOMEN HAVE FOLLOWED THE
BASIC RULES OF SELECTING SUITABLE, TIMELESS
CLOTHES THAT THEY CAN WEAR FOR YEARS. AND
IN BASIC COLORS LIKE BLACK, WHITE, GRAY [...]
BUSY PRINTS OR BUSY LINES IN A DRESS GET TIRING.'

– Marilyn Monroe, The *Los Angeles Times*, 1956 (Lane, 1956)

was the creator of this fluid frock, which was basic in shape and didn't restrict the body. Monroe made it look wonderful and Baron would go on to say the images were some of the best he had ever taken. His androgynous silhouettes were groundbreaking after the fitted fashions of the '50s and his initial designs worn by Monroe proved she could indeed look lovely wearing something more straightforward.

Sportswear in Monroe's closet at first meant wearing outfits for youthful modelling stints. Images of her dressed in tennis or gym outfits, often barefoot, skipping, running and jumping, captured her youth and charm time and again during the mid 1940s and very early 1950s, when she was trying to find her place as a Hollywood actress. Discussing photographs of Marilyn, Terence Pepper, curator of the National Portrait Gallery, points out that 'there's something about the earliest pictures. She would appear on magazine covers before anybody knew who she was. Her image was established before people knew who she was, but she was selling magazines' (Bolton et al, 2015). Her

wholesome appeal was something that captured the public's imagination long before the bombshell persona did, and while many of her preliminary films clad her in slinky attire, in *Clash by Night* (1952) she plays the role of Peggy, wearing a modest stripy shirt and working in a very unglamorous fish cannery works. The film is largely remembered for Monroe's small but convincing role, rather than the allure of her seductive starlet costume.

Marilyn knew the ease of a plain shirt; in her memoir, she describes the two white blouses that she owned and how she wore them on rotation. While crafting her career, she used her dressy clothes to get herself noticed, but behind the scenes it was a closet of shirts that she drew upon for day-to-day wear. She bought Jax silk chemises by the armful in favoured neutrals, but she also had a selection of demure button-ups, daintily decorated with tiny bows or sprigged prints. In those roles where Monroe occasionally wore a shirt, the characters prove to have substance behind the styling. In *Niagara* (1953), the iconic femme fatale Rose Loomis shows she

means business when wearing a crisp white conservative shirt. In *The Misfits* (1961), Monroe's most challenging role as Roslyn benefits from a basic blouse and jeans to defend against the heat of the day and the demands of the desert. Eve Arnold was one of the *Life* photographers commissioned to take images of Monroe while on location in Nevada and her candid shots are some of the most wistfully beautiful of Marilyn's career; almost all show her wearing the favoured plain blouse. Likewise, Milton Greene's most mesmerising imagery of Marilyn, taken in 1953 at Joseph Schenck's house in LA, depicts her wearing ankle-swinging capri pants and a slightly oversized shirt.

The humble shirt has a long history, worn by stars like Katharine Hepburn and Patti Smith, and appearing in the collections of designers such as Caroline Herrera and Karl Lagerfeld. The appeal of its androgynous shape has become a timeless staple and was a fashion essential for Monroe.

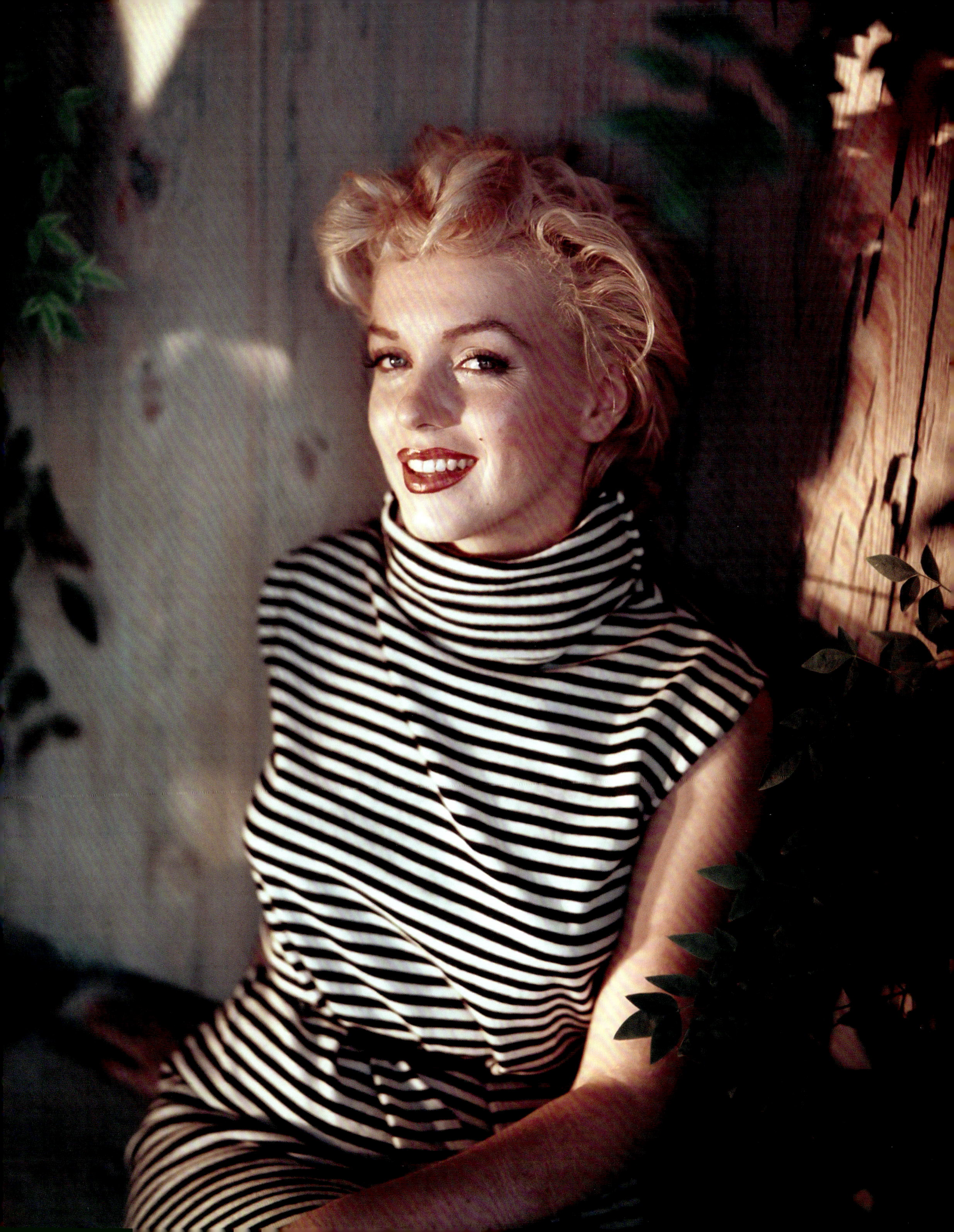

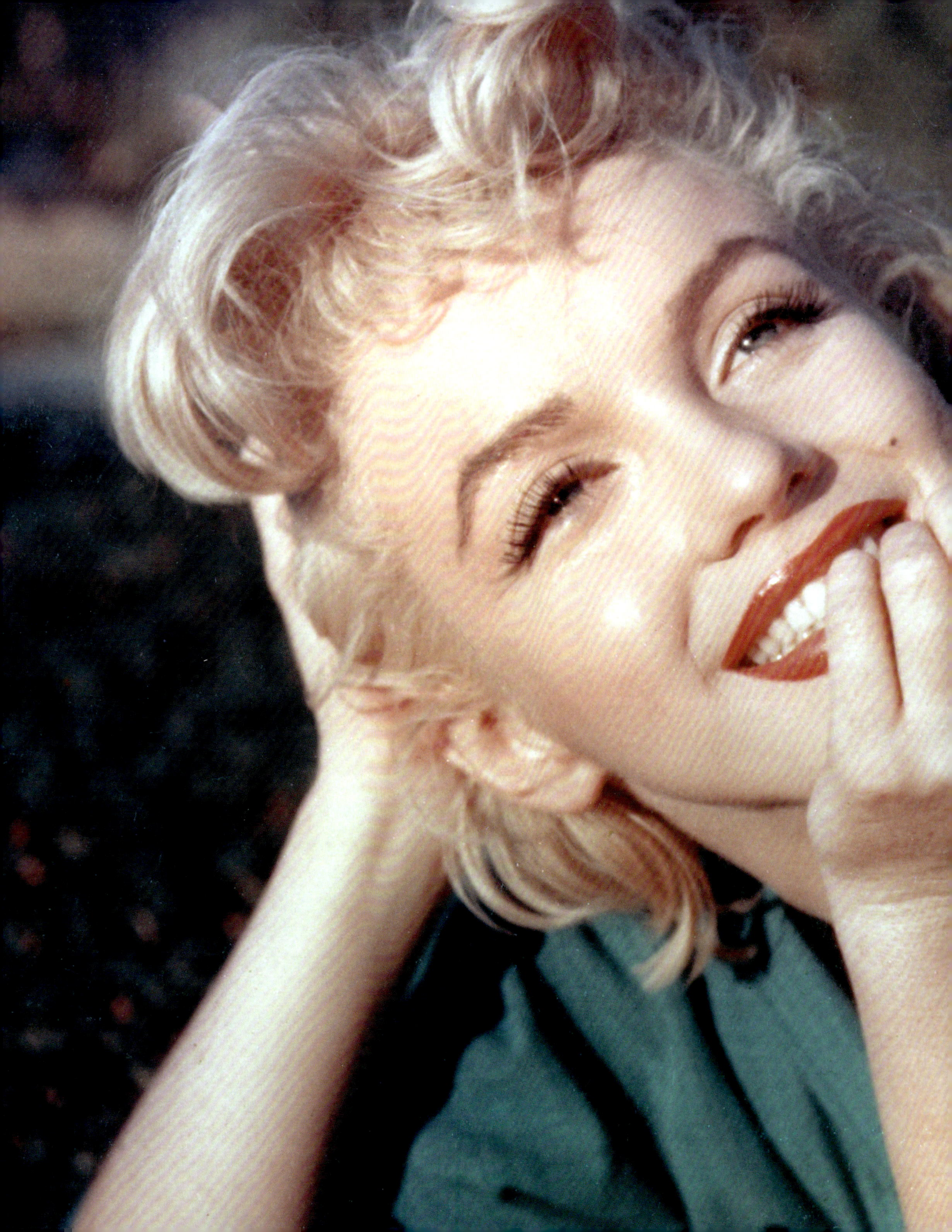

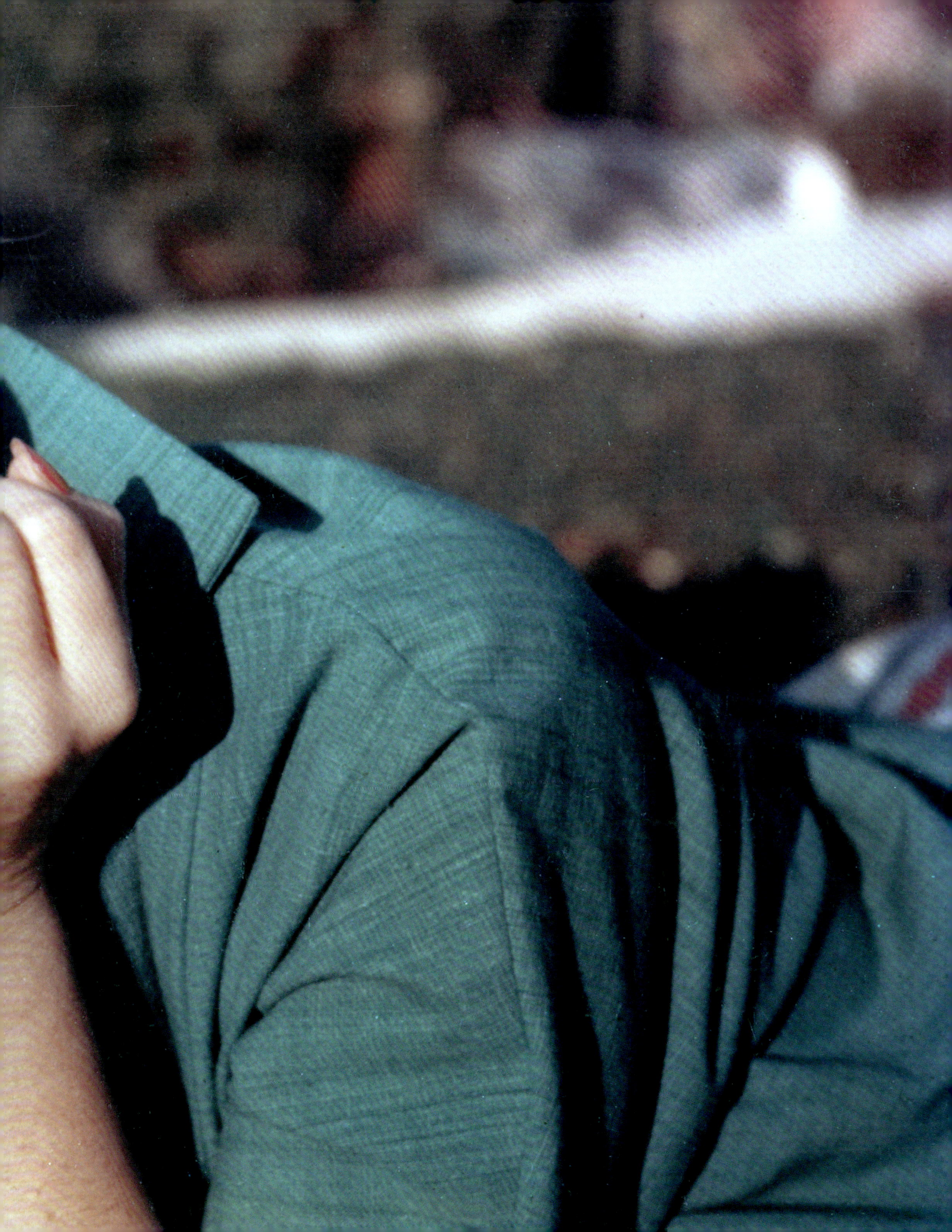

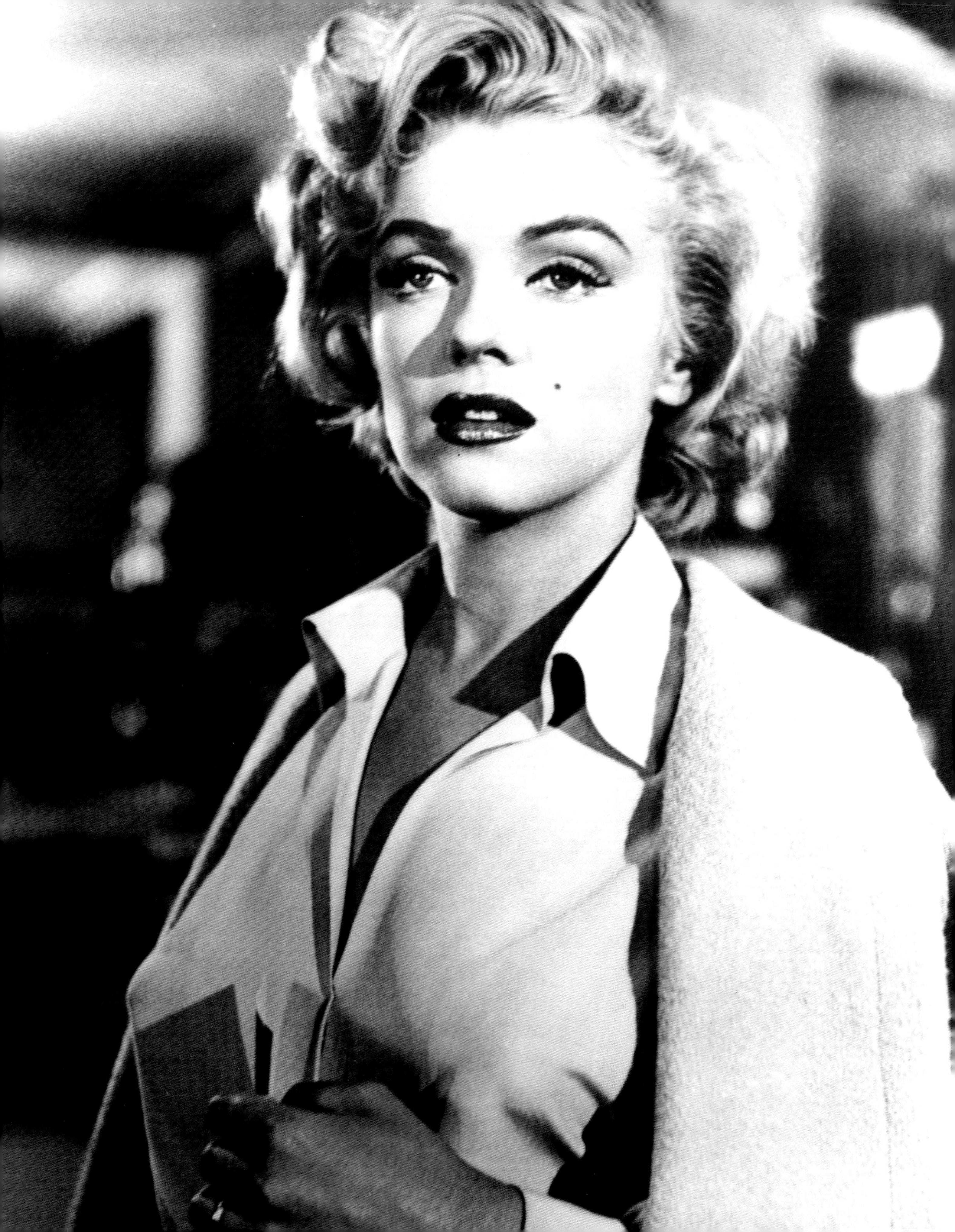

Left: Marilyn in *Niagara* (1953), wearing one of her casually chic outfits

Below: Marilyn looking chic and sporty, 1950s

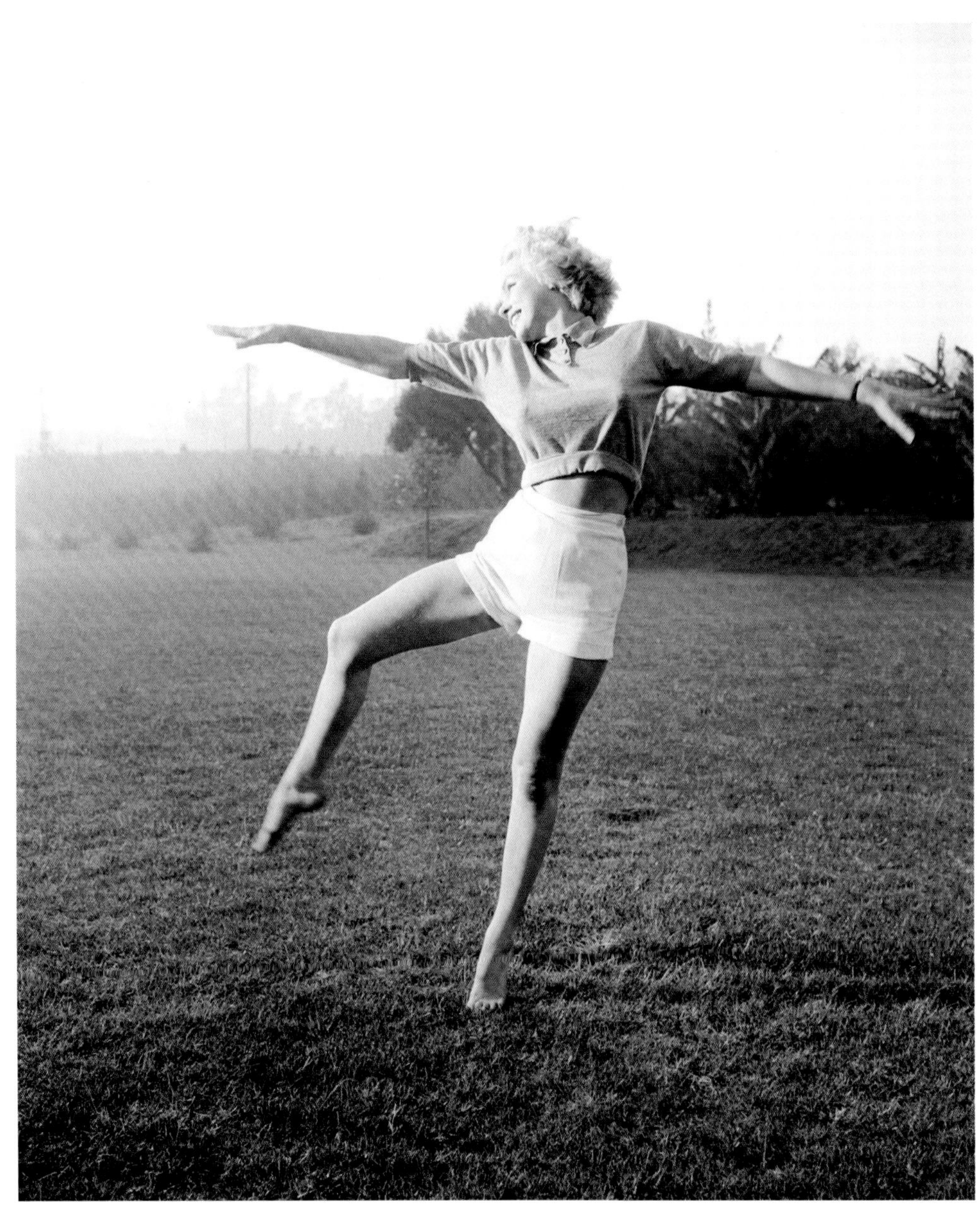

Overleaf: Marilyn looking casual but chic as she and new husband Arthur Miller leave for a picnic the day after their wedding, 1956

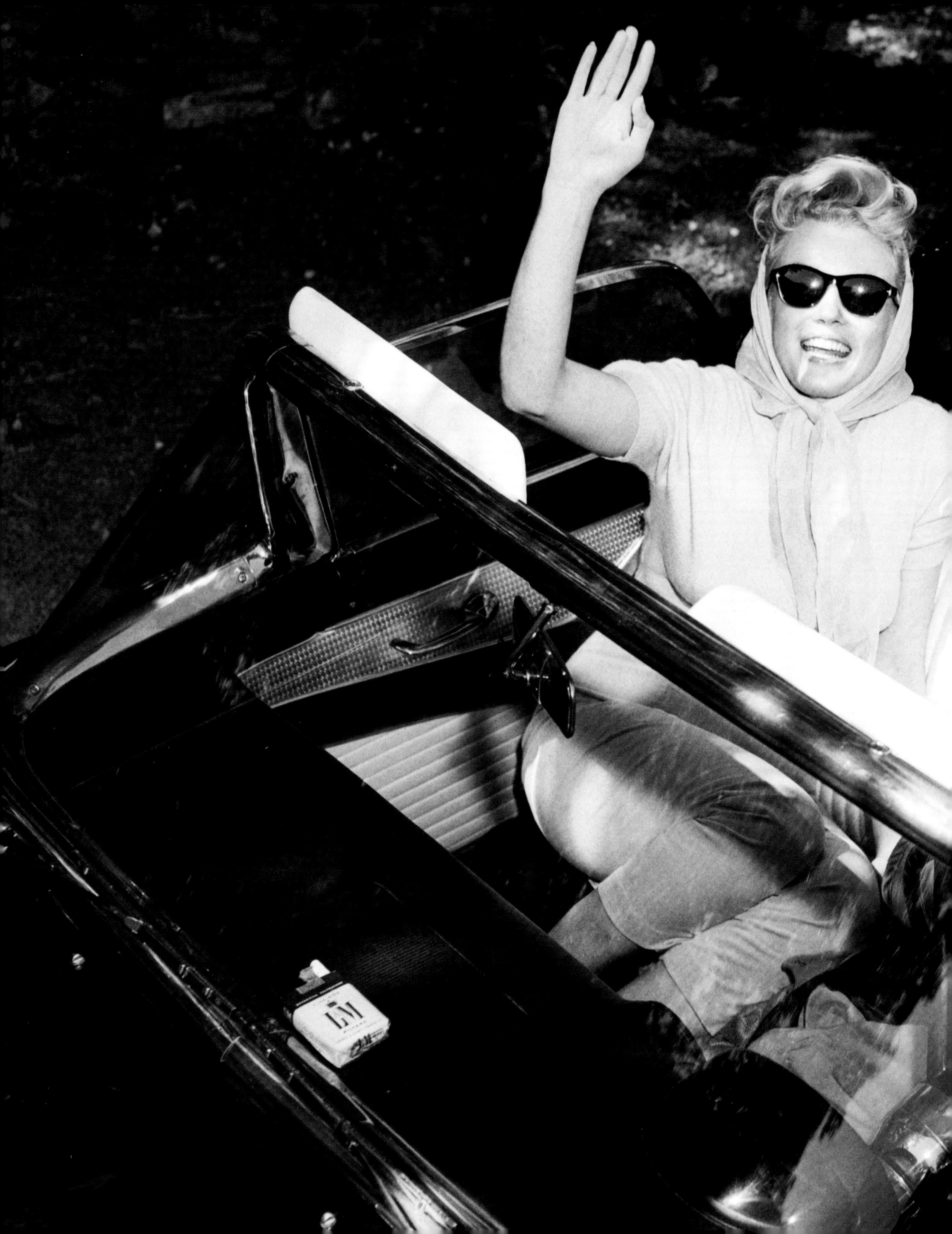

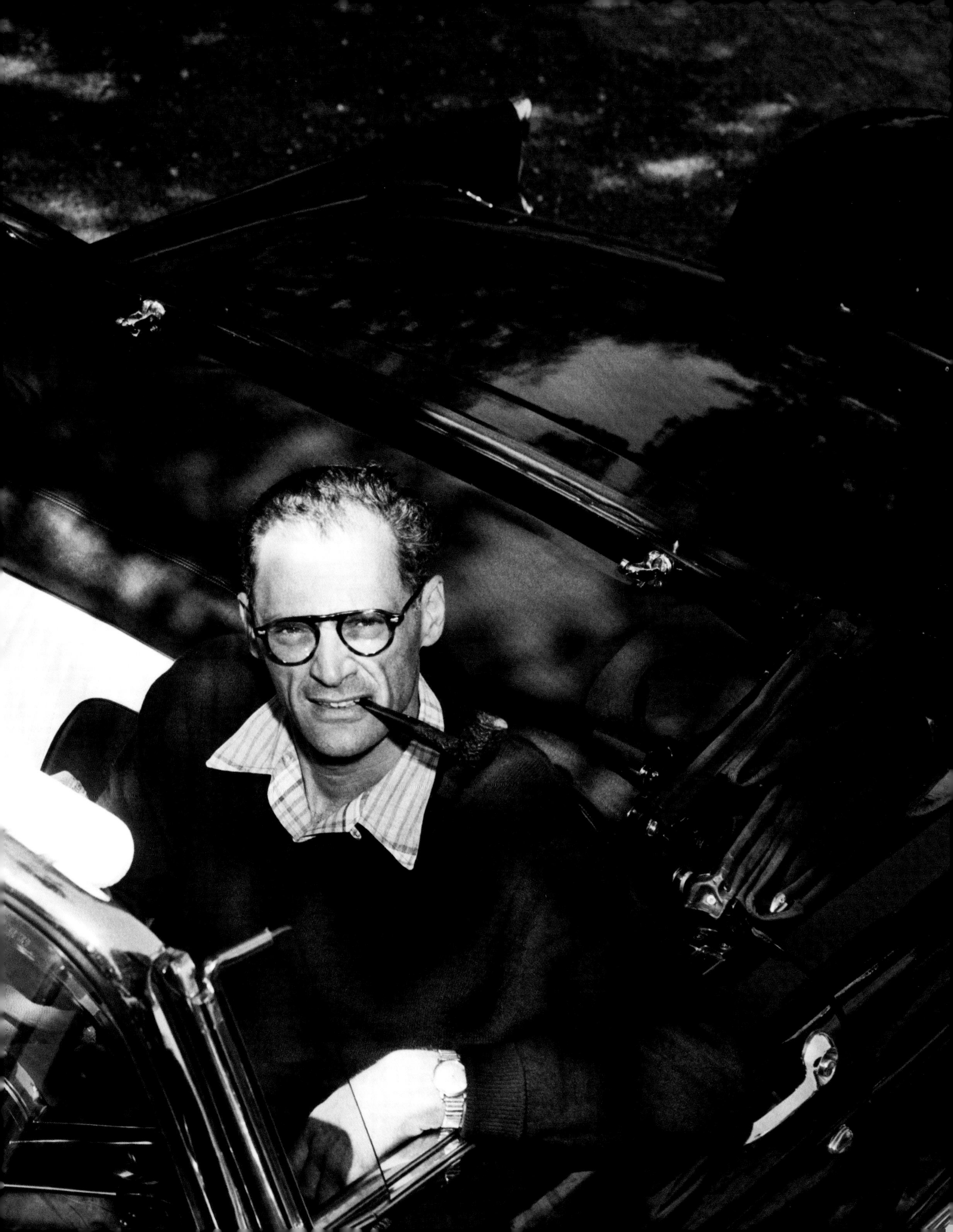

DAYDRESSES

'I DO NOT OWN A VAST UNPAID-FOR WARDROBE.
THE OTHER DAY, I SPLURGED ON TWO BLACK
DRESSES, BUT I PAID CASH FOR THEM BOTH.'

– Marilyn Monroe, 1951

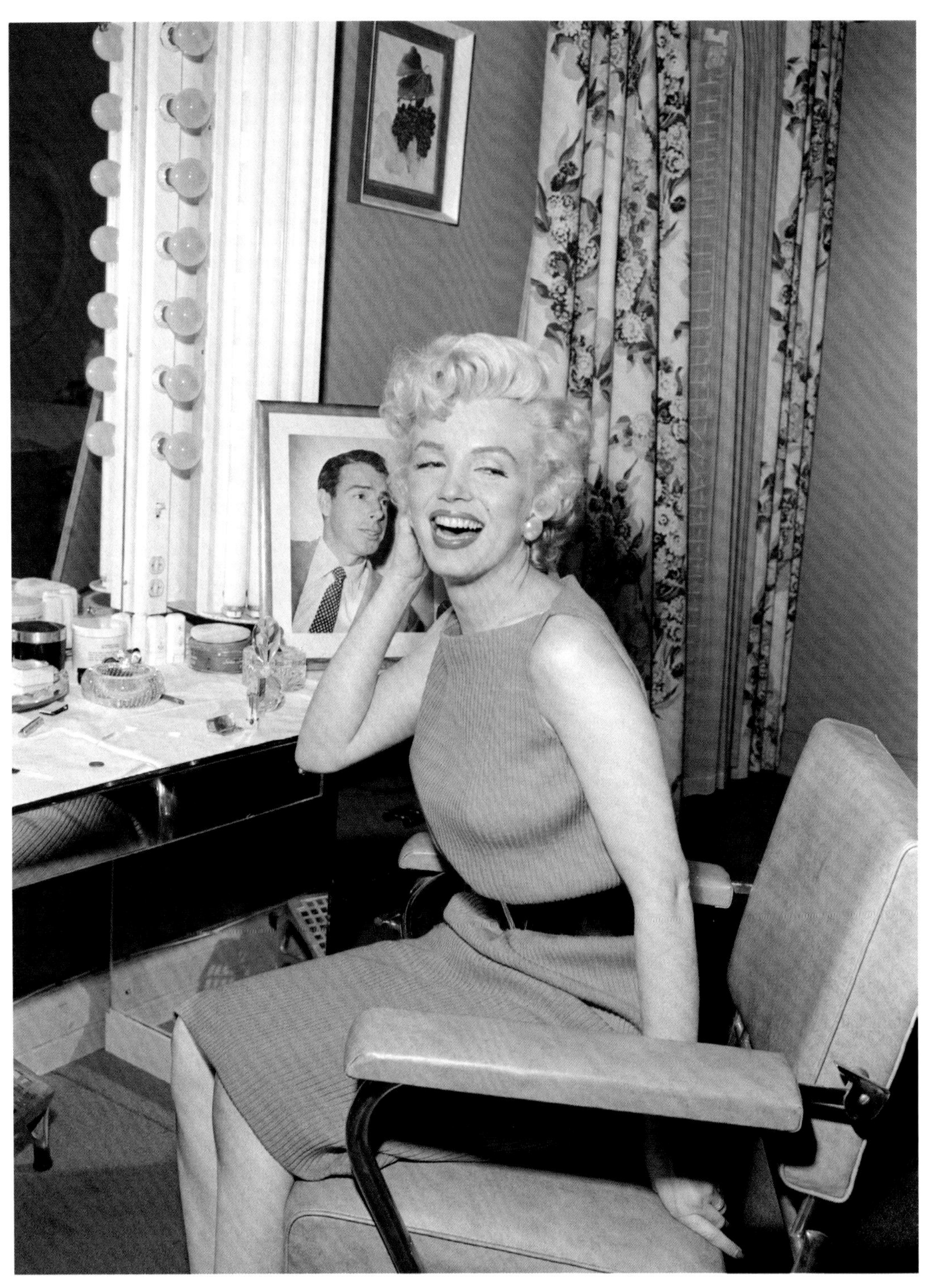

Marilyn in her dressing room, looking stylish in a simple shift dress with a belt, 1954

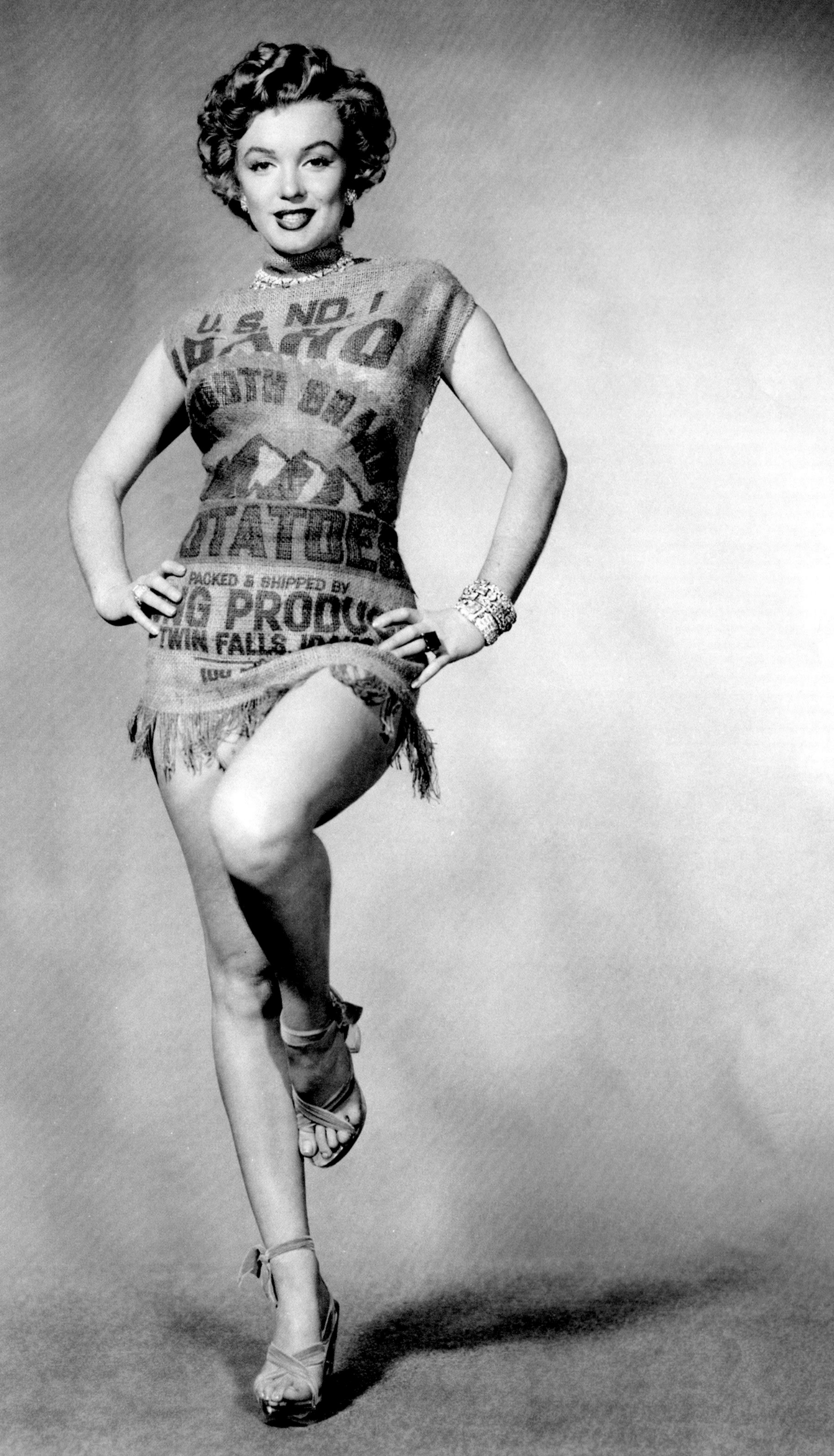

U.S. NO. 1
IDAHO
POTATOES
PACKED & SHIPPED BY
PRODUCE
TWIN FALLS, IDAHO

WHEN MARILYN was about
12 years old, she enrolled at Emerson
Junior High School in Westwood,
California, and lived with Ana Lower,
her 'aunt', who looked after her. In a
1951 interview, Marilyn remembers
how this was 'just at the age when
clothes were beginning to be important'.
She continues:

> '*I couldn't help but notice
> that mine weren't as pretty or
> varied as the other girls. One
> day, one of my classmates
> made a comment about
> the dress I was wearing,
> and I came home crying.
> I was so self-conscious
> and miserable that I never
> wanted to go back to school.'*
> (Monroe, 1951)

As a child, Marilyn wore cheap sneakers
and sandals and clothes where the
seams had been let out time and again.
She made do and mended what little she
had. Her small, unfashionable wardrobe
wasn't unusual at a time when much of

America was still experiencing economic
hardship following the Great Depression.
Rural areas were considerably affected
and there was a keen sense that nothing
could be wasted. This included feed
sacks which would once have held flour,
sugar, seeds or animal feed; these were
made from cotton and women would
ingeniously upcycle them into a variety of
items, including underwear and dresses.
Marilyn wore a version of these thrifty
dresses in 1951 for a Twentieth Century
Fox publicity stunt – by this time, she
was a well-known emerging actress
with a successful modelling career. The
photographer, Earl Theisen, shot her
wearing a bespoke hessian potato bag
because, reportedly, a journalist had
remarked on a gown Marilyn had worn at
a Beverly Hills Hotel party, saying it was
'cheap and vulgar' and she'd be better
off wearing a sack. This time, instead of
going home and weeping because people
were being mean about her wardrobe,
Monroe turned the tables on her critics.
The pictures by Theisen were fantastic,
and funny, and Fox got their story. Their
actress could make anything look good.

For work, Marilyn wore a rotation of
figure-hugging dresses and, when
necessary, she would borrow outfits
from the set of movies she was making
or wear her own clothes on camera,
when asked. The simple, slim-fit frock,
embellished with a pretty bow that
she wore to play her character Victoria
Parker in the 1954 film *There's No
Business Like Showbusiness* made
another appearance a year later, when
Marilyn flew to Idlewild Airport to begin
filming New York location shots for
The Seven Year Itch (1955). At that
time, Hollywood studios wanted their
stars to inhabit their personas and for
this reason the clothes Monroe wore
when she was not 'being Marilyn' are
fascinating to scrutinise. During different
phases of her life, she either turned up
or turned down the bombshell Monroe
character she had created.

Many of the dresses sold at Christie's
auction of her personal property indicate
that Marilyn had more of an affinity for
a casual look. Sleeveless white and
baby-blue striped shirt dresses from

the Women's Haberdashers store on Madison Avenue, ivory silk shifts by Jax, and loose-fitting frocks and tunics that she asked designers to copy and remake in a variety of colours, are all part of her behind-the-scenes outfits. Two sweet lace-trimmed summer frocks, one of which Monroe wore to an Abraham Lincoln exhibition in September 1955, indicate her penchant for prettiness. Occasionally, this was reflected in her film roles, too. Playing Harriet in *As Young as You Feel* (1951), she is outfitted by Hollywood costume designer Renié, in a crisp white-lace, square-necked dirndl dress.

During Monroe's short marriage to Joe DiMaggio, she would often wear more demure, high-necked frocks, in tune with the wifely role he wanted her to assume. Hence the alleged cause of their marriage break-up when she wore her famous white halterneck dress by Travilla in *The Seven Year Itch* (1955), which billowed around her while standing on a subway grating. The legendary baseball player was not happy with the world seeing his wife's underwear. She revealed in a letter that Joe 'hated all my clothes. When I told him I had to dress the way I did, that it was part of my job he said I should quit that job. But who did he think he was marrying when he was marrying me?' (Spoto, 1993).

When she was living in New York and studying at the Actors Studio, she met and fell in love with Arthur Miller. This was a time when she distanced herself from Hollywood, wanting more from her career, and this is reflected in part by the clothes she was seen wearing, which tended towards the more formally chic. Plain black shifts became a wardrobe

essential, very much influenced by her stay with Milton Greene and his wife Amy, who took her shopping uptown. While visiting England in 1956 to film *The Prince and the Showgirl*, she wore one of her favourite dresses by the designer John Moore; made in beige silk with bracelet sleeves, it is grownup, elegant and restrained. Moore was a friend who knew what she liked, creating the modest white gown she wore to marry Miller in 1956. In the celebrated pictures taken by Sam Shaw in 1957 at the house she shared with Arthur Miller in Roxbury, Connecticut, Marilyn wears a countrified pale-blue dress that echoes her bucolic environment. She never gave up on her work wardrobe, however, and when the occasion arose, she pulled out all the sartorial stops.

In September 1959, *The New York Times* reported that the most coveted invitation in town was a ticket to lunch with Nikita Khrushchev, who was visiting Hollywood. The newspaper headline declared it had become 'one of the angriest social free-for-alls in all the uninhibited and colorful history of Hollywood', and a seat at the feast with the Soviet premier was secured by only the biggest and brightest celebrities (quoted in Carlson, 2009). Spyros Skouras, the president of Twentieth Century Fox and the brains behind Fox Studios and Twentieth Century Pictures merger in 1935, insisted that Marilyn Monroe attend. He was a father figure to Marilyn, who called him 'Papa Skouras'. Skouras in turn had made happen some of Monroe's most famous films, including *Gentlemen Prefer Blondes* (1953) and *The Seven Year Itch* (1955). Lena Pepitone, Monroe's maid, recalled in her memoir: 'they told Marilyn that in Russia, America meant two things, Coca-Cola and Marilyn

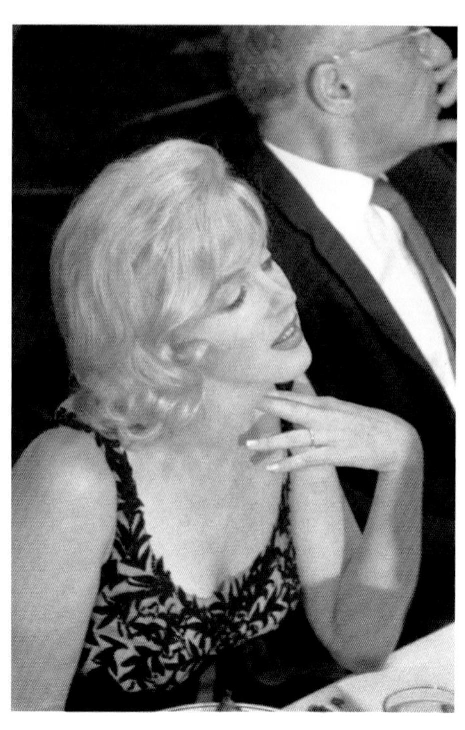

Monroe. She loved hearing that and agreed to go [...]. She told me that the studio wanted her to wear the tightest, sexiest dress she had' (Pepitone, 1979). And the dress she wore? A simple black shift with an embellished torso designed by John Moore.

Right: Marilyn with second husband Joe DiMaggio, 1954

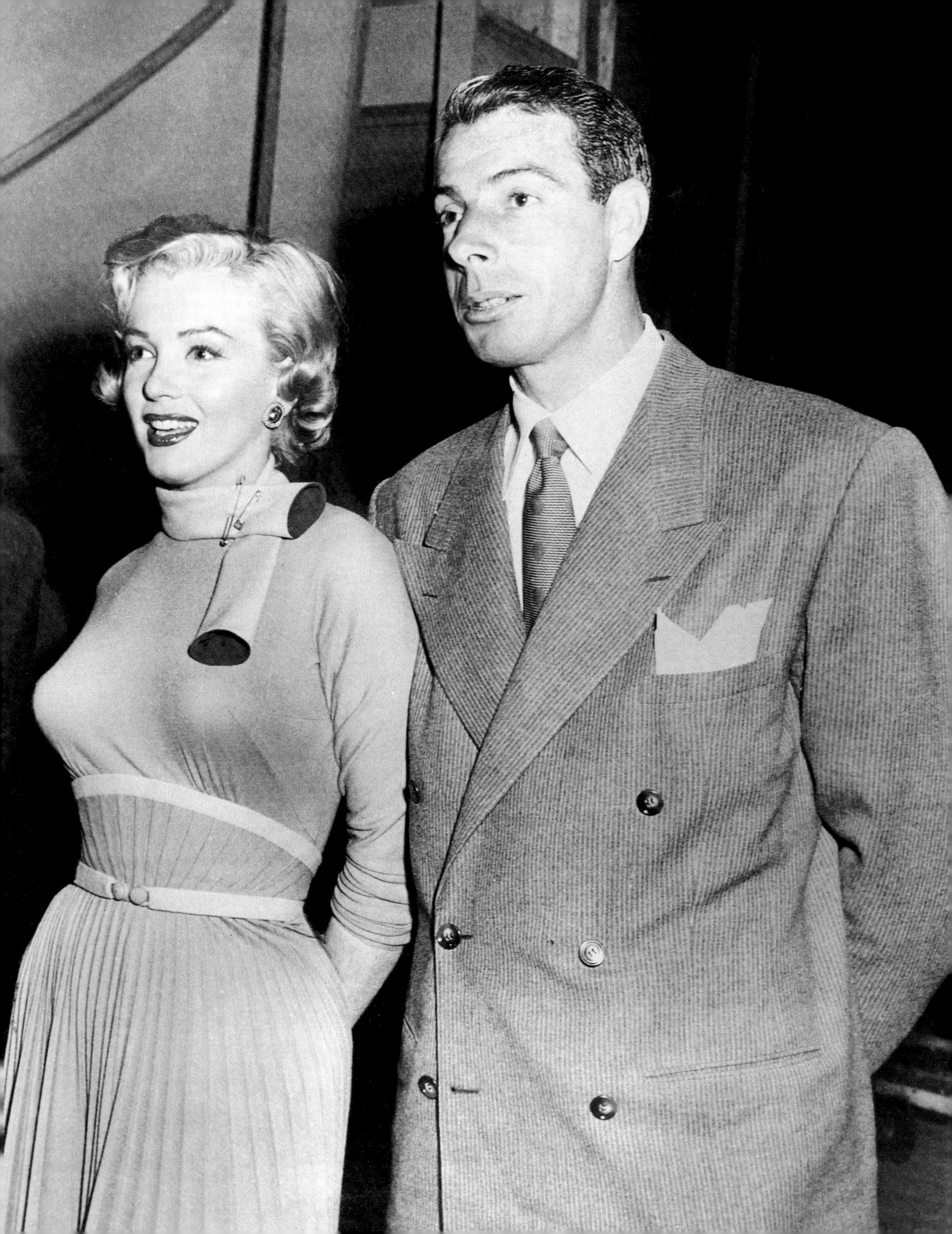

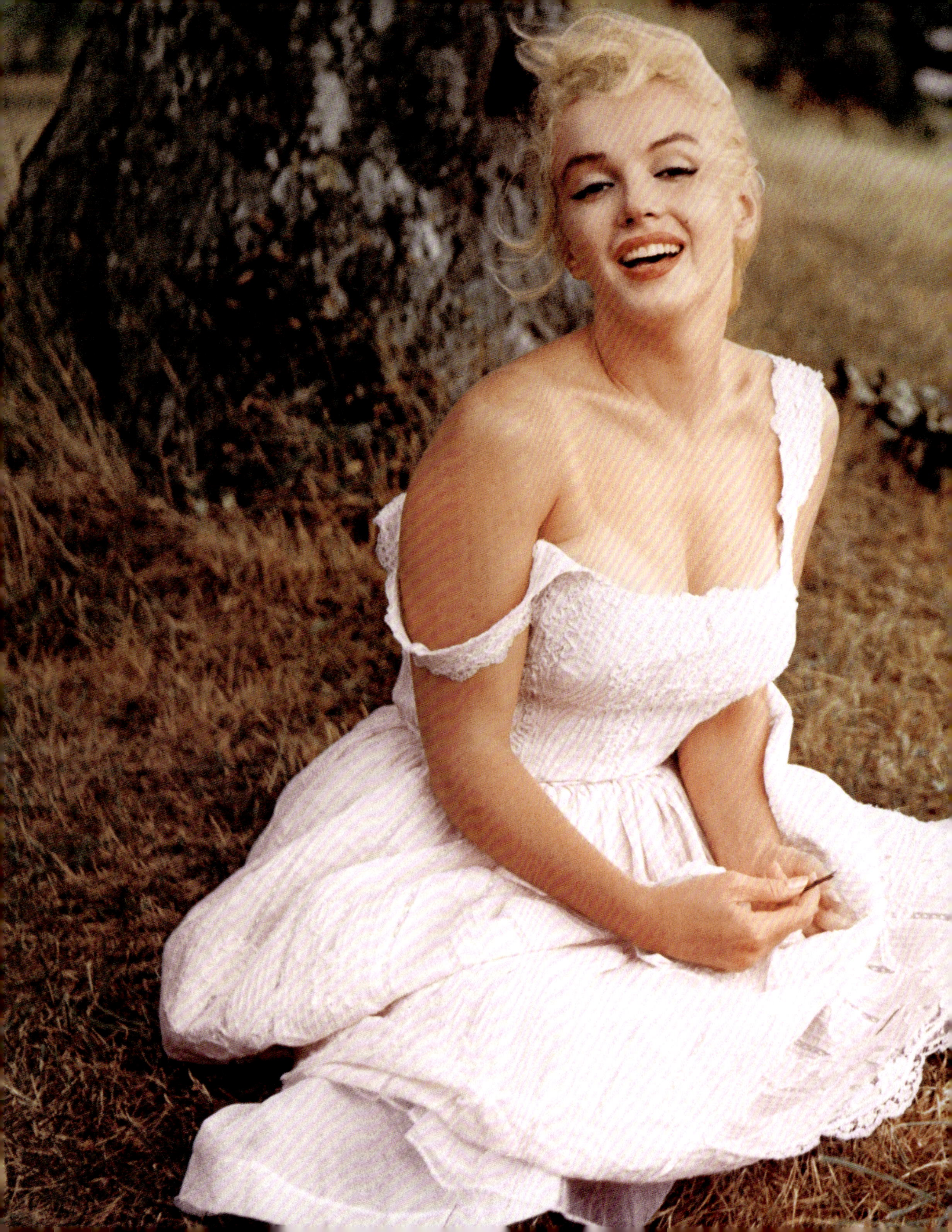

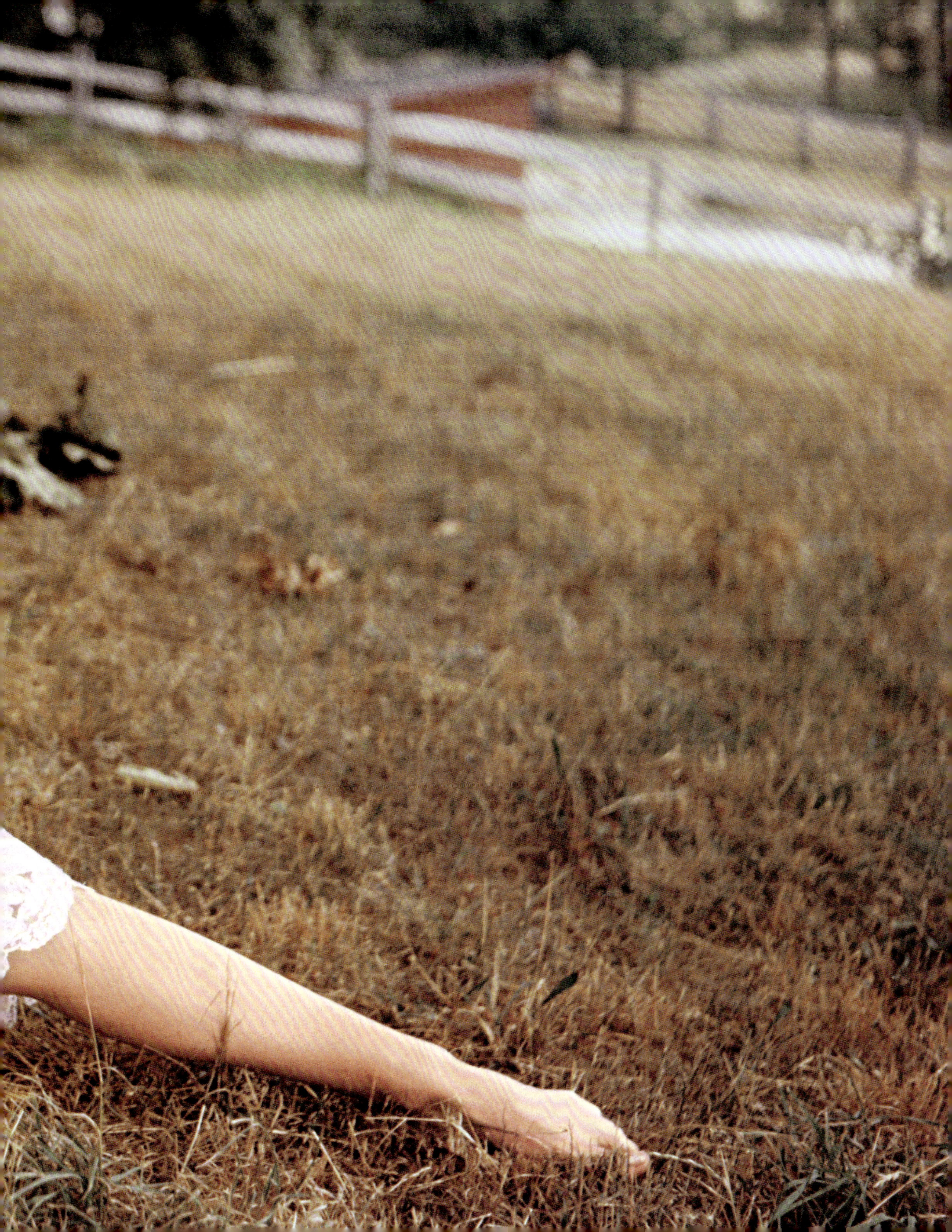

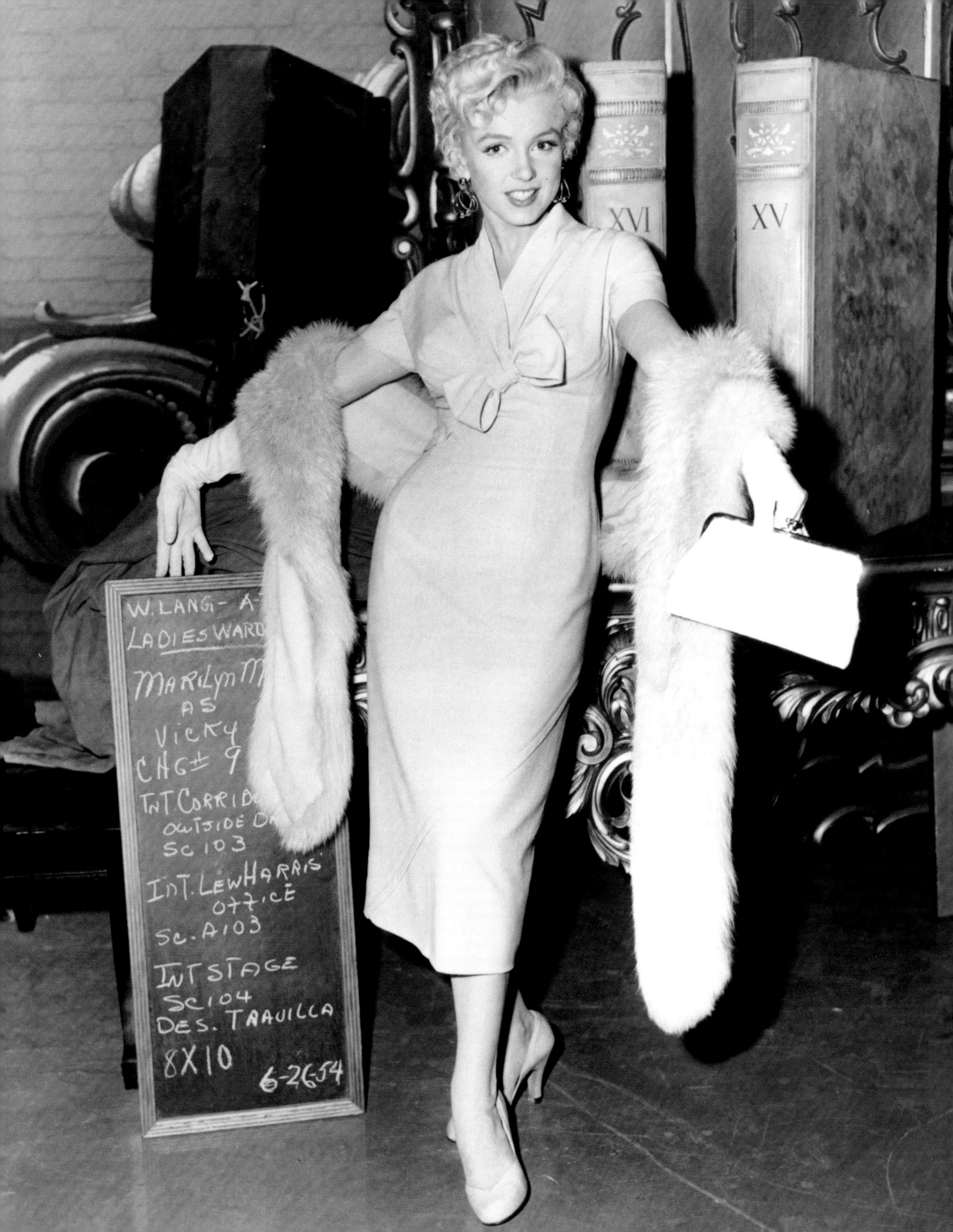

W. LANG - A
LADIES WARD
MARILYN M
AS
VICKY
CHG# 9
INT CORRID
OUTSIDE D
SC 103
INT. LEW HARRIS
OFFICE
SC. A103
INT STAGE
SC 104
DES. TRAVILLA
8X10
6-26-54
XVI
XV

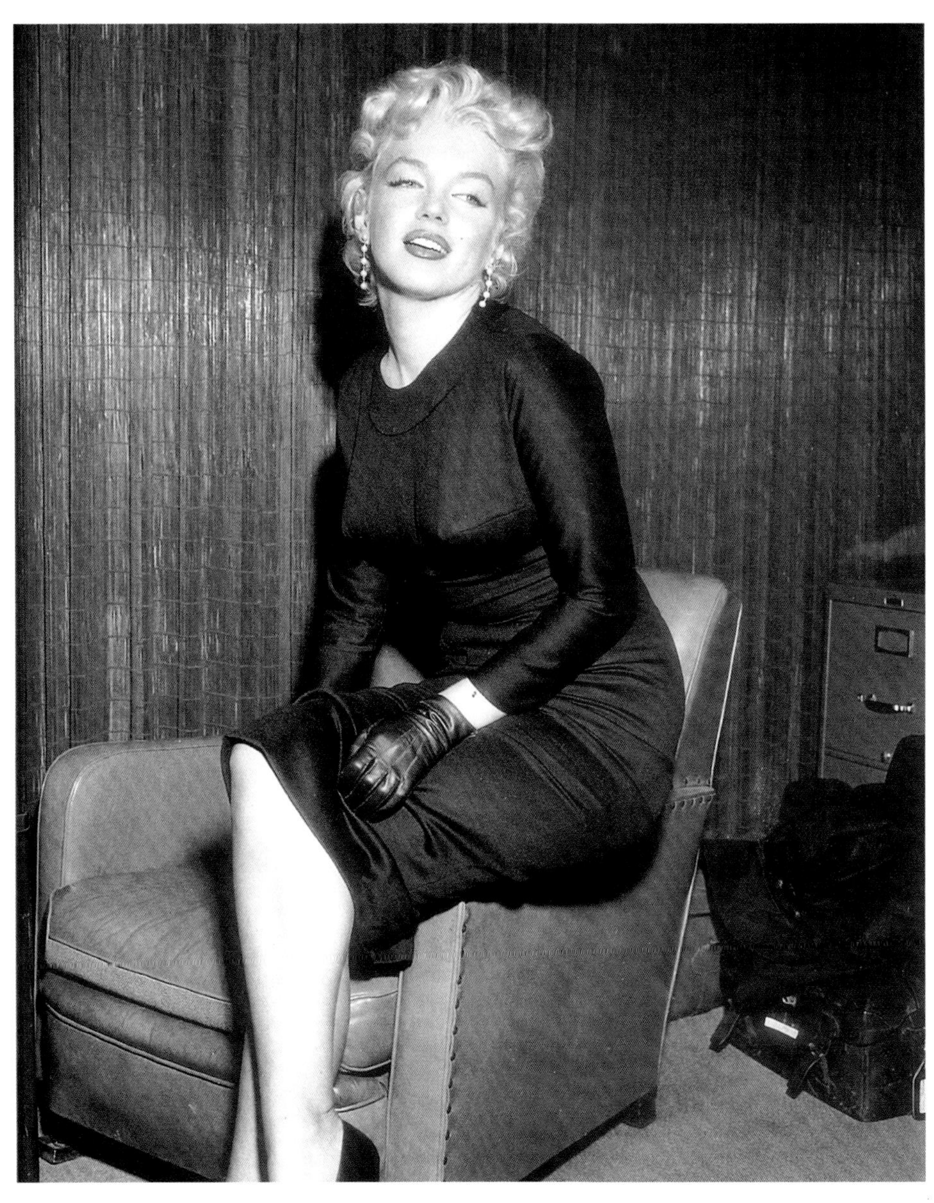

Marilyn posing for a costume test photo ahead of filming
There's No Business Like Show Business (1954)

Marilyn at the Idlewild Airport in New York, just before leaving
for Los Angeles, 1956

COATS WRAPS & FURS

'I USED TO THINK AS I LOOKED OUT ON THE HOLLYWOOD NIGHT, "THERE MUST BE THOUSANDS OF GIRLS SITTING ALONE LIKE ME DREAMING OF BECOMING A MOVIE STAR".'

– Marilyn Monroe, *My Story* (1974)

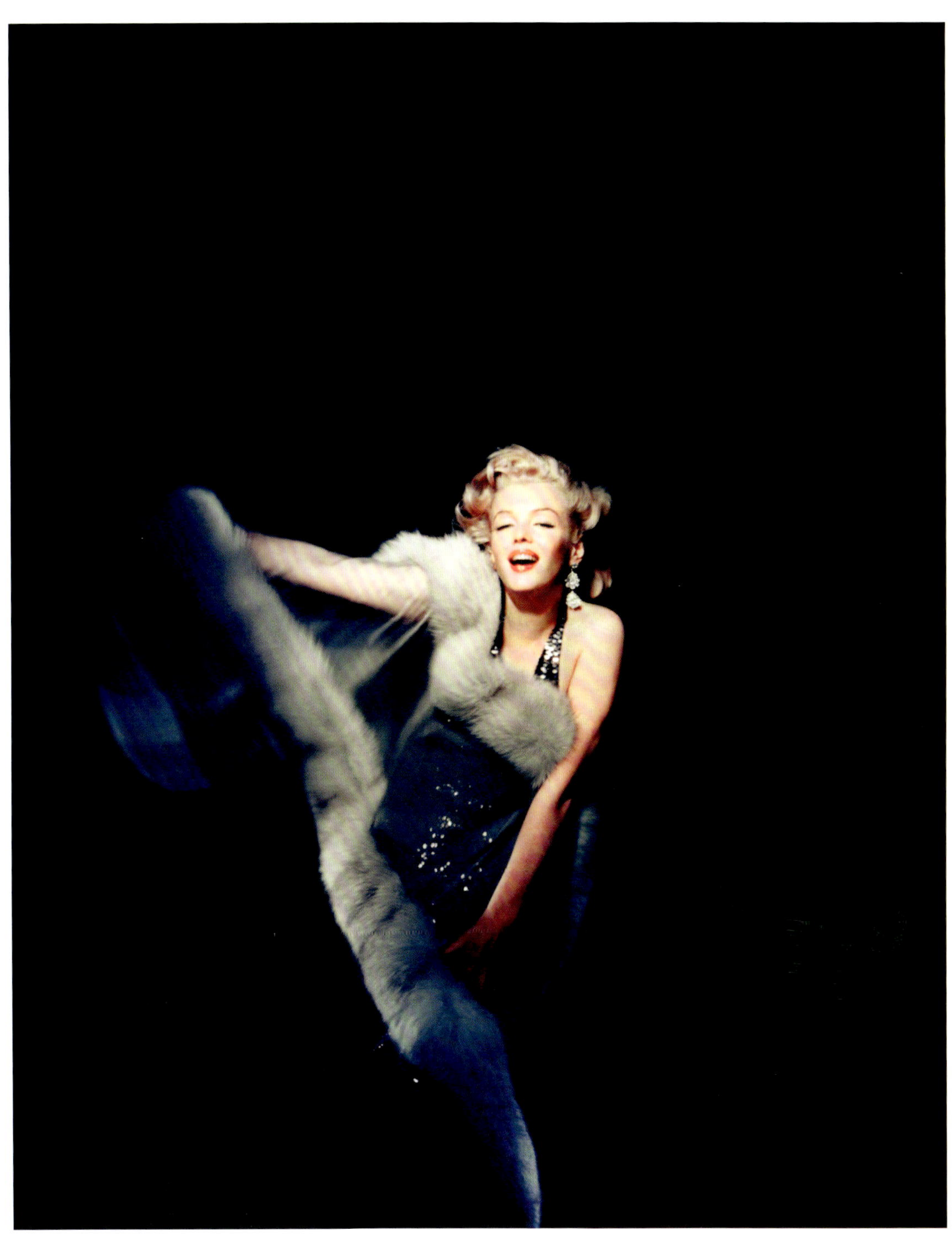

Marilyn in *The Prince and the Showgirl* (1957)

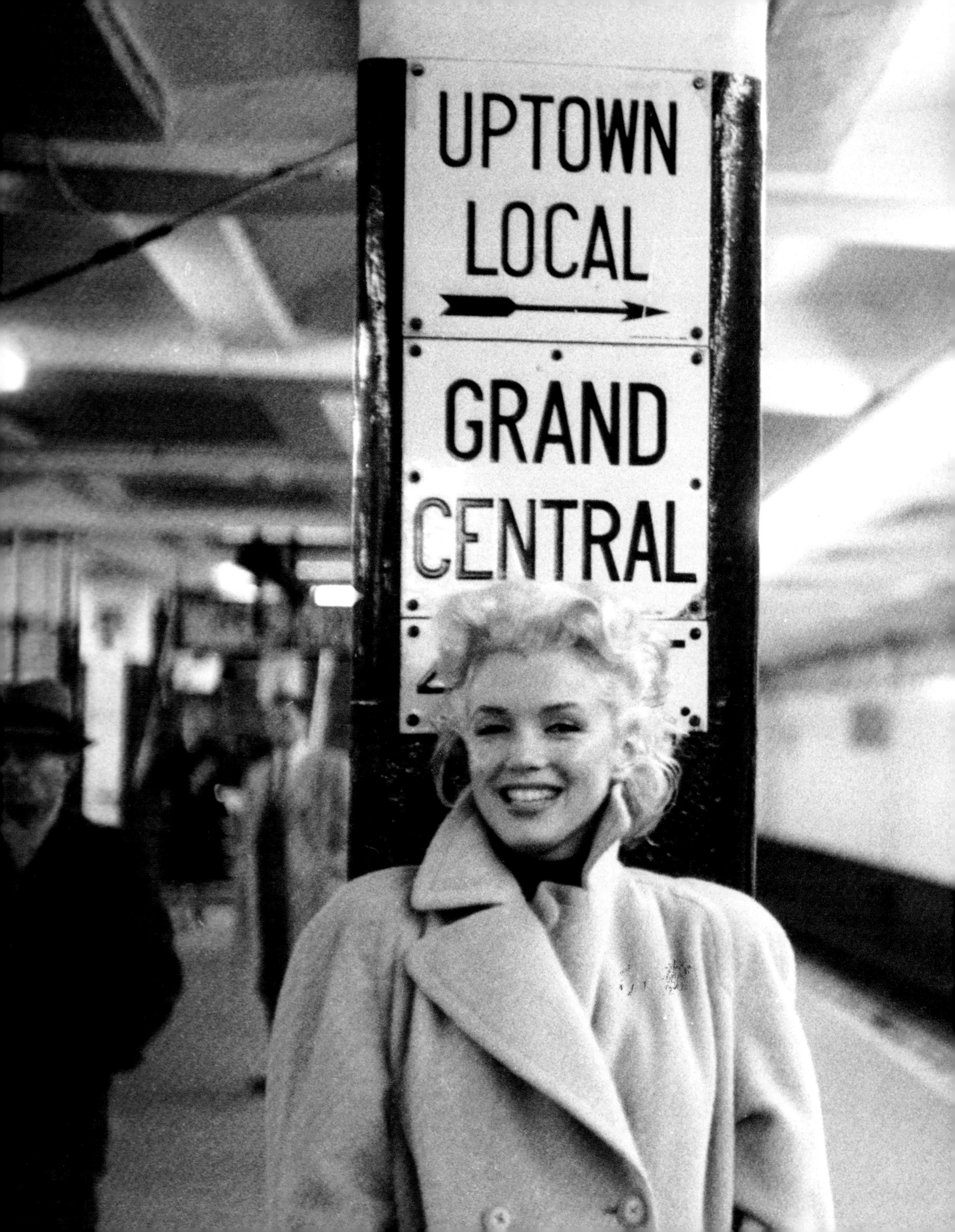

UPTOWN
LOCAL
GRAND
CENTRAL

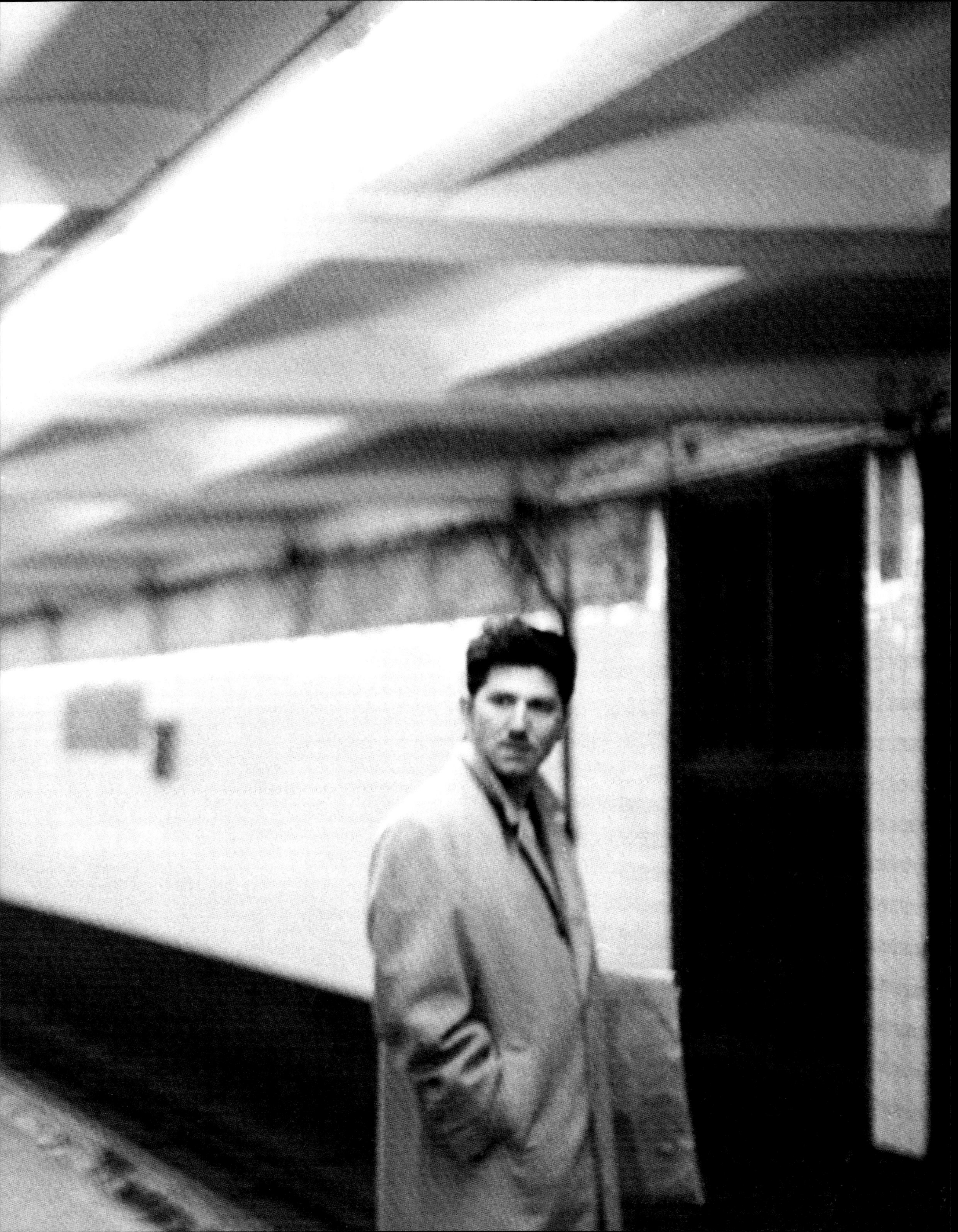

MARILYN MET JOHNNY

Hyde when she was 22, working hard at becoming a star and looking for a break. Hyde, the vice president of the William Morris agency, made it his mission to help her. Monroe described him as 'willing to act as my agent even though the only coat I had was a beat-up polo coat and I went to interviews without stockings before it was fashionable because I couldn't afford any' (quoted in Spoto, 1993). Although Marilyn's onscreen image was singularly sensational, behind the scenes she relied often on that 'beaten-up' coat to keep her warm. In an interview with Richard Meryman, Marilyn revealed:

'Sometimes wearing a scarf and a polo coat and no makeup and with a certain attitude of walking, I go shopping or just look at people living. But then you know, there will be a few teenagers who are kind of sharp and they'll say, "Hey, just a minute. You know who I think that is?" And they'll start tailing me. And I don't mind. I realise some people want to see if you're real.' (Quoted in Meryman, 2007)

She certainly looked real in her beat-up coat, without any adornment; but her natural chic still shone through. The polo coat began life back in Britain in the 1900s as something worn by polo players between breaks in the game. It was originally designed without buttons and just a belt and was similar in structure to the beloved bathroom robe Marilyn wore often as a comfort blanket. Even as it evolved into the more well-known Ivy League double-breasted silhouette, it was by no means a feminine choice. Nevertheless, it was Monroe's go-to coat when she was off camera. She had many practical coats – trenches from Jax and shapeless but useful houndstooth wool ones from Women's Haberdashers which she would shrug on over daywear styles for paparazzi pictures, looking casually smart. Later, she would buy a camel coat from Dior – a signature 'Marilyn piece' that she wore time and again when she lived in New York. When it came to dressing up, Monroe favoured velvet opera coats with bracelet sleeves and enjoyed wearing a favourite Rudi Gernreich for Walter Bass ivory satin coat with large mother-of-pearl buttons and a belt.

The 1940s and '50s were decades when fur governed glamorous wardrobes and although Monroe owned a beige faux-fur coat by Claire McCardell, she wore and was photographed in many real ones. There was doublethink about animal skins at that time, the semiotics of which reflected an aristocratic, monied elegance that told the world you had made it. Marilyn was a huge animal lover and owned dogs, including Hugo, the black-and-white Basset Hound she had when she was with Arthur Miller, as well as Maf Honey, a Maltese–Poodle cross, yet she didn't think twice about wearing mink. Furs were in vogue and were expected to be worn by Hollywood stars, with top photographers and magazines having no compunction about featuring them. A series of images taken by Richard Avedon for *The Prince and the Showgirl* (1957) sees Monroe wrapped in fur and Bert Stern's celebrated Last Sitting portraits, commissioned by *Vogue* magazine in 1962, also feature her dressed in a floor-length animal skin. Furs were like diamonds: luxury presents given to a wife or lover, or simply to dispense largesse.

After they founded their MM Productions deal in 1954, Milton presented Marilyn with a snow-white fur coat, and photographed her in it. Joe DiMaggio gave her a full-length brown mink coat for Christmas and, in 1958,

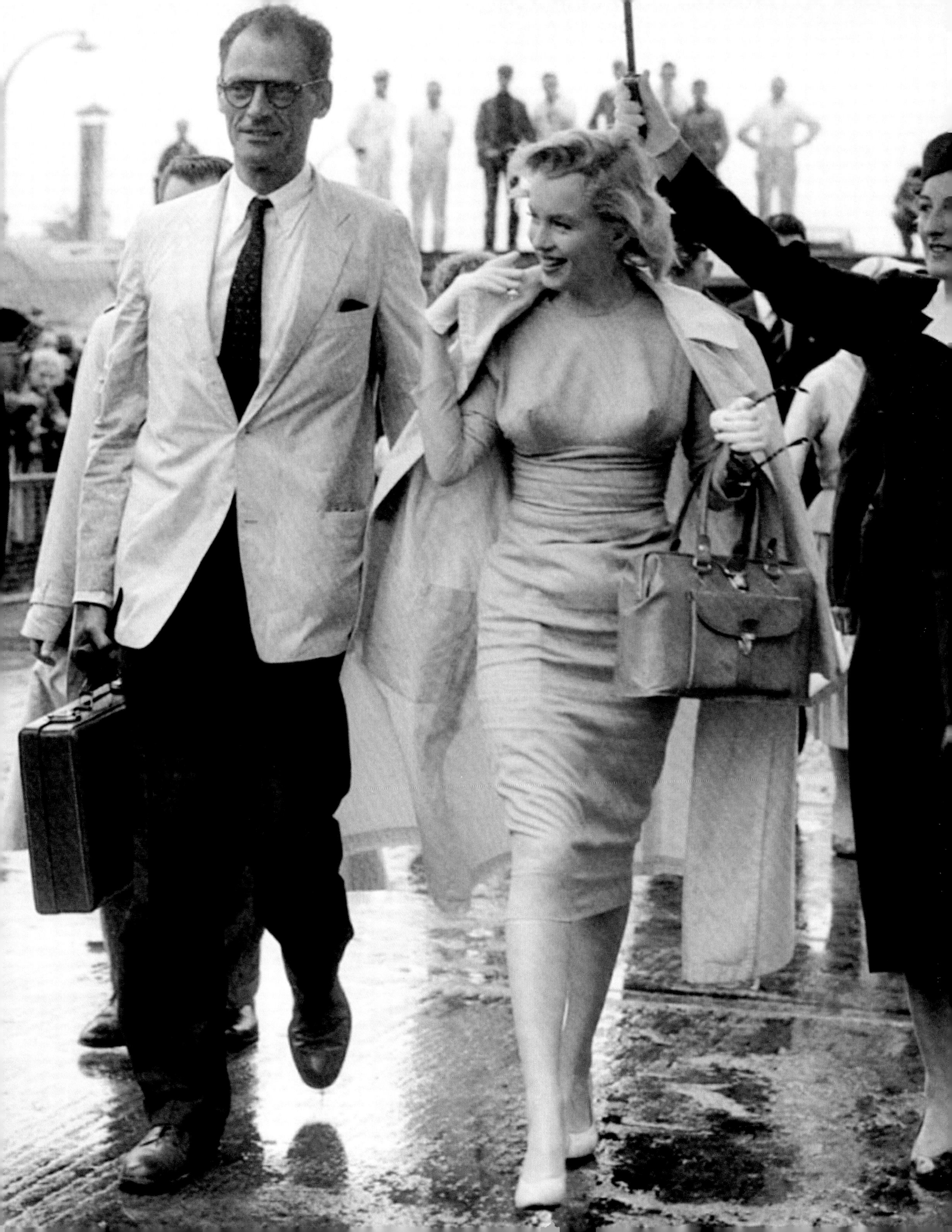

Arthur Miller gave Marilyn an oyster-white beaver coat from Teitelbaum Furs, which cost $1,337 at the time. Fur was also one of the few luxuries that Marilyn would invest in for herself. A white fox-fur stole with a triple-pleated ivory silk lining and a label reading 'Teitelbaum Furs, Beverly Hills' was the first fur she owned. She used it multiple times to imaginatively adorn sleeves, collars of coats and cardigans, as seen in her 1961 film *The Misfits*. For the sparkling world premiere on 14 November 1953 of *How to Marry a Millionaire*, everything Marilyn wore she had borrowed, with the exception of the furs. She would wear the stole again to the Photoplay Awards ceremony in 1953, and again to the premiere of *The Seven Year Itch* in 1955. The piece was originally sold in the 1999 Christie's auction of her possessions, where the final price realised was $9,775. At the Christie's memorabilia sale in November 2003, it was sold again for $17,925, with proceeds going to the World Wildlife Fund.

In 1954, Marilyn met the legendary jazz singer Ella Fitzgerald, before she hit the big time. Fitzgerald divulged that she was having trouble getting gigs at the bigger venues, and Marilyn then 'personally called the owner of the Mocambo [Charlie Morrison], and told him she wanted me booked immediately, and if he would do it, she would take a front table every night' (quoted in Ponder, 2022). Marilyn did so, wearing her finest black fur wrap and dressed to impress to show her support, bringing her friends Judy Garland and Frank Sinatra along for the first night. In a 1972 *Ms Magazine* interview, Fitzgerald reflected: 'The press went overboard [...] After that, I never had to play a small jazz club again' (quoted in Ponder, 2022).

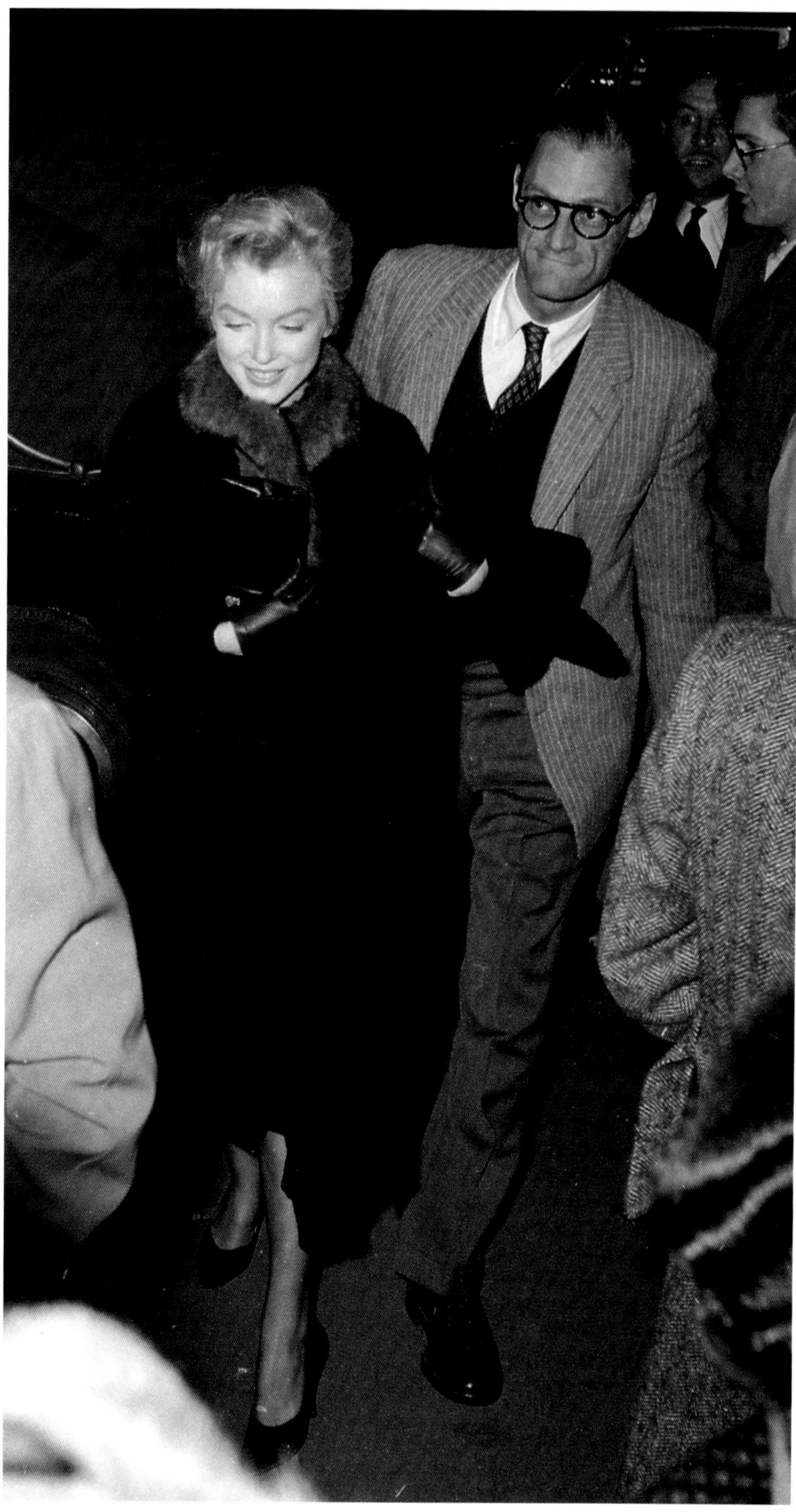

Overleaf: Marilyn with Ella Fitzgerald at a jazz session at the Tiffany Club in Hollywood, 1954

Right: Marilyn attends the benefit premiere of *East of Eden*, looking glamorous in a tight-fitting gown and fur stole, 1955

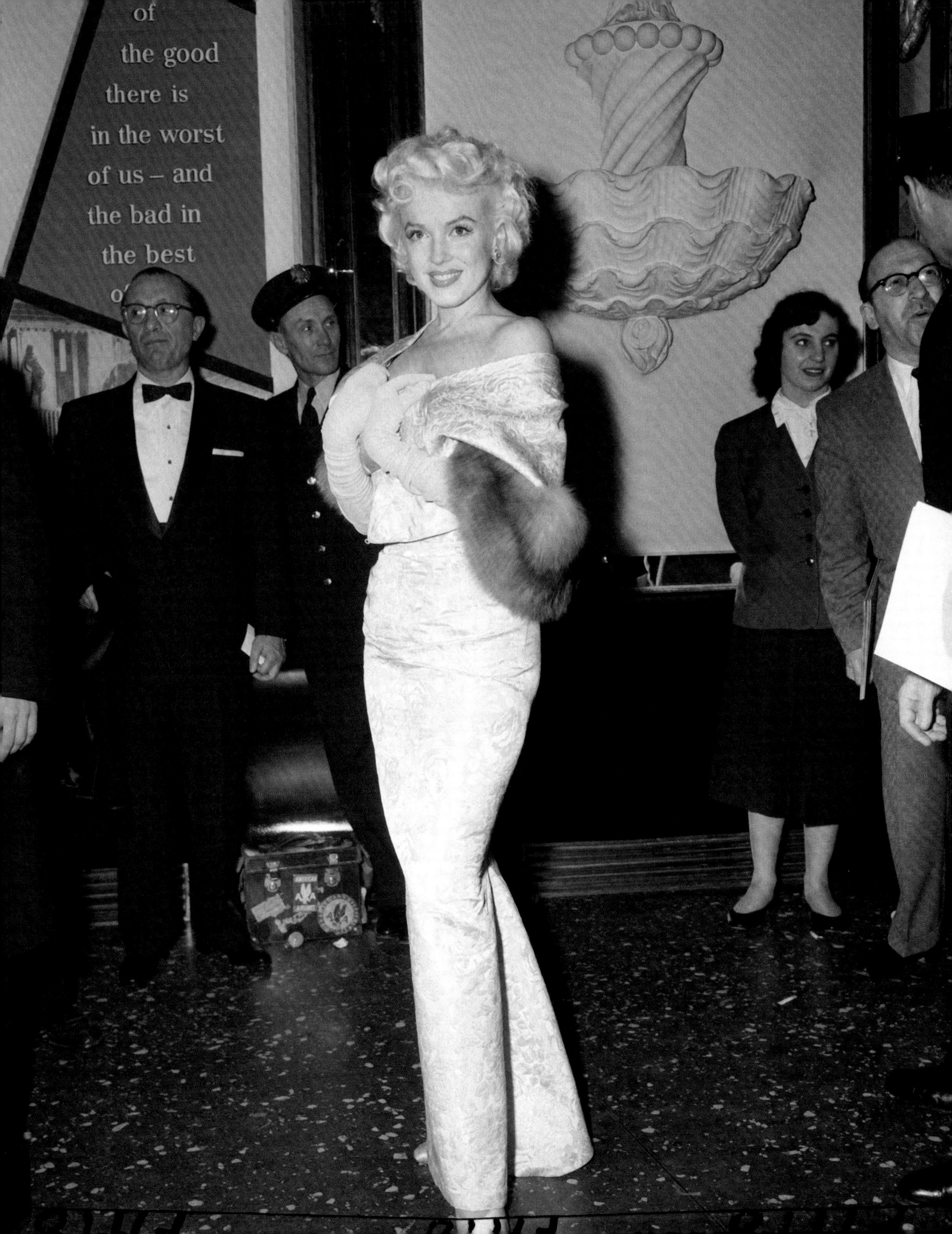
of
the good
there is
in the worst
of us – and
the bad in
the best
of

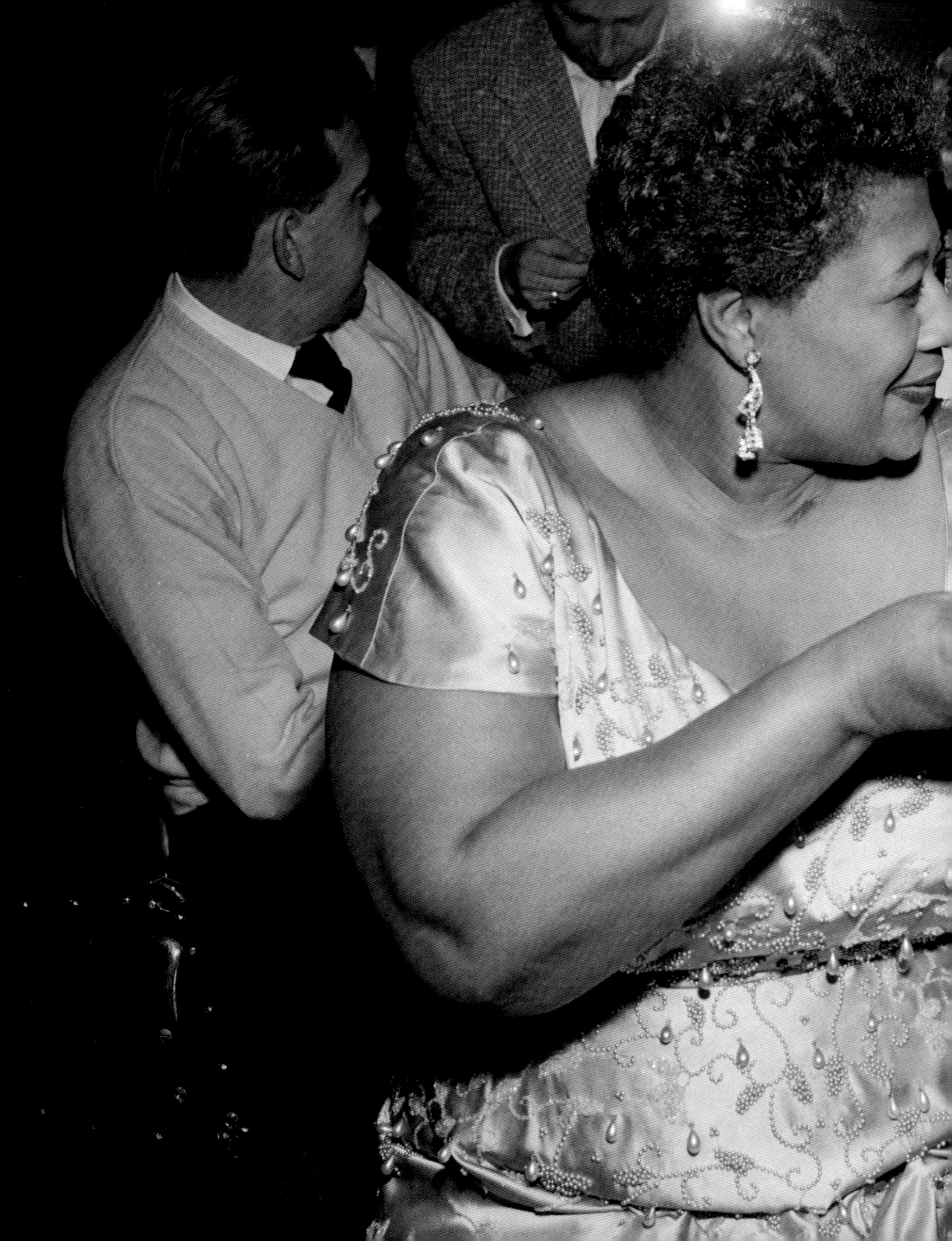

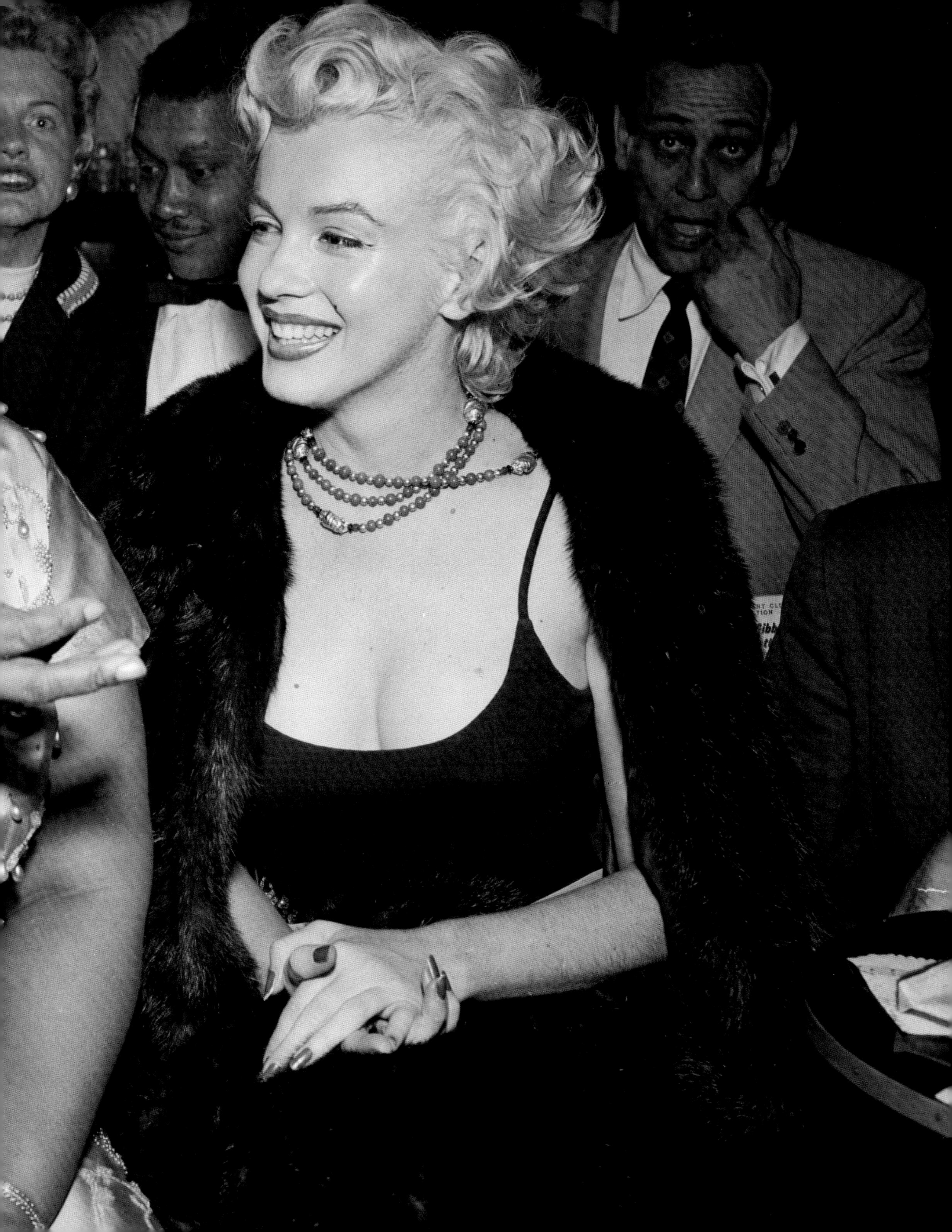

SUITS

'I'M THE SAME PERSON, IT'S JUST A DIFFERENT SUIT.'

– Marilyn Monroe, 1956 (Marilyn Monroe History, 2014)

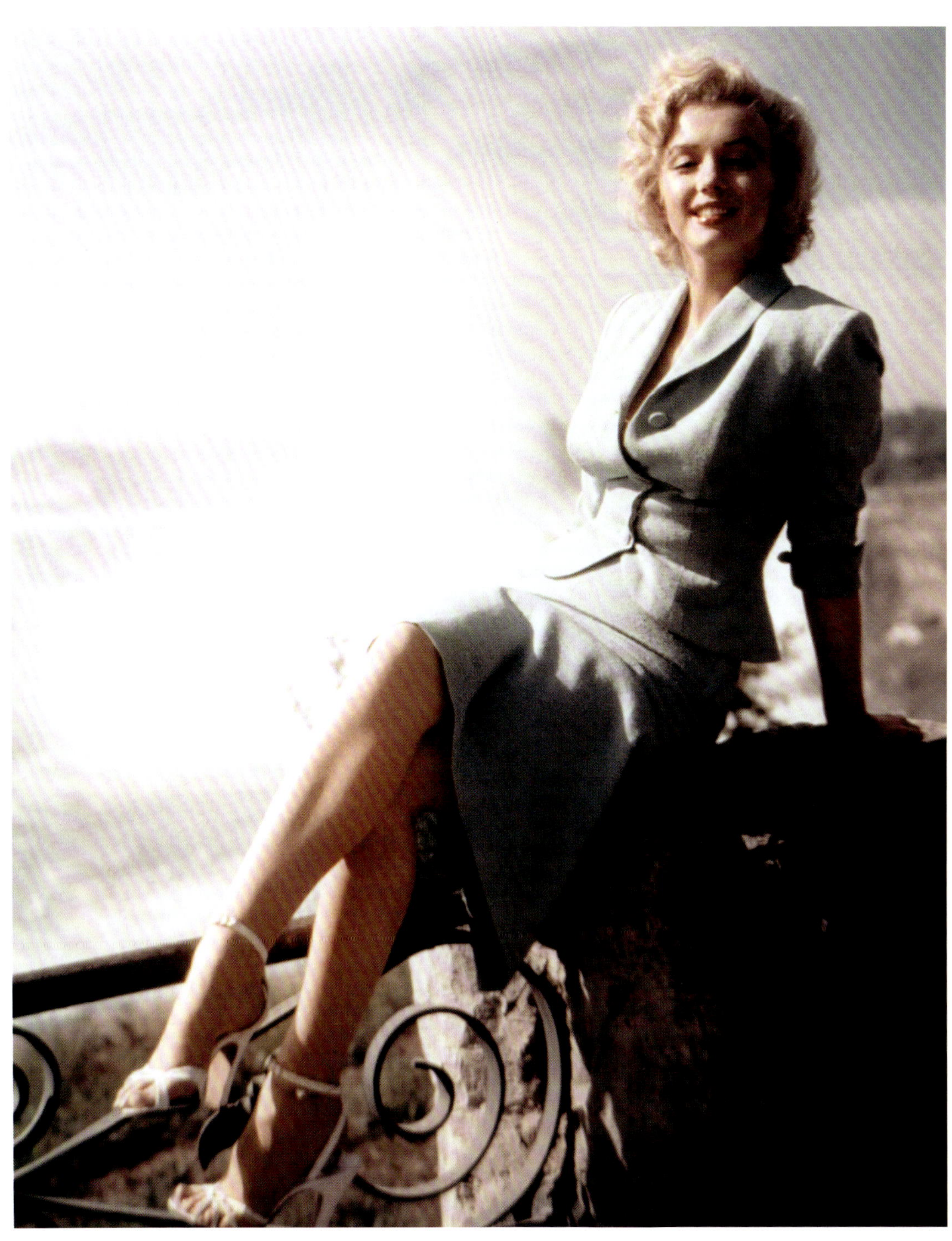

Looking fresh and stylish in a pale blue suit,
Marilyn poses on the set of *Niagara*, 1953

A SUIT is not typically remembered as a Marilyn Monroe outfit, but it was a choice she returned to time and again, with each telling a different story of moments in her life and films. Traditionally infused with propriety and tradition, a well-cut suit is both formal and feminine and embodied women's fashion throughout the 1940s and '50s. During the Second World War, tailoring was a practical option, with utility fabrics featuring simple, unadorned lines with few embellishments and pockets. Padded shoulders, however, were *de rigueur* and a boxy silhouette, with a hint of the military about it, pervaded. Mainbocher, the American creative who opened a fashion house in Paris before relocating back to New York at the start of the war, was known for his elegant ballgowns and tweed dinner suits. He also famously reworked the uniform worn by women in the American Navy and Red Cross.

At this time, the work of British designer Edward Molyneux and his svelte suiting was in great demand, selling at the smart department store Bergdorf Goodman's 'Custom Salon', where affluent customers would visit for bespoke orders. Similarly, Bonwit Teller's 'Salon de Couture' provided an upscale environment where Parisian designers sold top of the range two-pieces. Often the designs would trickle down to the mass market where comparable versions would sell at cheaper prices, off the rack. An early 1941 shot of Marilyn shows her wearing an inexpensive smart skirt suit, most probably her only one, and is plain to the point of austere, echoing the prevailing fashion for an unfussy and minimal shape. The outfit reflects the wardrobe of a thousand aspiring young professional women, who either sewed their own clothes or bought copies of high fashion-house designs.

One of Marilyn's first appearances in a magazine was modelling a 'Hollywood Star Suit' from the company Arnold's of Hollywood on Hollywood Boulevard, which cost $16.98 plus postage (Nickens & Zeno, 2012). Post-war women's tailoring reflected the re-established feminised role of women and became less no-frills and more chic, accessorised with gloves, hats and mini handbags. Marilyn's character Bobbie Stevens in her 1951 film *Love Nest*, is an ex-member of the Women's Army Corps and reflects this changing fashion in her wardrobe of chic two-piece suits designed by Renié Conley, all with matching gloves and tiny hats.

When Monroe was filming *Niagara* in 1952, director Henry Hathaway requested she wear some of her own clothes. It wasn't an unusual request at that time, and Marilyn had worn her own clothes in films before. This time, however, she 'replied without embarrassment that she possessed only slacks, sweaters and one black suit, which she bought for [American talent agent] Johnny Hyde's funeral'. She purportedly said, 'that's why I have to borrow clothes from the studio when I go out. I don't have any of my own' (quoted in Spoto, 1994). Hyde, with whom Marilyn was having an affair, had suffered a heart attack in December 1950 and the suit Marilyn had bought for the occasion was still treasured two years later. As required, the outfit makes an appearance in the film, an off-the-peg, double-breasted, elegant suit from I. Magnin & Co., the exclusive Beverly Hills department store. Marilyn's character in *Niagara* is a seductive femme fatale, most known for her

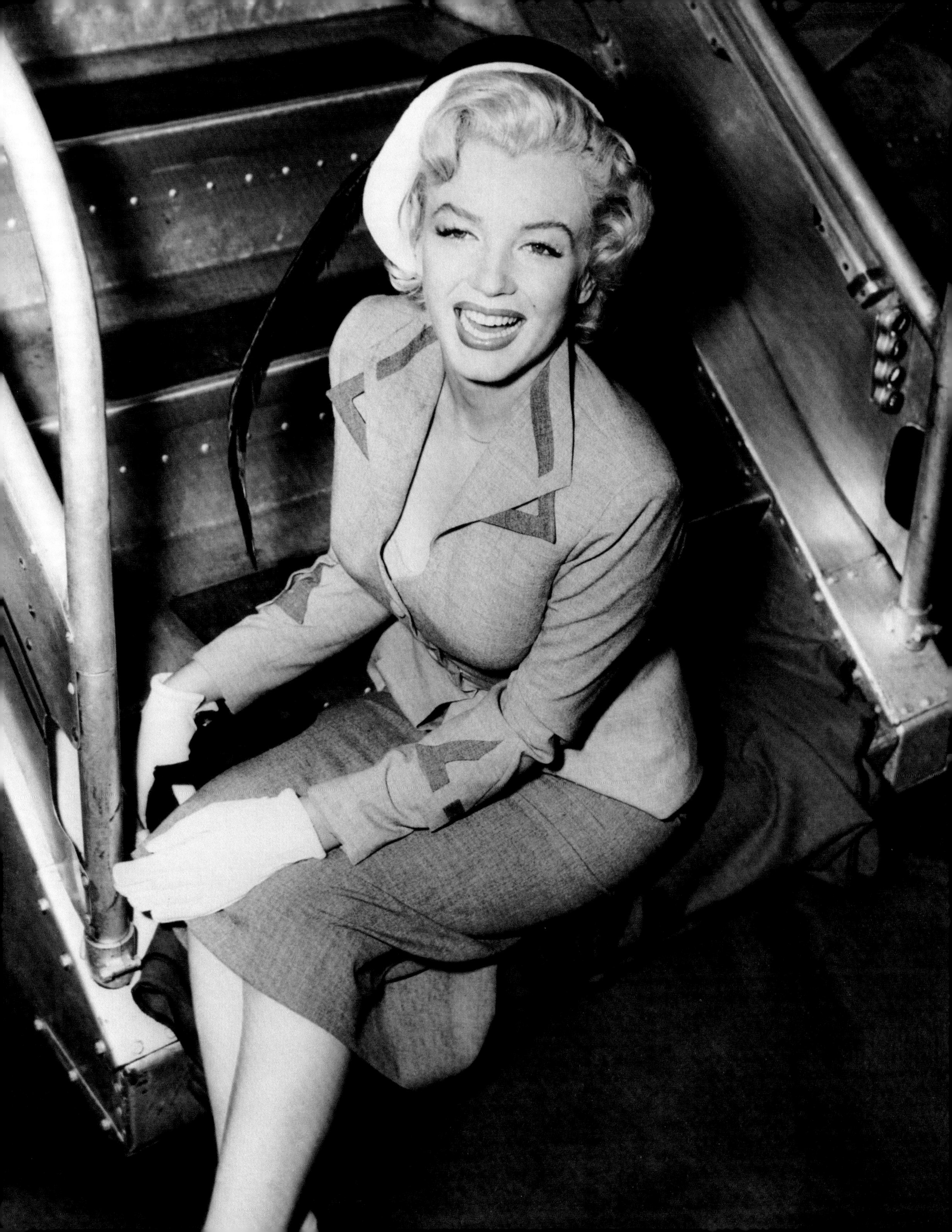

slinky dresses. But the suit has become famous in Marilyn legend as the outfit she wears while performing 'the longest walk in cinema history' while trying to escape from her husband, George, played by Joseph Cotten.

When Johnny Hyde passed away, Marilyn braced herself and dressed for the burial in the distinguished suit: it was elegant, showed off her curves but was also protective. Marilyn would return to I. Magnin & Co. to buy a chocolate brown suit to meet King Paul of Greece and his wife on a Twentieth Century Fox tour in November 1953. She wore the suit once again to get married to Joe DiMaggio in 1954, which was typical of Marilyn's habit of shrewdly reusing her wardrobe. The suit was a conservative choice but in keeping with the persona she appeared willing to adopt as a new wife.

In February 1956, after founding her own production company, Marilyn conducted a press conference at LAX to discuss her victory, wearing a black knee-length pencil-skirt suit, a satin shirt and coordinating tie by designer George Nardiello, to whom she had been introduced by Amy Greene. It was an extraordinarily masculine look for an actress notable for her bombshell appeal, but it showed off her significant new stature. In the 30 January 1956 edition, *Time* magazine celebrated her win, reporting that 'there was persuasive evidence that Marilyn Monroe is a shrewd businesswoman', a fact to which her settlement with the studio attested.

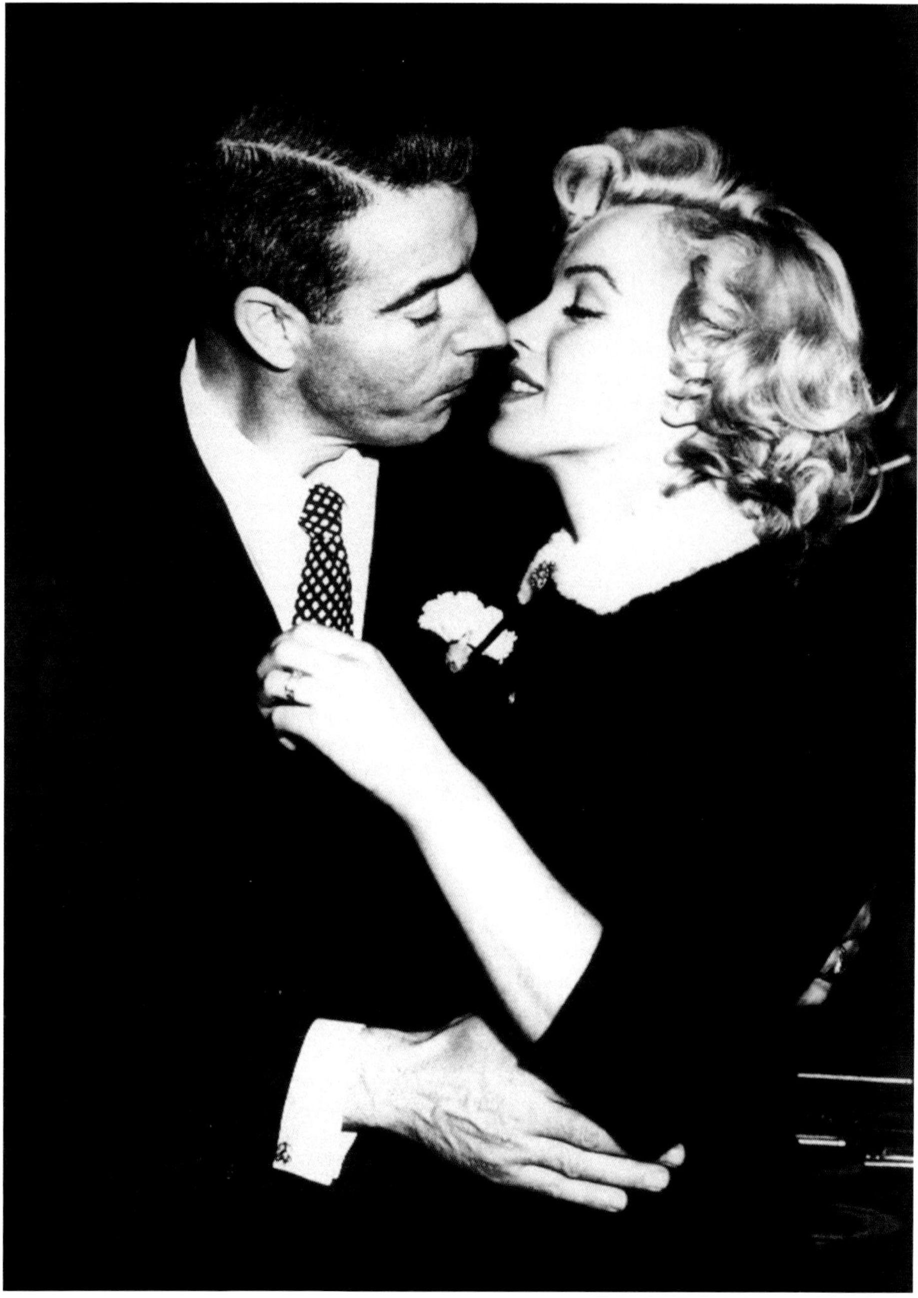

Marilyn and Joe DiMaggio shortly after getting married, 1954

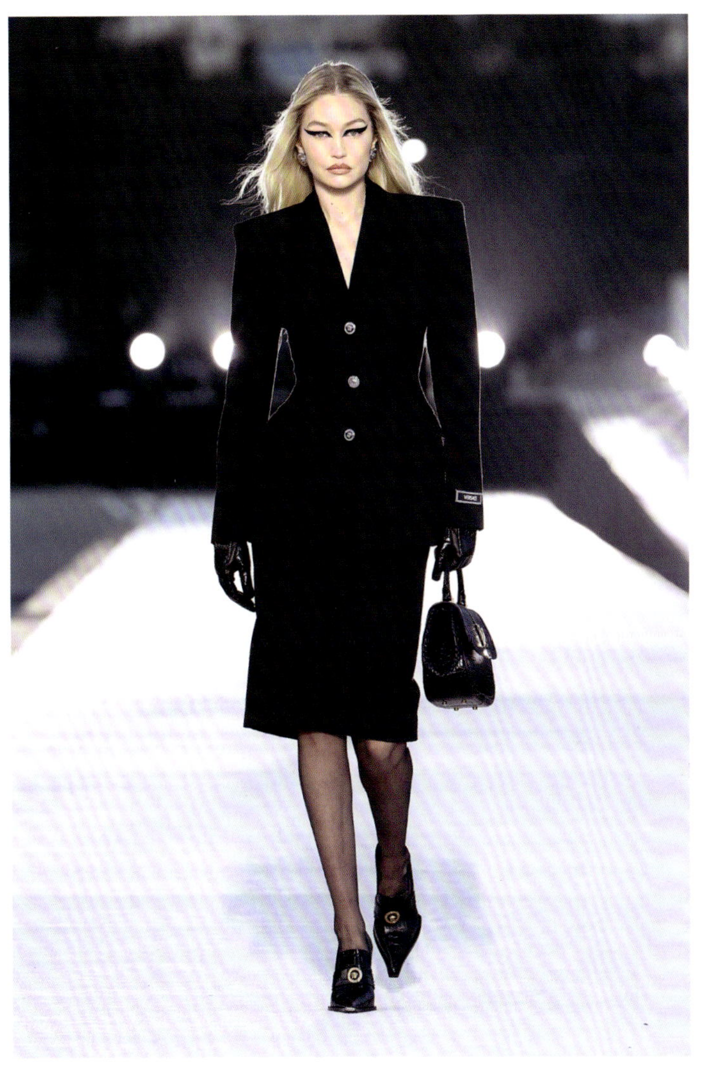

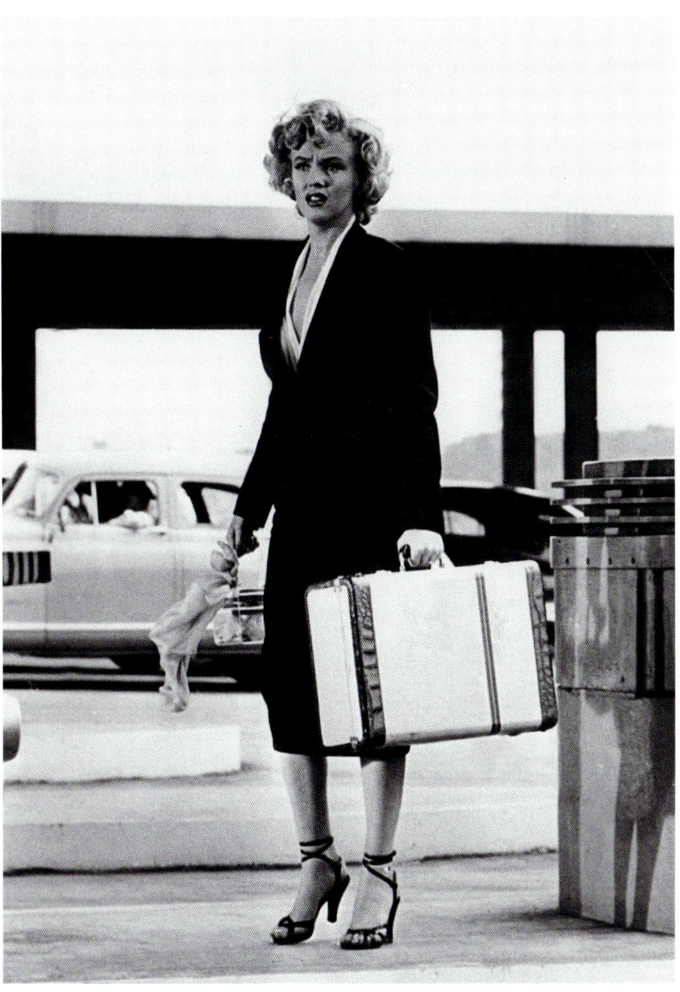

Gigi Hadid walks the catwalk for the Versace FW23 Show in West Hollywood, wearing a Marilyn-inspired suit, 2023

Marilyn wears the suit she wore to Johnny Hyde's funeral on the set of *Niagara*, 1953

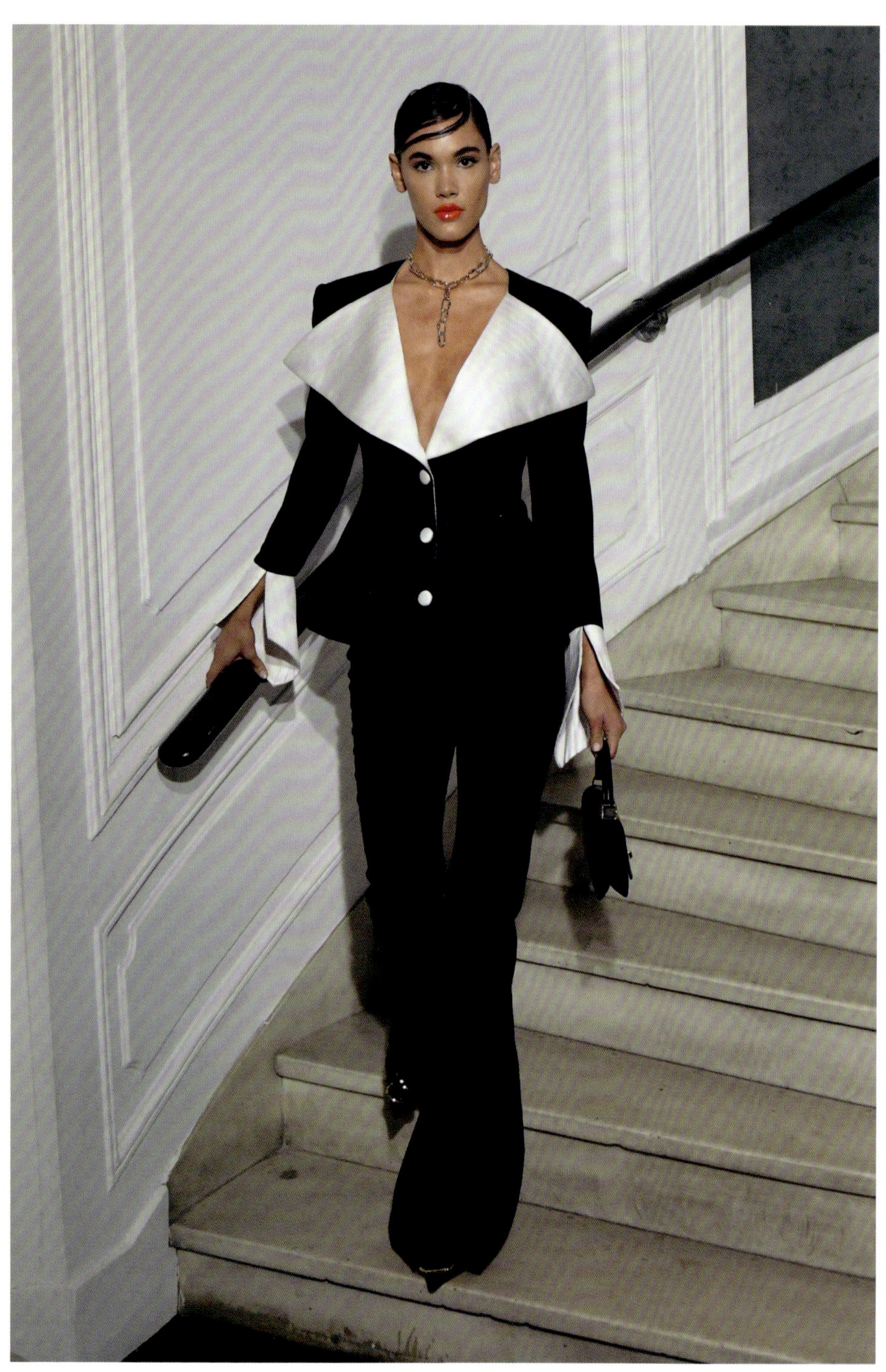

Above: A model at the Spring 2023 fashion show in New York, showcasing a Christian Siriano outfit inspired by the suit Marilyn wore in *Gentlemen Prefer Blondes* (1953)

Right: Marilyn posing for a costume test photo ahead of filming *Gentlemen Prefer Blondes*, 1953

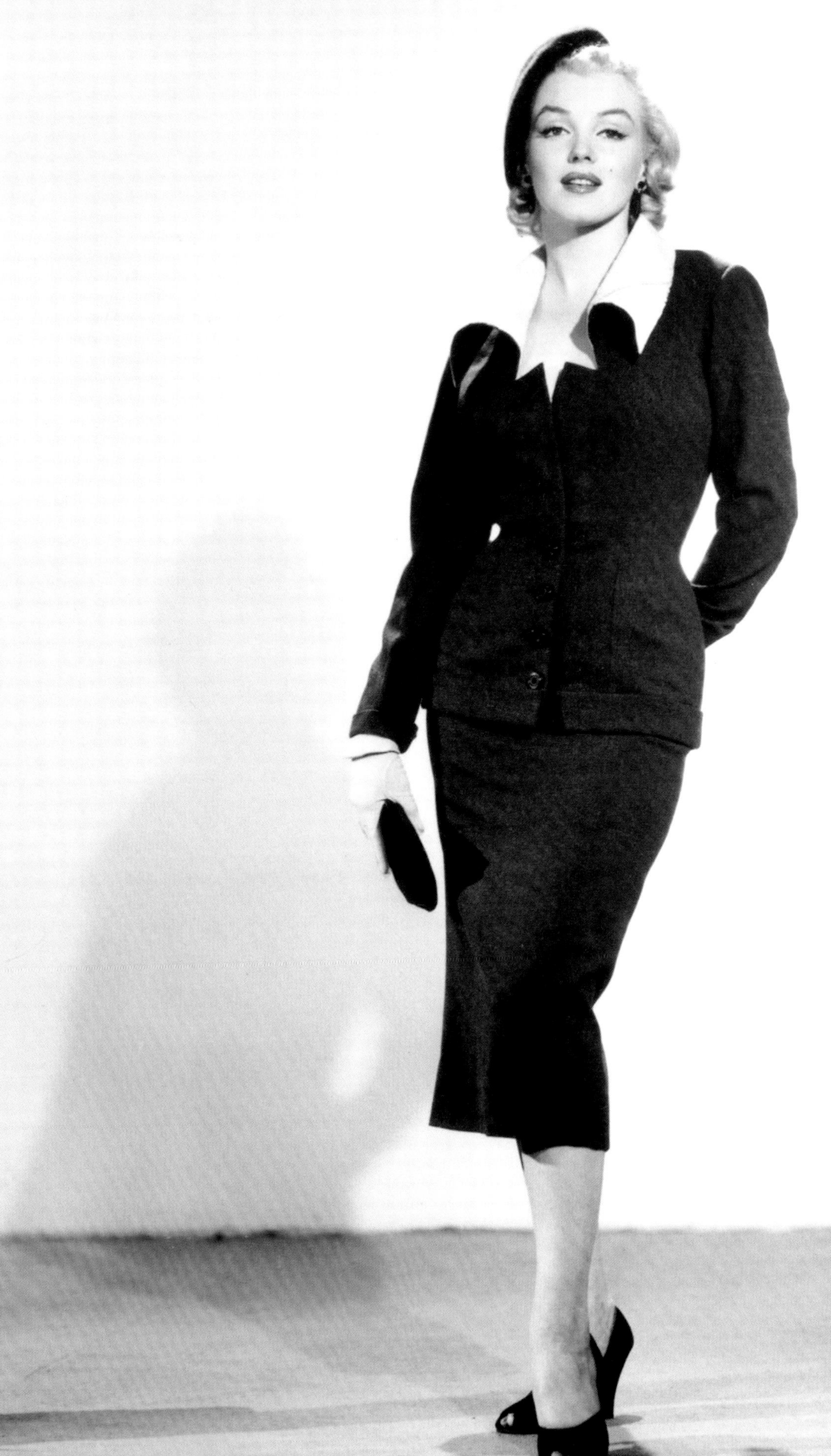

KS-A-698
ILYN MONROE
ORELEI
12
S MONTAGE
3
HOTEL
BBY 64,66
ANAGER'S
E 65
ABARET
67
AXI 68
TRAVILLA
31/52

ACCESSORIES

'SOMETIMES WEARING A SCARF AND A POLO COAT
AND NO MAKEUP AND WITH A CERTAIN ATTITUDE
OF WALKING, I GO SHOPPING [...]'

– Marilyn Monroe, quoted in Meryman, 2007

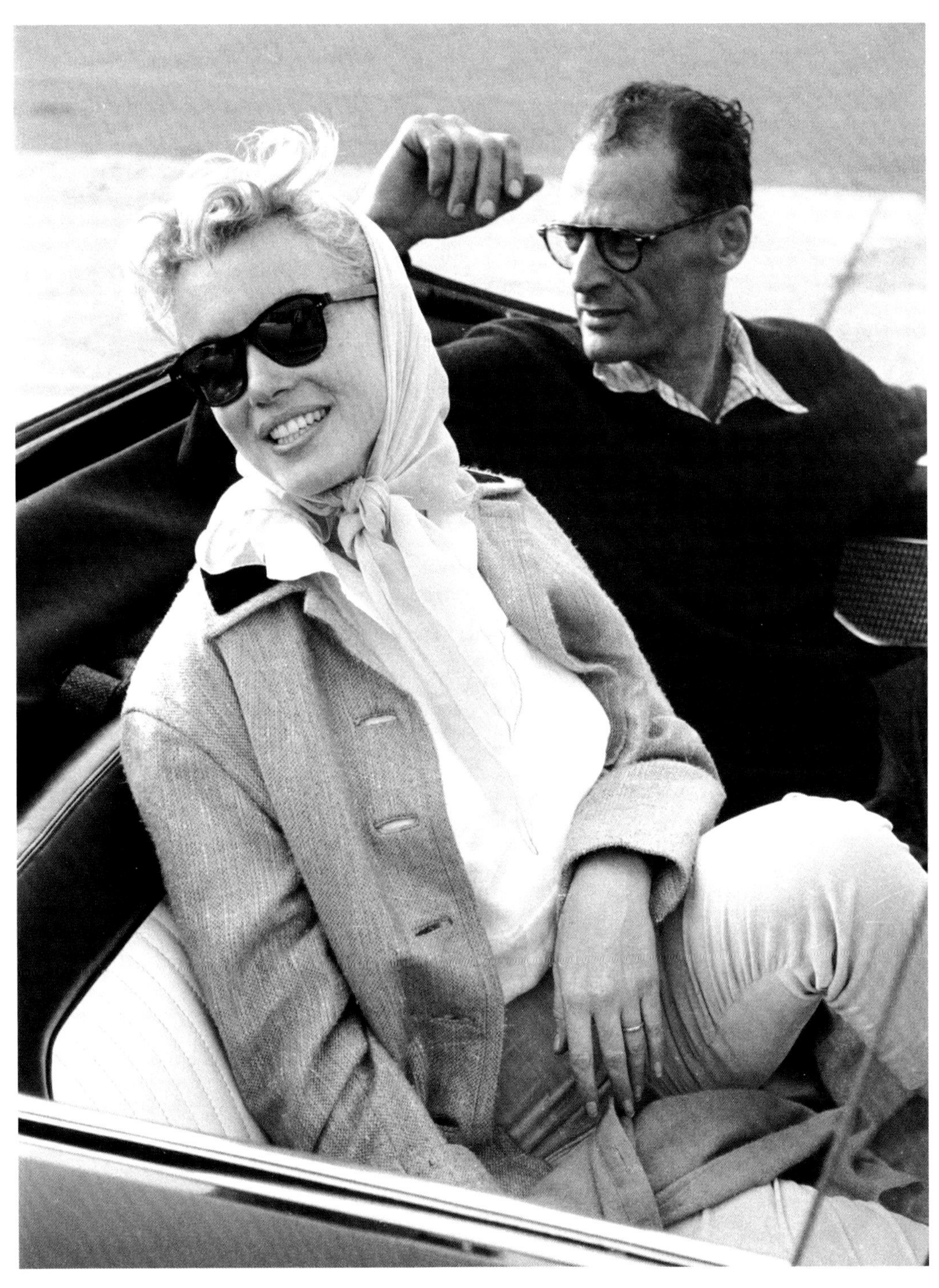

Marilyn looks relaxed and glamorous as she sits in a Thunderbird
with her newly wed husband, Arthur Miller, 1956

A FASHIONABLY formal 1950s outfit was unfinished without a hat and Marilyn wore them as a matter of course: they weren't left for special occasions, but a wide variety donned every day. From berets and pillboxes in Monroe's 1953 film *Gentlemen Prefer Blondes* to close-cropped black satin skullcaps and chic netted saucers in *There's No Business Like Show Business* (1954), iconic hats completed many of her character outfits. Off-screen, as a casual alternative, she liked to wear headscarves tied loosely under the chin. Accessorised with sunglasses, they offered a definitive Hollywood incognito look that was both dashing and debonair. A scarf also helped cover Monroe's hair when brunette roots started peeking through – she reportedly had it dyed every three weeks to keep it in top condition and had a hairdresser on call. For the beach, she owned sandals, handbags, and fashionable boaters made of straw: one in natural and black, and another trimmed with flowers.

A May 1956 *Vogue* editorial featured Bill Cunningham's 'William J.' straw bonnets as a 'witty and wise' choice for a trip to the seaside – and Monroe was a fan. A top milliner who made fashion just a little more thrilling with his striking designs, Cunningham would go on to make an even bigger name for himself as a celebrity and street-fashion photographer. When it came to glasses, Marilyn favoured a pair of Dorr Beverly Hills sunglasses, and although she was rarely seen wearing her prescription spectacles, her unforgettable portrayal of Pola Debevoise wearing cat's-eye glasses in the 1953 film *How to Marry a Millionaire* set the bar for librarian chic from that moment on.

The finesse of a fine accessory could not be understated in the 1950s and Marilyn owned a whole wardrobe of gloves in a rainbow of colours and a variety of fabrics, from crochet and velvet to nylon and leather. Her opera gloves were fabulously camp and helped add maximum charge to evening wear.

When it came to jewellery, whether she wore pieces that cost thousands of dollars or something far more modest, Marilyn made everything sparkle. When she sang 'Diamonds Are a Girl's Best Friend' in *Gentlemen Prefer Blondes* (1953), the jewels she twirled in her pink-satin gloved hands were only rhinestones, but they glittered just as exquisitely as genuine diamonds. Monroe's performance was equally full of nuance, as she sang the song satirically, with a humour and magnetism that has gone down in history as one of Hollywood's most absolutely fabulous moments. Off-camera, Monroe had a glittering selection of paste jewels, including pretty star hairclips and crystal necklaces. These were the accessories she reached for when going to parties and premieres and what she wore when she hoped to sparkle the most.

A treasured timepiece that Marilyn owned was by Blancpain, the Swiss luxury watchmaker, bought in 1932 by trusted company member Betty

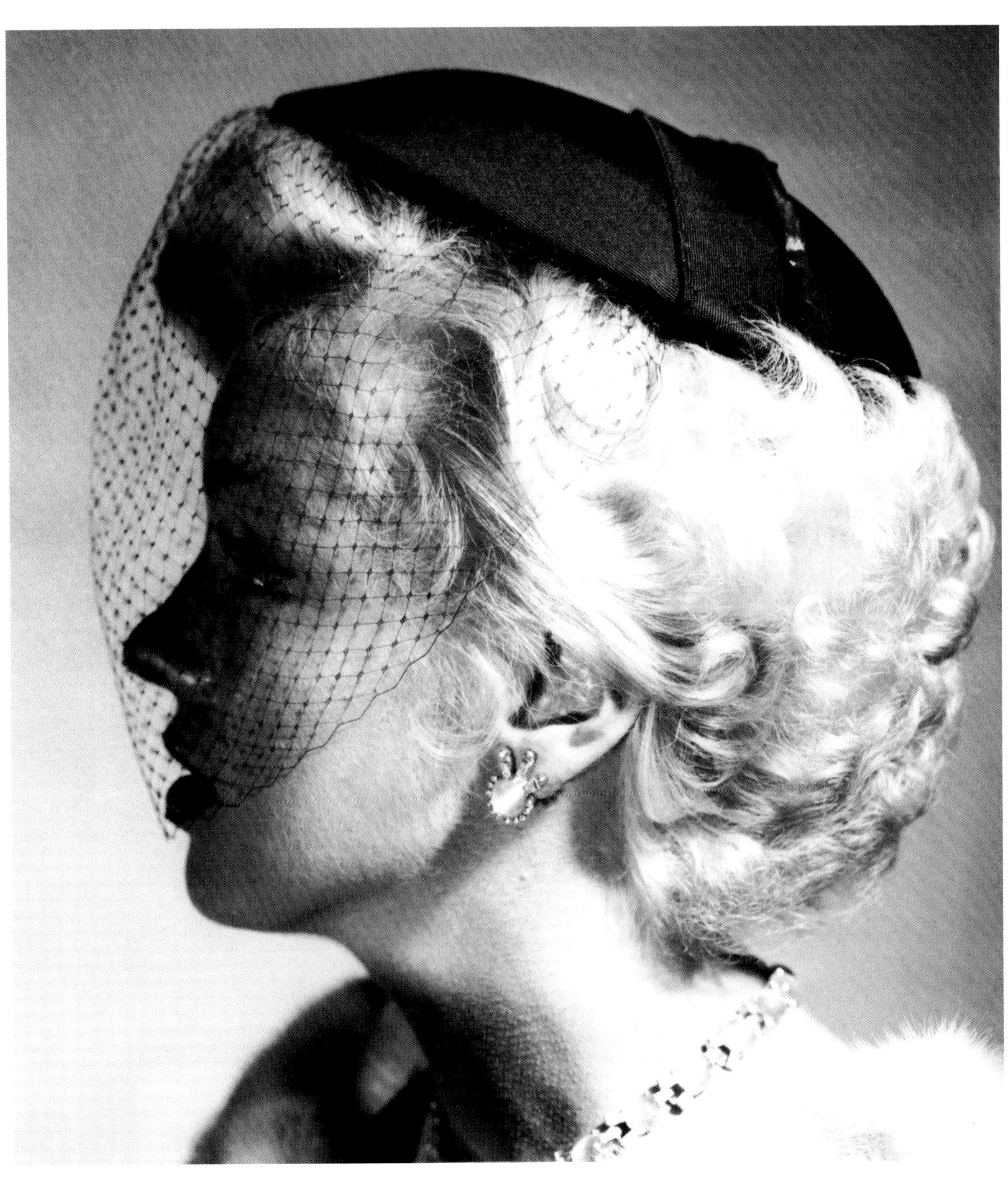

Marilyn poses for a photo test for costume hat and make-up ahead of the film
There's No Business Like Show Business, 1954

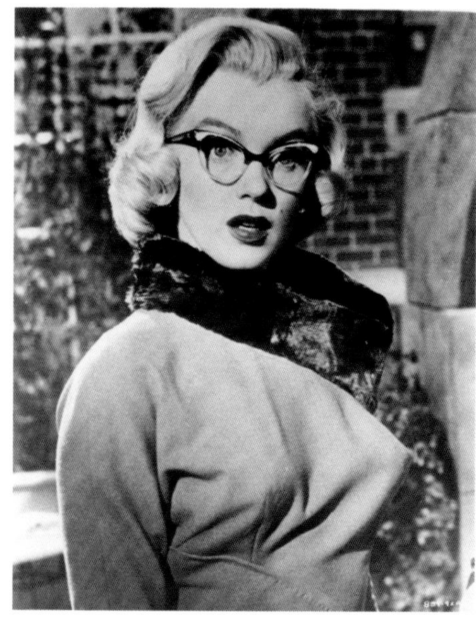

Fiechter. The first female owner of a leading watch company, Fiechter oversaw the development of some of Blancpain's most profitable creations, which prioritised women's designs and established a line of elegant art deco-inspired wristwatches that Marilyn loved. Other small items found in her jewellery case, such as a Star of David gold pendant and an unusual coral pendant, feel equally evocatively personal.

In 1954, Monroe wore a stunning pair of diamanté chandelier earrings for the Photoplay Awards ceremony where she picked up the award for the most popular film actress of 1953. Following her wedding to Joe DiMaggio that same year, he bought her a platinum eternity band with 35 baguette-cut diamonds. Among her faux-pearl necklaces was a string of 44 Akoya pearls – a gift from DiMaggio while they were on honeymoon in 1954. Monroe would wear this again in court during the couple's divorce proceedings later that year in October.

The break-up would lead Monroe to live in New York and Connecticut with the photographer Milton Greene and his wife Amy, who made it her job to teach Marilyn about the world of fashion.

Famously, Monroe will be forever associated with Salvatore Ferragamo heels, but Amy also introduced her to the Rome-based handmade footwear brand Dal Co', after she spotted Ava Gardner wearing shoes by this designer. Greene, like Monroe, believed in buying in multiples and reportedly splashed out on 25 pairs of shoes for her friend.

Marilyn would also shop locally when in LA for inexpensive footwear. The strappy gold sandals that she famously wore in 1954 to sing to the troops in South Korea, were from The French Room, a fashion-forward collection made by Chandlers, who had shops on Hollywood, Wiltshire, and Westwood Boulevards. A pair of white fox-fur plexiglass slippers she owned were made by Juel Park, the Beverly Hills lingerie designer who created underpinnings and boudoir-wear for Hollywood royalty. Fittingly enough, Delman of New York and Paris who, according to the Metropolitan Museum of Art, was 'the great showman of the New York footwear industry', also made shoes for Marilyn. A pair of white satin pumps had their soles embossed in gold with the words 'Especially for Marilyn Miller' – heels she wore while married to her third husband Arthur.

Right: Marilyn wearing her treasured 1930s platinum cocktail Blancpain watch, set with 71 round-cut and two marquise-cut white diamonds, 1952

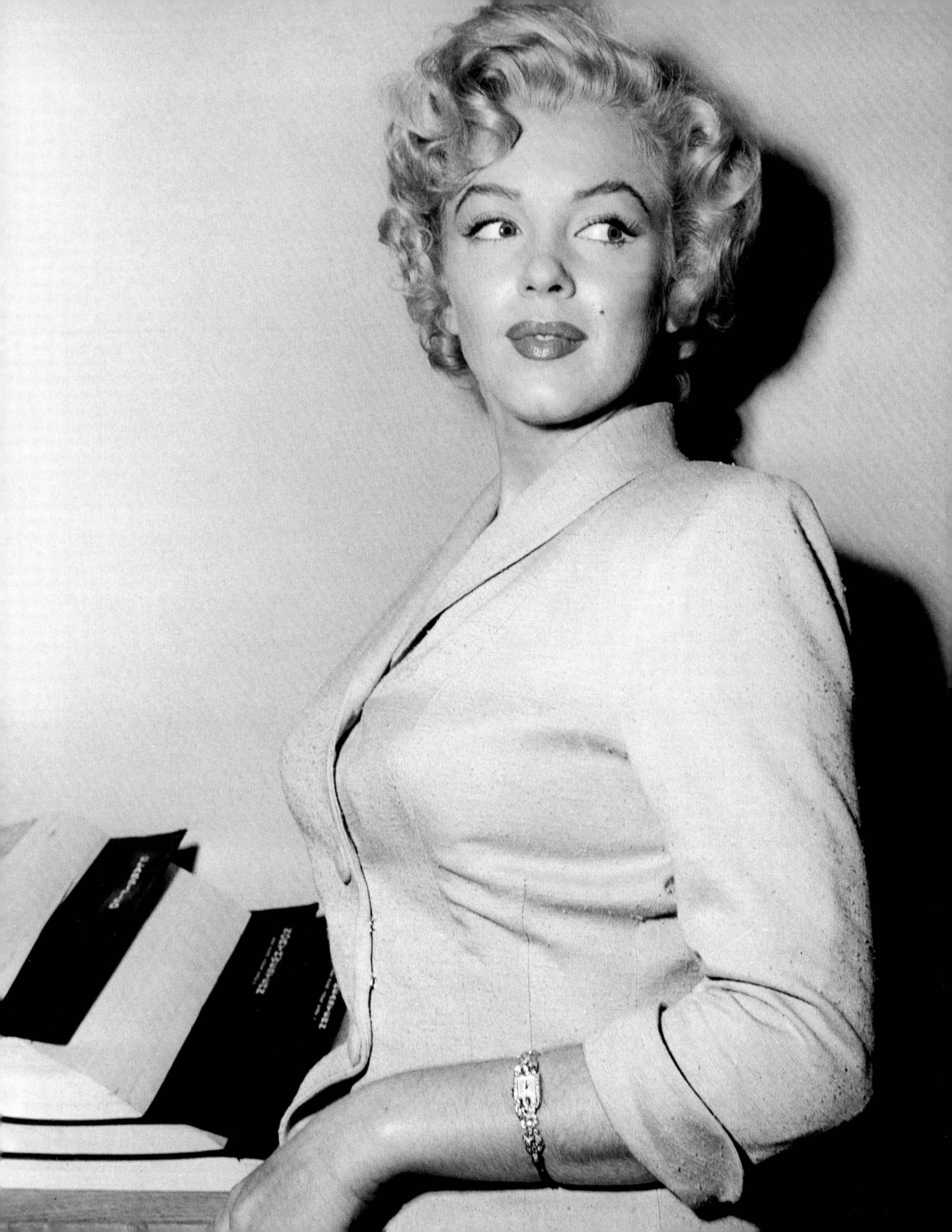

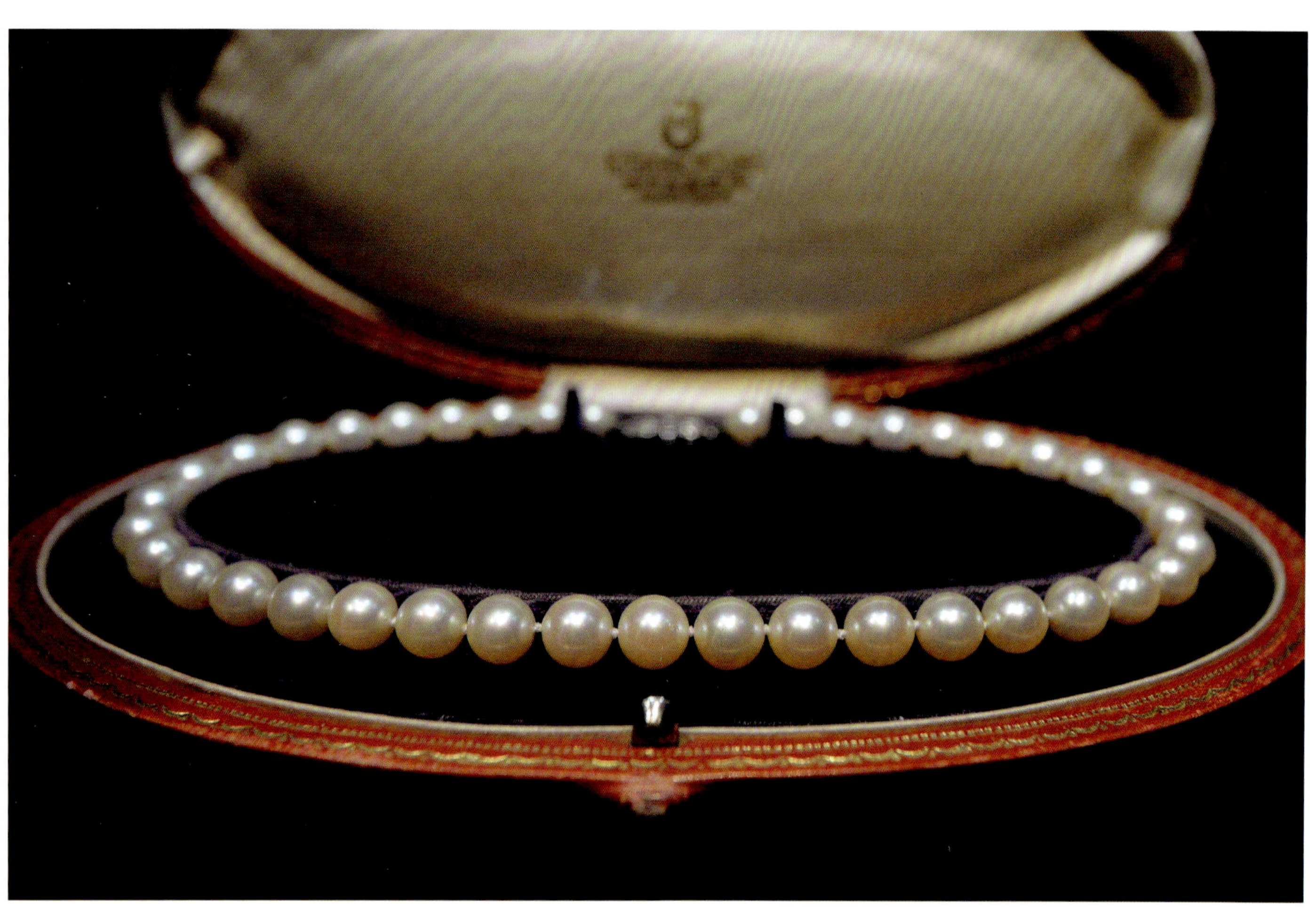

Above: Marilyn's string of Akoya pearls, a gift from Joe DiMaggio, her second husband, in 1954

Right: Marilyn in *Gentlemen Prefer Blondes*, 1953

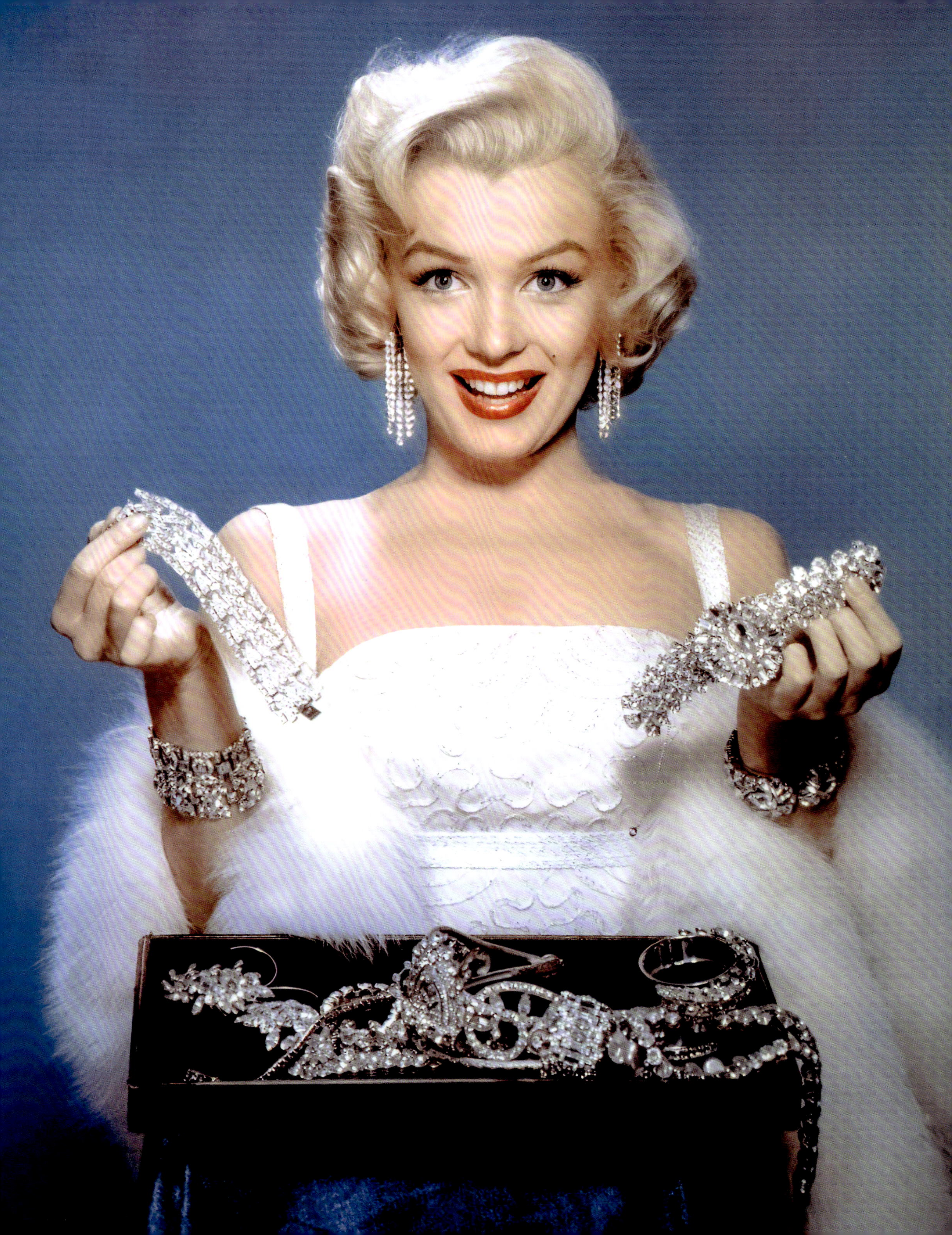

'I BELIEVE YOUR BODY SHOULD MAKE YOUR CLOTHES LOOK GOOD – INSTEAD OF MAKING THE BODY CONFORM TO WHAT IS CONSIDERED FASHIONABLE AT THE MOMENT.'

– Marilyn Monroe, *Movieland Magazine*, 1952

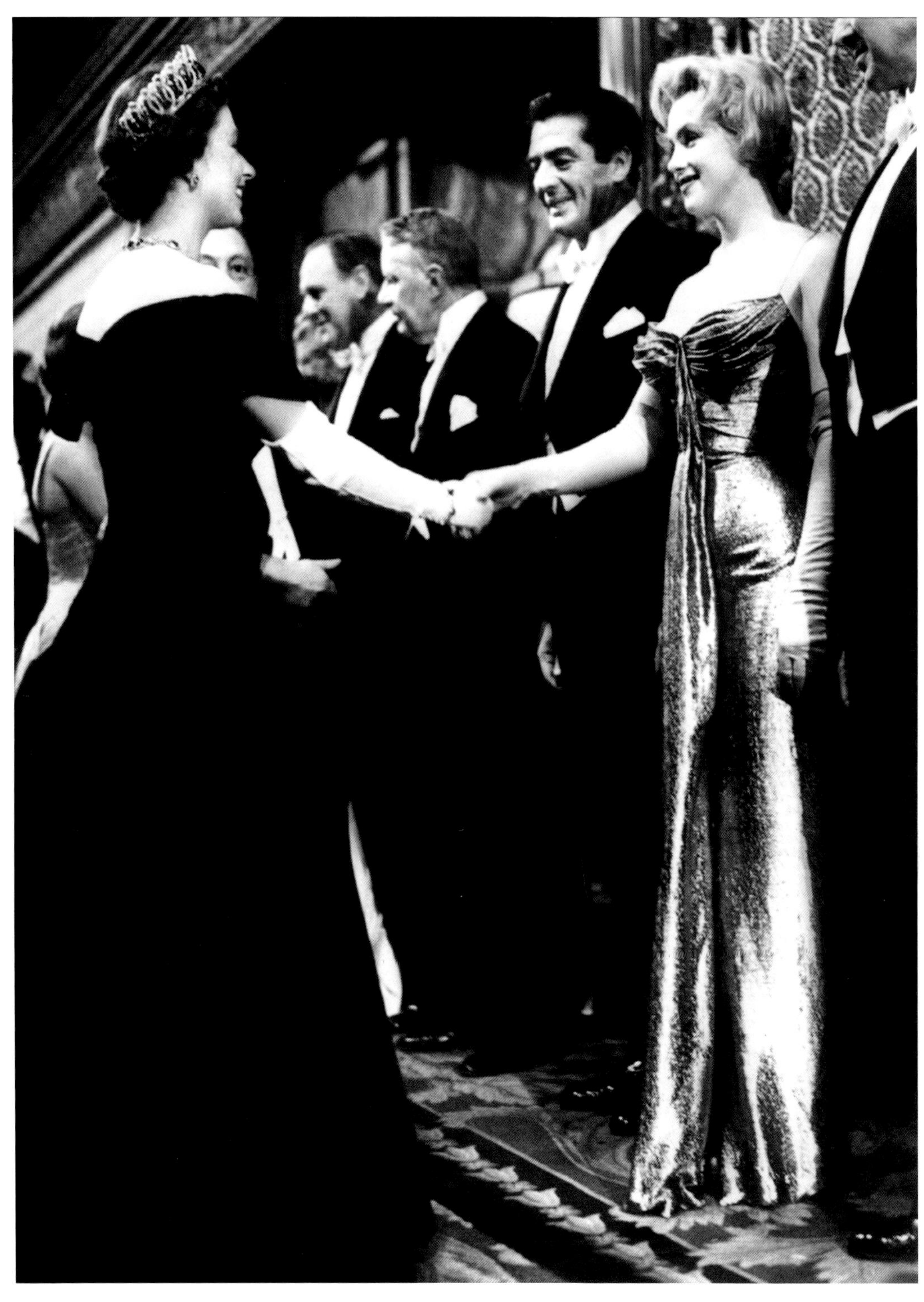

Marilyn meets Queen Elizabeth II at the Royal Command Performance at the Empire Theatre
in London, looking stunning in a gold lamé gown, 1956

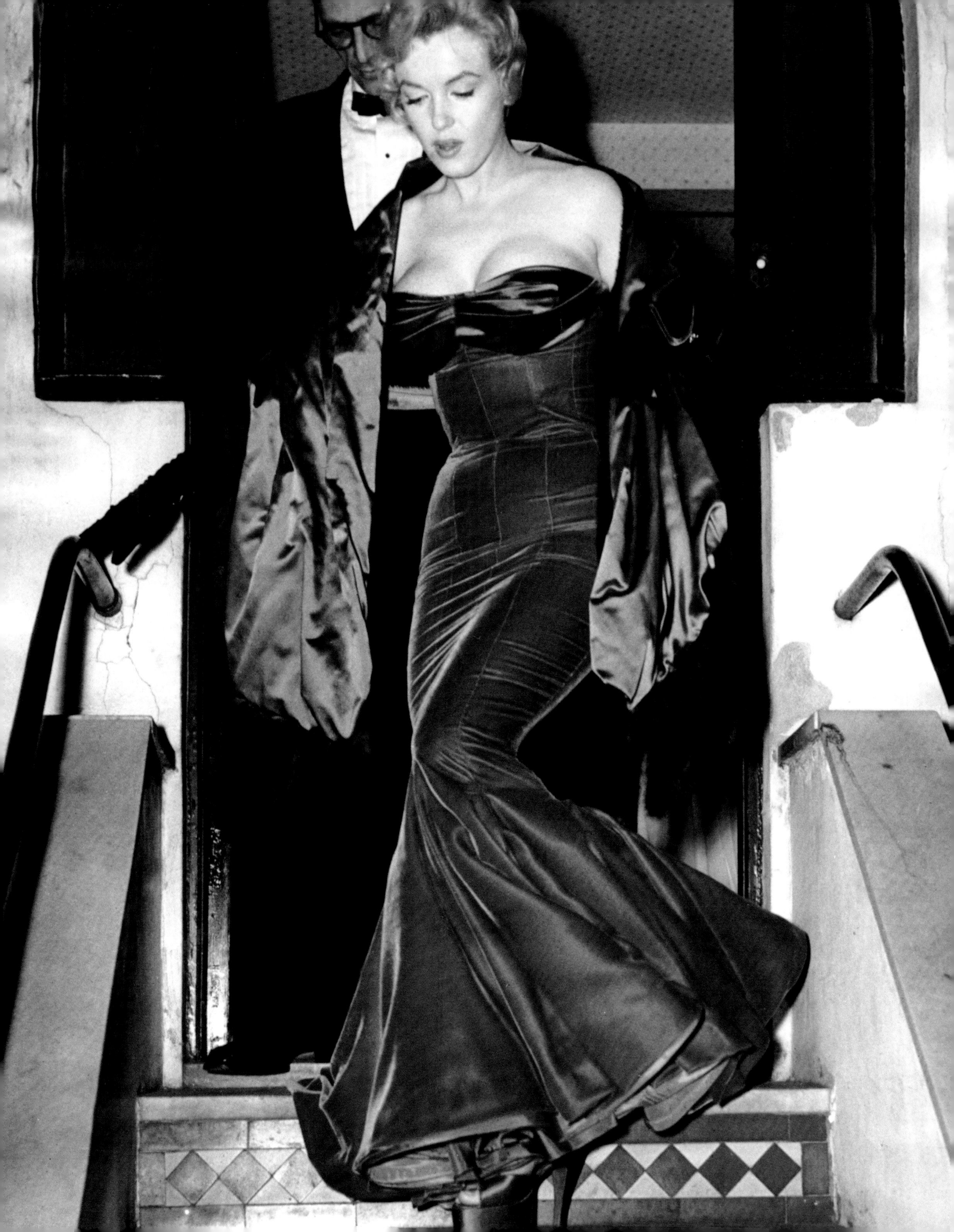

ACCORDING TO Arthur Miller, his first impression of his wife-to-be was that she was 'almost ludicrously provocative', wearing a dress that was 'blatantly tight, declaring rather than insinuating that she had brought her body along and that it was the best one in the room' (quoted in Bigsby, 2009). Marilyn's evening wear came in many shapes and sizes but ultimately all were designed with a singular aim: to show off her body. Back when she was first enrolled at the Blue Book Modeling Agency, there was only one issue with her modelling career. Monroe recalled that 'the problem, if you can call it that, was my figure. Miss Snively said nobody was paying attention to the clothes because my dresses or blouses or bathing suits were too tight. In other words, they were looking at me, and to hell with the clothes' (quoted in Spoto, 1993). However, when Marilyn was on duty, meeting her public or promoting herself at Hollywood parties, she chose her outfits with exactitude. She would always wear what would most beneficially advance her career and get her noticed. From mermaid silhouettes to luxuriously voluptuous slip dresses, Monroe's iconography is forever connected with the most va-va-voom gowns of the 1950s and '60s.

While in many ways Marilyn functioned outside of the fashion system and wore what suited her purpose rather than following trends, the evening wear she chose reflects the decades' ideologies of female roles in society. Objectifying women was par for the course, and gender divisions strictly binary. To succeed in Hollywood, Monroe had assumed the role of showgirl, and it was a part she played for a great deal of her life, both onscreen and off, to international and eternal applause. She was ultimately her own construct and quickly learned that the clothes she wore announced she meant business.

Marilyn's 'lucky dress' was the black-and-red strapless gown she wore to attend the *Photoplay* Awards on 11 February 1952; the following year she would be given the honour of 'fastest rising star'. It seems that Marilyn knew exactly what a shrewd investment the dress had been: 'As soon as I could afford an evening gown, I bought the loudest I could find. It was a bright-red, low-cut gown and it infuriated half the women in the room because it was so immodest. I was sorry in a way to do this, but I had a long way to go, and I needed a lot of advertising to get there' (quoted in Banner, 2012). It was expensive and, according to one of her biographers, she bought it from the department store I. Magnin, where she opened up one of her first charge accounts and where Dorothy Jeakins, who would go on to become one of Monroe's wardrobe stylists, had once worked. Monroe was drawn to the frock's fishtail shape and would later enlist the American designer John Moore to create another in the same style, this time in red lace with a sweetheart bustier neckline. She would wear it over again throughout the '50s.

The fishtail is a silhouette that featured heavily on the pages of *Vogue*. Their September 1950 editorial from Paris details French couturier Jacques Fath's mermaid line, 'importantly in ruby satin'. The way Marilyn wore this particular design was, however, entirely different to the models in *Vogue* who were reed-thin and seemed even more bound by the corsetry involved in the shape. Monroe's physicality, with its usual styling demands, instead seemed to engulf the dress with more sensuality.

Moore was also a talented interior designer and, in 1957, he helped refurbish the New York apartment on 57th Street that Marilyn shared with Arthur Miller, suggesting she paint the walls white to match the piano she owned. He became a friend and would continue to create some of her most high-profile gowns, such as the one worn to the 1959 premiere of *Some Like It Hot* at Loew's Capitol Theatre. It was a white sheath, embellished with shiny bugle beads in a nod to the 1920s flapper fashion featured in the film. In the way that her wardrobe would mutate from real life to the silver screen, she also wore the shimmering plunged-backed fringed dress in the 1960 film *Let's Make Love*. During one of the film's highlights – singing 'Specialization' in a duet with Frankie Vaughan – she accessorises the dress with long lamé gloves. Marilyn adored the look and Moore made an identical one in black, which she wore in Philippe Halsman's celebrated 'jumping' portrait of her which appeared on the cover of *Life* magazine, 9 November 1959.

For her first appearance on television on *The Jack Benny Show* in September 1953, and then again in November at the premiere of *How to Marry a Millionaire*, Marilyn wore a white lace Travilla gown that she borrowed from the studio. Although by this time she was a well-known star – in June 1953 she had been invited along with Jane Russell to leave handprints at Grauman's Chinese Theatre – her finances were still relatively modest. She had been paid the weekly contract rate of $500 for an actress, while Russell had earned $200,000 in total for *Gentlemen Prefer Blondes*, even though, as Marilyn pointed out when requesting a dressing room, she was the film's blonde. The amount she had spare for dressy clothes wasn't limitless and the Travilla gown, worn twice, was returned to the wardrobe department.

Although she relied on costume designers to guide and mould her characters, she was never styled by anyone, apart from when she lived with Amy and Milton Greene on and off between 1954 and 1957 at their home in Connecticut. Amy became Monroe's supporter and, for a time, dedicated herself to revamping Marilyn's wardrobe which she considered cheap and tacky. The result was a newly sophisticated Marilyn who, equipped with more understated designer pieces, embarked on a fashion phase more to Amy's liking.

Black slips and cocktail dresses replaced the statement dresses of Monroe's early years. The clothes she wore while living in New York and with the Greenes coincided with a time in her career when she was beginning to take more control – founding her production company with Milton and renegotiating contracts. It also felt in tune with her New York persona. She wore an elegant, plain-black slip to the December 1955 premiere of *The Rose Tattoo*. The minimal silhouette spoke to Monroe's more confident poise, although from time to time she would instinctively revert to what she knew worked best for her when she needed to dazzle: low-cut, skin-tight and ultra-sensual. In October 1956, when she met Queen Elizabeth II at the Royal Command Performance at the Empire Theatre, she thrilled in a body-hugging gold lamé gown with the lowest possible cleavage and cantilevered to its best possible advantage, despite the dress code dictating modesty. The outfit hit headlines around the world.

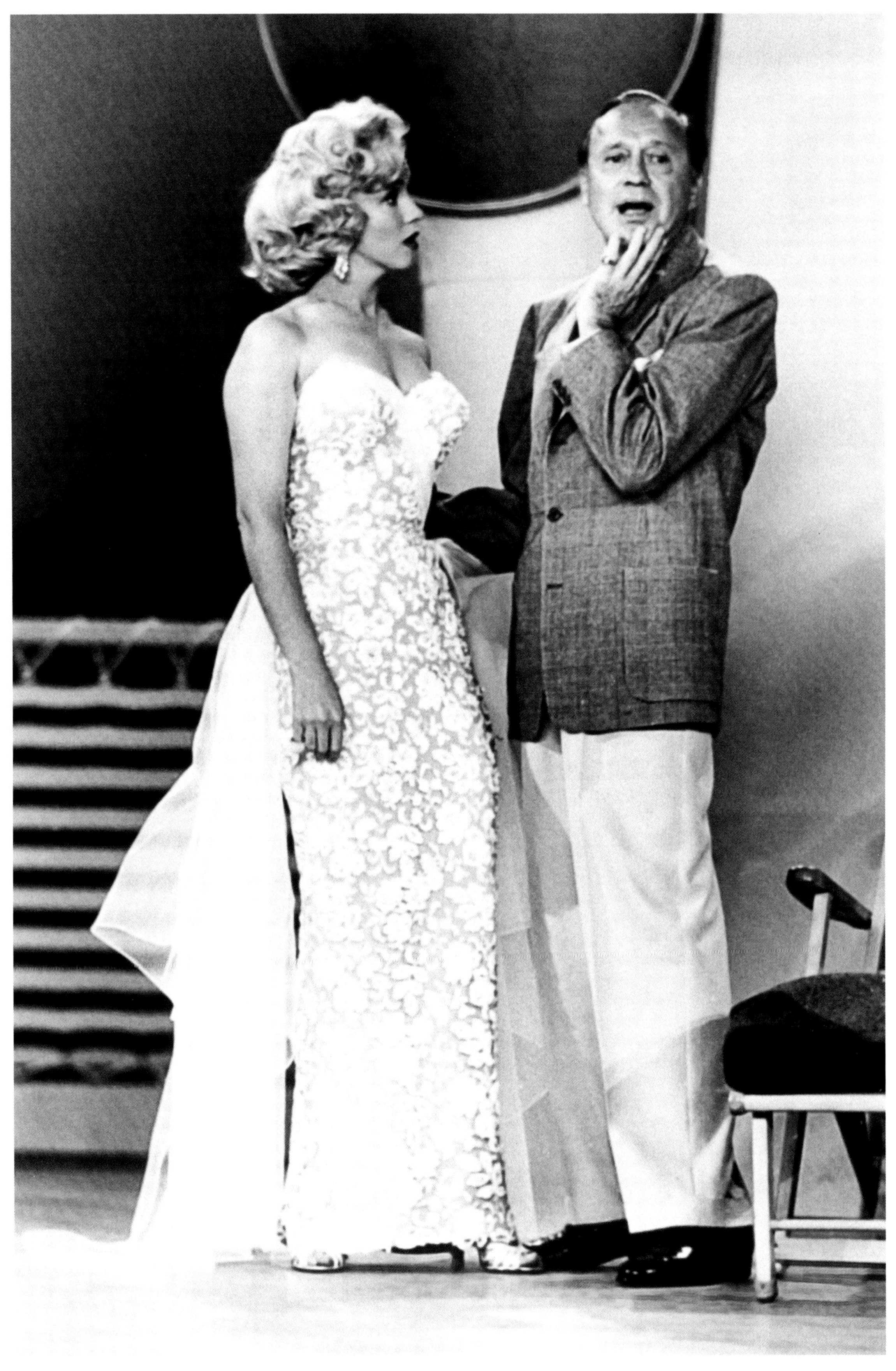

Marilyn with Jack Benny, shimmering in a bugle bead dress on *The Jack Benny Show*, 1953

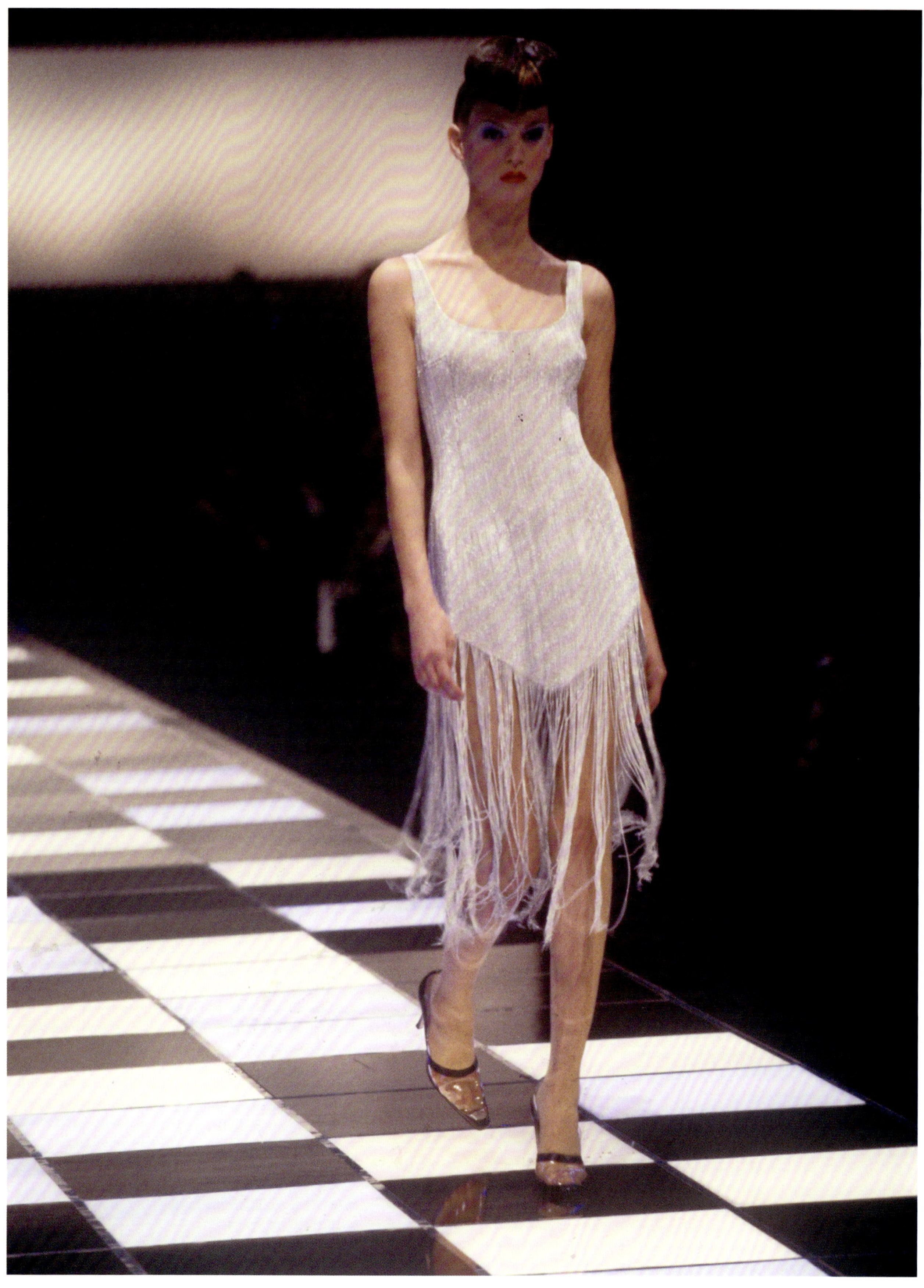

A model walks down the catwalk at the Givenchy Autumn/Winter 1998 show in Paris
in a beaded slip dress with fringe hemline, designed by Alexander McQueen,
reminiscent of Marilyn's beaded fringe dress in *Let's Make Love* (1960)

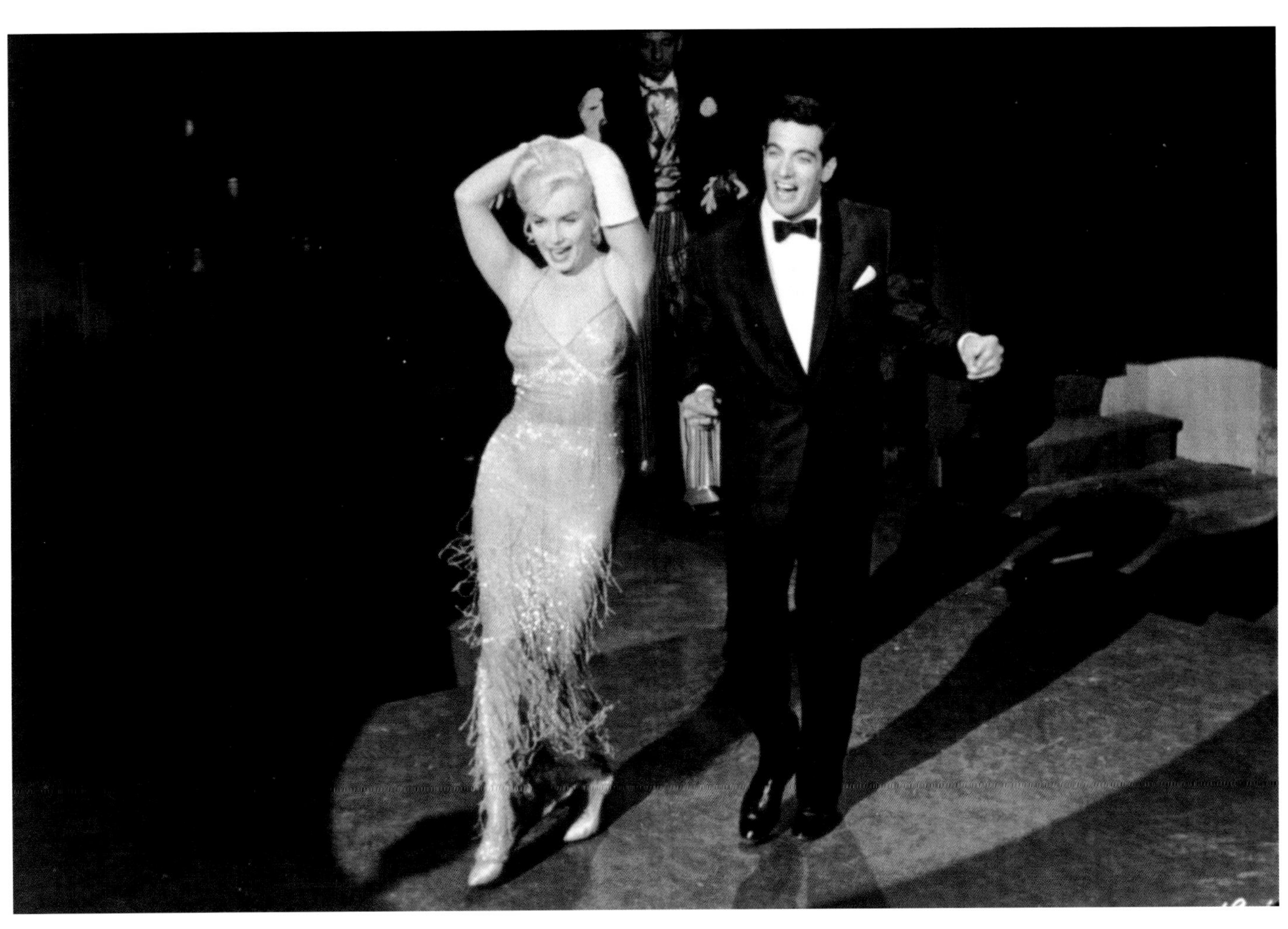

Marilyn wearing a shimmery beaded dress with fringed hem on the set of
Let's Make Love (1960) with Frankie Vaughan

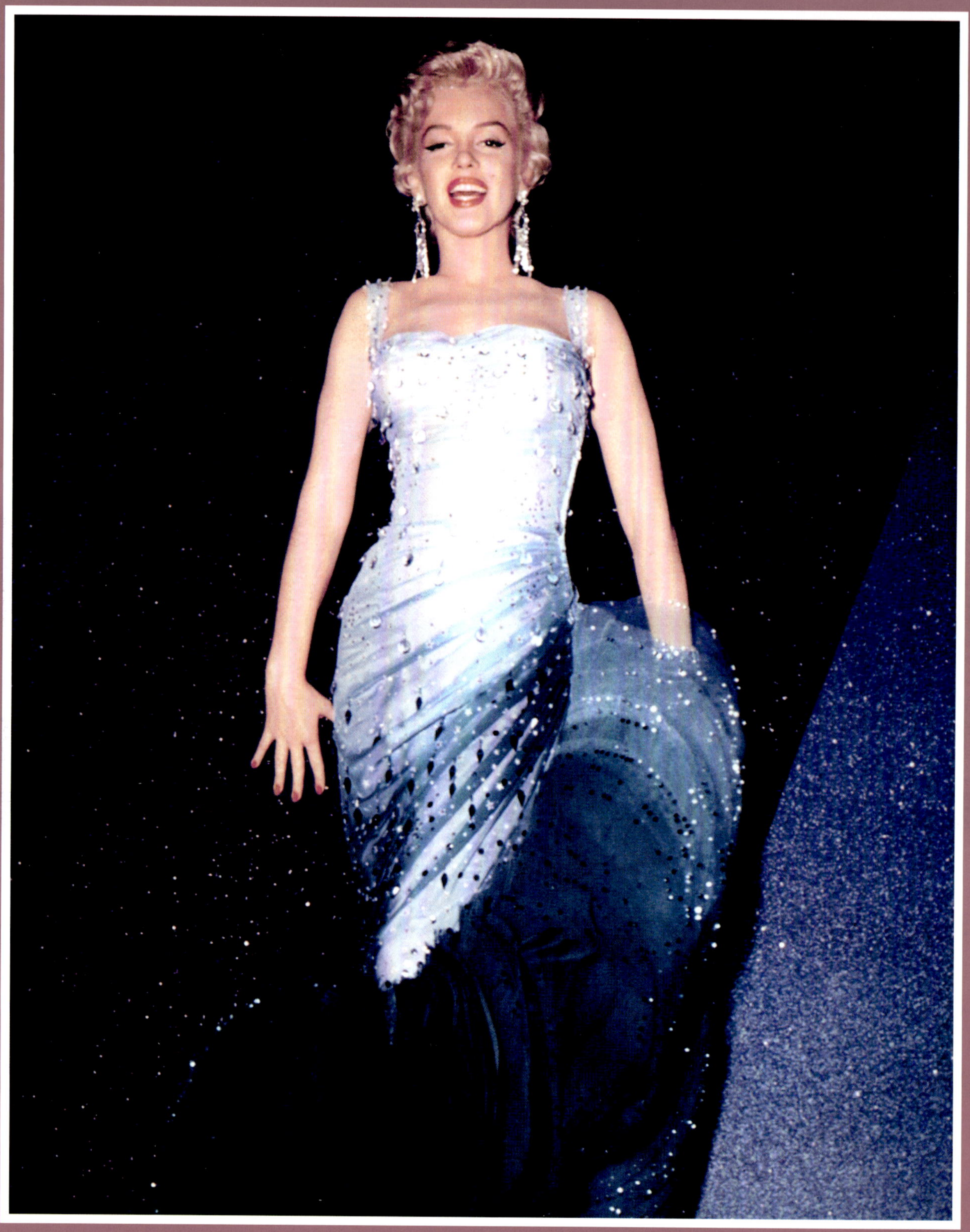

MARILYN
AND THE DESIGNERS
SHE WORE

Much of Marilyn's wardrobe was bespoke, created for the films she starred in, and she would habitually wear favourite pieces to parties and premieres. Travilla, Orry-Kelly and Jean Louis were just some of the names that are synonymous with Marilyn's look, but she supplemented what she borrowed with a sharp selection of high-profile designer wear, too. She was a savvy stylist, wearing white blouses by Gucci, silky Pucci separates, coats by Claire McCardell, footwear by Ferragamo, dresses by Ciel Chapman, Anne Klein, Pauline Trigère and George Nardiello, as well as modish Rudi Gernreich casual coordinates designed for Walter Bass, alongside Jeanne Lanvin couture and James Galanos. Although Monroe appeared on countless consumer magazine covers, she wasn't taken very seriously by haughty high-fashion journals. In 1954, *Harper's Bazaar* published publicity images of Monroe and the director of *The Seven Year Itch*, Billy Wilder, taken by photographer Richard Avedon. The derisive caption which ran alongside, however, is less than complimentary, highlighting Wilder as 'one in the long line of skilful illusionists who have

helped a calendar pin-up girl parlay her own not inconsiderable resources into the image of the All-American Good Time Girl' (Gefter, 2020).

Later in 1956, Cecil Beaton shot Marilyn for *Harper's Bazaar*, too, and, while he was charmed by her, she was not like the aristocratic mannequins he was used to meeting. He later reflected, 'if this star is an abandoned sprite, she touchingly looks to her audience for approval. She is strikingly like an over-excited child asked downstairs after tea. The initial shyness over, excitement has now got the better of her. She romps, she squeals with delight, she leaps on to the sofa. She puts a flower stem in her mouth, puffing on a daisy as though it were a cigarette. It is an artless, impromptu, high-spirited, infectiously gay performance. It will probably end in tears' (Beaton, 2014).

While there was no arguing that Marilyn was a star and courted by Dior, who sought her custom, American *Vogue* would not request an editorial with her until Bert Stern was

Marilyn in *There's No Business Like Show Business* (1954), looking stunning in a glittering Travilla gown

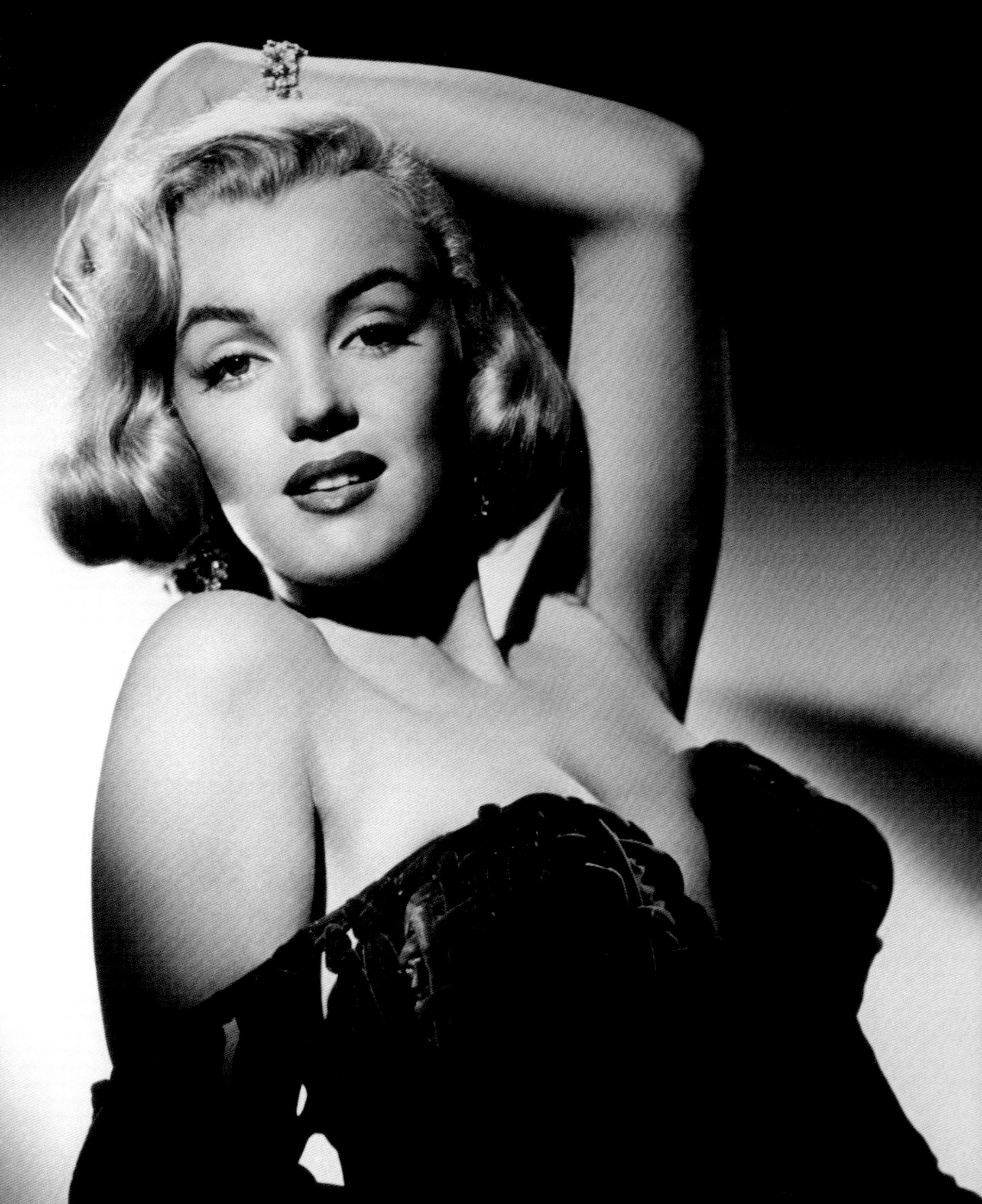

commissioned in June 1962 to undertake a
shoot that would result in the now-celebrated
Last Sitting series of images. Marilyn
instinctively spun in her own fashion orbit
and picked and mixed famous designers who
connected with her personal style schema.
To be in fashion inevitably means that at
some point you will be out of fashion. Trends
disappear and re-emerge as the cycle of
design revolves. But Monroe trod a fashion
path of her own. In January 1952 she turned to
Oleg Cassini, a well-born Parisian of Russian
descent who had studied under the French
couturier Jean Patou.

Cassini would famously dress Jackie Kennedy
when she became first lady in 1962, but
10 years earlier a young Monroe visited his
salon and selected a deep-red mermaid gown
to wear to collect the Henrietta Award for
'Best Young Box Office Personality'. It caught
press attention with journalists marvelling at
how it daringly exposed her décolleté. Monroe
was at the start of her career and knew
she needed to heighten her profile, cannily
choosing designers who helped her work a
room. American creative Ciel Chapman, whose
cocktail attire often featured in *Vogue*, was
a designer Monroe called on time after time.
In 1954, Chapman created the sparkling slip
Monroe wore when she sang to the American
troops stationed in South Korea. Following
Marilyn's death in 1962, a British Pathé news
report would reflect on how her tour had
'brought GIs beauty and vivacity that made her
an undisputed symbol in her time. As soldiers
adored her, so did men wherever in the world
her films were played and that was everywhere'

(*The Untimely Passing of Marilyn Monroe,*
1962). She donned the frock, despite the
freezing cold, and her image was sent around
the world.

Chapman knew what Monroe liked and
replicated her favourite halterneck dresses for
day- and evening wear in a variety of colours
and fabrics, some embellished, some plain.
Amy Greene introduced her to American
fashion designer Norman Norell, whose
sophisticated aesthetic looked stunning on
Marilyn. A particular favourite was a short
white Norell dress. It would come in handy for
the night Amy and Marilyn went to see Sinatra
at The Copacabana; he had sold out, but
Marilyn insisted she could get them a table.
She wore the white mink, bought for her by
Milton Greene, over the Norell dress. When
the maître d' saw her, he immediately rushed
to find a table for her and her friends.

Norell would dress Monroe at pivotal moments
in her life. In 1956, when she married Arthur
Miller, he created her delicate chiffon wedding
dress. Then, for the 1962 Golden Globes
where Monroe won the World Film Favourites
Award, he produced the green sequin gown
she dazzled in. This emerald floor-length
frock made a reappearance in 2022 when Kim
Kardashian wore it later in the evening after
her famous Met Ball entrance in Monroe's
Jean Louis creation. Its enduring silhouette
felt contemporary and fresh and is testament
to Norell's timeless designs. The simple
couture slip that Norrell created for Marilyn
became her signature dress for a while, and
she would ask fashion designer George

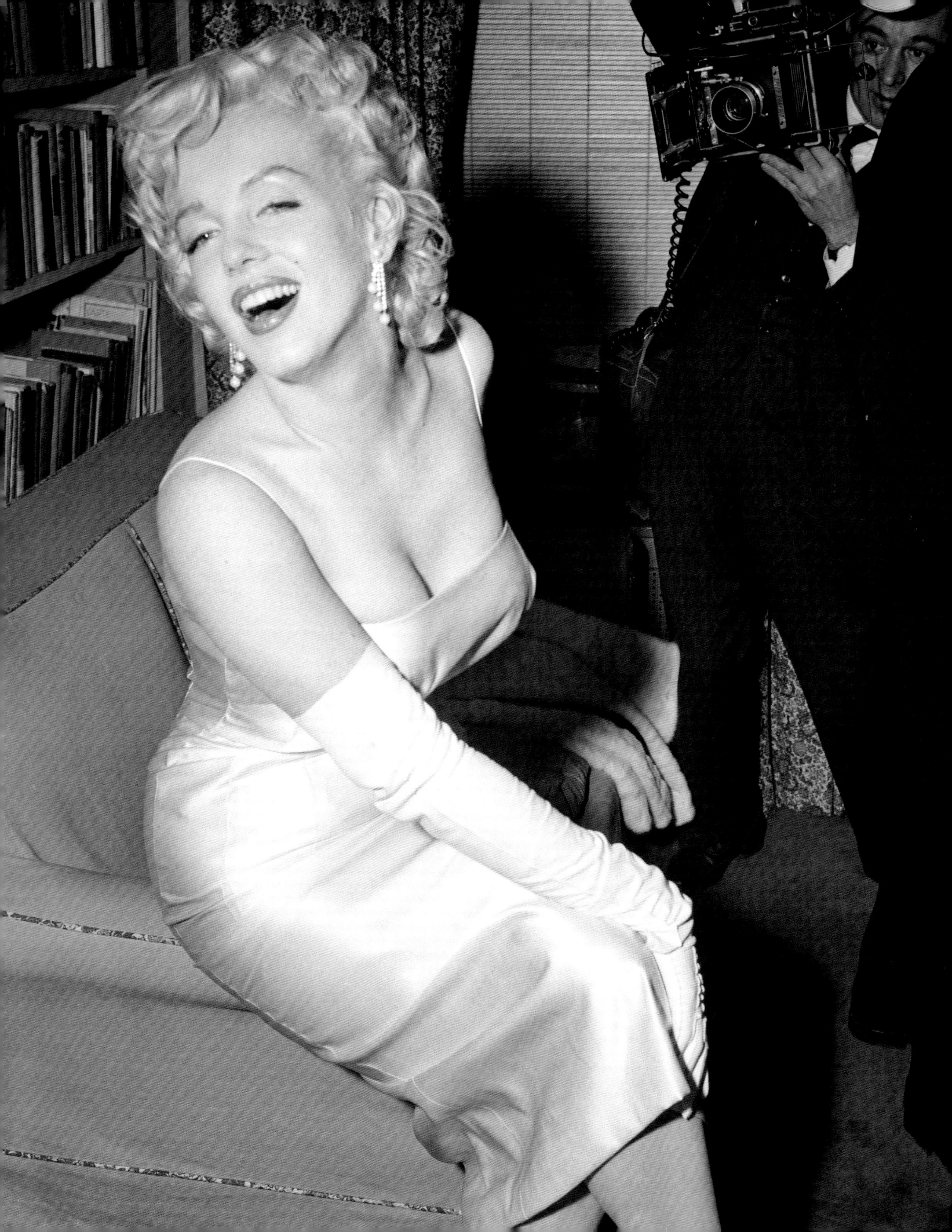

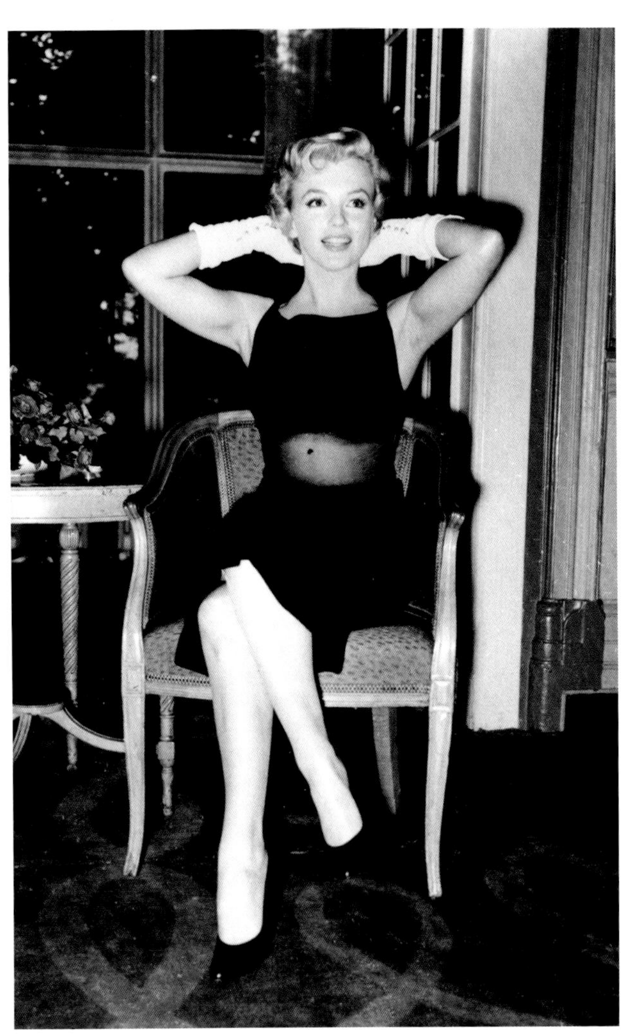

Niardello, with whom she became friends, to make her copies. Niardello is famously featured alongside Milton and Marilyn in a candid 1955 16mm film, shot by 14-year-old fan Peter Mangone, who spotted Monroe in New York airily walking down 5th Avenue, blowing kisses and laughing at the camera (Little, 2013). She is spontaneously relaxed in front of the camera, partly because that was her superpower but also because she was always confident in the clothes she had chosen to wear and she understood what they communicated. With the help of the right designers, she succeeded in turning heads wherever she went.

Above: Marilyn wearing a James Galanos dress with sheer panel, 1956

Left: Marilyn wearing a dress by Norman Norell at a cocktail party thrown by attorney Frank Delaney in New York, 1955

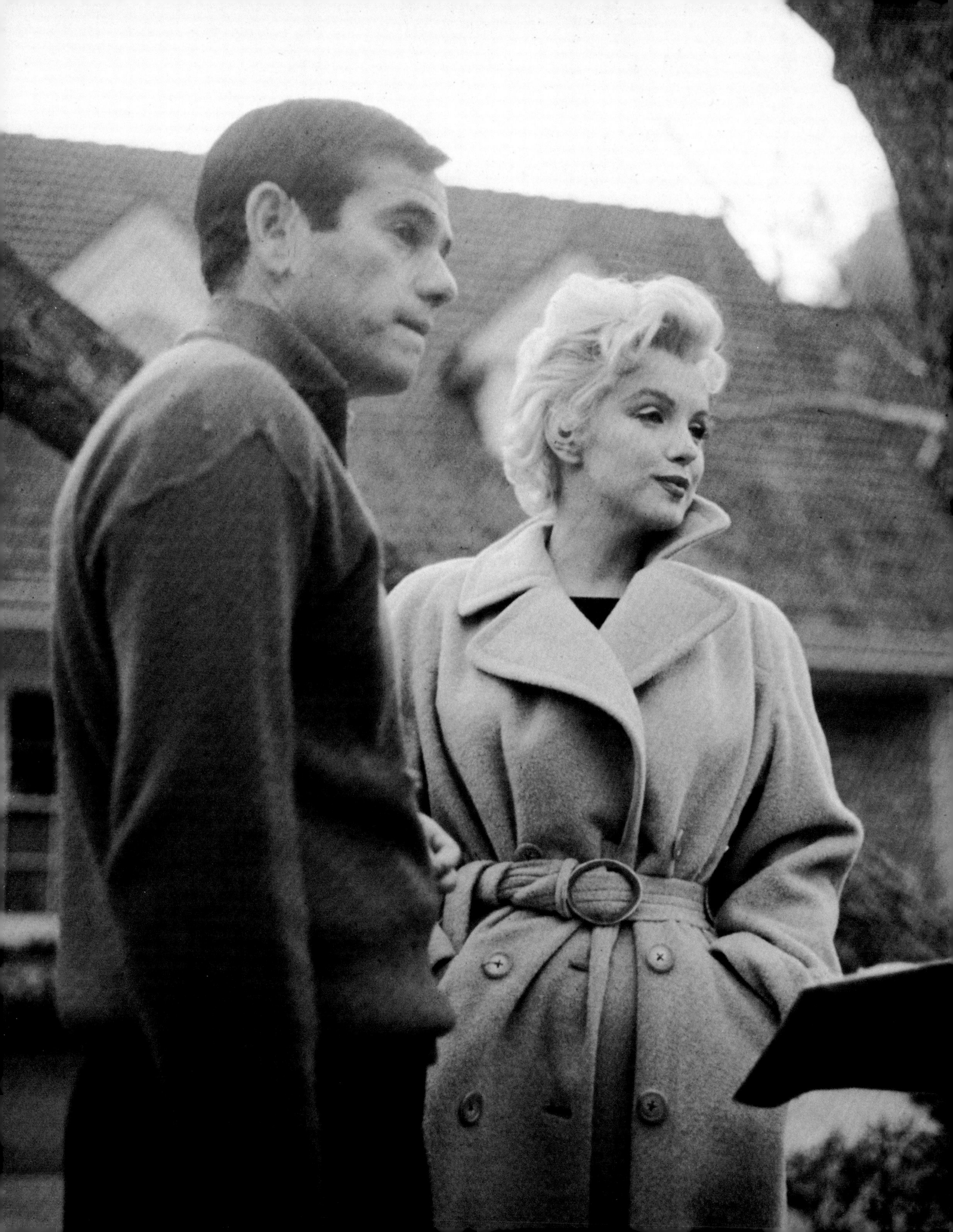

MARILYN
AND DIOR

In 1952, Marilyn Monroe confessed to *Movieland Magazine* that her favourite suit was designed by Christian Dior, the distinguished couturier. There were items in Monroe's wardrobe that she was careless of and there were those that she loved and took great care of. A blanket-like, belted, camel Dior coat she wore time and time again, most famously when photographed by Milton Greene, is one trusty example. A sales receipt, from Polly's at 480 Park Avenue where Marilyn bought it, details 'this Christian Dior coat ought to be very good for you both here and in California' (Julien's Auctions, 2016c). It cost $350, along with a black wool dinner dress charged at $290. Fashion in the '50s saw women the world over dressing in copies of Dior's structured, corseted, hourglass-shaped clothes, first shown on graceful models in the atelier's elegant Parisian drawing rooms and replicated by seamstresses all over. It was this ultra-feminine silhouette that defined the character of the era.

Marilyn was courted by Dior; in March 1958, in anticipation of a visit to Paris, the couture house sent a letter in an attempt to entice her to pay them a visit, and they wired a telegram informing her they would send design sketches. The following year, they contacted her to suggest creating gowns for the Cannes Film Festival if she were to attend. In 1962, Monroe wore Dior for *Vogue*'s September issue, photographed by

Bert Stern for part of a series that famously would become 'The Last Sitting'. Although at this point in her career Monroe was refusing all requests, Stern 'wanted to put an image on the page that would be delicious and utterly memorable'. He felt that 'the definitive picture of *her* had yet to be taken' and was determined to do so, revealing, 'Marilyn Monroe was that magic image for me, as she was for millions of other American men' (Stern, 1982).

Styled by American *Vogue*'s fashion editor Babs Simpson, the black, backless Dior dress was chosen to help distinguish the iconic image Stern eventually took. The final shot shows Marilyn looking as refined and resplendent as an English princess. Moreover, with her signature white-blonde locks swept back by the famous hairdresser Kenneth Battelle, known to his friends and clients simply as Mr Kenneth, Monroe appears insouciant and blasé of the high-profile magazine editorial set-up that day at the Hotel Bel-Air in California. What comes across on camera is Marilyn's innate ability to intuitively inhabit the clothes she wore, to make them her own. A decade earlier, she accessorised her preferred Dior suit with red roses, sometimes real, sometimes fake, because she loved flowers. She didn't need a *Vogue* editor to dress her because she knew what made her look good.

Marilyn with Milton Greene outside her home in California, wearing her Dior camel-wool coat, 1956

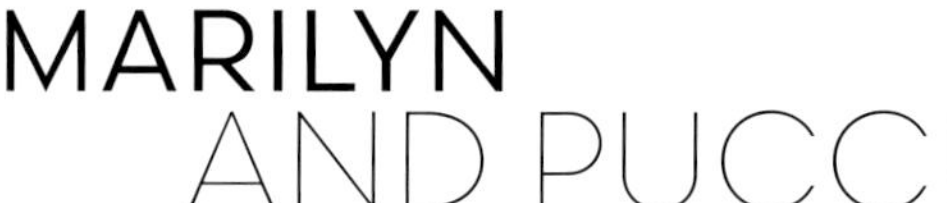

MARILYN
AND PUCCI

– Buddy Greco, quoted in *Mail Online*, 11 May 2009

As the 1960s blossomed and a new decade began to retune its fashion and culture, Marilyn, now in her mid-thirties, would introduce her own new look. With the introduction into law of the Equal Pay Act of 1963 and the Civil Rights Act of 1964, 'discrimination on the basis of race, colour, religion, sex, or national origin' would be prohibited. Although Monroe would not live to witness the world changing, passing away in August 1962, her wardrobe had already begun to reflect the laid-back cool of what ultimately would become the Swinging Sixties.

Off camera, simplicity had always been at the heart of the clothes she wore, and even for parties, she felt comfortable dressing in a monochrome and neutrally toned palette with the occasional alpha-red shade adopted for the very glitziest of occasions. When Marilyn discovered the Italian designer Emilio Pucci, she fell in love with his unfussy silhouettes and embraced a new appreciation of print.

Emilio Pucci, Marchese di Barsento, was an Olympic skier with a keen eye for style and created his own sports clothing to wear on the slopes. After he returned from the Second World War, in which he had served as a pilot, he changed course by launching a couture house. Pucci's jewel-coloured collections conjured up the colours of the Island of Capri, where he founded his first boutique back in 1949. The modern, elegant cut of his work, combined with his signature psychedelic prints, were very fashion-forward and by the 1960s, felt very much in tune with its liberated and more freethinking styling of the times, which were a million miles away from the elaborate femininity of the 1950s.

Monroe bought Pucci by the armful and was photographed sporting his boat-neck dresses and tops in tangerine and lime shades, as well as geometric-patterned boxy shirting paired with Jax trousers. The iconic photographs of George Barris, shot in June 1962, just two weeks before she passed away, show Marilyn frolicking barefoot at the house of his friend, Tim Leimert, wearing pink and purple Pucci separates, looking untroubled and carefree. She also wears a shirt printed with Pucci's famous Specchi print, now a choice archive pattern revisited in modern collections by the fashion house.

Earlier that year, Willy Rizzo, the Italian photographer and furniture designer, had been commissioned to shoot a *Paris Match* cover of Monroe; again, she chose Pucci to wear for the high-profile magazine editorial. Bert Stern's 'Last Sitting' images for American *Vogue* see Marilyn wearing a silk jersey shift dress by Pucci, this time repeat-printed with fuchsia- and pea-shaded ovals. She wore Pucci often, including the weekend before she died, when visiting her friends Frank Sinatra and pianist Buddy Greco at Cal Neva Lodge in Lake Tahoe. Images of the few days she spent there show her colour-blocking Pucci's lively chartreuse chemise top with the same shade scarf, shoes and matching trousers. Heartbreakingly, five days later, she would be found in her home, 12305 Fifth Helena Drive in Brentwood, Los Angeles, dead from a barbiturate overdose. She was buried at Pierce Brothers Westwood Village Memorial Park, wearing a treasured plain Pucci shift dress in lawn-green silk, with her favourite song playing, 'Somewhere Over the Rainbow', sung by Judy Garland.

Marilyn wears Pucci as she poses for George Barris for a *Cosmopolitan* magazine photoshoot, Los Angeles, 1962

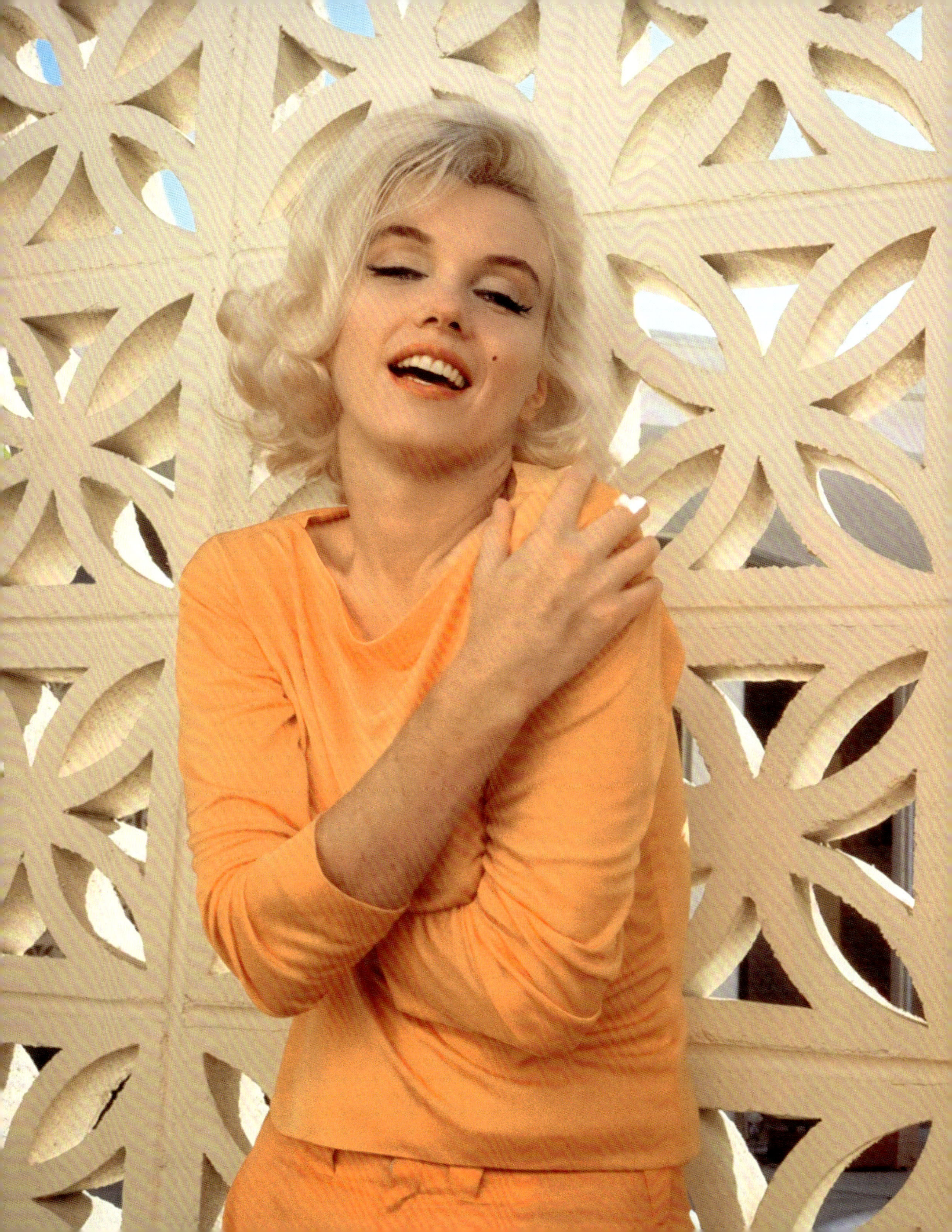

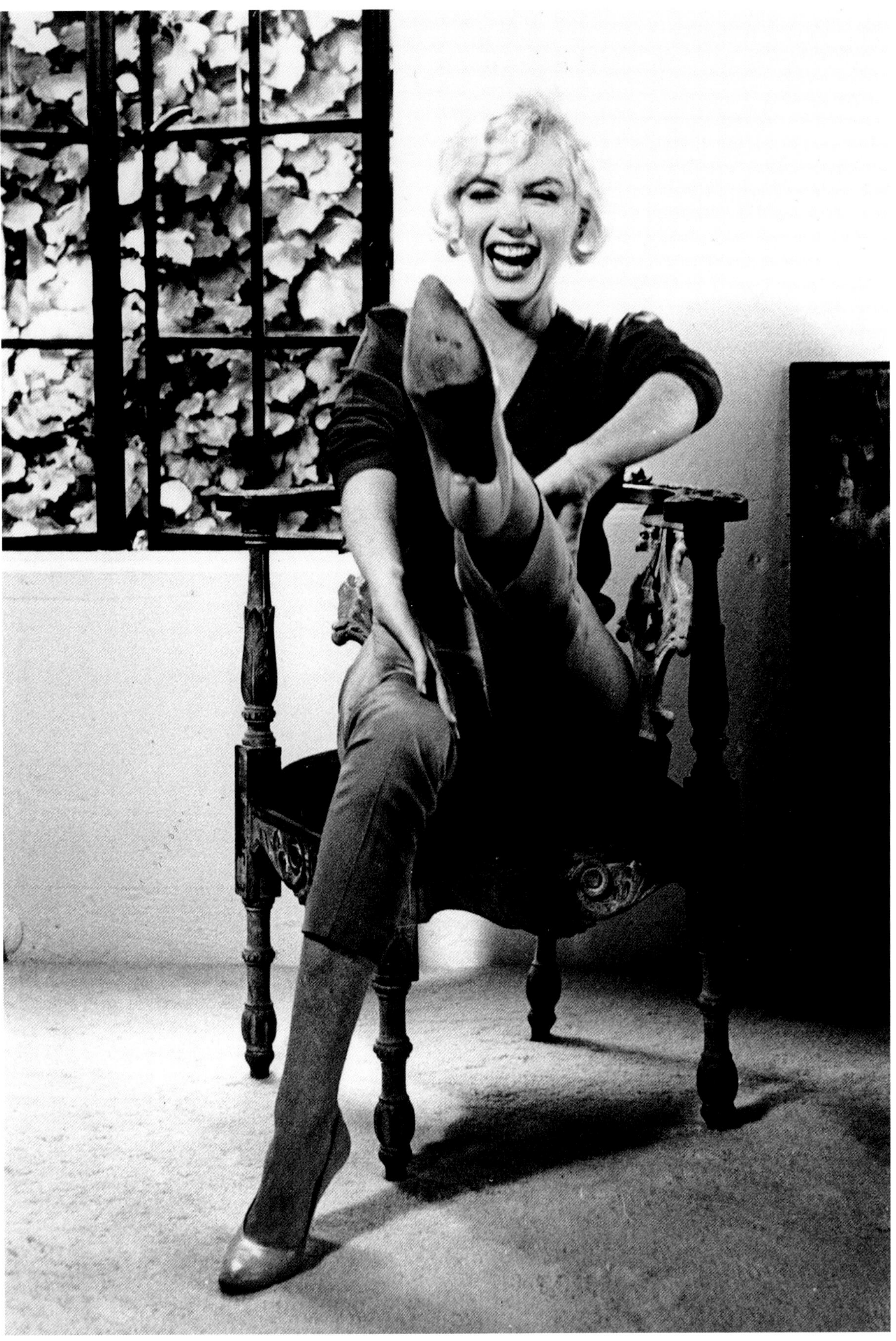

Marilyn wearing Ferragamo heels, posing at her home in Brentwood, California, 1962

MARILYN
AND FERRAGAMO

It feels very apt that one of Marilyn's favourite songs was Judy Garland's 'Somewhere Over the Rainbow'. Having both lived in the Hollywood movie mill from a young age, Judy and Marilyn had a close connection and were good friends. When it came to fashion, they were both great fans of the Italian 'shoemaker of dreams', Salvatore Ferragamo, who famously created the 1938 suede rainbow wedge for Garland and the legendary red rhinestone heels for Monroe, which were gloriously reminiscent of Garland's ruby slippers in *The Wizard of Oz* (1939). In 1999, Christie's auction of Monroe's possessions sold the shoes for over $48,000 to Ferragamo, who today keeps them secure in the house archive. A 2015 Ferragamo capsule collection celebrates both the wedges and the sparkle shoes, recreating contemporary versions to commemorate the originals.

The appeal of Ferragamo's shoes lay in their craftsmanship, but also its DNA is strongly aligned with the magic of the silver screen. In 1923, Salvatore Ferragamo took over the Hollywood Boot Shop, where he would take orders from film stars such as Joan Crawford, Pola Negri and Marilyn's muse, Jean Harlow. It would be only a matter of time before Monroe herself would become a loyal customer. She visited the Park Avenue Ferragamo shop in New York to buy her pumps and occasionally ordered directly from their workshop in Italy. Although Salvatore never met Monroe, he felt he knew his customers well and categorised them as either a Cinderella, Venus or Aristocrat. He anointed Marilyn a Venus, revealing that a 'Venus is usually of great beauty, glamour, and sophistication, yet under her glittering exterior she is often essentially a home body loving the simple things of life. Because these two characteristics are mutually contradictory the Venus is often misunderstood. People accuse her of too much luxury-loving and frivolity' (Ferragamo, 1957).

Marilyn also loved wearing Ferragamo's classic court shoes and famously bought many pairs of her preferred Filetia and Viatica styles in a variety of colours, all with a four-inch heel that she could comfortably walk in. She wore them on screen and off: Sugar Kane's black stilettoes in *Some Like It Hot* (1959), Amanda Dell's pink satin heels in *Let's Make Love* (1960) and Roslyn Tabor's white pumps in *The Misfits* (1961) are all by Ferragamo. In June 2012, to commemorate the 50th anniversary of her death, the Ferragamo fashion house curated an exhibition in Florence to honour their relationship with Monroe. Although a rumour suggested she had her heels made a little shorter on one foot to enhance walking with a wiggle, inspection of the footwear on display reportedly showed no signs of this customisation, proving that Marilyn's famous walk was her own.

More recently, the debut collection from Ferragamo creative director Maximilian Davis (Spring/Summer 2023) took inspiration from the shoes the brand made for Marilyn and sprinkled red crystals over garments. For the same year's Autumn/Winter collection, he explains:

> *'Ferragamo started making shoes for films in the 1930s, and that grew into building relationships with movie stars like Sophia Loren and Marilyn Monroe in the 1950s [...] I was interested in using their glamour and beauty, and their way of dressing, as a reference, but looking at how we could make it feel modern for today.'* (Quoted in Madsen, 2023)

That Marilyn is still influencing designers more than 60 years after her death is testament to what a style icon she really was.

MARILYN AND CHANEL

– Marilyn Monroe, April 1960 (quoted in Martin, 2013)

Marilyn could dazzle wearing simple, unfussy clothes in a neutral palette. Having grown up during the lean years of the Great Depression, she was not overly frivolous when it came to her off-camera wardrobe and instead opted for chicly minimal separates – a cashmere cardigan, white shirt and capri pants with pumps. Similarly, a luxe austerity was the backbone of the aesthetic championed by Gabrielle 'Coco' Chanel who, like Marilyn, largely grew up in an orphanage. One of the earliest designs Chanel created in 1917 was an effortless cream silk-jersey tie-front jacket, not dissimilar to Monroe's favourite bathrobe silhouette.

Chanel is one of the most celebrated fashion houses today, dedicated to a clientele who are drawn to the exclusivity of its CC-ed elegance. When Coco began her work, however, it was closely aligned to an egalitarian sensibility that drew inspiration from boyish silhouettes and fabrics and contingent on her strong-minded good taste. A 1931 feature in *The New Yorker* describes how Chanel 'utilized the ditch-digger's scarf, made chic the white collars and cuffs of the waitress, and put queens into mechanics' tunics' (quoted in Fury, 2023). When Marilyn was relaxing and taking time off from 'being Marilyn', the clothes she wore on rotation showed a fondness for the same fuss-free, functional standards.

When leaving Columbia University's Presbyterian Medical Center in Manhattan after a few weeks of convalescence, Marilyn looked chic with 'an elegantly casual new champagne-coloured coiffeur that matched her beige cashmere sweater and skirt and identically dyed shoes' (Spoto, 1993) – a very 'Chanel-like' outfit in its sophisticated simplicity. The formal connection between Chanel and Monroe, however, revolves around her love of an invisible accessory: the Chanel No. 5 perfume, originally introduced in 1921. Just over 30 years later in 1952, for Monroe's first *Life* magazine cover feature, she was famously asked what she wore to bed, replying, 'Chanel No. 5'. Later in 1960, during an interview with editor-in-chief of *Marie Claire France*, George Belmont, she mused, 'I said I wore Chanel No. 5 because it's the truth' (quoted in Martin, 2013).

The House of Chanel would go on to delight in the association in 2013, creating an advertising campaign for the scent using a 1955 Ed Feingersh portrait of Marilyn dousing herself with Chanel No. 5, before heading out to see Tennessee William's play *Cat on a Hot Tin Roof* at the legendary Morosco Theatre. The legend of Marilyn and Chanel No. 5 has become synonymous with the fashion house's narrative and, although Madame Coco was the first face of the scent, it is Monroe who has become its most famous embodiment, which continues to this day.

Marilyn splashes on her favourite Chanel No. 5 as she gets ready to go and see the play *Cat on a Hot Tin Roof* at the Morosco Theatre in New York City, 1955

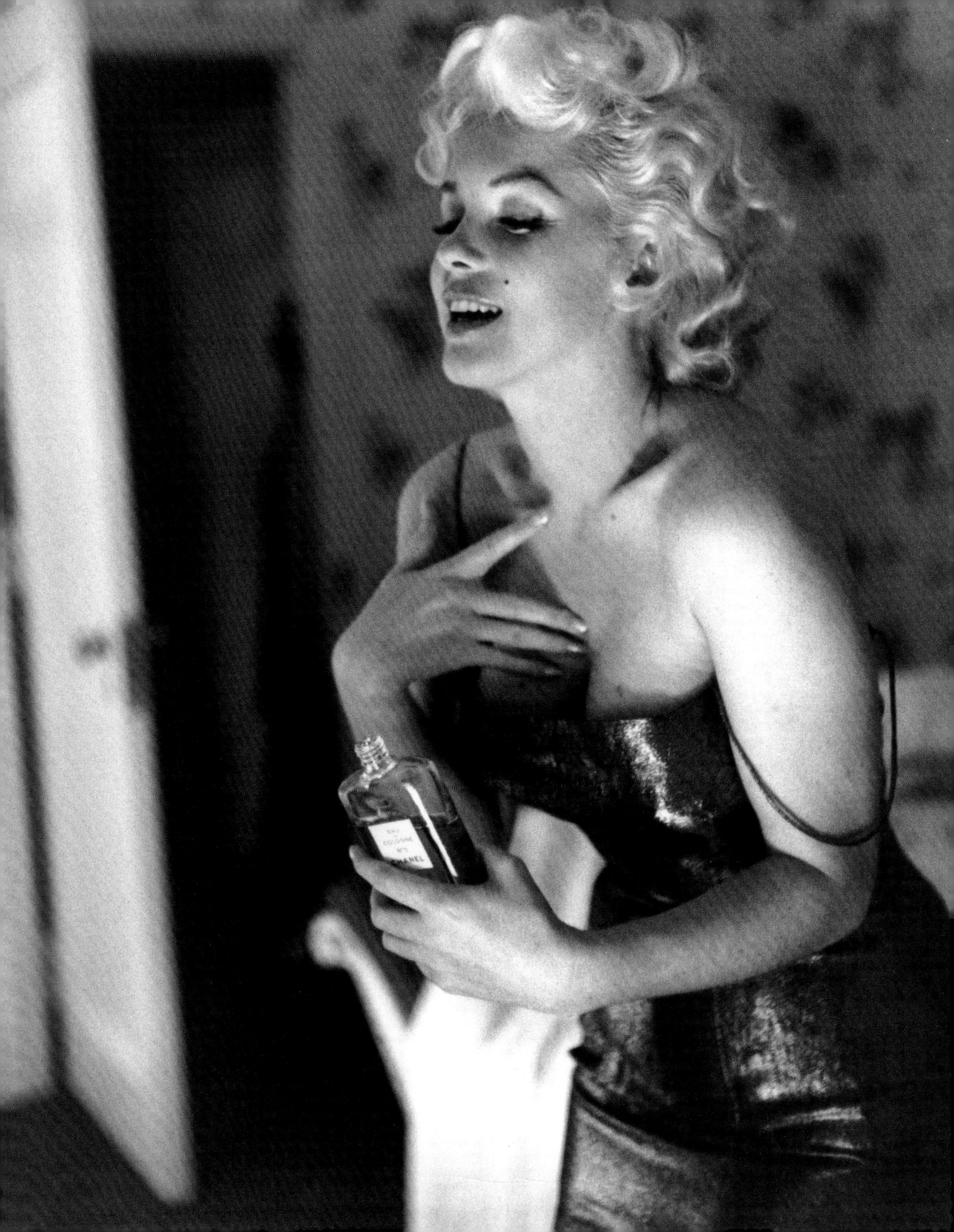
EAU
COLOGNE
N°5
CHANEL

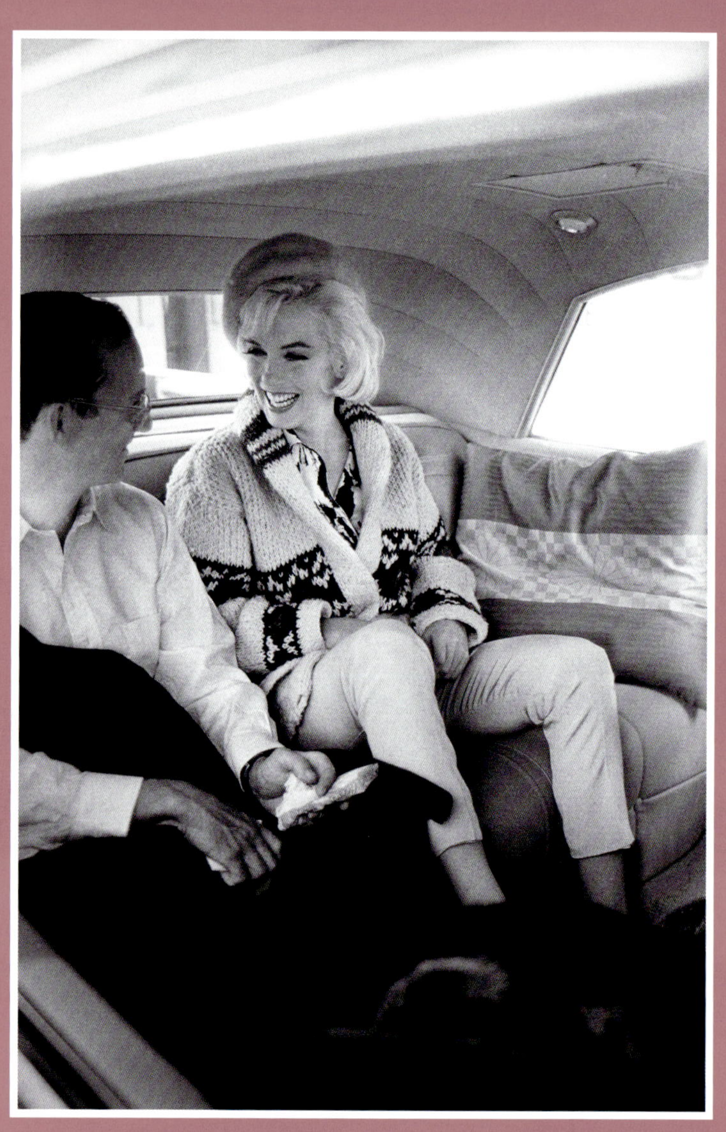

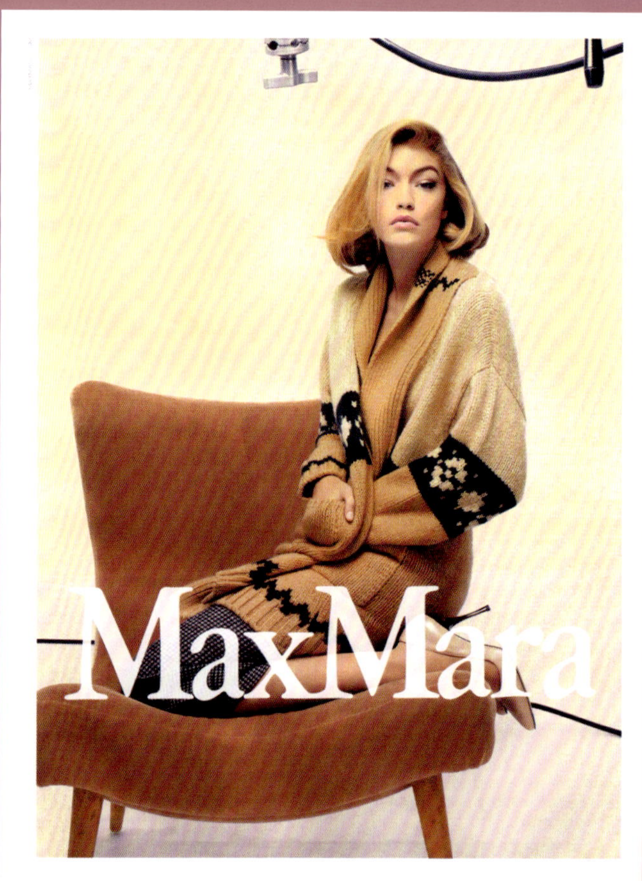
MaxMara

MARILYN
AND THE DESIGNERS
SHE INFLUENCED

Marilyn Monroe sported a spectrum of fashionable looks, and designers today continue to track her multifaceted style chapters as a mood board to inspire their work. Marilyn's wardrobe embraced not just sensual femininity but low-key minimalism and practicality, too, and creatives from Comme des Garçons to Yves Saint Laurent have picked and mixed her dress codes, refreshing and reinventing her enduring sartorial appeal on their catwalks. Monroe's glittering red-carpet attire has helped pilot the direction of many a designer's collection. The pink dress she wore to sing 'Diamonds are a Girl's Best Friend' in 1953 has been reliably reimagined, most recently by English singer-songwriter Raye who wore a version to the 2021 BRIT Awards. John Galliano's Dior Couture Autumn/Winter 2002–03 show revised Monroe's *The Seven Year Itch* white halterneck dress in ivory chiffon and silk. The backless Dior dress by Marc Bohan, in which Monroe was photographed by Bert Stern, was recreated by the House's artistic director Bill Gaytten in 2011, and subsequently exhibited at the Dior show in Denver in 2018.

Less well-known is how her simple daywear is routinely referenced. Copies of Marilyn's oversized cardigans and camel coats, white shirts and denim jeans similarly find their way into key designer collections. Italian label Max Mara, recognised for its pared-down chic, embodied Monroe's casual wardrobe on their Autumn/Winter 2015 catwalk, which was inspired by George Barris' 1962 shoot with Marilyn and included near exact copies of her now-famous Mexican cardigan and taupe wrap coat. Everything, from her bathing costumes to siren suits, have been eagerly remade for consumers who wanted to copy the film-star look. As a pop-cultural touchstone, her face has become part of fashion iconography, printed on T-shirts and sweats by streetwear giants such as Supreme, as well as avant-garde designers like Dries van Noten and Junya Watanabe, whose collections have included Marilyn motifs.

Every fashion season, designers platform a fresh twist on past silhouettes, at the same time following their creative instinct to express the zeitgeist. Christian Siriano, the youngest designer to win Project Runway in 2008, has since dressed prominent customers from Michelle Obama to Zendaya. But for his Spring/Summer 2023 show, he looked to Marilyn as his muse:

'We all have a little bit of that Old Hollywood glamour in us, so my hope is that the collection transports you to a different time and helps you channel your inner style icon. [...] it isn't just about what's next for Spring, but rather about being inspired in the moment. I wanted to do something that our customer will be excited about right now as well as stand the test of time.' (Quoted in Vernose, 2022)

Equally, New York-based, Nepalese–American creative Prabal Gurung looked to Monroe in 2014 and based his fresh looks on not just the clothes Marilyn wore, but her emotional resonance, too:

'Marilyn Monroe was the most idolized, most wanted woman, but yet she was so lonely and melancholic. The melancholic feel to her was what I wanted to create and suggest with the music and the setting. I wanted to give an ode to her, a nod to her.' (Quoted in King, 2013)

His work aimed to 'put her in a modern context', and the creations he produced were based heavily on the glamour and poignancy of Bert Stern's famous 1962 Last Sitting session (Phelps, 2013).

Marilyn is the perfect muse: her looks can be recalibrated in a kaleidoscopic variety of ways and her symbolism has been tapped to evoke myriad moods. In 2018, Prada referenced Monroe's *The Seven Year Itch* Travilla gown in their Neon Dream advertising campaign which featured an army of blonde lookalikes wearing the dress while marching through a Hollywood vista. Vivienne Westwood's acclaimed Spring/Summer 1985 Mini-Crini collection was fused with a subversive reappraisal of English heritage, while the house model, Sarah Stockbridge, who became the face of the look, wore her hair in platinum Marilyn waves while conjuring Monroe's winking sexuality. Menswear equally has benefited from Marilyn's magic. Jonathan Anderson's Autumn/Winter 2019 Paris show for Loewe featured a selection of flowing chemises embellished with Marilyn's face, while Comme des Garçons Shirt Spring/Summer 2024 Show collaborated with the Andy Warhol Foundation to produce Marilyn imagery shirts and sweats printed with her judicious quotation, 'Dogs don't bite me. Just humans'.

Marilyn's influence and resonance on the world of fashion endures beyond all trend cycles, however. She wasn't just one kind of muse. Throughout her life, she explored many ways of being a woman, all of which are represented by the clothes she wore. While there is a cultural context to Marilyn's visual and transformative performance, she pervades as a graphic symbol of womanhood and designers continue to pay homage to it today.

'WHEN PEOPLE LOOK AT ME, THEY WANT TO SEE A STAR.'

– Marilyn Monroe, quoted in Spoto, 1993

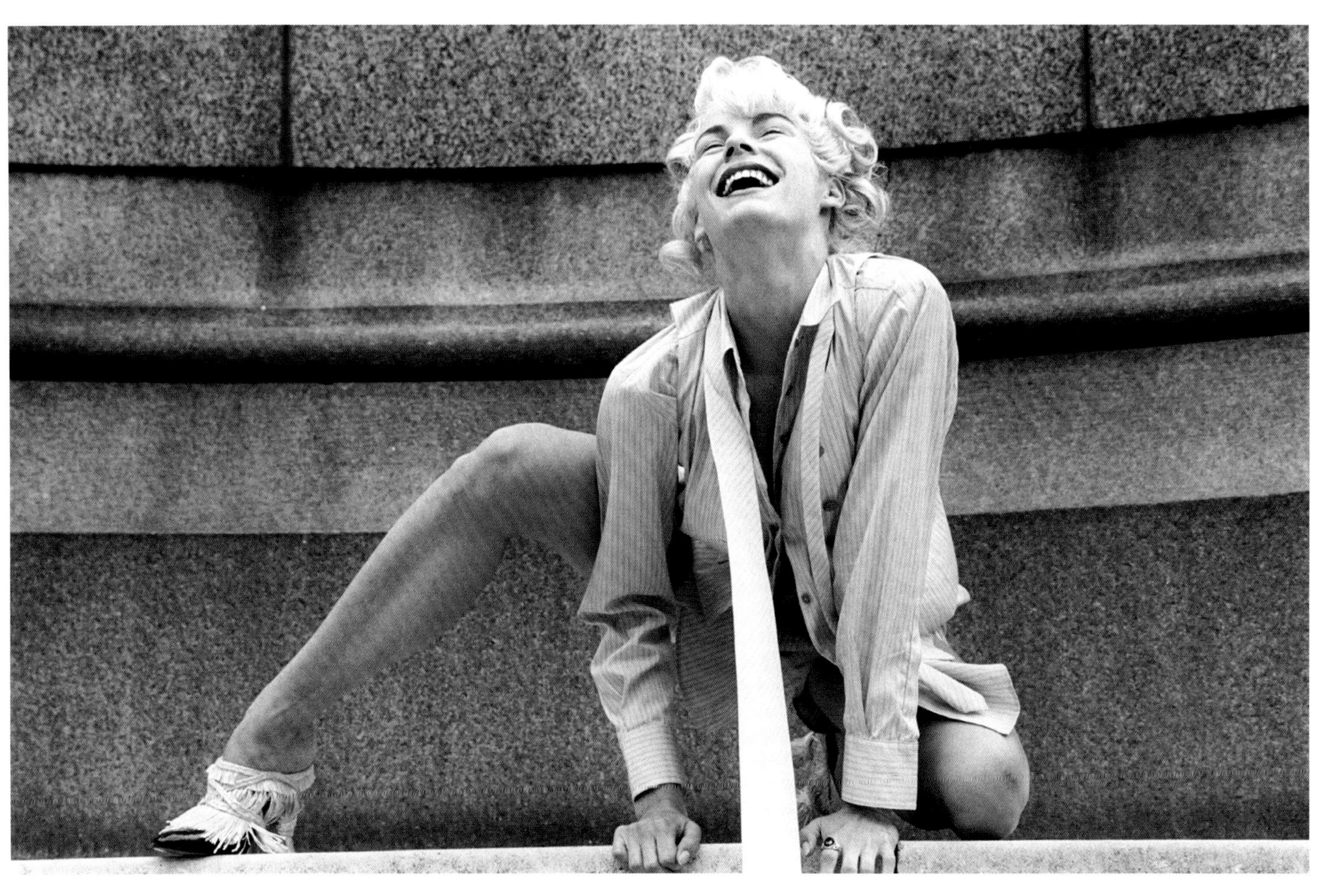

Model Sarah Stockbridge with Marilyn platinum waves, strikes a pose for
Vivienne Westwood's 1985 Mini-Crini collection

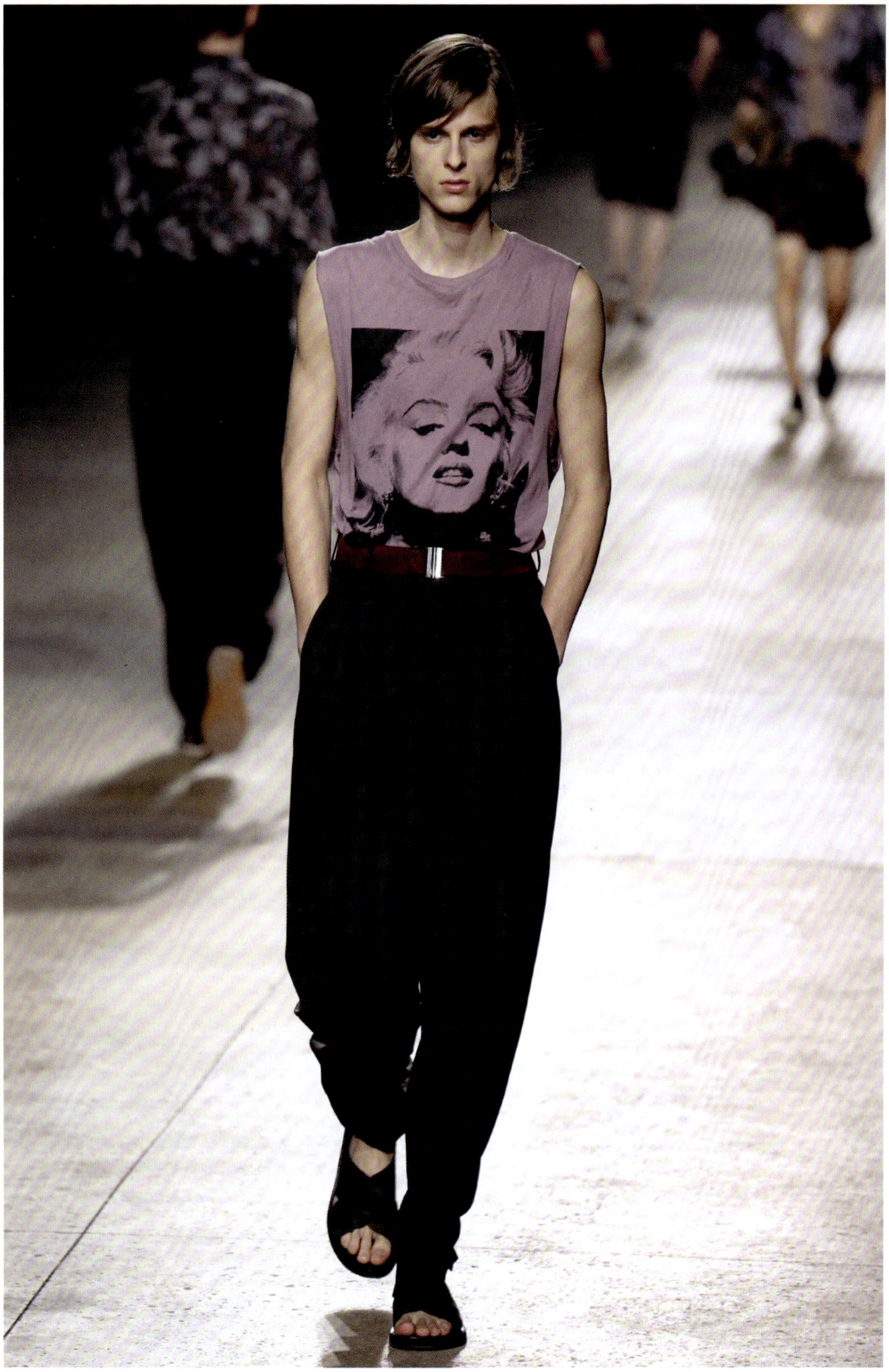

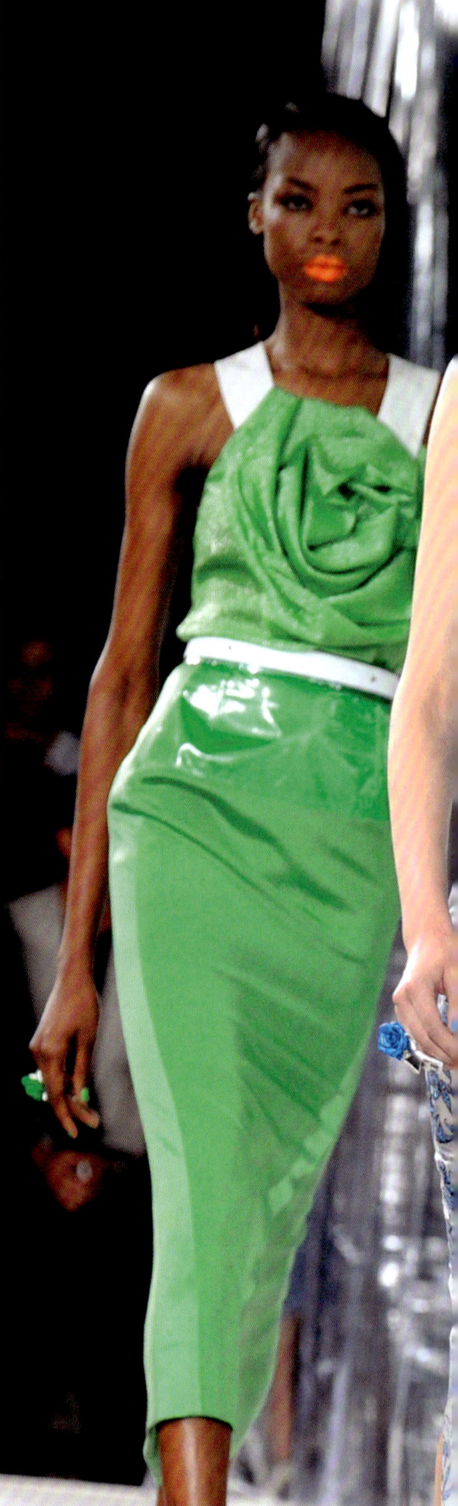

Dries Van Noten gives a nod to Marilyn in his Men's Spring/Summer
2015 collection in Paris

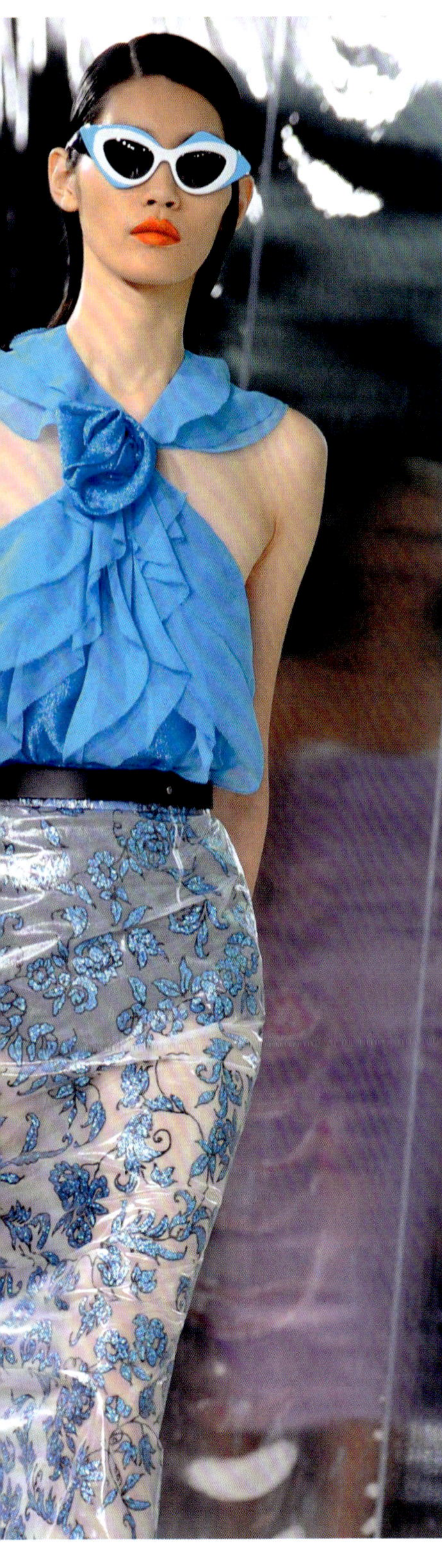

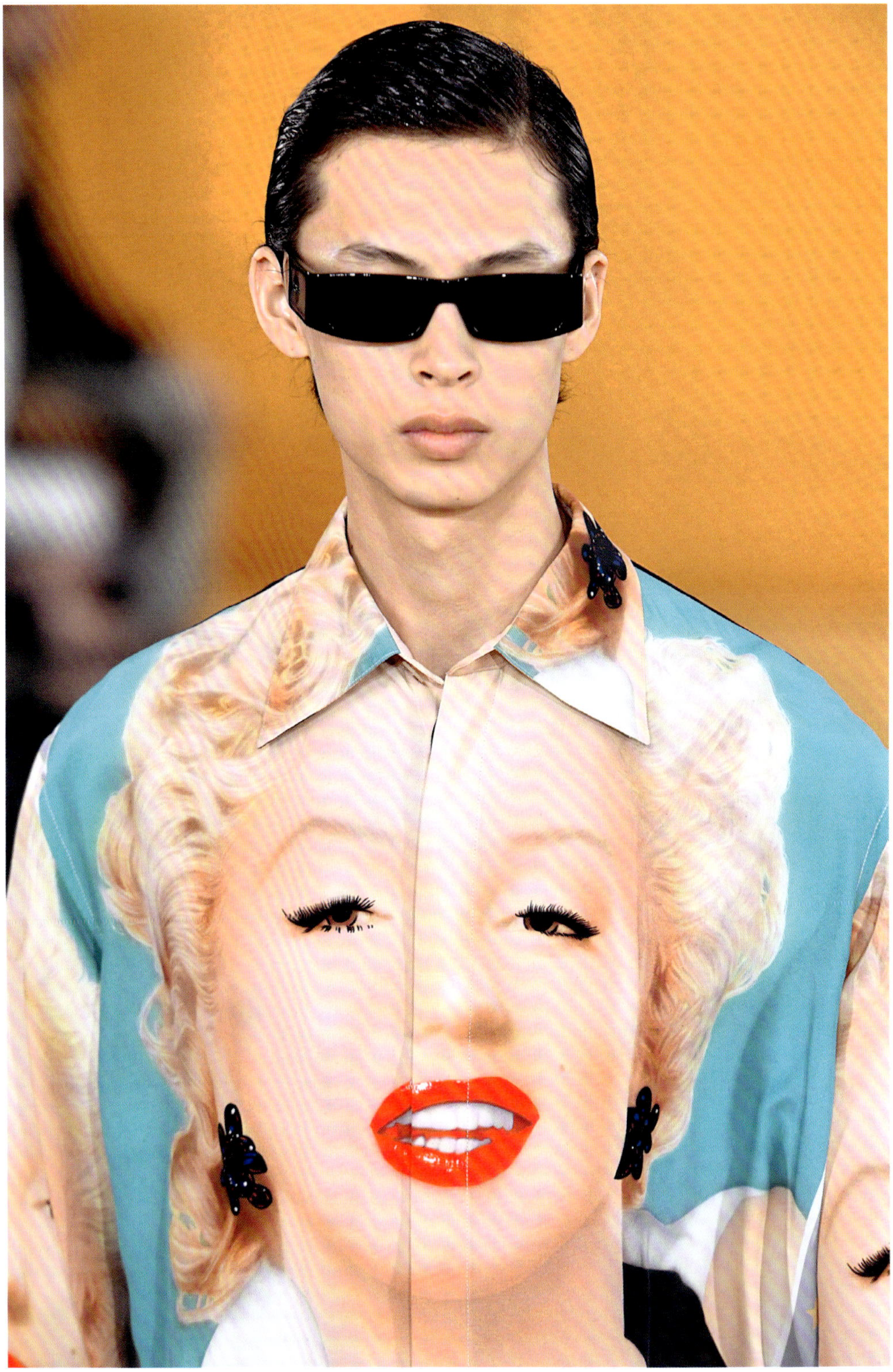

Above left: The Prabal Gurung Spring/Summer 2014 collection puts the clothes Marilyn wore into a modern context

Above: The Loewe Menswear Autumn/Winter 2019–20 collection at Paris Fashion Week features a selection of chemises embellished with Marilyn's face in vivid colours

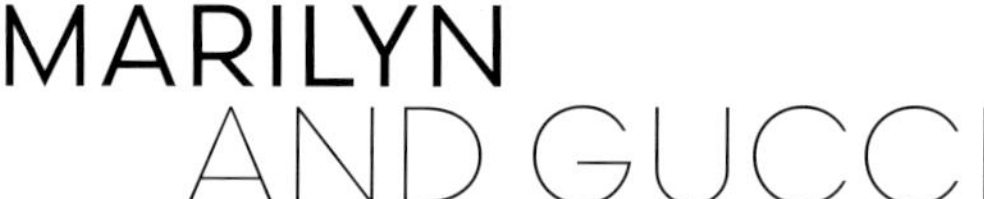

MARILYN
AND GUCCI

When designer Alessandro Michele namechecked Marilyn Monroe during his tenure as creative director at Gucci for the Spring/Summer 2022 Love Parade catwalk show, it was because he grew up living her Hollywood dreams. 'My mom was really obsessed with American movies and cinema,' he explained. 'For her it was like a religion' (quoted in Bowles, 2019). Michele's love of American film, 'the dark and the light both', has spurred his creativity. While his reverie of the life Marilyn lived in Hollywood is romantic, the clothes Marilyn wore, even when employed at a studio, weren't always lavish. The image we have of Monroe as a screen goddess is just one of her wardrobe chapters. Her personality transformed with how she dressed, and could spin from super-chic, such as her 'Happy Birthday Mr. President' Jean-Louis gown, decorated in thousands of shimmering rhinestones, to ever-so-stylishly geeky, with standard stay-at-home slacks and cat's-eye spectacles.

Gucci is a fashion house extraordinaire, founded by Guccio Gucci who, like Marilyn, came from humble origins. Inspired by the elegance of the guests and their luggage at the Savoy Hotel in London, where he worked as a bellhop, Gucci returned to Florence in 1921 and began making luxury leather accessories. Today, his heritage brand has become the master of reinvention and is driven by making a connection with its customers who are faithful to the GG logo, much like Marilyn made it her aim to connect with her fans, giving them the glamour and the romance of Hollywood, all wrapped up in a down-to-earth girl-made-good.

Gucci's Spring/Summer 2022 homage to Marilyn celebrates the legend of her glamorous armour – the clothes she wore to dazzle and become an icon. Under Alessandro Michele, the Gucci label played outside the rules of conventional fashion, championing the 'outsider' look, so their nod to Marilyn feels very apt. Michele explains his thinking behind his collection:

'In my work, I caress the roots of the past to create unexpected inflorescences, carving the matter through grafting and pruning. I appeal to such ability to reinhabit what has already been given. And to the blending, the transitions, the fractures, the concatenations. To escape the reactionary cages of purity, I pursue a poetics of the illegitimate.' (Michele, *Crash*)

With his 'blending' of Marilyn's Hollywood glitz and glamour with Gucci's equestrian roots, the catwalk was an eclectic fusion of (faux) fur, diamanté, lace and shimmering fabrics with camel-coloured suits, oversized jumpers and riding accessories. To top it off, digital screens surrounding the catwalk showed classic 'Marilyn quotes'. Existing in the spotlight, but always with the feeling that she didn't belong, Marilyn would attend premieres and events, dressed to the nines. But afterwards, she would often forego the after-parties, changing into trousers and a shirt, and drive herself home.

A few Gucci possessions of Marilyn's still remain. She bought a leather Gucci address book a couple of years after the fashion house opened its first store in NYC in 1953. The book is monogrammed with MM on the cover and inside is a fascinating glimpse of her world at that time – carefully listed are the addresses and phone numbers of Lee Strasberg, the Actors Studio and close friends including Marlon Brando. She also bought a signature Gucci horse-bit bracelet. A robust and tomboyish piece of jewellery in silver, it is far from the diamonds she sang about in the 1953 film *Gentlemen Prefer Blondes*. But perhaps the Gucci item that most reflects who Marilyn really was is the simple white Gucci shirt (later auctioned by Christie's after her death), which was one of her favourites, and speaks of the modest, unpretentious style that Marilyn favoured off-screen.

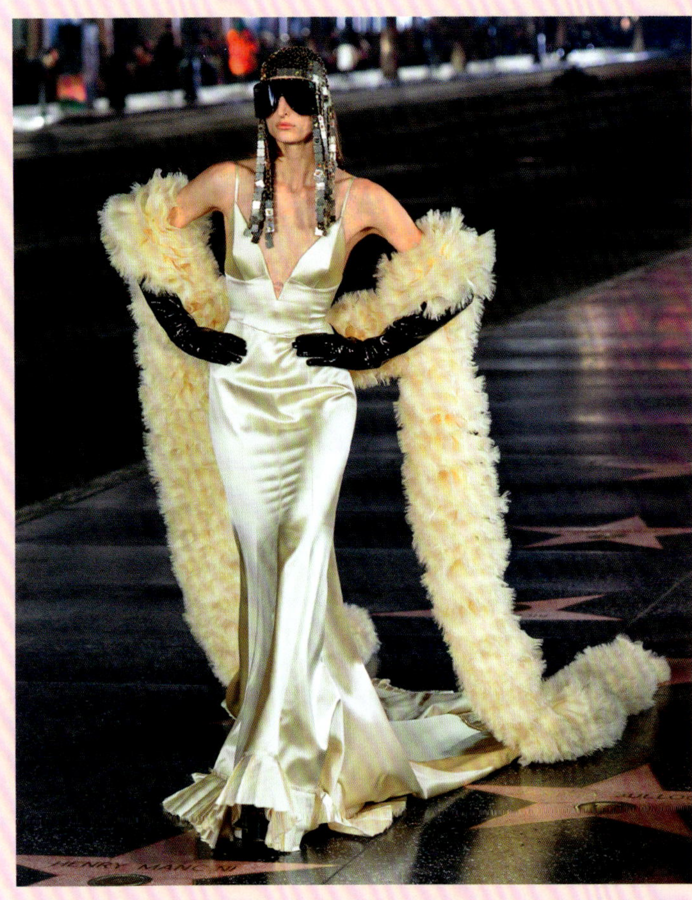
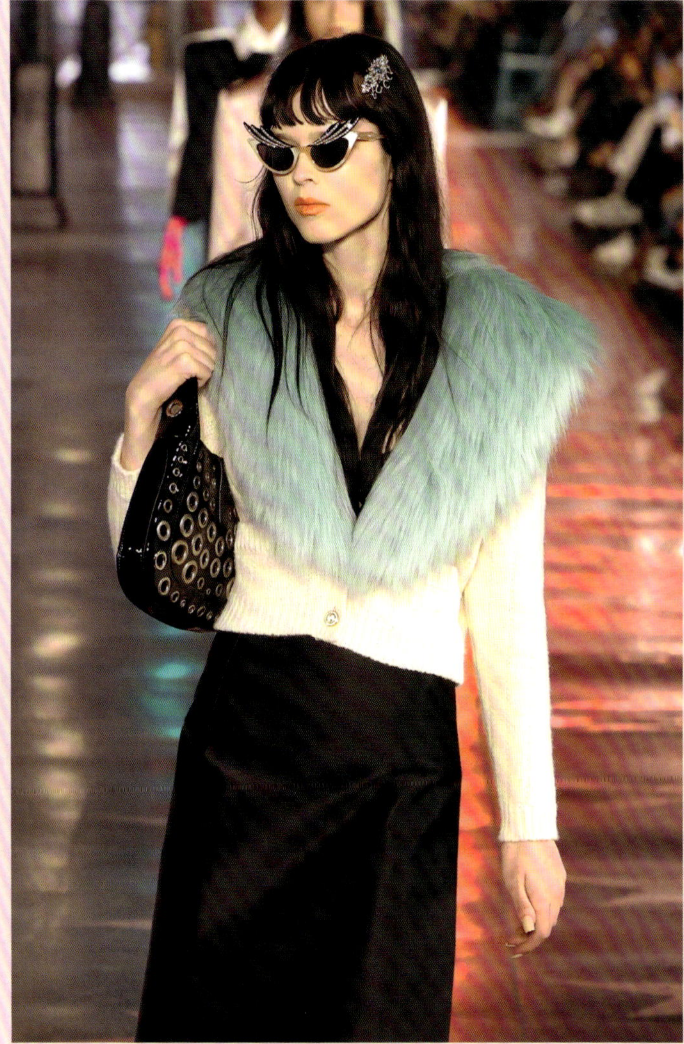

Models walk the Hollywood Walk of Fame at the Gucci Love Parade
on Hollywood Boulevard, exuding true Marilyn glamour, 2021

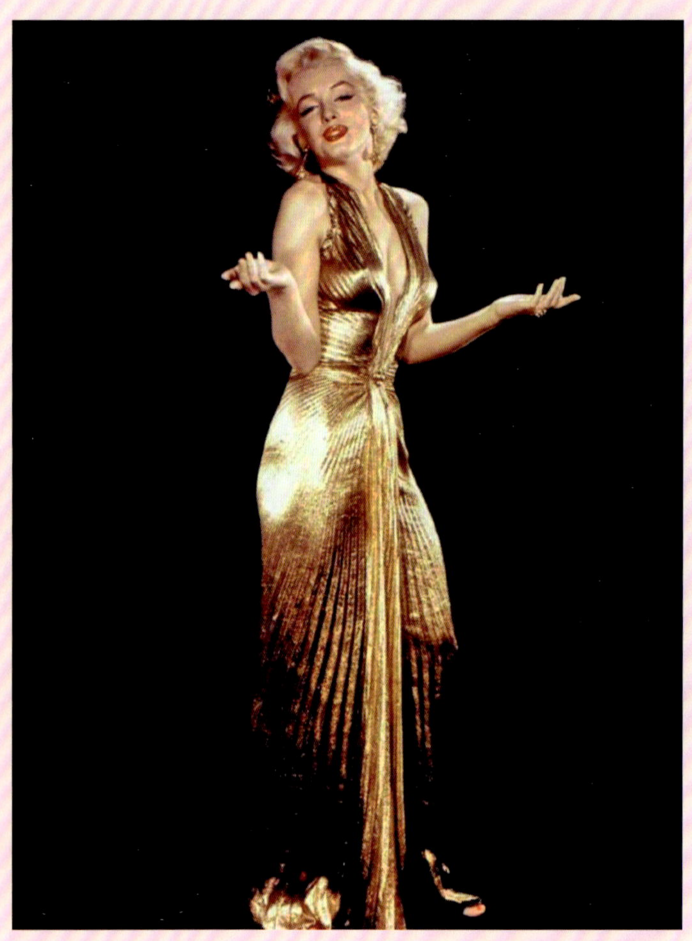

Marilyn wearing the famous gold lamé Travilla dress designed for her role in *Gentlemen Prefer Blondes*, 1953

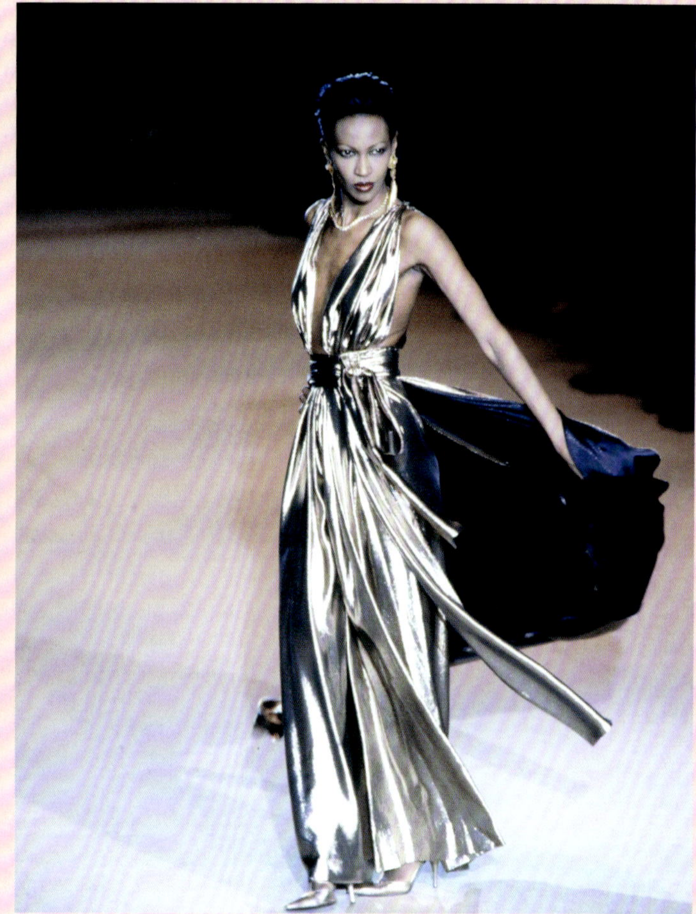

Amalia Vairelli models Yves Saint Laurent's take on Travilla's gold lamé dress for the Spring 2002 Couture Collection

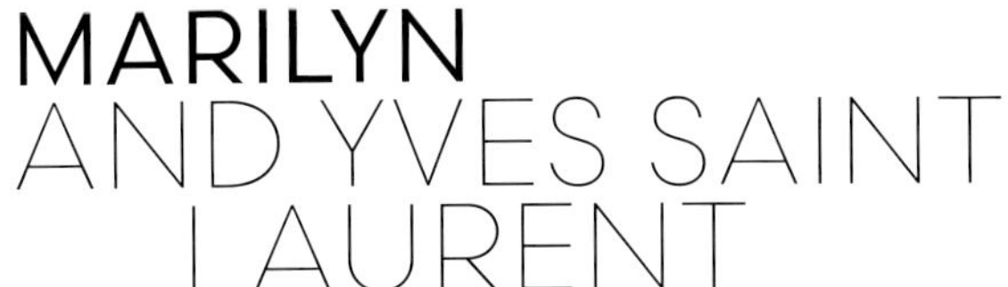

'SAINT LAURENT, WHO'S HOTTER THAN HE'S BEEN IN YEARS, IS MAD ABOUT MM THIS SEASON, AND PART OF THE COLLECTION HE UNVEILS WEDNESDAY WILL BE AN HOMAGE TO THE SEXY STAR [MARILYN]. IN ONE WHITE LACE DRESS [...] YSL PERFECTLY SUMS UP THE NEW HOT ATTITUDE: SHORT, SEXY, AND TIGHT, WITH A CORSET-LIKE BODICE THAT PUSHES THE BREASTS TO THE SKY.'

– 'Yves likes it hot', *WWD*, 1990

Yves Saint Laurent's January 1990 Paris couture collection featured a strapless white dress worn with satin opera gloves and a snowy fur wrap. Afterwards he spoke to the fashion industry's trade journal, *WWD*, about the clothes he had shown on the catwalk, saying they were 'an homage to Marilyn with the kind of light, sexy, spirited clothes I associate with her'. The white look was similar to a John Moore dress she had often favoured while married to Joe DiMaggio in the 1950s; she wore it regularly accessorised with white gloves and stole. More than anything, though, the Yves version had Monroe's stylistic energy flowing through its fabric. He transported the silhouette to his preferred model that season, Rochelle Redfield, an auburn-haired Texan who was, on first glance, quite unlike his muse, Marilyn. However, Saint Laurent explained how, like Monroe, Redfield was 'a real woman. A woman with hips and breasts and a body' (quoted in *WWD*, 1990).

Saint Laurent and his partner, Pierre Bergé, had originally launched the fashion house in 1961 with the intention of shifting the rigid conventions of the couture industry. YSL experimented with fashion and took it beyond its traditionally ordered strictures. Post-war, the voguish shape and sensibility was bone-thin and aristocratically confident, confined again by Christian Dior's New Look corsetry. Yves' designs were created to empower women and dared to liberate them, whether it was dressing them in an androgynous suit or bearing a scandalous nipple. His message was that all women were beautiful and he was one of the first designers to include a diverse cohort of models on his catwalk.

Marilyn didn't try to change her naturally Grecian curves to fit the prevailing trend and instead went her own way, inadvertently heralding the liberating body inclusivity movement we welcome today. In 2002, on Yves' retirement, the house staged a grand retrospective: the most memorable show of his life. Among the wave after wave of iconic couture that rolled down the catwalk were more Saint Laurent tributes to Marilyn – including pieces in homage to her gold, pleated halterneck Travilla dress and the legendary pink bustier gown worn in *Gentlemen Prefer Blondes* (1953), masterfully reinterpreted. One of the last looks was worn by another preferred Saint Laurent Texan model, Jerry Hall, who strode the catwalk in a slinky floor-length slip and fur shawl in full Marilyn mode.

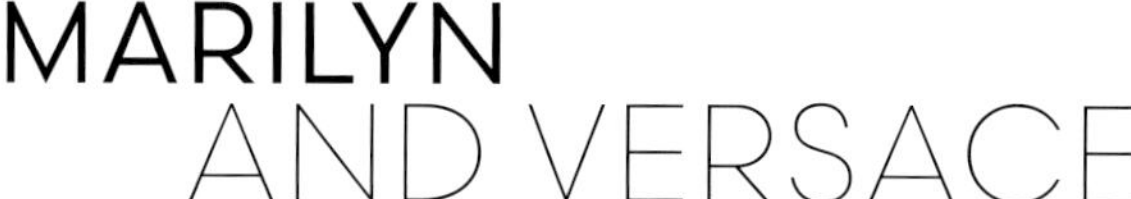

MARILYN
AND VERSACE

'THIS WAS KIND OF A NO-BRAINER,
I MUST SAY. I WAS LIKE, "I HAVE TO WEAR
THIS". IT HAS MARILYN MONROE ON IT
AND I'M OBSESSED WITH HER.'

– Elle Fanning, quoted in Frey, 2017

Fashion branding became a persuasive part of the lingua franca of style in the 1990s. Gianni Versace's signature ready-to-wear collections, signified by his famous Medusa and Greco prints, combined baroque Italian luxe, gold hardware and opulent jewel colours which became synonymous with the designer, who grew up in Reggio Calabria where his mother ran a dressmaking studio. In a resounding fashion moment of excess, Versace's Spring/Summer 1991 Pop Art catwalk took Andy Warhol's celebrated 1962 screen-print of Marilyn's 1953 *Niagara* publicity shot and platformed an unrivalled holy trinity of the 20th century's most enduringly recognisable imagery in his now iconic Pop collection. The supermodels on his Milan catwalk, including Naomi Campbell and Christy Turlington, wore rhinestone-encrusted leggings, jackets and jeans, featuring Warhol's Marilyn print.

The eternal energy of Monroe's charm was something Warhol had been fascinated with since he was a child. Transfixed by the spell of the big screen, like Marilyn had been herself, he collected film magazines and autographs of the film stars who deigned to reply to his enquiring letters. Warhol's 1962 New York show of Pop silkscreens at the Stable Gallery would include his *Marilyn Diptych* – later part of Versace's own art collection. In 2010, the 'Marilyn Monroe: Life as a Legend' exhibition at the Andy Warhol Museum in Pittsburgh displayed Warhol's 'Marilyns' together with his personal collection of 120 Monroe photographs. Warhol was famously obsessed with Marilyn and with how celebrity reflected modern culture.

Versace's 1991 collection encapsulated the dreams and iconography of both, fusing it with his own conspicuously transformative design aesthetic. He, too, was a man captivated with celebrity and, years before it became part of the typical fashion cycle, regularly commandeered a front row of glamorous jetsetters, and featured his famous friends in campaigns. Monroe, Warhol and Versace were a match made in fashion heaven and would be revisited once again in 2018 by Donatella Versace as a commemorative tribute to her brother, following Gianni's sudden death in 1997, when she took over the helm of the company.

The collection has become a modern classic, examples of which are now kept in the Metropolitan Museum of Art in New York: Monroe's glossy version of voluptuous womanhood infused with optimism equated with Versace's mindset. In a 1977 interview with Warhol's *Interview* magazine, Gianni muses on his creative approach: 'I watch women continuously. I want them to look beautiful, I am not interested in making them funny, but just beautiful' (quoted in Morera, 2014). Today, Marilyn-Versace-Warhol pieces are coveted by collectors and red-carpet attendees alike, and have been worn by a whole host of celebrities, actresses and musicians, from Elle Fanning to Cardi B and Keyshia Ka'Oir, who are drawn to the art of fashion.

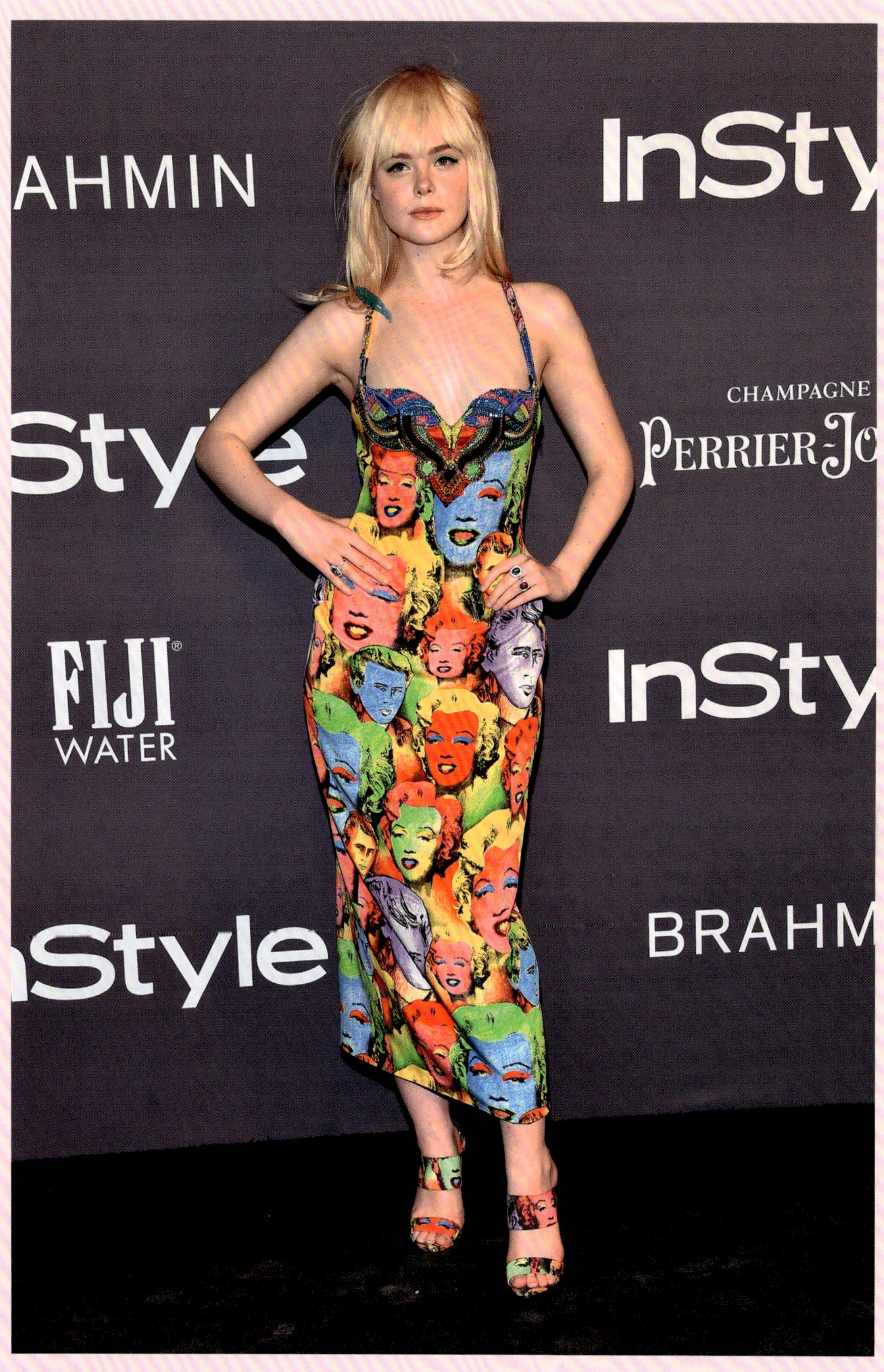

Elle Fanning arrives at the InStyle Awards in 2017 wearing a Versace
Marilyn Monroe-printed dress with perfectly matched shoes

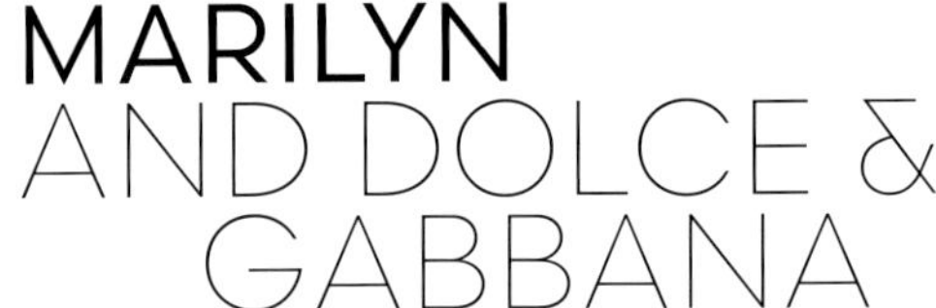

MARILYN AND DOLCE & GABBANA

'BEAUTY AND FEMININITY ARE AGELESS […] REAL GLAMOUR, IT'S BASED ON FEMININITY. I THINK THAT SEXUALITY IS ONLY ATTRACTIVE WHEN IT'S NATURAL AND SPONTANEOUS.'

– Marilyn Monroe, *Life* magazine, 17 August 1962

Dolce & Gabbana, the Sicilian–Italian duo who launched their eponymous label in 1985 at Milan Fashion Week, have built their fashion empire by designing clothes that celebrate the sensuality of women. Their commanding styles are empowering, yet never shy away from emphasising a voluptuous silhouette, and their collections show a keen understanding of the contemporary female form that synchronises with the aesthetic legacy of Marilyn Monroe. Dolce & Gabbana collections showcase glamour, sexuality and a timeless elegance that defies trends; whether it be perfectly cut suits or laced and embellished corsetry, all speak to a customer who is confidently assured. Their Autumn/ Winter 2009 catwalk featured a direct homage to a favourite muse: on the catwalk among the silk tuxedos and suits, appeared models wearing satin spaghetti-strapped prom gowns, pencil-slim sheath dresses, dirndl skirts and sporty tank tops, branded with an array of iconic monochrome images of Marilyn, including one of her wearing the legendary Dorothy Jeakins gown featured in *Niagara*. American actress Scarlett Johansson, who sat front row at the Dolce & Gabbana show, became the face of the brand's perfume and cosmetic campaigns. In 2010, photographer Sølve Sundsbø shot

Johansson for Dolce & Gabbana styled as Monroe. With smoky eyes and red lipstick and her hair blonde and coiffured, the actress looked radiant as she inhabited Marilyn's look. The brand continued to channel an old Hollywood sensibility in subsequent commercials with Johansson, which led to her being described as 'the modern Marilyn' in *Cosmopolitan* magazine (Kovacs, 2013).

Dolce & Gabbana connected with Monroe once again in their collaborative Summer 2023 collection with Kim Kardashian. Kardashian's well-known love of Marilyn manifested in the short black-and-white video she released ahead of the show, where she wore a lace dress and flourished platinum locks, looking every inch a 1950s' bombshell. The catwalk equally paid homage with a series of body-con gowns and sheer bodices that would not have looked out of place in Monroe's own wardrobe.

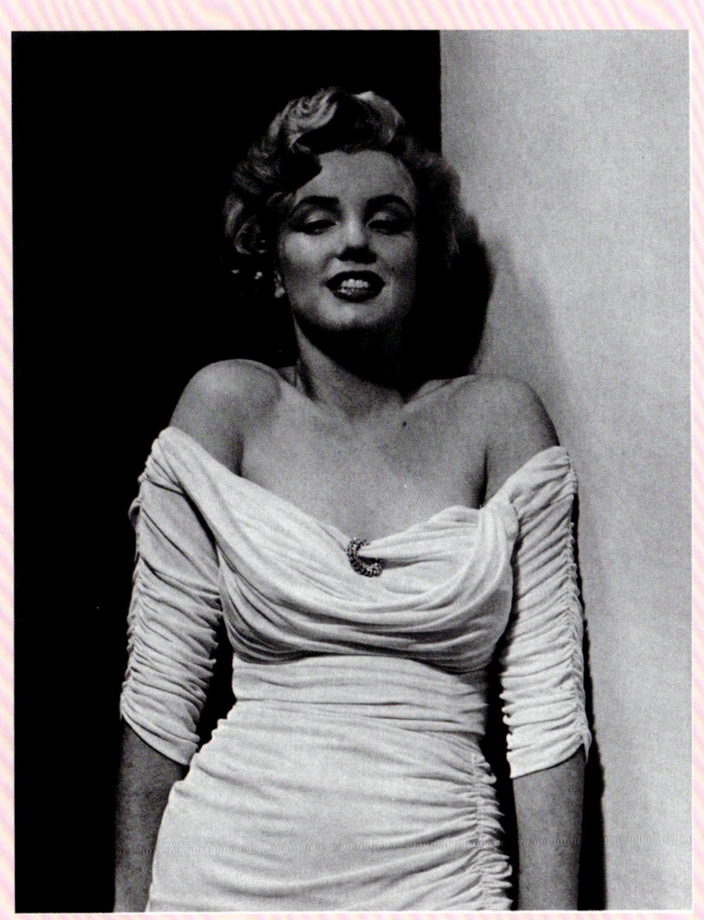

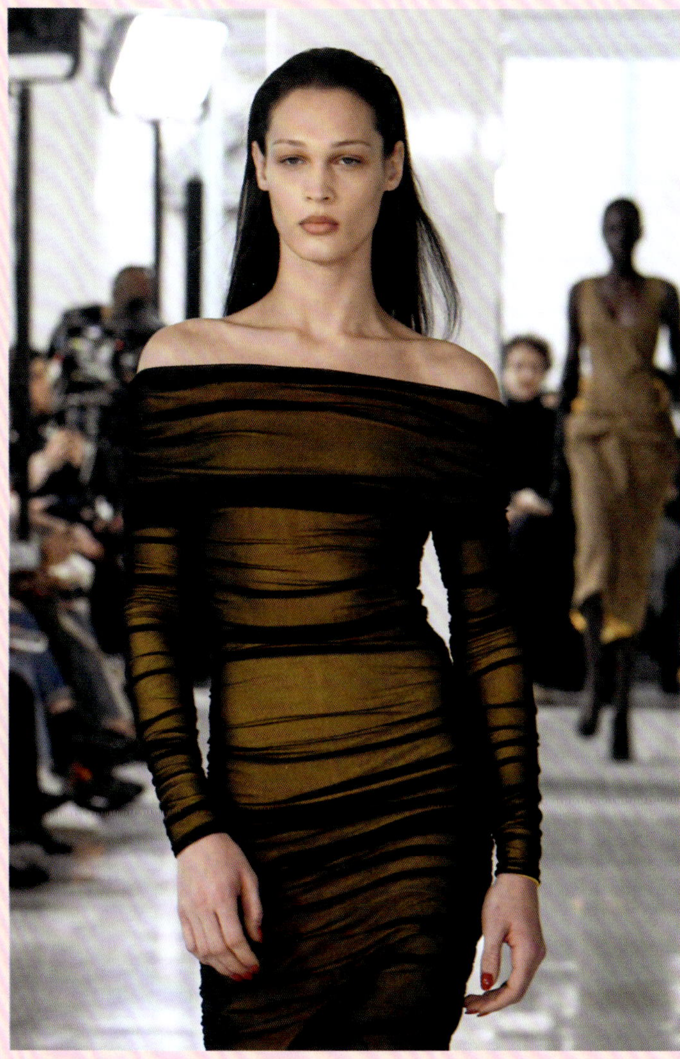

Marilyn poses for *Parade* magazine in an off-the-shoulder dress, July 1952

Dolce & Gabbana showcase Marilyn Monroe glamour in their collection for Milan Fashion Week, 2024

194–195

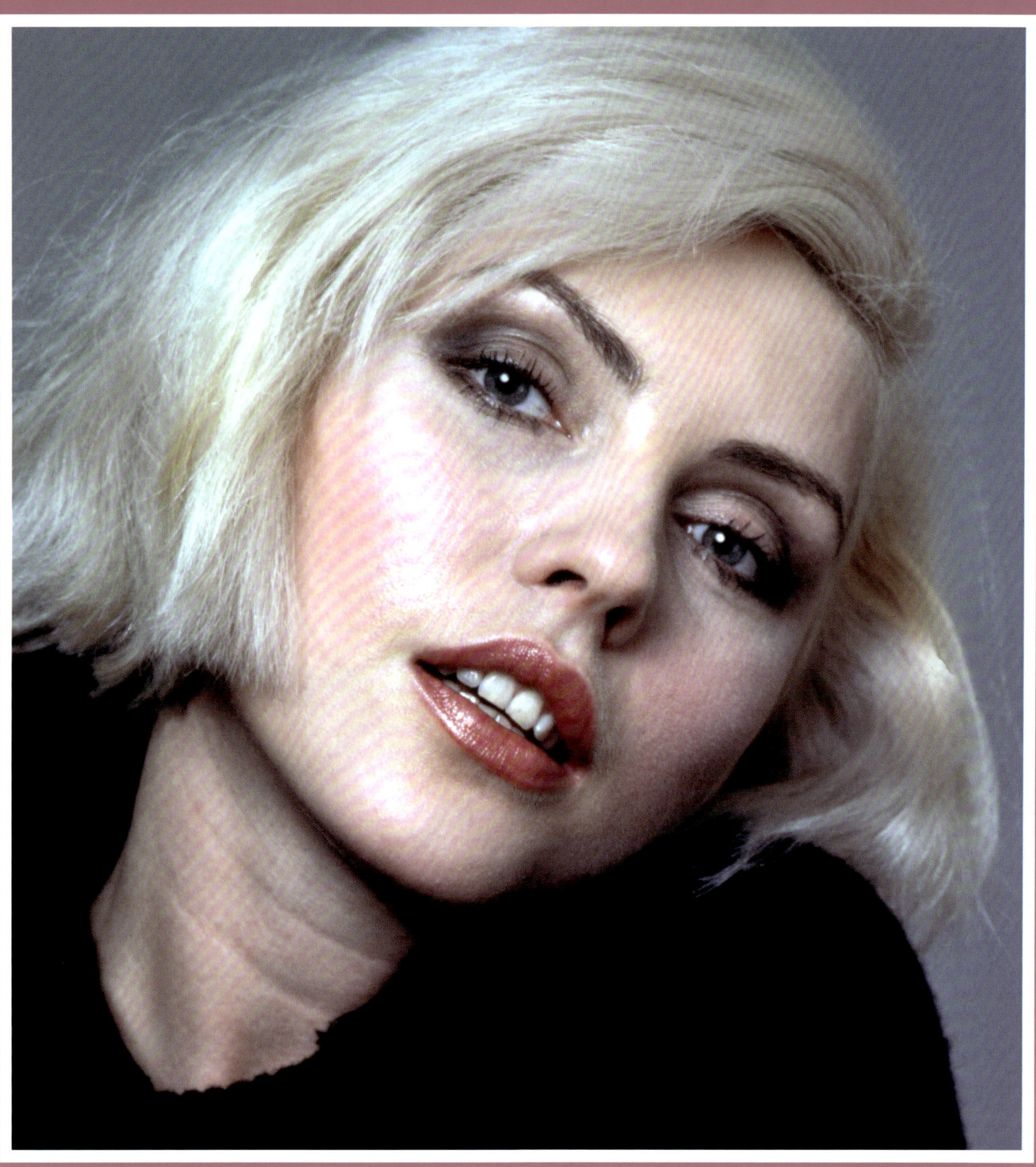

MARILYN
AND THE CELEBRITIES
SHE INFLUENCED

'I FELT RELATED TO MARILYN SPIRITUALLY.'

– Debbie Harry, *Vice*, 2012

Fashion is about transformation and Marilyn's career evidenced the wide possibilities of the power of an electrifying appearance. She took everything to the stage when it came to dressing up for an audience and spent hours in front of the mirror refining her looks. It was a formula that still inspires celebrities today to interpret Monroe's style and is testimony to her enduring status as a film goddess. In 1956, when Marilyn filmed *The Prince and the Showgirl* in London, the newspapers typically went crazy about her, with the *Daily Mirror* describing Marilyn as 'the sleek, the pink and the beautiful' while *The Spectator* pointed out that she was 'as intelligent as she was pleasant as she was pretty' (quoted in Spoto, 1993). Monroe was not simply courting an audience with her clothes, but the paparazzi and the media, too. She was shrewd enough to know she needed them onside to succeed in her career and because she always delivered, without fail, they kept coming back for more.

This symbiotic relationship is commonplace now in times of myriad digital platforms. In a series of 1961 interviews, Marilyn spoke of how she 'has to look a certain way – be beautiful – and act a certain way, be talented,' yet at the same time admitting, 'it's a relief to get in sloppy clothes and not worry about the impression you're making – any of it. But it's part of my career – my life! – and I accept it' (quoted in Weatherby, 1989). Red carpet appearances are a well-established routine today, yet in an overcrowded showground, still one of the most sure-fire ways of magnetising attention is to revisit one of Marilyn's iconic outfits. There are many to choose from and the thrill of seeing the juxtaposition of reinterpretation rarely fails to hit the headlines.

According to fashion historian Darnell-Jamal Lisby, Monroe 'was probably one of the first to use dress as a tool for that kind of attention and to be quite clever about it. She was just a lot smarter than people thought and she knew exactly what she was doing in those moments' (quoted in Lang, 2022). One of the key female musicians to fuse their persona with Marilyn's was Debbie Harry, who headed the New Wave group Blondie, formed in 1974. She explains in a 1990 MTV interview:

> *'I think for the first time, a singer took a visual cue. I really was inspired by film actresses and the blonde sex symbol. So, I combined images, which I don't think had been done up until that point. I was inspired by Marilyn, and Jean Harlow…and all these vivacious women…it was surprising to people and caught on'* (Cliporama, 2018b)

Andy Warhol agreed, and in 1980 Harry was screen-printed in the same way he had pictured Marilyn, reiterating the bond further. The metanarrative of Marilyn is fun to perform, and Monroe's sartorial story never tires for those who connect with her symbolic legend as well as the dazzle of her glamorous gowns. In 2005, the artist Banksy recreated Warhol's 'Marilyn' featuring Kate Moss as Monroe. Most recently, in 2024 at the age of 50, Moss appeared as Monroe in Charlotte Tilbury's 'Hollywood Beauty Icons' red lipstick advert, imitating Monroe's character, Lorelei Lee, from *Gentlemen Prefer Blondes* (1953) when Lee sings 'Diamonds are a Girl's Best Friend'.

Madonna is another celebrity who has connected with Marilyn on many occasions, including her own seminal interpretation of Lorelei for her 'Material Girl' video in 1985. Then again, in 1991 at the Oscars, she donned a white gown and wrap – reminiscent of

Marilyn's outfit by Travilla that she wore at the premiere of *How to Marry a Millionaire* in 1953 – and curled her hair like Monroe's. In her 2012 video for 'Give Me All Your Luvin'' with rappers M.I.A. and Nicki Minaj, all three give their own rendition of Monroe's *The Seven Year Itch* subway tableau, wearing their hair blonde and dressed in white frocks. Minaj adopted the Marilyn theme again that year with a track titled 'Marilyn Monroe', which included the lyrics 'Sometimes I feel like Marilyn Monroe. I'm insecure, yeah, I make mistakes'.

Marilyn could be whatever her audience wanted her to be, and this has metamorphosed into a constellation of celebrities who seize on her magic. From Taylor Swift to Travis Barker, Saweetie to Scarlett Johansson, and even Ryan Gosling at the 2024 Oscars, the biggest, best and brightest have added shine to their allure by being just a little more like Marilyn.

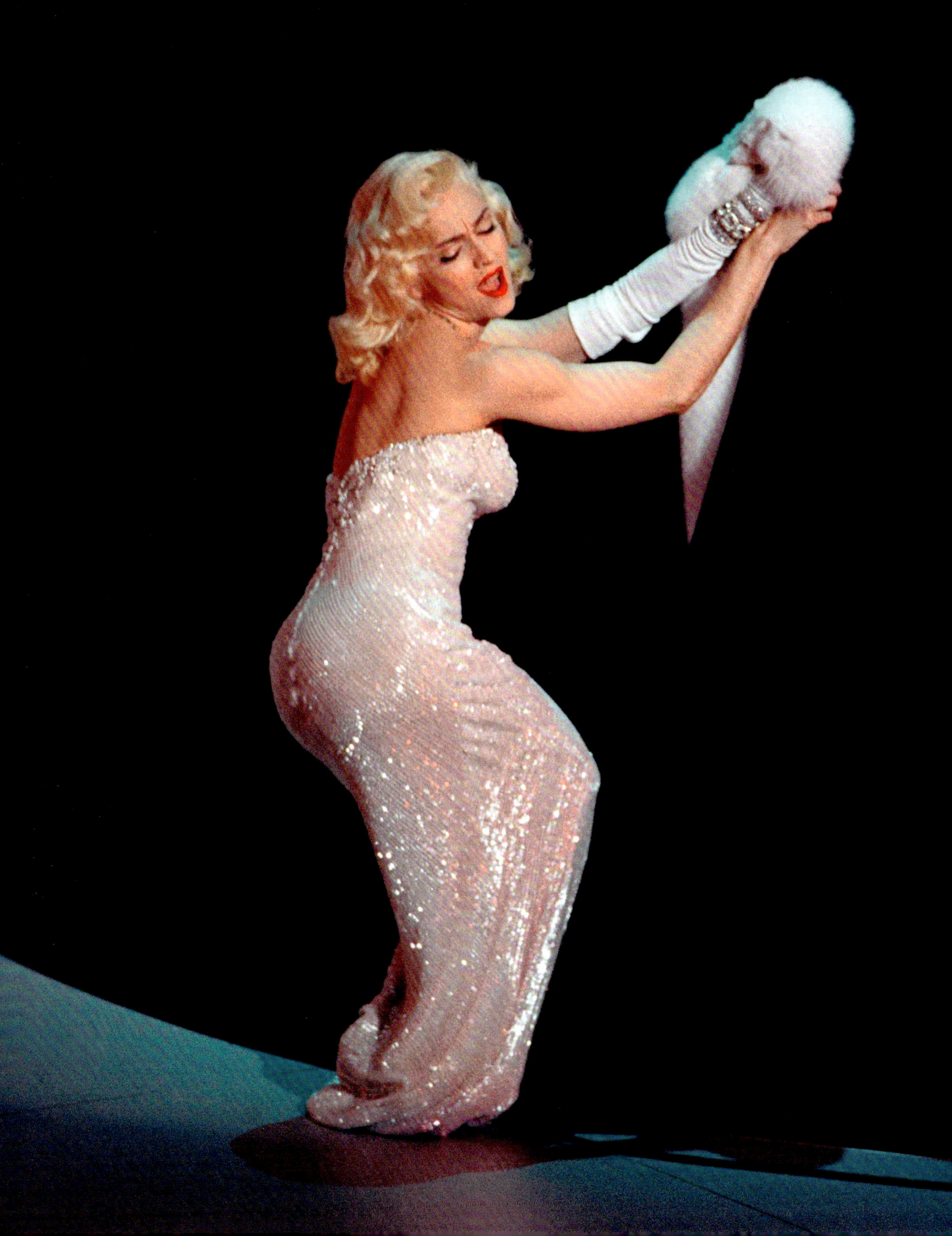

Seeing Marilyn at the Actors Studio in 1956, Gloria Steinem recalls how 'she sat by herself, her body hidden in shapeless black sweater and slacks, her skin luminescent as she put her hands up to her face, as if trying to hide herself' (Steinem, 2014). Monroe had recently launched her own production company and, as a result, signed a better deal with the Hollywood giant Fox. She was a woman who wanted to be known for more than her body. Despite her inner turmoil, her traumatic childhood and her difficult emergence into the limelight out of the shadows of the often-unscrupulous Hollywood elites, she was growing in stature. Among her many ace cards was a shrewd fashion sense.

Six years later, she walked onto the grand stage at Madison Square Garden, wearing the most famous Jean Louis dress ever made. She had told the designer she wanted it to look like she was wearing nothing at all. Sketched by the fledgling King of Bling, Bob Mackie, the finished frock, made from soufflé gauze and crystals, did indeed give the illusion of being naked. *Time* magazine reported:

> *'The figure was famous. And for one breathless moment, the 15,000 people in Madison Square Garden thought they were going to see all of it. Onto the stage sashayed Marilyn Monroe, attired in a great bundle of white mink. Arriving at the lectern, she turned and swept the furs from her shoulders. A slight gasp rose from the audience before it was realized that she was really wearing a skin-tight, flesh-toned gown.'* (*Time*, 1962)

Monroe was there to sing to her purported lover in the most high-profile, scandalous style – at President Kennedy's 45th birthday celebration and a Democratic Party fund-raiser. According to Bob Mackie, Marilyn 'looked amazing and accomplished exactly what she intended to. Her figure was at its peak, the dress was a classic shape of fashion at the time' (Brockington, 2022). Wearing a dress that fit like a glove and arriving brazenly late, Monroe knew exactly what she was doing. Showing herself off on her terms, she was clearly in control of the moment.

Fast-forward 60 years and Kim Kardashian, one of today's most famous celebrities, caused almost equal affront by borrowing the same gown and wearing it to the 2022 gilded glamour-themed Met Gala. She told her 309 million Instagram followers that she was 'so honoured to be wearing the iconic dress' and revealed that she only dared wear it for the entrance and photo call, changing into a duplicate for the party proper. Talking to *Vogue* about her idol, Kardashian reflected: 'For me the most Marilyn Monroe moment is when she sang "Happy Birthday," to JFK, it was *that* look' (Nnadi, 2022)). Later on, she paid tribute to Monroe again by wearing the green sequinned Norman Norell gown that Marilyn had worn to the 1962 Golden Globes where she won the Henrietta Award for World Film Favourite Female.

It seemed that the whole world had an opinion about Kardashian's look for the evening, with her dress choice hitting every headline for days afterwards. CNN reported: 'The gown Kardashian wore represents a particular aspect of Monroe's celebrity—infamy rather than fame—and Monroe's unique ability to take something scandalous and embrace it rather than allow herself to be shamed by it' (Gates, 2022). There's no doubt the dress shone bright when shimmied in and, losing 16lb (7.25kg) to fit into it, Kim clearly had a compulsion to sample some of its charisma. In Kim Kardashian's universe, and at the 2022 Met Gala, it's the red carpet where image control is key; it's also the ultimate space where dreams are played out, reframed and pinged around the world. Kim and her body possessed their very own magical moment at The Met that night in May and she showed everyone who she wanted to be, even if it was only make-believe for a twinkling.

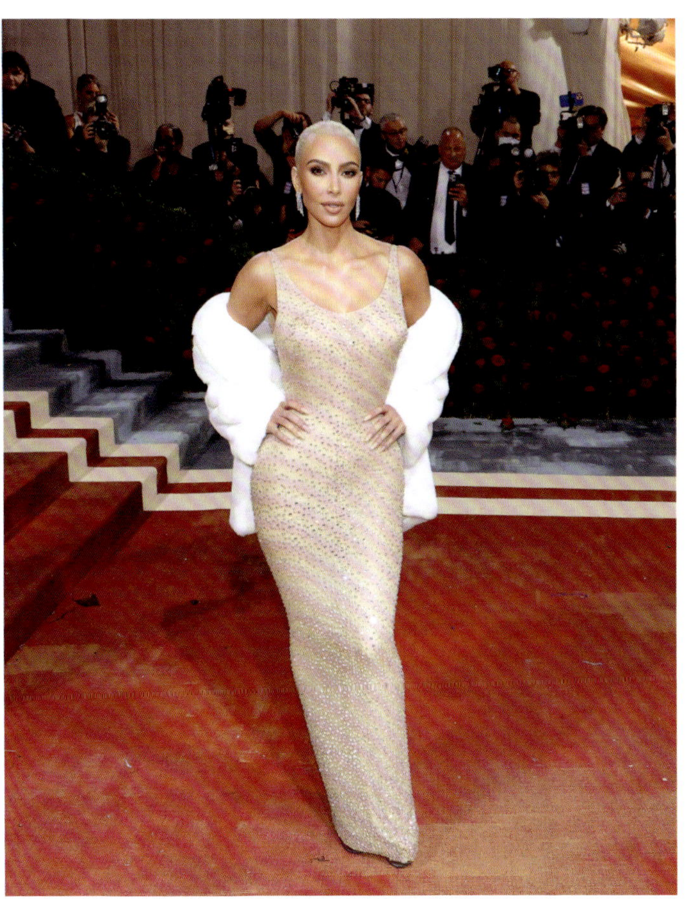

Kim Kardashian arrives on the red carpet for the Met Gala wearing Marilyn's nude Jean Louis dress, 2022

'IT WILL FOREVER BE ONE OF THE GREATEST PRIVILEGES OF MY LIFE TO BE ABLE TO CHANNEL MY INNER MARILYN IN THIS WAY, ON SUCH A SPECIAL NIGHT.'

– Kim Kardashian, Instagram, April 2022

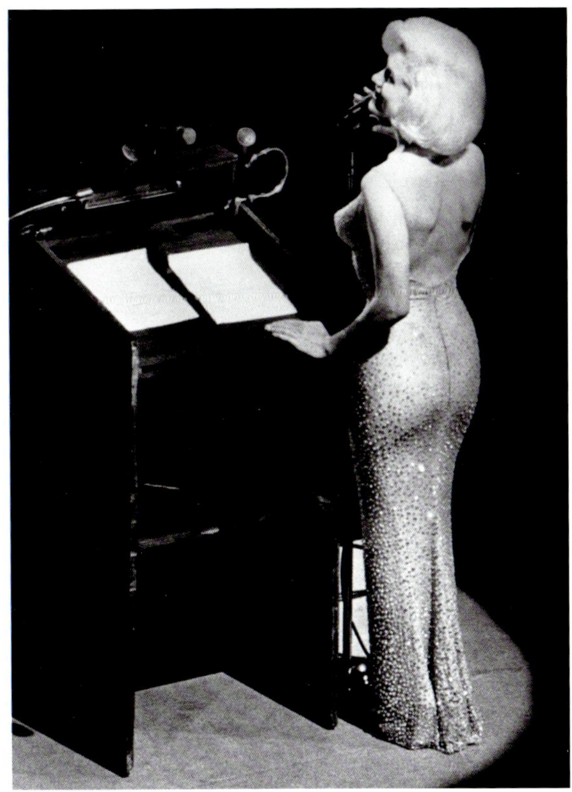

Marilyn sings 'Happy Birthday ' to President John F. Kennedy at Madison Square Garden in New York City, wearing the most famous Jean Louis dress ever made, 1962

MARILYN
AND BILLIE EILISH

When Billie Eilish arrived at the Met Gala in 2021, she embodied the theme of 'America: A Lexicon of Fashion' by taking a leaf out of Marilyn Monroe's style book. The Oscar de la Renta peach tulle dress she wore was, as stylist Dena Giannini revealed, inspired by the black Charles LeMaire gown worn by Monroe to present the award for Best Sound Recording at the Academy Awards in March 1951. Monroe had borrowed the original from Twentieth Century Fox's wardrobe department and it would be seen on the big screen in May that same year, donned by the actress Valentina Cortesa in *The House on Telegraph Hill* (1951).

The dress was a poised statement for the 19-year-old singer who had, up till then, been most famous for a bold and baggy goth-skate-anime wardrobe, which she admits to wearing in order to hide her body. Blossoming on the red carpet, Eilish revealed how she felt 'it was time for this. I feel like I've grown so much over the last few years and my confidence has gotten so much better and I've always wanted to do this' (*Vogue*, 2021). Eilish matched the dress with Monroe's hair style, too, wearing it in a loosely waved platinum bob, reminiscent of Marilyn in *Let's Make Love* (1960), and her jewellery was all Cartier, who loaned pieces to all the biggest stars at the Met Gala that evening. When asked what had inspired her look, Eilish replied, 'it's inspired by all the dresses I wanted to wear growing up and how I wanted to look' (Access Hollywood, 2021).

A year later, Eilish gave another fashion nod to Monroe, this time in the baggy style that she is known for. On her world tour, she appeared on stage in Glasgow wearing an oversized T-shirt and matching cycling shorts covered in a repeating black-and-white image of Marilyn's face. The designer, Doug Wiggins, specialises in recycled fashion, combining it with his penchant for screen printing. 'Nowadays, fast fashion is

crazy. I hate it,' he says. 'I think taking a step back and realizing what you are wearing and how it was made is important. [...] being able to get big artists like Billie Eilish, for example, to be wearing a used shirt that I made her, it shows other people that it's cool.' (Quoted in Gomez, 2022).

Having spent years wearing hand-me-down clothes and borrowing from studio wardrobe departments, Marilyn would probably have been very much on board with Wiggins' ethos.

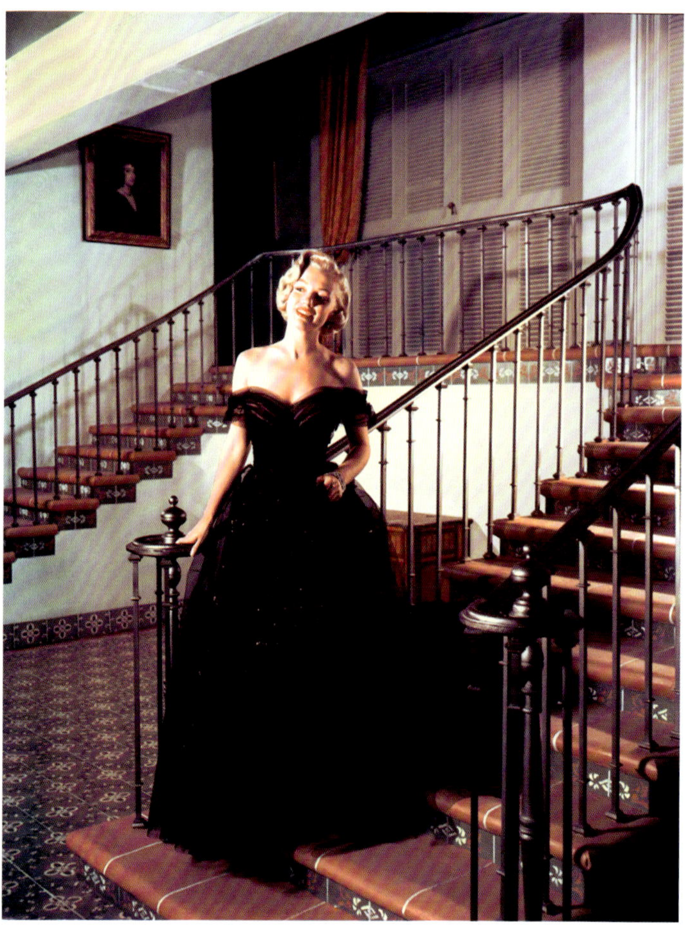

Marilyn wears a black off-the-shoulder Charles LeMaire tulle gown to the
23rd Annual Academy Awards in 1951

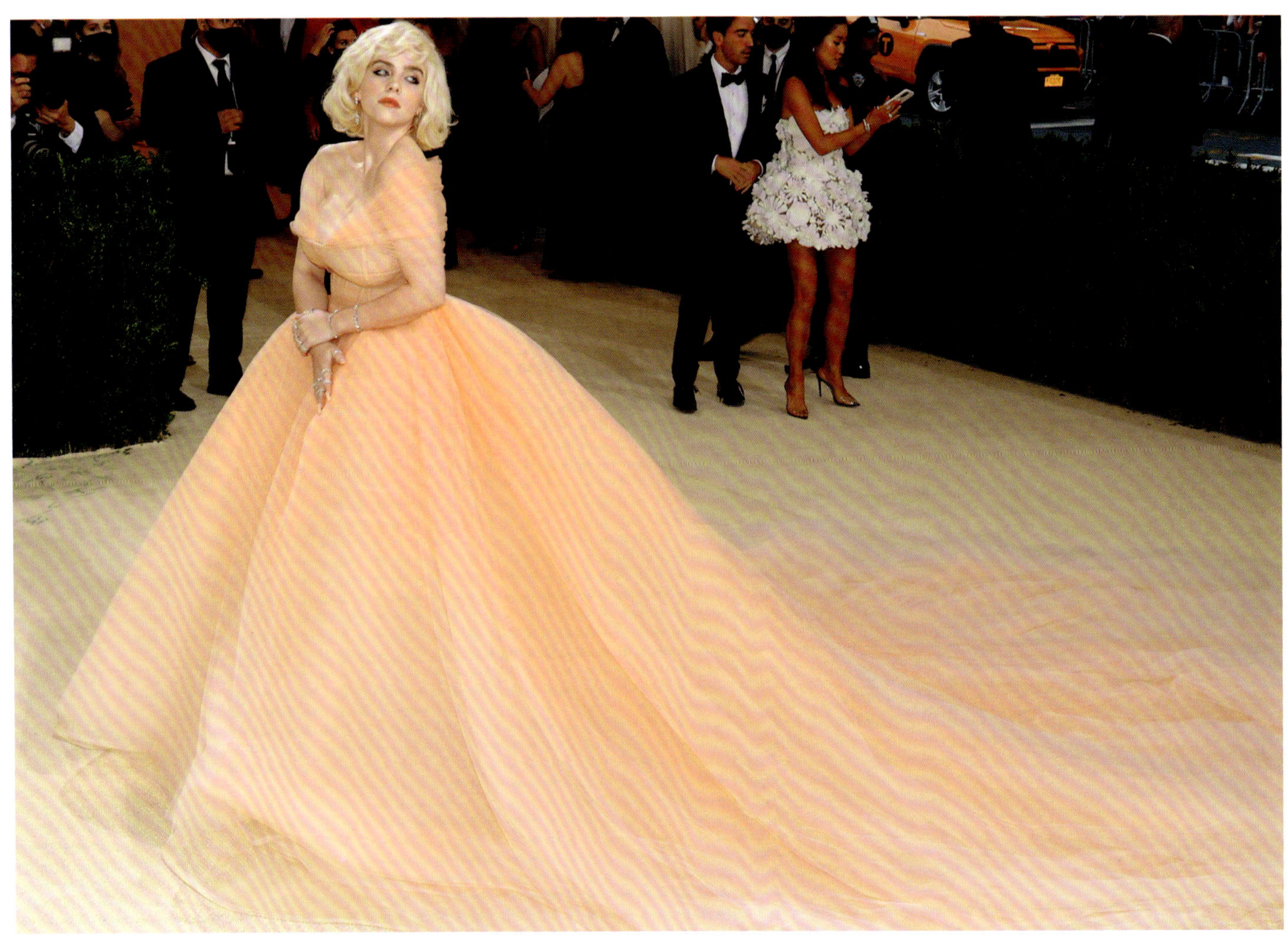

Billie Eilish arrives at the 2021 Met Gala wearing a Marilyn-inspired
Oscar de la Renta tulle dress, with platinum locks to match

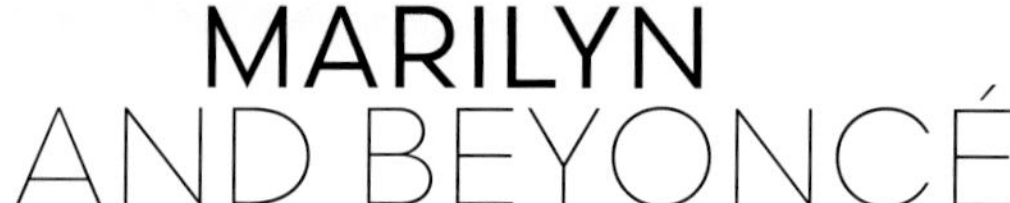

MARILYN
AND BEYONCÉ

Beyoncé's affinity with Marilyn crystallised in 2007 when she wore an Elie Saab plunge-front gold halterneck gown to the Golden Globes. She had been nominated for Best Actress for her role as Deena Jones in *Dreamgirls* (2006) and the dress she wore was a tribute to the celebrated William Travilla design that Monroe had worn in her 1953 film *Gentlemen Prefer Blondes*. Although in the film the audience glimpse the frock for only a second (as, reportedly, the censors felt it was too daring), the knife-pleated lamé frock has become iconic and is testimony to the timelessness of Monroe's styling. Saab's Monroe homage for Beyoncé felt relevant and contemporary and in 2024, *Vogue* nominated it as one of the best Golden Globe dresses of all time.

The history of the dress is somewhat controversial, however. Marilyn chose it to wear to the Photoplay Awards to accept her win as Fastest Rising Star of 1952; it was a big night for her, and a great promotion. The dress was tight; indeed, she had been sewn into it. When Monroe walked up to the stage to collect her plaque, the audience whooped their approval. Not everyone appreciated the dress, though. Veteran star Joan Crawford told reporter Bob Thomas exactly what she thought: 'It was like a burlesque show,' she said, cattily.

> *'The publicity has gone too far. She is making the mistake of believing her publicity. Someone should make her see the light. She should be told that the public likes provocative feminine personalities; but it also likes to know that underneath it all, the actresses are ladies.'*
> (Quoted in Robinson, 2017)

When Beyoncé wore the Elie Saab gown, she hit the best dressed lists; Marilyn, meanwhile, was castigated. Rising to the challenge, she spoke to a friendly member of the press, Louella Parsons – one of the most powerful gossip columnists at the time – who printed her response to the public brouhaha. Monroe countered Crawford saying:

> *'At first, all I could think of was why should she select me to blast? She is a great star. I'm just starting. And then, when the first hurt began to die down, I told myself she must have spoken to Mr. Thomas impulsively, without thinking.'* (Quoted in Robinson, 2017)

Beyoncé's inner Monroe appeared again later that year when she appeared in Giorgio Armani's Emporio Armani Diamonds perfume advert. Directed by Jake Nava, she sang an updated version of Monroe's 'Diamonds are a Girl's Best Friend'. It was perfect casting and Beyoncé gave the classic song a contemporary pulse and resonance. Likewise in 2014, the USA's favourite LGBTQ magazine *Out* styled Beyoncé as a modern-day Marilyn, shooting her in black and white, wearing a platinum wig and rhinestones. The sartorial reference to Marilyn, as well as her life story, underwrote the choice editor-in-chief Aaron Hicklin had made. There is a powerful correlation between the marginalised heroism of Monroe, Beyoncé and the LGBTQ+ community. Upon uniting the two icons for the cover imagery, Hicklin reflected: 'Getting Beyoncé for *Out* felt like an endorsement of the magazine's place as a cultural force, and while she did not identify as queer, there was no question that she resonated in the lives of queer people […] She was an outsider who had worked to make her success' (Street, 2022).

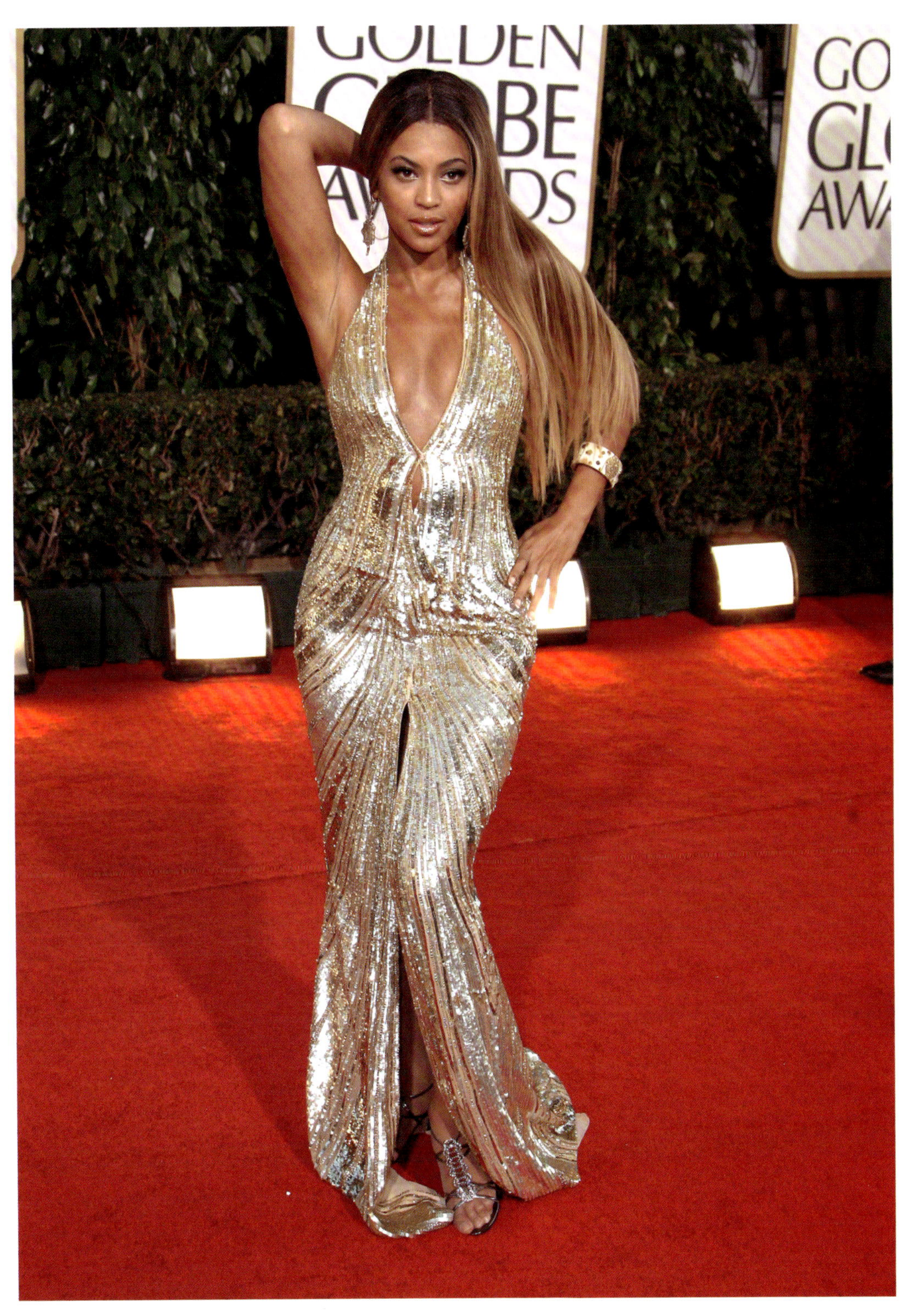

Beyoncé arrives at the 2007 Golden Globes ceremony wearing a gold plunge halterneck
Travilla gown in a nod to Marilyn's *Gentlemen Prefer Blondes* (1953) outfit

MARILYN
AND LANA DEL REY

Whether she is wearing a blonde wig or not, Lana Del Rey chooses visual cues that are firmly rooted in the legacy of Marilyn Monroe. Monroe symbolises Americana, beauty, sadness and hope: all metaphors Del Rey explores in her work. Lana's beauty is infused with the glamorous 1950s and '60s aesthetic of Monroe: hair that is set but tousled, clothes that emphasise a wayward femininity. And while Del Rey's wardrobe is always fashion-forward, there is a parallel world where what she wears might just be found in Marilyn's closet. She is a super-fan, keeping 'a magazine cut-out of Marilyn Monroe tacked to a window in the bathroom', according to *Harper's Bazaar* (Cooper Jones, 2023).

Direct tributes by the New York singer are repeated occurrences. At the 2015 Golden Globes, nominated for Best Original Motion Picture Song for 'Big Eyes', the title track of Tim Burton's film, Lana elected to wear a vintage William Travilla, floor-length, halterneck evening dress – a turquoise version of Marilyn's famous 'golden gown'. Del Rey accessorised the dress with vintage shoes and a Ferragamo clutch – another nod to Monroe's favourite Italian accessory designer.

In 2012, Lana's draw towards Marilyn manifested in the video for 'National Anthem', which featured a breathy invocation of Monroe's 1962 version of 'Happy Birthday Mr. President', sung to JFK in Madison Square Garden. Del Rey wore a nude sheath dress reminiscent of the iconic Jean Louis gown Marilyn had sparkled in. The connection continued with the art film she released to support the track, 'Candy Necklace' from the 2023 album *Did You Know That There's a Tunnel Under Ocean Blvd.* This time Del Rey referenced Monroe's minimal wardrobe. Wearing a simple black turtleneck sweater and cigarette trousers matched with a blonde wig, she was unmistakably Marilyn, as shot by the German American photojournalist Alfred Eisenstaedt for his 1953 *Life* magazine 'Marilyn at Home' portraits. Fans of Del Rey were equally thrilled with her performance at the MITA Festival in Rio de Janeiro; her first 'full' concert for four years, it was an occasion to emulate her Hollywood idol once more by wearing her hair styled 'Marilyn platinum' once again.

'FROM WHEN I WAS YOUNGER, SEEING HER IN PICTURES AND MOVIES, I JUST GOT THAT SHE WAS SWEET. AND SHE COULD BE FUCKING FUNNY. IT'S JUST LIKE, THAT'S MY GIRL. BUT I GUESS EVERYONE WHO LIKES THAT KIND OF THING PROBABLY FEELS LIKE THAT. SHE MIGHT HAVE, YOU KNOW, THE MOST RECOGNIZABLE FACE – THIRD TO JESUS, AND WHO ELSE?'

– Lana Del Rey, *The Hollywood Reporter*, 2023 (quoted in O'Connell, 2023)

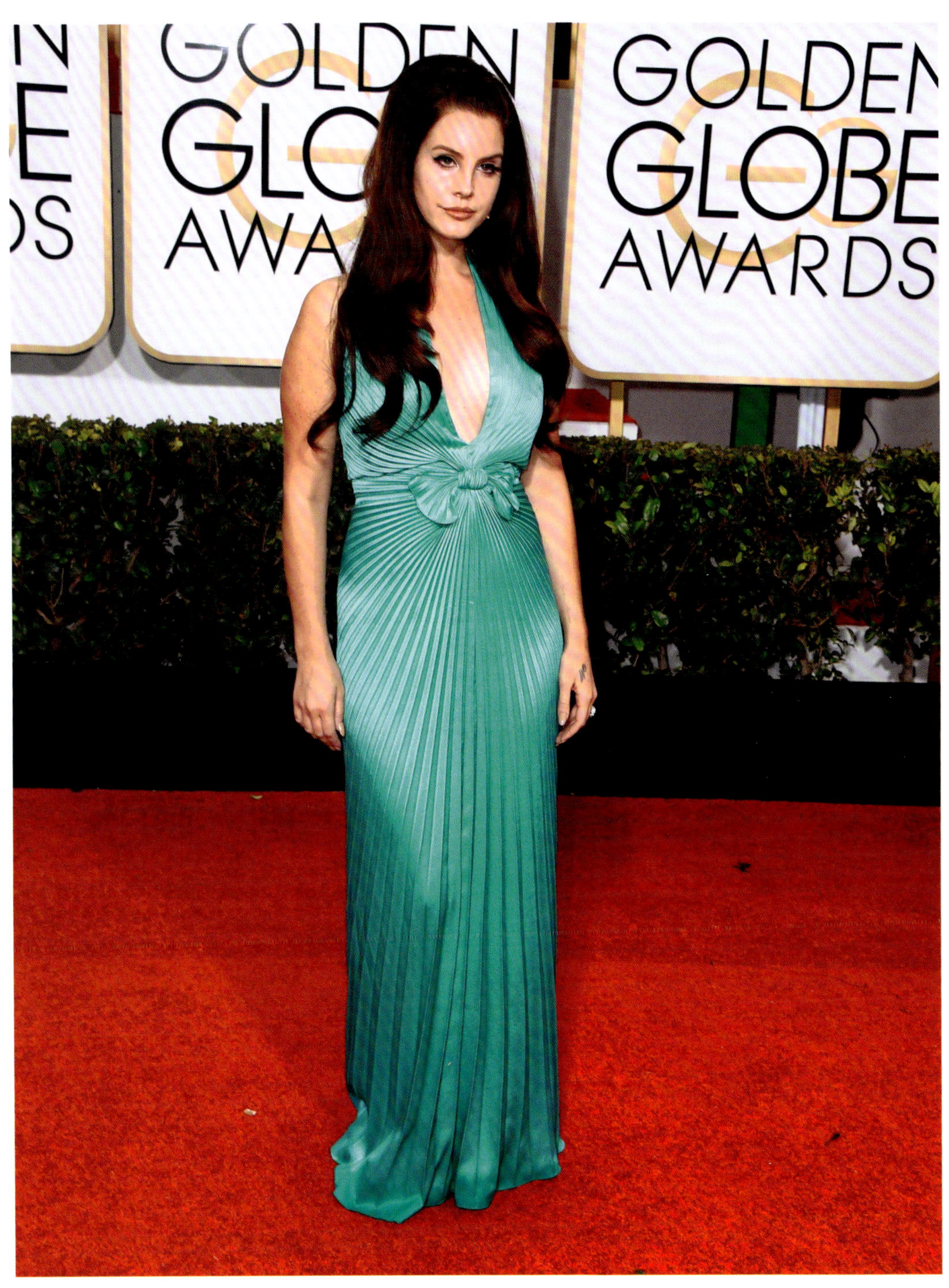

Lana Del Rey arrives at the 2015 Golden Globe Awards wearing a turquoise version
of Travilla's famous dress that Marilyn wore in *Gentlemen Prefer Blondes* (1953)

AFTERWORD

Marilyn Monroe's wardrobe was central to the superstar she became. Through the clothes she wore, she crafted a playfully sexy persona adored by both men and women, and her legendary outfits are today instantly recognisable.

Growing up during the Great Depression, Marilyn lived through lean years which gave agency to her ambition to succeed. As a young up-and-coming actress, she had only meagre funds which meant being resourceful, so the few outfits she had, she wore both on screen and off, accessorising them to change her look. She quickly learned how to look good on camera and worked hard to craft a visual brand that sold in Hollywood. So successful was she at the sensationally seductive, witty and warm roles she played, that her fans expected the 'onscreen Marilyn' off-screen, too. And she never disappointed. In February 1954, despite the freezing cold, she sang to the American troops stationed in South Korea wearing only a bugle-beaded, sequin shift dress. In her characteristically upbeat fashion, she described the trip as 'the best thing that ever happened to me. I never felt like a star before in my heart' (National Portrait Gallery, n.d.)

In her downtime, she chose effortlessly stylish pieces and made them her own. Discreetly chic white shirts, cashmere sweaters and ballet slippers were her go-to daywear; while at home, she often pulled on a towelling bathrobe for comfort. In 1955, when she set up her own production company with Milton Greene and began to attend the Actors Studio in New York, she was spotted regularly wearing a favourite beatnik black turtle-neck jumper and stripy capri pants, an outfit that was not dissimilar to one she had worn for a photoshoot in 1953 with Alfred Eisenstaedt. Cropped capris and a simple sweater were as much her sartorial signature as her most high-octane red-carpet wear. Such is the impact that Marilyn has had on fashion culture, that even the Keds sneakers she teamed with jeans in the 1952 film *Clash by Night* were revisited by the heritage American brand in 2022.

Marilyn knew what looked good and chose designers who understood the fashion language she employed onscreen. Two of her most famous dresses are the gold lamé halterneck dress, chosen to make a sensational entrance at the 1953 Photoplay Awards and worn for just a moment in *Gentlemen Prefer Blondes*, and the legendary white gown featured a couple of years later in *The Seven Year Itch*. Similar in silhouette, albeit different lengths and fabrics, both were crafted by one of her favourite designers, William Travilla.

Today, all aspects of Marilyn's style choices continue to inspire, and what better proof than the multiple reinterpretations of her chosen outfits by key fashion houses, modelled by the biggest celebrities at the highest profile events, especially on the red carpet. Jessica Chastain hit headlines at the 2015 Met Gala, shining in a Givenchy reworking of the celebrated gold Travilla dress; at the 2017 Oscars, a gown by Dior worn by Charlize Theron paid equal tribute, as did the sequinned Burberry design modelled by Naomi Campbell at the 2014 Evening Standard Theatre Awards in London, establishing the iconic evening dress as a modern classic and showcasing Monroe's fashionable legacy. The sparkling nude dress that she wore to sing 'Happy Birthday' to JFK at Madison Square Garden in New York, created by French designer Jean Louis, has informed myriad 'naked' dresses worn by fashion connoisseurs: in 1999, Angelina Jolie wore a jewelled Randolph Duke interpretation to the Golden Globes; in 2014, Rihanna accepted the CFDA Fashion Icon Award wearing an Adam Selman version; and in 2015, Jennifer Lopez glittered in a gold Zuhair Murad couture homage at the *Vanity Fair* Oscar party.

Marilyn Monroe's influence on fashion has endured over three-quarters of a century. A self-made success, she used her canny knack for style to help her accomplish her ambitions. What she wore, and the stories her clothes tell, influence not just celebrities but everyone who values the transformative appeal of fashion.

Marilyn wears her own clothes while modelling for Milton Greene in Laurel Canyon for *Look* magazine, 1953

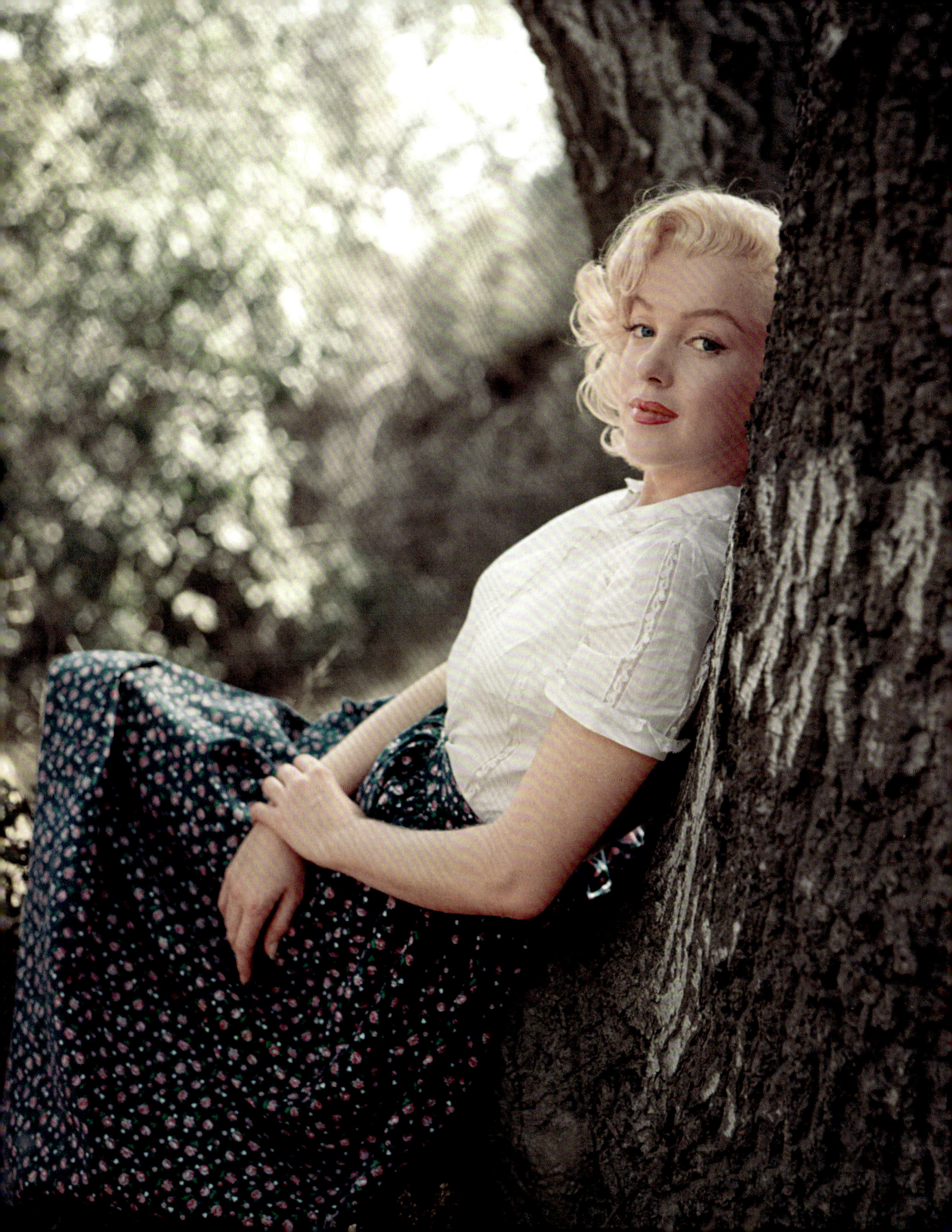

BIBLIOGRAPHY

A _______________________

Access Hollywood (2021) 'Billie Eilish Says She Feels "Squished" in 2021 Met Gala Look', *YouTube*, 14 September 2021. Available at: https://www.youtube.com/watch?v=k3S80UILAMc. Accessed: Feb 2024.

ACMI (2015) 'Uncovering Orry-Kelly with Gillian Armstrong', *YouTube.* Available at: https://www.youtube.com/watch?v=wx-9WxeBcNjl. Accessed: Feb 2024. Accessed: Mar 2024

Ahmed, Osman (2015) 'The YSL Collection That Shook Classic Couture to its Core', *AnOther Magazine*, published online 30 November 2015. Available at: https://www.anothermag.com/fashion-beauty/8078/the-ysl-collection-that-shook-classic-couture-to-its-core#:~:text=One%20of%20the%20models%2C%20a,"She%20was%20very%20sexy. Accessed Feb 2024.

AlainSky (2013) 'Marilyn Monroe – Person to Person – Edward R. Murrow – April 8, 1955' *YouTube.* Available at: https://www.youtube.com/watch?v=Vv7zQWw-6JOE. Accessed: March 2024.

American Masters Digital Archive (2006) *Gloria Steinem, Marilyn Monroe: Still Life*, WNET. 21 February, 2006. Available at: https://www.pbs.org/wnet/americanmasters/archive/interview/gloria-steinem/. Accessed: March 2024.

Anderson, LaDale (2010) 'Interview with Marilyn Monroe Photographer Bill Carroll', *Canyon News*, published online 27 June 2010. Available at: http://divinemarilyn.canalblog.com/archives/2010/07/05/29364687.html. Accessed Feb 2024.

Arnold, Eve (1960) *Magnum Editions: Marilyn Monroe on the set of "The Misfits", 1960*, [online article]. Available at: https://www.magnumphotos.com/shop/collections/marilyn-monroe/magnum-editions-marilyn-monroe-on-the-set-of-the-misfits-1960/#:~:text=Arnold%20noted%20Monroe%27s%20fragile%20state,point%3A%20

"I%27ve%20been Accessed: March 2024.

Arnold, Rebecca (2007) 'Modern Fashions for Modern Women: The Evolution of New York Sportswear in the 1930s', *Costume*, 41:1, 111–125.

B _______________________

Banner, Lois (2012) *Marilyn: The Passion and the Paradox*, Bloomsbury USA.

Beaton, Cecil (2014) *Cecil Beaton: Portraits and Profiles*, Frances Lincoln.

Beauvoir, Simone de (1946) *The Second Sex*, Vintage Classics (this edition 1997).

Berle, Milton (1974) *Milton Berle: An Autobiography*, Applause Theatre & Cinema Books

Berry, Sarah (2000) *Screen Style: Fashion and Femininity in 1930s Hollywood*, University of Minnesota Press.

Bigsby, Christopher (2009) *Arthur Miller: 1962–2005*, Phoenix.

Bolton, L., Adams, L., Witt, H.D., Edgar, D., Freestone, C. and Pepper, T. (2015) 'Curating Marilyn Monroe: Interviews with the British Film Institute and the National Portrait Gallery'. *Film, Fashion & Consumption*, 4(2–3), pp.197–220.

Bowles, Hamish (2019) 'Inside the Wild World of Gucci's Alessandro Michele', *Vogue*, 15 April 2019 [online publication]. Available at: https://www.vogue.com/article/gucci-alessandro-michele-interview-may-2019-issue#:~:text="My%20mom%20was%20really%20obsessed,at%20the%20local%20coffee%20shop. Accessed: Feb 2014.

Brockington, Ariana (2022) 'Bob Mackie says Kim Kardashian wearing Marilyn Monroe's dress was a "big mistake"', Today, 17 May 2022 [online publication]. Available at: https://www.today.com/style/celeb-style/bob-mackie-says-kim-kardashian-wearing-marilyn-monroes-dress-was-big-m-rcna29290. Accessed: April 2022.

C _______________________

Capote, Truman (1980) *Music for Chameleons*, Random House.

Carlson, Peter (2009) 'Nikita Khrushchev Goes to Hollywood', *Smithsonian Magazine*, July edition. Available at: https://www.smithsonianmag.com/history/nikita-khrushchev-goes-to-hollywood-30668979/. Accessed: March 2024.

Christie's (1999) Christie's NYC sale, [online catalogues]. Available at: https://www.christies.com/en/auction/the-personal-property-of-marilyn-monroe-9645/ Accessed: April 2024.

Church Gibson, Pamela (2015) 'Marilyn and Her Female Audiences: Consumption, Transgression, Emulation', *Film, Fashion and Consumption*, 4(2&3), pp.159–175.

Cliporama (2018a) 'Shelley Winters on Marilyn Monroe – Diva on Diva', *YouTube*, 2 July 2018. Available at: https://www.youtube.com/watch?v=cRvw-jm3eq3g. Accessed: Feb 2024.

Cliporama (2018b) 'Debbie Harry on Marilyn Monroe – Diva on Diva', *YouTube*, 12 August 2018. Available at: https://www.youtube.com/watch?v=hVi5vvT5wHs. Accessed: Feb 2024.

Cooper, Anna (2023) *The American Abroad. The Imperial Gaze in Postwar Hollywood Cinema*, Bloomsbury Publishing.

Cooper Jones, Chloé (2023) 'Lana Del Rey Leads With Her Heart', *Harper's Bazaar*, 21 November 2023 [online publication]. Available at: https://www.harpersbazaar.com/culture/art-books-music/a45862475/lana-del-rey-interview-2023/. Accessed: Feb 2024.

The Untimely Passing of Marilyn Monroe (1962) [Tape; online]. *News of the Day*, British Pathé. Available at: https://www.britishpathe.com/asset/98290/. Accessed: Feb 2024.

D _______________________

de Klerk, Amy (2019) 'The house of Karl Lagerfeld pays tribute to late designer with celebrity collaborations', *Harpers Bazaar*, 18 September 2019 [online publication]. Available at: https://www.harpersbazaar.com/uk/fashion/fashion-news/a28360235/karl-lagerfeld-white-shirt-tribute/#. Accessed: March 2024.

de la Haye, Amy (2020) 'Essay: Haute Couture Under Occupation', *ShowStudio*, published online 1 July 2020. Available at: https://www.showstudio.com/projects/fashion-in-a-time-of-crisis/haute-couture-under-occupation#:~:text=By%20February%201943%2C%20just%2047,reduced%20to%20feature%20only%2060.&text=As%20ever%2C%20haute%20couture%20remained,than%201%25–of%20women. Accessed: Feb 2024.

Downey, Lynn (2016) *Levi Strauss: The Man Who Gave Blue Jeans to the World*, University of Massachusetts Press.

Durrer, Preston (2005) 'Books of Plays Published by Fred A. Woodress', *87th Infantry Division Legacy Association,* 25 June 2005 [online publication]. Available at: http://87thinfantrydivision.com/preston-durrer/book-of-plays-published-by-fred-a-woodress. Accessed: April 2024.

E _______________________

Emery, Joy Spanabel (2014) *A History of the Paper Pattern Industry: The Home Dressmaking Fashion Revolution*, Bloomsbury.

F _______________________

Fernandez, Ivan (2010) 'Marilyn Monroe Photographer Bill Carroll Talks About Working With a Young Norma Jeane', *LA Weekly*, published online 28 June 2010. Available at: https://www.laweekly.com/marilyn-monroe-photographer-bill-carroll-talks-about-working-with-a-young-norma-jeane/. Accessed: Feb 2024.

Ferragamo, Salvatore (1957) *Shoemaker of Dreams –The Autobiography of Salvatore Ferragamo*, Harrap, London.

Frey, Kaitlyn (2017) 'Elle Fanning Says Choosing the Vibrant Pop Art Versace Gown She Wore to the "InStyle" Awards Was "A No-Brainer"', *People*, 24 October 2017 [online publication]. Available at: https://people.com/style/elle-fanning-marilyn-monroe-versace-dress-instyle-awards/. Accessed: Feb 2024.

Fury, Alexander (2023) 'The Radical History and Philosophy of Coco Chanel', *AnOther Magazine,* 22 September 2023. Available at: https://www.anothermag.com/fashion-beauty/15125/the-radical-history-and-philosophy-of-coco-chanel-v-and-a-chanel-exhibition. Accessed: Feb 2024.

G _______________________

Garcia-Furtado, Laia (2022) 'This Reissued '50s Handbook Is A Trove Of Brilliant (And Frequently Hilarious) Fashion Advice', British *Vogue*, published online 18 September 2022. Available at: https://www.vogue.co.uk/arts-and-lifestyle/article/claire-mccardell-what-shall-i-wear#:~:text=It%20is%20not%20an%20exaggeration,in%20the%201940s%20and%20%2750s. Accessed: Feb 2024.

Gates, Racquel (2022) 'Opinion: Kim Kardashian gives us a glimpse of how hard it was to be Marilyn Monroe, the star', *CNN Opinion* [online publication], 10 May 2022. Available at: https://edition.cnn.com/2022/05/10/opinions/marilyn-monroe-kim-kardashian-met-gala-dress-gates/index.html. Accessed: April 2024.

Gefter, Philip (2020) 'Richard Avedon, Marilyn Monroe, and Hollywood's Blond Mania', *Literary Hub*, 27 October 2020. Available at: https://lithub.com/richard-avedon-marilyn-monroe-and-hollywoods-blond-mania/. Accessed: Feb 2024.

Goles, Kelly (2023) 'What Not to Wear: Clothing Rationing During World War II', Law Library of Congress, published online 19 January 2023. Available at: https://blogs.loc.gov/law/2023/01/what-not-to-wear-clothing-rationing-during-world-war-ii/#:~:text=The%20order%20specified%20the%20amount,hoods%2C%20and%20scarves%20were%20banned. Accessed: Feb 2024.

Gomez, Adrian (2022) 'ABQ artist transforms discarded garments into elevated, recycled pieces', *Albuquerque Journal*. Available at: https://www.abqjournal.com/news/local/abq-artist-transforms-discarded-garments-into-elevated-recycled-pieces/article_d39fef89-2397-5153-862d-3eb255b8b091.html. Accessed: April 2024.

Greene, Amy (2006) 'Marilyn Monroe: Still Life', American Masters Digital Archive (WNET). April 4, 2006. Available at: https://www.pbs.org/wnet/americanmasters/archive/interview/amy-greene/. Accessed: Feb 2024.

Greene, Joshua (2017) *The Essential Marilyn Monroe: 50 Sessions*, ACC Art Books

H _______________________

Hanks, Tara (2021) 'Marilyn Inspires "Sweater Dress" Trend', *The Marilyn Report*, 5 October 2021 [online blog]. Available at: https://themarilynreport.com/2021/10/15/marilyn-inspires-sweater-dress-trend/. Accessed: March 2024.

Hanks, Tara (2022) 'Billie Eilish is "Happier Than Ever" With Marilyn', *The Marilyn Report*, 4 July 2022 [online blog]. Available at: https://themarilynreport.com/2022/07/04/billie-eilish-is-happier-than-ever-with-marilyn/. Accessed: April 2024.

Hansford, Andrew (2017) *Dressing Marilyn: The Timeless Dresses of William Travilla. Designed for a Hollywood Star*, Carlton Books ltd.

Hansford, Andrew & Karen Homer (2011) *Dressing Marilyn: How a Hollywood Icon Was Styled*, Wellbeck Publishing.

Head, Edith (1983) *Edith Head's Hollywood*, Dutton.

Hyer (2024) 'Did you hear about the cowboy who walked into the cobbler shop?'. Available at:

https://hyerboots.com/pages/about-us#:~:text=C.H.%20Hyer%20listened%20as%20the,of%20the%20boot%20more%20easily. Accessed: March 2024.

J ______________________

Jenkins, Dan (1967) 'Life With the Jax Pack', *Sports Illustrated*, June 10, 1967. [Online at *Sports Illustrated Vault*]. Available at: https://vault.si.com/vault/1967/07/10/life-with-the-jax-pack. Accessed: March 2024.

Jorgensen, Jay and Donald L. Scoggins (2015) *Creating the Illusion: A Fashionable History of Hollywood Costume Designers*, Running Press.

Julien's Auctions (2010) 'Marilyn Monroe Black Jax Pants', Lot#812. Hollywood: Julien's. Available at: https://www.julienslive.com/lot-details/index/catalog/6/lot/1141?url=%2Fsearch%3Fkey%3Dralph%2B-greenson%26xclosed%3D0. Accessed: April 2024.

Julien's Auctions (2016a) 'Marilyn Monroe Received Letter from Dorothy Jeakins', Lot#512. Hollywood: Julien's. Available at: https://www.julienslive.com/lot-details/index/catalog/180/lot/83397/MARI-LYN-MONROE-RECEIVED-LET-TER-FROM-DOROTHY-JEAKINS. Accessed: March 2024.

Julien's Auctions (2016b) 'Marilyn Monroe Communi-cations from Christian Dior', Lot#385. Hollywood: Julien's. Available at: https://www.julienslive.com/lot-details/index/catalog/180/lot/83270/MARILYN-MONROE-COMMUNI-CATIONS-FROM-CHRISTIAN-DI-OR?url=%2Fsearch%3Fkey%3D-Monroe%2Bdior%26x-closed%3D0. Accessed: April 2024.

Julien's Auctions (2016c) 'Marilyn Monroe Fashion Invoice', Lot#384. Hollywood: Julien's. Available at: https://www.julienslive.com/lot-details/index/catalog/180/lot/83269/MARI-LYN-MONROE-FASHION-IN-VOICE. Accessed: April 2024.

K ______________________

Kauffman, Stanley (1991) 'Album of Marilyn Monroe', *The American Scholar*, 60, No.4 (Fall 1991).

Kazan, Elia (1997) *Elia Kazan: A Life*, Da Capo Press.

King, Joyann (2013) '5 Minutes With: Prabal Gurung, Spring 2014', *Harpers Bazaar* [online], 7 Sep-tember 2013. Available at: https://www.harpersbazaar.com/fashion/designers/a1060/five-minutes-with-prabal-gurung-spring-2014/. Accessed: Feb 2024.

Kotsilibas-Davis, James (1994) *Milton's Marilyn. The Photo-graphs of Milton H. Greene.* Schirmer/Mosel., Munich.

Kovacs, Shannon (2013) 'Scarlett Johansson does barely there make-up for *Harper's Bazaar* shoot', *Cosmopolitan*, 6 August 2013. Available at: https://www.cosmopolitan.com/uk/beauty-hair/news/a21727/scarlett-johansson-does-bareley-there-makeup-for-harpers-ba-zaar-shoot/. Accessed: May 2024.

L ______________________

Lane, Lydia (1956) 'New Marilyn Radiates Confidence and Aplomb, Indicates She Sees No Excuse for Wallflowers', *The Los Angeles Times*, 24 June 1956, p.93. Available via Newspapers.com at: https://www.newspapers.com/article/the-los-angeles-times/133419280/. Accessed: April 2024.

Lang, Brett (2021) 'Marilyn Monroe's "Some Like It Hot" Was a Troubled Production That Produced a Classic Movie', *Variety*, 1 June 2021. Available at: https://variety.com/2021/film/news/marilyn-monroe-some-like-it-hot-troubled-production-movie-classic-1234984318/. Accessed: Feb 2024.

Lang, Cady (2022) 'Why Marilyn Monroe's Legacy in Fashion Is Still So Influential', *Time* [online publication], 27 September 2022. Available at: https://time.com/6216202/blonde-mari-lyn-monroe-fashion-legacy/. Accessed: Feb 2024.

Little, Myles (2013) 'Marilyn, Moving and Still: One Fan's 16mm Film', *Time*, 13 September 2013. Available at: https://time.com/3802370/marilyn-moving-and-still-one-fans-16mm-film/. Accessed: Feb 2024.

M _______________________

Madsen, Anders Christian (2023) '5 Things to Know About Ferragamo's Futuristic Glamour AW23 Show', British *Vogue*, 25 February 2023. Available at: https://www.vogue.co.uk/fashion/gallery/ferragamo-aw23. Accessed: Feb 2024.

Mail Online (2009) 'The last ever pictures of Marilyn Monroe, taken the weekend before she died', 11 May 2009. Available at: https://www.dailymail.co.uk/tvshowbiz/article-1180108/The-pictures-Marilyn-Monroe-taken-weekend-died.html. Accessed: Feb 2024.

Making 'The Misfits' (2002) Gail Levin (documentary; DVD), Thirteen / WNET, Little Bird Production, NHK.

Marilyn Monroe: Beyond the Legend (1987) Dir. by Gene Feldman and Suzette Winter [documentary; DVD], Wombat Productions, DeVillier Donegan Enterprizes, Cinemax, Janson Media.

Marilyn Monroe History (2013a) 'Marilyn Monroe – Larry King Live, 35th Anniversary Special 1997', *YouTube*. Available at: https://www.youtube.com/watch?v=TweqbfFqueA. Accessed: Feb 2024.

Marilyn Monroe History (2013b) 'Eyewitness – Marilyn Monroe: Why? VERY RARE! 1962 television special', *YouTube*. Available at: https://www.youtube.com/watch?v=JGf5yEDe_r4&t=0s. Accessed: Feb 2024.

Marilyn Monroe History (2014) 'Marilyn Monroe in New York City (Documentary)', *YouTube,* 2 Jan 2014. Available at: https://www.youtube.com/watch?v=Ub9r-Hp1zhw. Accessed: March 2024.

Marilyn Monroe History (2023) 'Rare Interview With Emmeline Snively (Blue Book Modeling Agency) About Marilyn Monroe In August 1962', *YouTube*. Available at: https://www.youtube.com/watch?v=XP7uGcX-IqBE. Accessed: June 2024.

Marilyn Monroe Video Archives (2011) 'Marilyn Monroe – Photoplay Awards 1953', *YouTube*, 29 April 2011. Available at: https://www.youtube.com/watch?v=en-12ah0e7gM. Accessed: April 2024.

Marilyn Monroe Video Archives (2016) 'Rare Footage of Marilyn Monroe Costume Tests "The Misfits"', *YouTube*, 17 Nov 2016. Available at: https://www.youtube.com/watch?v=W76ZX-pY_BYg. Accessed: Feb 2024.

Martin, Pete (1956) 'The New Marilyn Monroe', *The Saturday Evening Post*, May 5–9, 1956. Republished in the April 25, 2016 online edition. Available at: https://www.saturdayeveningpost.com/2016/04/marilyn-monroe/. Accessed: March 2024.

Martin, Rebecca (2013) 'When Marie Claire Met Marilyn Monroe…Something Iconic Happened', *Marie Claire*, 17 October 2013. Available at: https://www.marieclaire.co.uk/news/beauty-news/when-marie-claire-met-marilyn-monroe-something-iconic-happened-100533. Accessed: Feb 2024.

Mau, Dhani (2021) 'Billie Eilish Goes Full "Holiday Barbie" in Oscar de la Renta at the Met Gala', *Fashionista*, 13 September 2021 [online publication]. Available at: https://fashionista.com/2021/09/met-gala-2021-billie-eilish. Accessed: Feb 2024.

McCardell, Claire (1956) *What Shall I Wear?: The What, Where, When, and How Much of Fashion*, Simon and Schuster, New York.

McDermott, Kerry (2021) 'Billie Eilish's Oscar De La Renta Met Gala Gown Is An Ode To Marilyn Monroe', British *Vogue*, 13 September 2021 [online publication]. Available at: https://www.vogue.co.uk/fashion/article/billie-eilish-met-gala-2021#:~:text=Eilish%20%E2%80%93%20a%20co%2Dchair%20of,attend%20the%20Oscars%20in%201951. Accessed January 2024.

McDowell, Colin (1997) *Forties Fashion and the New Look*, Bloomsbury Publishing.

Meryman, Richard (1962a) 'Last Talk with a Lonely Girl: Marilyn Monroe', *Life* magazine, 17 August 1962.

Meryman, Richard (2007) *Great Interviews of the 20th Century: Marilyn Monroe by Richard Meryman 1962*, Guardian News & Media.

Michele, Alessandro (n.d.) 'Gucci Aria Collection', *Crash Magazine* [online publication]. Available at: https://www.crash.fr/gucci-aria-collection/. Accessed: Feb 2024.

Minowa, Y., Maclaran, P & Stevens, L. (2019). 'The Femme Fatale in Vogue: Femininity Ideologies in Fin-de-siècle America', *Journal of Macromarketing*, *39*(3), pp270–286.

Monroe, Marilyn (1951) 'I was an orphan', *Modern Screen* magazine, February edition, pp.40–41 & 64–65. Available at: https://archive.org/details/modernscreen4243unse/page/n165/mode/2up?view=theater. Accessed: March 2024.

Monroe, Marilyn (1974) *My Story*, written with Ben Hecht, Stein & Day.

Morath, Inge (2001) 'The Misfits: Story of a Shoot', *Magnum*. Available at: https://www.magnumphotos.com/arts-culture/cinema/misfits-story-shoot-inge-morath-arthur-miller/. Accessed: Feb 2024.

Morera, Daniela (2014) 'New Again: Gianni Versace', *Interview*, 25 June 2014. [Online publication]. Available at: https://www.interviewmagazine.com/fashion/new-again-versace. Accessed: Feb 2024.

Morris, Bernadine (1977) 'Jax Bounces Back', *The New York Times*, March 7, 1977. Available at: https://www.nytimes.com/1977/03/07/archives/jax-bounces-back.html. Accessed: Feb 2024.

Mosby, Aline (1952) 'Actress Admits Nude Calendar Girl is She', *The Terre Haute Tribune*, Thursday, 13 March 1952, p19.

Movieland Magazine (1952) '"I Dress for Men" says Marilyn Monroe', Movieland Inc, New Jersey, USA.

Mulvey, Laura (2017) 'Thoughts on Marilyn Monroe: emblem and allegory', *Screen*, *58*(2), Summer 2017, pp202–209.

N _______________________

National Portrait Gallery (n.d.) 'Marilyn Monroe, Korea, 1954: Newly discovered portraits by David Geary'. Available at: https://npg.si.edu/exh/marilyn/intro.htm. Accessed: May 2024.

Nickens, C. & Zeno, G. (2012) *Marilyn in Fashion: The Enduring Influence of Marilyn Monroe*, Running Press.

Nnadi, Chioma (2022) 'Kim Kardashian Takes Marilyn Monroe's "Happy Birthday, Mr. President" Dress Out for a Spin', *Vogue*, 2 May 2022 [online publication]. Available at: https://www.vogue.com/article/kim-kardashian-met-gala-2022. Accessed: Feb 2024.

O _______________________

O'Connell, Mikey (2023) 'Lana Del Rey Forgives You', *The Hollywood Reporter*, 20 September 2023 [online publication]. Available at: https://www.hollywoodreporter.com/news/music-news/lana-del-rey-billie-eilish-olivia-rodrigo-critics-waffle-house-1235593189/. Accessed: Feb 2024.

Ogilvie, Jessica P. (2013) 'Marilyn Monroe's Depressed Letter to Lee Strasberg to Be Auctioned', *LAist*, 28 March 2013 [online publication]. Available at: https://laist.com/news/entertainment/marilyn-monroes-depressed-letter-to. Accessed: April 2024.

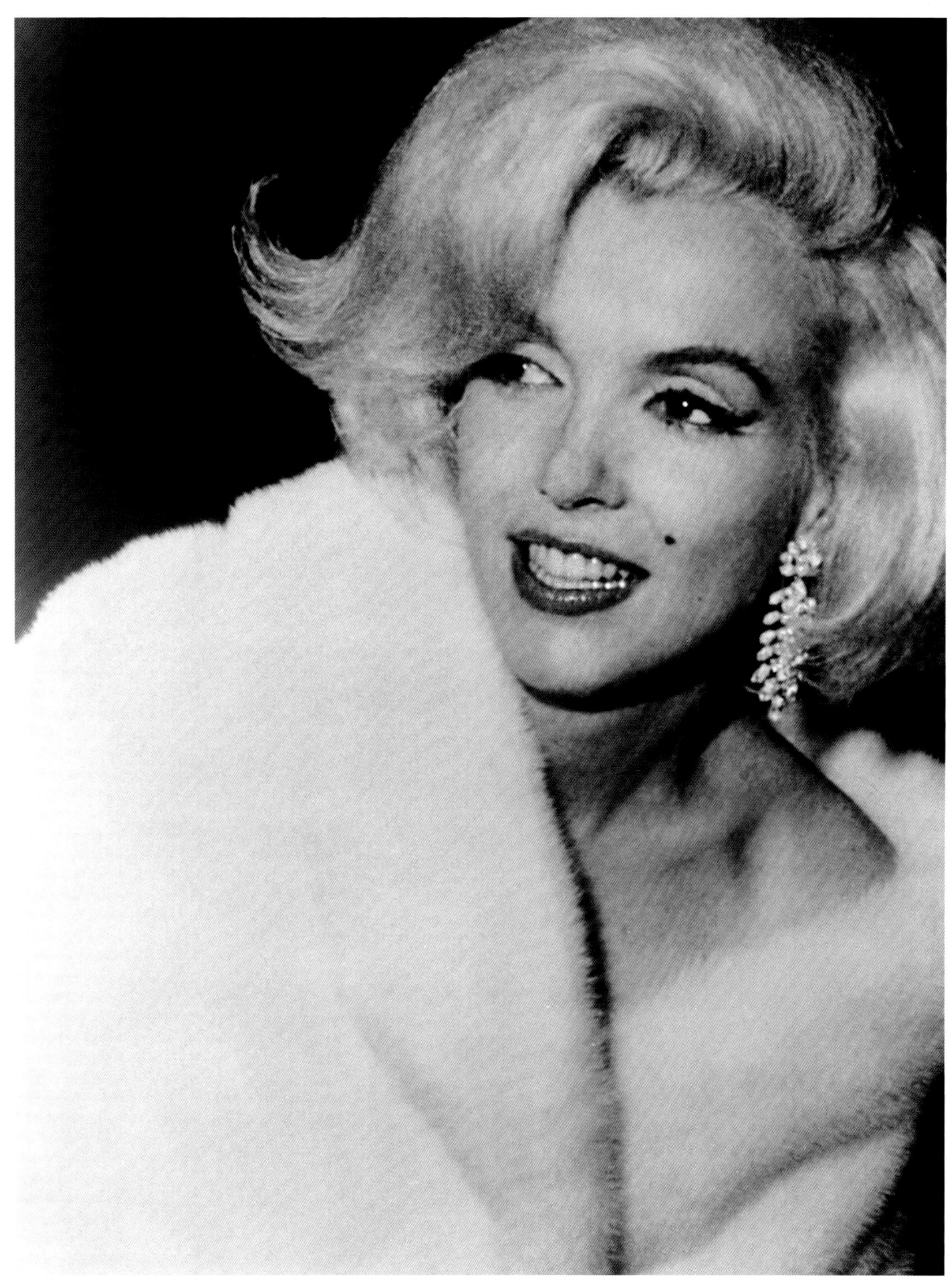

Marilyn at JFK's birthday gala in 1962

O'Hara, Helen (2015) 'Marilyn Monroe vs. Hollywood', *Vancouver Sun*, 4 June 2015, [online publication]. Available at: https://vancouversun.com/entertainment/movies/marilyn-monroe-vs-hollywood. Accessed: March 2024.

P ___________________

Pepitone, Lena (1979) *Marilyn Monroe Confidential: An Intimate Personal Account*, Simon & Schuster

Phelps, Nicole (2013) 'Prabal Gurung Spring 2014 Ready-to-Wear', *Vogue* [online publication], 6 September 2013. Available at: https://www.vogue.com/fashion-shows/spring-2014-ready-to-wear/prabal-gurung. Accessed: Feb 2024.

Photoplay Magazine (1952) Argus Press, London.

Photoplay Magazine (1965) Argus Press, London.

Ponder, Jon (2022) 'The Truth about that Famous Photo of Marilyn Monroe and Ella Fitzgerald', *West Hollywood History*, 15 May 2022 [online publication]. Available at: https://www.westhollywoodhistory.org/the-truth-about-that-famous-photo-of-marilyn-monroe-and-ella-fitzgerald/. Accessed: March 2024.

Pryor, Thomas M. (1954) 'Marilyn Monroe Suspended by Fox', *The New York Times*, Tuesday 5 January 1954. Available at: https://timesmachine.nytimes.com/timesmachine/1954/01/05/84092778.pdf?pdf_redirect=true&ip=0. Accessed: March 2024.

R ___________________

Riese, Randall & Neal Hitchins (1987) *The Unabridged Marilyn: Her Life from A to Z*, McGraw-Hill Contemporary.

Robinson, Joanna (2017) '*Feud*: Why the Real Fight Between Joan Crawford and Marilyn Monroe Was Even Nastier and Juicier', *Vanity Fair*. Available at: https://www.vanityfair.com/hollywood/2017/03/feud-joan-crawford-marilyn-monroe-golden-globes-photoplay-dress. Accessed: Feb 2024.

Russell, Jane (1986) *Jane Russell: My Path & My Detours, an Autography*, Thorndike Press.

S ___________________

Spoto, Donald (1993) *Marilyn Monroe: the Biography*, Chatto & Windus.

Steinem, Gloria (2014) *The Essential Gloria Steinem Reader: As If Women Matter*, Rupa Publications India Pvt. Ltd.

Stern, Bert (1962) 'The Last Sitting', *Vogue*, September 1962.

Street, Mikelle (2022) 'Miss Shalae Recreates Out's Iconic Beyoncé Cover', *Out*, 25 July 2022 [online publication]. Available at: https://www.out.com/print/2022/7/25/miss-shalae-recreates-outs-iconic-beyonce-cover. Accessed: Feb 2024.

T ___________________

Time (1952) 'Cinema: Something for the Boys', Monday 11 August 1952. Available at: https://content.time.com/time/subscriber/article/0,33009,857350,00.html. Accessed: Feb 2024.

Time (1955) 'Fashion: The American Look', 2 May 1955, pp.85–90. Available online at: https://msa.maryland.gov/megafile/msa/speccol/sc3500/sc3520/013500/013581/pdf/time2may1955.pdf. Accessed: March 2024.

Time (1956) 'Cinema: Who Would Resist?', Monday, 30 January 1956. Available at: https://content.time.com/time/subscriber/article/0,33009,891689,00.html. Accessed: March 2024.

Time (1962) 'The Presidency: Happy Birthday', Friday, 1 June 1962. Available at: https://content.time.com/time/subscriber/article/0,33009,938361,00.html

Thakur, Pradeep (2010) *Madonna: Unstoppable!* Pradeep Thakur & Sons

Truhler, Kimberly (2014) 'Style Essentials—Stardom Strikes Marilyn Monroe as GENTLEMEN PREFER BLONDES', *GlamAmor*. Available at: http://www.glamamor.com/2014/05/MarilynMonroe-GentlemenPreferBlondes-Travilla.html. Accessed: Feb 2024.

V ___________________

Vernose, Vienna (2022) 'Spring/Summer 2023 Christian Siriano', *CR Fashion Book*, 8 September 2022. Available at: https://crfashionbook.com/every-look-from-christian-siriano-spring-summer-2023/. Accessed: Feb 2024.

VICE (2012) 'VICE meets Debbie Harry', *YouTube*, uploaded by defdumbandblonde, 5 September 2012. Available at: https://www.youtube.com/watch?v=p3FO-PnFZChQ. Accessed: Feb 2024.

Vitacco-Robles, Gary (2014) *Icon: The Life, Times, and Films of Marilyn Monroe Volume II 1956 to 1962 & Beyond*, BearManor Media.

Vogue (1929) 'Chic at High Tide: New Costumes for Sand and Sea', 1 June 1929. Greenwich, Ct, USA. Conde Nast Publications, Inc.

Vogue (1936) 'Fashion: Bravura on the Beach', 87(10), pp.58–59, 110. Greenwich, Ct, USA. Conde Nast Publications, Inc.

Vogue (1942) 'Industrious Diamonds', 1 July 1942. pp.36–37. Greenwich, Ct, USA. Conde Nast Publications, Inc.

Vogue (1943) 'Fifty Years from Now', 15 November 1943. Greenwich, Ct, USA. Conde Nast Publications, Inc.

Vogue (1944) 'Fashion: Smart Girl', 104(3), pp.112–117, 191. Greenwich, Ct, USA. Conde Nast Publications, Inc.

Vogue (1950) 'Fashion: From Fath: Mermaid Line/From Dresses: Tunic Dress', 116(4), pp.126–27. Greenwich, Ct, USA. Conde Nast Publications, Inc.

Vogue (1953) 'Fashion: 1953 Fashion Announcement: The summer sweater', 121(10), pp.92, 94–101. Greenwich, Ct, USA. Conde Nast Publications, Inc.

Vogue (1956) 'New Beach Dressing—Suits and Hats', 15 May 1956. Greenwich, Ct, USA. Conde Nast Publications, Inc.

Vogue (2021) 'Billie Eilish on Her Holiday Barbie Met Look & Confidence / Met Gala 2021 with Keke Palmer / Vogue', *YouTube*, 15 September 2021. Available at: https://www.youtube.com/watch?v=qEvQa6xayYE. Accessed: April 2024.

W ___________________

Wang, Jessica (2017) 'This will change everything you thought you knew about Marilyn Monroe – see the rare photos', *HelloGiggles* [online publication]. Available at: https://hellogiggles.com/essential-marilyn-monroe-milton-greene/. Accessed: April 2024.

Weatherby, WJ (1989) *Conversations with Marilyn: Portrait of Marilyn Monroe*, Sphere Books.

White, Constance C.R. (1998) 'Celebrating Claire McCardell', *The New York Times*, 17 November 1998. Available at: https://www.nytimes.com/1998/11/17/style/celebrating-claire-mccardell.html. Accessed: March 2024.

Wilder, Billy & Cameron Crowe (1999) *Conversations with Wilder*, Knopf.

Winder, Elizabeth (2017) *Marilyn in Manhattan: Her Year of Joy*, Flatiron Books.

Women He's Undressed (2015) Directed by Gillian Armstrong, Damien Parer Productions, Australia.

Y ___________________

'Yves likes it hot' (1990) *WWD*, Vol. 159, No. 15, 22 January 1990 [online publication].

Z ___________________

Zolotow, Maurice (1960) *A Biography by Maurice Zolotow: Marilyn Monroe*, Harcourt, Vrace.

INDEX

Page numbers in **bold** refer to images

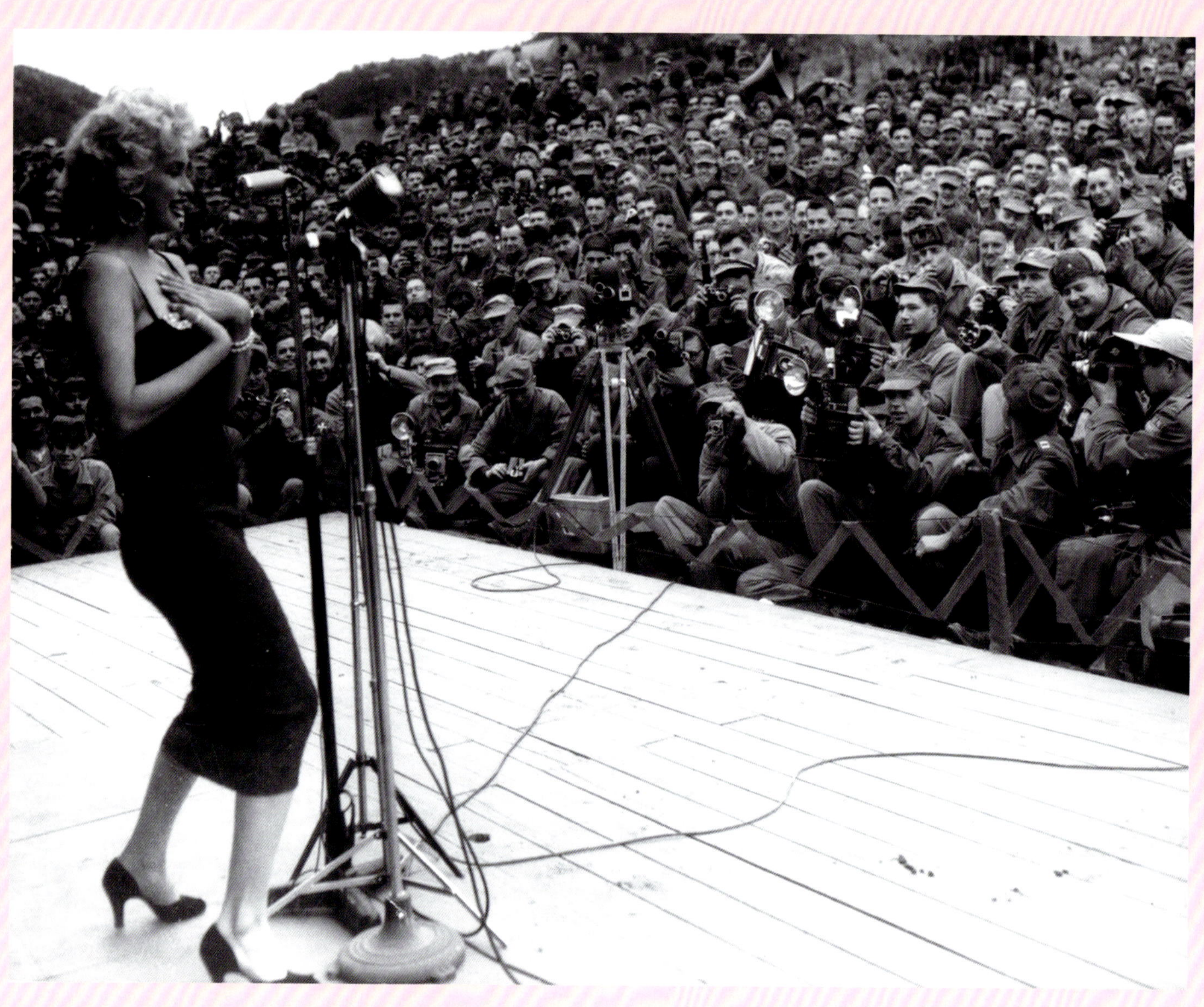

Marilyn singing to the US troops in South Korea
to keep up morale, 1954

PICTURE CREDITS

ACKNOWLEDGEMENTS
AND BIOGRAPHY

Page 161 Allstar Picture Library Ltd / Alamy Stock Photo
Page 162 Keystone Press / Alamy Stock Photo
Page 165 Entertainment Pictures / Alamy Stock Photo
Page 166 Fairchild Archive / Penske Media / Getty Images
Page 167 Entertainment Pictures / Alamy Stock Photo
Page 168 Archivio GBB / Alamy Stock Photo
Page 170 Archivio GBB / Alamy Stock Photo
Page 172 Bettmann / Bettmann / Getty Images
Page 173 Trinity Mirror / Mirrorpix / Alamy Stock Photo
Page 174 Gene Lester / Archive Photos / Getty Images
Page 177 GTCRFOTO / Alamy Stock Photo
Page 178 Landmark Media / Alamy Stock Photo
Page 181 Photo by Ed Feingersh / Michael Ochs Archives / Michael Ochs Archives / Getty Images
Page 182 (left) Photo © 1962 by Lawrence Schiller, All Rights Reserved
Page 182 (right) PageGrzegorz Czapski / Alamy Stock Photo
Page 185 PA Images / Alamy Stock Photo
Page 186 (left) PATRICK KOVARIK / AFP / Getty Images
Page 186–87 Associated Press / Alamy Stock Photo
Page 187 (right) Victor VIRGILE / Gamma-Rapho / Getty Images
Page 189 (left) Image Press Agency / Alamy Stock Photo
Page 189 (right) Taylor Hill / WireImage / Getty Images
Page 190 Pictorial Press Ltd / Alamy Stock Photo
Page 190 Photo by Dominique Maître / Penske Media / Penske Media / Getty Images
Page 193 AFF / Alamy Stock Photo
Page 195 (right) Victor VIRGILE / Gamma-Rapho / Getty Images
Page 195 (left) Keystone Press / Alamy Stock Photo
Page 196 Anthony Barboza / Archive Photos / Getty Images
Page 199 Associated Press / Alamy Stock Photo
Page 201 (left) Bettmann / Bettmann / Getty Images
Page 201 (right) UPI / Alamy Stock Photo
Page 202 Sunset Boulevard / Corbis Historical / Getty Images
Page 203 UPI / Alamy Stock Photo
Page 205 Steve Granitz / WireImage / Getty Images
Page 207 Steve Granitz / WireImage / Getty Images
Page 209 Photographed by Milton H. Greene © 2024 Joshua Greene www.miltonhgreene.com
Page 214 Everett Collection Inc / Alamy Stock Photo
Page 220 Alexandros Lavdas / Alamy Stock Photo

Many thanks to Carrie Kania at C&W Agency as well as James Smith, Alice Bowden, Mariona Vilarós, Corban Wilkin, and all at ACC Art Books. Thanks also to Samuel Dorame and Tracy Panek at Levi's. Last but not least, thanks to Andrew, Freddie and William Newman, Mick Rooney, Gina Gibbons, Pippa Healy, Michael Costiff, Francine Bosco and Jo Unwin for their love and encouragement.

Terry Newman is a fashion historian who worked in the industry for over 15 years as a journalist and stylist and now writes about fashion, art and culture. She currently lectures at Regents University London. Recent books include *Legendary Authors and the Clothes they Wore*, *Legendary Artists and the Clothes they Wore*, *Harry Styles and the Clothes He Wears* and *Rihanna and the Clothes She Wears*, *Billie Eilish and the Clothes She Wears*, *Taylor Swift and the Clothes She Wears*, and *Beyoncé and the Clothes She Wears*. During the 1990s, she was employed as Shopping Editor at *i-D* magazine, Associate Editor at *SelfService* magazine, and Consumer Editor at *Attitude* magazine, and as a TV presenter for Channel 4 fashion programmes. Her journalism has been published in *The Guardian*, *The Times* and *The Sunday Times*, *Viewpoint* and *The Big Issue*, among others, and she has contributed to *i-D*'s *Fashion Now*, *Fashion Now 2* and *Soul i-D* books. Newman lives in London with her husband and two sons.

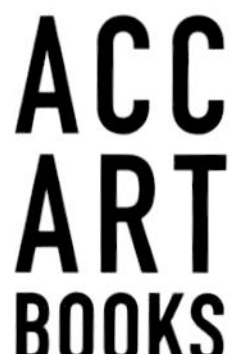